VARIETIES OF EARLY CHRISTIANITY

Blackwell Ancient Religions

Ancient religious practice and belief are at once fascinating and alien for twenty-first-century readers. There was no Bible, no creed, no fixed set of beliefs. Rather, ancient religion was characterized by extraordinary diversity in belief and ritual.

This distance means that modern readers need a guide to ancient religious experience. Written by experts, the books in this series provide accessible introductions to this central aspect of the ancient world.

Published

Ancient Greek Divination
Sarah Iles Johnston

Magic in the Ancient Greek World
Derek Collins

Religion in the Roman Empire
James B. Rives

Ancient Greek Religion, Second Edition
Jon D. Mikalson

Ancient Egyptian Tombs: The Culture of Life and Death
Steven Snape

Exploring Religion in Ancient Egypt
Stephen Quirke

Greek and Roman Religions
Rebecca I. Denova

Varieties of Early Christianity
Rebecca I. Denova

VARIETIES OF EARLY CHRISTIANITY

THE FORMATION OF THE WESTERN CHRISTIAN TRADITION

Rebecca I. Denova

WILEY Blackwell

© 2023 by John Wiley & Sons Inc. All rights reserved.

Published by John Wiley & Sons, Inc., Hoboken, New Jersey.
Published simultaneously in Canada.

No part of this publication may be reproduced, stored in a retrieval system, or transmitted in any form or by any means, electronic, mechanical, photocopying, recording, scanning, or otherwise, except as permitted under Section 107 or 108 of the 1976 United States Copyright Act, without either the prior written permission of the Publisher, or authorization through payment of the appropriate per-copy fee to the Copyright Clearance Center, Inc., 222 Rosewood Drive, Danvers, MA 01923, (978) 750-8400, fax (978) 750-4470, or on the web at www.copyright.com. Requests to the Publisher for permission should be addressed to the Permissions Department, John Wiley & Sons, Inc., 111 River Street, Hoboken, NJ 07030, (201) 748-6011, fax (201) 748-6008, or online at http://www.wiley.com/go/permission.

Trademarks
Wiley and the Wiley logo are trademarks or registered trademarks of John Wiley & Sons, Inc. and/or its affiliates in the United States and other countries and may not be used without written permission. All other trademarks are the property of their respective owners. John Wiley & Sons, Inc. is not associated with any product or vendor mentioned in this book.

Limit of Liability/Disclaimer of Warranty
While the publisher and author have used their best efforts in preparing this book, they make no representations or warranties with respect to the accuracy or completeness of the contents of this book and specifically disclaim any implied warranties of merchantability or fitness for a particular purpose. No warranty may be created or extended by sales representatives or written sales materials. The advice and strategies contained herein may not be suitable for your situation. You should consult with a professional where appropriate. Neither the publisher nor author shall be liable for any loss of profit or any other commercial damages, including but not limited to special, incidental, consequential, or other damages. Further, readers should be aware that websites listed in this work may have changed or disappeared between when this work was written and when it is read. Neither the publisher nor authors shall be liable for any loss of profit or any other commercial damages, including but not limited to special, incidental, consequential, or other damages.

For general information on our other products and services or for technical support, please contact our Customer Care Department within the United States at (800) 762-2974, outside the United States at (317) 572-3993 or fax (317) 572-4002.

Wiley also publishes its books in a variety of electronic formats. Some content that appears in print may not be available in electronic formats. For more information about Wiley products, visit our web site at www.wiley.com.

Library of Congress Cataloging-in-Publication Data:

Names: Denova, Rebecca I., author.
Title: Varieties of Early Christianity: The Formation of the Western Christian Tradition/ Rebecca I. Denova
Description: Hoboken, NJ: John Wiley & Sons, 2023. |Series: Blackwell ancient religions | Includes bibliographical references and index.
Identifiers: LCCN 2022060569 (print) | LCCN 2022060570 (ebook) | ISBN 9781119891246 (paperback) | ISBN 9781119891253 (pdf) | ISBN 9781119891260 (epub)
Subjects: LCSH: Christianity--Origin. | Jesus Christ--Historicity. | Bible. New Testament--Criticism, interpretation, etc.
Classification: LCC QR111. P333 2022 (print) | LCC QR111 (ebook) | DDC 579/. 1757--dc23/eng/20221005
LC record available at https://lccn.loc.gov/2022060569
LC ebook record available at https://lccn.loc.gov/2022060570

Cover Image: © PaoloGaetano/Getty Images
Cover design by Wiley

Set in 10.5/13pt MinionPro by Integra Software Services, Pondicherry, India.
SKY10041687_012323

CONTENTS

Preface		*vii*
I	Shared Concepts of Ancient Religions	1
II	The History of Israel	21
Excursus I	The Origins and Evolution of Satan, the Devil	51
Excursus II	Introduction to the Gospels	59
III	The Origins of Christianity	79
IV	Martyrdom	99
Excursus III	The Church Fathers	123
V	Classical Culture (*Paideia*)	127
VI	Greco-Roman Views on Life, Sex and Marriage: Christian "Innovations"	145
VII	The Challenge of Gnosticism, "Wisdom, Falsely So-Called"	159
VIII	Finding an Identity and Separating from Judaism	179
IX	Charismatic Christianity: Apocrypha and Pseudepigrapha	193
X	Institutional Development: Bishops and their Authority	205
XI	The Conversion of the Roman Empire: Constantine and Nicaea	221
XII	Asceticism and Monasticism: The Desert Fathers and the Cult of the Saints	239
Excursus IV	The Latin Fathers	251

XIII	Augustine (354–430)	257
Excursus V	Chalcedon and Beyond	271
Epilog	The Legacy of Christianity in the Western Tradition	277

Appendix I: A Brief Outline of the History of Rome — 291
Appendix II: Timeline for the Early History of Christianity — 293
Glossary — 297
Index — 323

PREFACE

Often described as a "revealed religion", Christianity did not arise in a vacuum. It took several centuries to constitute what became Christian **dogma**, or the essential concepts and rituals that Christians follow today. The word, "varieties" in the title reflects the fact that there was no central authority for three hundred years (such as the Vatican which evolved in the fifth century). Dozens of Christian communities worked out their own systems, often in competition with each other.

Throughout the Roman Empire there were groups collectively known as Jewish-Christians, Gentile-Christians, "proto-orthodox", Ebionites, Martyrs, Mandaeans, Encratites, Gnostics, Montanists, Manicheans, Arians, and Nestorians, to name only some of the largest. At the same time, the Christian equivalent of Greek philosophical schools emerged in various cities under the auspices of a master teacher ("**catechism schools**"). Dominating the views of these diverse groups was the continuing concern for the relationship between "the body and society." How to relate religious beliefs and concepts to everyday life? And how to ensure conformity throughout the Roman Empire?

In an age of diversity and diverse religious views, there has recently been an increased publication of historical surveys of Christianity in late antiquity. People are interested in the roots of church and state relations and especially the social and religious construction of gender identity and roles. What can this history teach us about these concepts in the modern world? Then as now various Christian communities struggled with changes over the decades, reinterpreting both Scripture and traditions as updated versions to provide meaning in their contemporary societies. This process continues.

The Myth of the Rise of Christianity

In the Western tradition, the rise and success of the new religion was described as "the triumph of Christianity." Thoroughly embedded in faith traditions, this history was presented in polarized and oppositional views of both Judaism and the dominant religious culture of the Roman Empire. The tradition was summarized as follows:

The history of Christianity and its triumph as the only religion of the Roman Empire was the result of "divine fulfillment". God, through the Prophets, had promised to restore his kingdom to Israel, but Judaism had become corrupt and meaningless. It was necessary for God to send his son to redeem the world from sin, which could not be accomplished through Judaism. From the beginning, Christianity grew by leaps and bounds with an unprecedented conversion rate (like "wild-fire"), providing a new community of brotherhood, in place of a paganism bereft of spirituality. The "spirit" could find no place in a world of sexual immorality and no respect for the dignity for the human body. Pagan religion had too many gods, too many philosophical schools, so that the average person dwelt in an "age of anxiety". Christianity created an egalitarian world order, where there was neither "Jew nor Greek, male nor female, slave nor free".

(Paul's letter to the Galatians 3:28)

The problem is that there is no historical evidence for any of the statements that summarize the history of Christianity. This view of Christianity is validated upon faith, but undemonstrated by historicity. "Growing like wild-fire" is difficult to verify. Scholars continue to apply Social Scientific methods to calculate raw data for Christian communities. By the year 300 CE, there is an estimated population in the Roman Empire of 60 million. This may have included 11 million Jews and 3 million Christians. But these statistics continue to be challenged in modern archaeological surveys of crop ratios, trade, infant mortality rates, and wars. We do have evidence for a broad expansion. Christian communities were established very early in the Middle East, North Africa, Spain, France, Britain, the Balkans and beyond, and half-way down the Nile in Roman Egypt. Another misconception is that Christians only attracted the poor and slaves, the "oppressed" of the Empire. On the contrary, Christianity appealed to all classes.

The traditional construction of this "triumph" consisted of two false assumptions: (1) "paganism", containing no spirituality and no morality, was already dying a slow death by the time Constantine converted (312 CE); and (2) after the destruction of the Second Temple in 70 CE, the Jews "turned inward", and had no further standing or influence in the ancient world. But paganism was alive and well and continued for centuries; Jewish communities continued to survive and flourish throughout the Empire.

Several modern scholars are beginning to question the use of the word, "triumph" for the history of Christianity. If Judaism and paganism were no longer viable, in what sense was this a "triumph?" Methodologically, the reconstruction of ancient Christianity remains problematic because of the nature of our evidence. The literature from this period is dominated by the educated classes, estimated to be anywhere from 1–5%. It is incredibly difficult to reconstruct the ways in which Christian teaching impacted the lower classes due to the absence of an equivalent body of literature.

Christianity began as a sect of Judaism in the first century, following the preaching of Jesus of Nazareth (ca. 26–36 CE.) His basic message was informed by what the Prophets of Israel had predicted, that the God of Israel would intervene in human history one more time ("in the final days") to institute his reign on earth ("the kingdom of God"). According to the gospels, Jesus claimed that this promise was fulfilled in both himself and his ministry, within his lifetime.

The first generation of the followers of Jesus (deemed *Christianoi*, the "followers of Christ" (*christos*, Greek for the Hebrew, "messiah," "anointed one")), were able to sustain this hope for 40 to 60 years after his death through reinterpretation of events. However, as the decades passed, and the kingdom did not come, the delay of the kingdom became problematic. Was Jesus a failed Prophet? Awaiting the kingdom was still the primary goal, but Christians began the process of how to live their daily lives in the interim, proleptically, as *if* the kingdom was already here. These teachings became the **Church**, as a separate, independent religion from Judaism beginning in the second century. The Church was then institutionalized as the basis for Christian government and society in the Western tradition.

The purpose of this textbook is to survey the history of Christianity in its first 500 years and to highlight the events and issues that helped form the origins of Christian belief. Many modern Christians remain unaware of the sources of Christian teaching. For example, all Christians are taught the formula of the **Trinity** ("father, son and holy spirit as one essence"), but without understanding the historical context of how and why this innovation became necessary; it is not in the Bible per se.

The study of origins is crucially important, not only to study the past, but to understand what gave rise to concepts and beliefs in their historical context. *Context determines content.* Many modern Christians consistently quote Biblical passages to validate their views not only on religion, but society and politics as well. The quotes help to validate one's faith, but different contexts create different meanings.

We are fortunate to have an enormous body of literature from this period (sermons, letters, treatises, and histories of the Roman Empire). The unfortunate element is that the literature is incredibly complicated and at times esoteric without knowing the historical, literary, and cultural contexts. This textbook will offer ways in which to navigate this Christian literature for the beginning student and public. Many histories of Christianity only focus on the unique elements of that tradition, to the neglect of historical events and changes in the dominant culture. At the same time, "Judaism" is reduced to the Christian utilization of its Scriptures, without reference to the fact that the continuing existence of Judaism and Jews created theological as well as community threats to the validation of the claims of the Church. This text will follow the history of both non-Christians as well as Jews to the sixth century.

A second purpose of the textbook is to serve as background reading for Syllabi in both secondary and university undergraduate courses on the history of early Christianity. There are literally thousands of books on the history of Christianity in various periods. Many of them are concerned with scholarly debates on various theories and utilize specific jargon that is unique to the discipline. This textbook will analyse both the scholarly and archaeological research in a comprehensible format. Having this material in one textbook will also reduce the cost of requiring additional texts for courses. This textbook focuses for the most part on the period after the first century. The beginning decades are summarized, but for a more detailed history and analysis of the origins in the first century see Denova, *Origins of Christianity and the New Testament* (Wiley-Blackwell, 2019).

The Academic Discipline of Religious Studies

Religious Studies is a relatively new discipline in the academy (in the past 70 years). It is important to recognize the differences between Theology (the study of God) and Religious Studies. Theology involves the study of the nature of God and the way in which God and humans interact. Theologians address such issues from a preconceived faith conviction. There are thousands of books and articles on the theological development of Christian theology.

Religious Studies (often referred to as "the academic study of religion") focuses on the origins of religious authority (institutions), beliefs, rituals, sacred texts, and ethics. Absent value judgments of which religions are right or wrong, Religious Studies analyses the people and societies who created religious traditions and the way in which they functioned in daily life.

Religious Studies utilizes a multidisciplinary approach and methodology that incorporates all the liberal arts and social sciences: classics, history, literature, anthropology, archaeology, sociology, philosophy, and psychology. In addition, the study of religion analyses economics, politics, ethnic studies, ritual studies, gender studies, the arts, global studies, and cross-cultural approaches. Religious Studies explores the human experience of religion in specific cultures over time, as a "system of meaning". This is the approach that is utilized in the following chapters. Working in tandem, a Religious Studies approach also sheds light on theological issues.

The Contents

To fully understand the development of Christianity, it is important to recognize the religious and cultural background of the two major contributors to Christian thought: Second Temple Judaism (450 BCE–70 CE) and Greco-Roman religion and culture.

Chapter I: Shared Concepts of Ancient Religions contains definitions of religious rituals and beliefs between the two.

Chapter II: The History of Israel, provides the background and history of Judaism, as told in their Scriptures. Jesus of Nazareth was a Jew, not a Christian (there was no such entity at the time). This chapter places him within that religious and historical context.

Excursus I: The Origins and Evolution of Satan

The concept of Satan, or the Devil, emerged over time and only became a more dominant figure after the rise of Christianity.

Excursus II: Introduction to the Gospels

The **gospels** are neither biographies nor histories. Scholars and theologians have developed methodology over the years on how to analyse the gospels in relation to comparable ancient concepts and literature. This chapter provides some of those tools in "the quest for the historical Jesus."

Chapter III: The Origins of Christianity, establishes the basic message and ministry of Jesus of Nazareth and how and why the movement began in Jerusalem and moved to the cities of the Eastern Roman Empire. The Acts of the Apostles narrates details on the spread of Christianity in the first century to non-Jews (**Gentiles**). A highlight of this chapter is understanding the mission and letters of **Paul**.

Chapter IV: Martyrdom

The Christians in the Roman Empire were persecuted and condemned for the crime of "atheism", or non-participation in the state cults. How do the magistrates go about this, and how do outsiders view Christianity in this light? This chapter will include several martyrologies, or stories of famous martyrs.

Excursus III: The Church Fathers

Christian leaders in the second century who created what became Christian dogma (a system of belief) are retrospectively deemed the "Church Fathers" for their contributions to the faith. We highlight several of the more important Church Fathers and their major treatises.

Chapter V: Classical Culture (*Paedeia*)

One of the greatest challenges to Christianity from the mid-second century onward was presented by the "religiousness" of Greco-Roman culture and the philosophical world-view(s) of late antiquity's *paideia*, or "higher learning." How does Christianity find a place within these various world-views and what arguments are presented to challenge "the presence of the gods?"

Chapter VI: Greco-Roman Views on Life, Sex and Marriage: Christian "Innovations" In the Jewish book of Genesis, humans were told to be "fruitful and multiply." Greco-Roman society viewed marriage and procreation as part of the natural order, a religious duty of every citizen for the welfare of his community. Influenced by both traditions, Christianity nevertheless opted for a conception of sex and marriage that is inferior, and at times opposed to, the ideal of Genesis, as well as their contemporary culture. Important in this context, is understanding the role and function of women in traditional Mediterranean society.

Chapter VII: The Challenge of Gnosticism, "Wisdom, Falsely So-Called"

Much of the early life of the Church was involved in family feuds--conflicts among Christians, rather than external opponents. The result became the innovation of the twin concepts of **orthodoxy** and **heresy**. What was the danger of "false teaching?" How did this differ from non-Christian views of religious pluralism? This chapter provides the background and concepts of Gnostic Christians.

Chapter VIII: Finding an Identity and Separating from Judaism

Beginning as an apocalyptic sect within Judaism in the first century, the large number of non-Jewish converts helped this movement emerge as a distinct belief system called "Christianity". How much of the parent religion should be retained? What is the relationship between the Judaism of the Jewish Scriptures and the new Christian sects?

Chapter IX: Charismatic Christianity: Apochrypha, Pseudepigrapha

Christian religious expression encompassed ecstatic behavior, such as "speaking in tongues", spirit possession resulting in prophecy, and often developed unique ideas on the uses and abuses of the body, including extreme fasting and life-long celibacy. As non-Christians asked, "Where does all this madness comes from?" How are such "overachieving" Christians viewed by both adherents and outsiders? By the second century, Christians had developed legendary stories of the Apostles and Christian missionaries that upheld what became some basic tenets of model Christian behavior.

Chapter X: Institutional Development: Bishops and Their Authority

Bishops became distinctive and unique leaders in the early Churches, while also borrowing styles of leadership from both Judaism and the dominant culture. What was the basis of their authority and how did they perceive themselves in relation to their flocks? This period also saw the development of Christian rituals and holidays. How much of this was borrowed from Judaism and how much from Greco-Roman culture?

Chapter XI: The Conversion of the Roman Empire: Constantine and Nicaea

When Constantine converted, the Empire did not become Christian overnight. What problems within the Church did Constantine inherit? How did his court and the subsequent conferences resolve the continuing problems of schism, the nature of God and the Trinity, and continuing co-existence with non-Christians?

Chapter XII: Asceticism and Monasticism: The Desert Fathers and the Cult of the Saints

Contrary to popular views, the "mad rush" to the desert was not the result of perceived tensions in worldly society, but the means to escape Christian feuds. What was the impetus for the ascetic ideal and what is the relationship of monastic communities to the rest of Christian society? The "saints" of Christianity will follow the concepts of patron/client inherent in Greco-Roman religion and society, adding the innovation of **relics**.

Excursus IV: Latin Fathers

Late antiquity provided the major contributions to Christianity from men who now wrote in Latin. We highlight their backgrounds and contributions: Ambrose, John Chrysostom, Jerome.

Chapter XIII: Augustine (354–430)

Augustine's work was the pinnacle of the Christianization of the Roman Empire and set the tone for the relationship between the body and society and between the Church and state in the subsequent development of Western Christianity. More than any other writer of late antiquity, Augustine was the most influential theologian for the way in which Catholicism developed in the later Middle Ages. Through the work of an ex-Augustinian monk, Martin Luther, Augustine contributed to the rise of the Protestant Reformation.

Excursus V: Chalcedon and Beyond

One of the largest of the Council meetings of late antiquity, Chalcedon completed the final explication of the combination of the two natures of Christ, simultaneously divine and human.

Epilog: The Legacy of Christianity in the Western Tradition

The original teachings of Christianity were condoned over time, but also subject to reinterpretation and continuing debate. The historical process of exegesis and re-interpretation of Scriptures continues in modern Christian debates, with the same "variety" we saw in the ancient world.

Features of this Textbook

Each of the chapters contains excerpts of primary documents and places the documents within their historical context. Examining both the world of ancient Christianity as well as scholarly methods of analysis often necessitates a vocabulary that is above and beyond the average reader. Throughout the text, words and concepts will appear in **bold print** and are then defined in a convenient **Glossary** at the end. Between the chapters, I have added what is called an **Excursus**, or a more detailed examination and summary of a topic or point of view.

Boxes

Understanding the background and nuances of ancient society and ancient texts requires years of study and analysis. **Boxes** are provided in the chapters that summarize issues or add detail to the background. For example, "Sexuality and Marriage in the Jewish Scriptures", and "Concepts of Monism and Dualism in the Ancient World".

Figures and **Timelines** appear within the chapters and highlight maps, schematics, and some of the archaeological sites associated with the development of Christianity. I have travelled and explored all these sites. When appropriate I have added a few details of each place.

Each chapter concludes with **Suggestions for Further Reading** for those who wish to explore the material in depth. The suggestions include both traditional studies and more recent articles and books.

Reconstructing the Past

The problem for the historian of any age is to carefully balance the literature with material remains (archaeology). In reconstructing the world of early

Christianity, we rely on established, written law-codes of both Judaism and the Roman Empire, to first, understand these societies. We then analyse innovations (or not) through Christian teaching. However, how do we know that all ancient people literally "followed the laws" in their everyday lives without parallel evidence? This remains especially problematic in analysing the separation of Christianity from Judaism. The Christian polemic against Judaism utilized the laws of Leviticus to prove that Judaism oppressed people. But we often have little information of how these "laws" were enforced (if ever), especially for Diaspora Jews (living outside the land of Israel), in their historical contexts. Much of Leviticus only applied when one was approaching the Temple. Later Christian writers consistently critiqued the Jewish Temple rituals, although the Temple had been destroyed by Rome in 70 CE.

As moderns, we tend to bemoan the fact that ancient literature is full of contradictions (including the Bible). This is because there was no centralized, authorized body that dictated "what everyone should believe and practice" in antiquity (unlike the later Christian "creed" or the Vatican). What we have are various beliefs and narratives that arose in various towns and cities over the centuries, in different contexts. Beginning with the myths of the Olympians, contradictory views of the divine were rampant. Dozens of cities all claimed to have the tomb of the Greek/Roman hero, Herakles/Hercules. There were countless views on the afterlife. Everyone read Homer's description of Odysseus' descent to Hades (the *Iliad*), where the dead exist as "shadows" and are eternally miserable. But as "shadows", they remain tactile; the dead still experience joy, but also pain and suffering.

We are also going to encounter contradictions in Christian literature. As we will learn, various Christian communities (including the international Councils) all declared what had to be believed and followed. But Councils continued to be re-called and re-constituted because oppositional teachings and opinions still flourished despite such declarations and bans on "false teaching".

Another problem is the one-sided literary evidence of ancient Christianity; our literature reflected the thoughts of elite, educated men. With a few exceptions, the masses did not produce an equivalent literature. It is difficult to reconstruct what ordinary Christians thought or how they lived. But sometimes we can "read between the lines". For example, Christian leaders adopted the cultural understanding that women should have no public or political voice. Some Christian women defied the customs and taught in the communities. We know this because the men consistently denounced such practices, naming names. In other words, for every general conclusion about ancient society and religion, there are always going to be exceptions.

And finally, I have taught a course on the "Varieties of Early Christianity" for over 25 years. Some students enter the course with more background than others, usually from Bible Study programs in their churches. In the beginning there is often some anxiety over the fear that an historical method will uncover something that will challenge their faith. "Faith" by its very nature is not subject to verification or scientific analysis. This text is not designed to challenge anyone's faith. It is to provide an understanding of how that faith originated in the first five centuries.

The study of the origins of Christianity is a fascinating subject. Learning how the ancients fully integrated their worldviews, politics, and daily life through these centuries can help us continue to articulate our own "systems of meaning" in the modern world.

SHARED CONCEPTS OF ANCIENT RELIGIONS

I

Concepts and Terminology

Religion

Polytheism and Monotheism

Religion and Society

Social Class

Slavery

Myth

Acts of Worship/Rituals

Cult

Official Cults

Voluntary Cults: The "Mysteries"

Religious Festivals

Divination: Astrology, Oracles, Magicians

Ancient Concepts of the Afterlife

Ancient Judaism

Ancient Greece and Rome

Greek and Roman Funerals

Funeral Games

Gentiles and Pagans (Problematic Terms)

Varieties of Early Christianity: The Formation of the Western Christian Tradition, First Edition. Rebecca I. Denova.
© 2023 John Wiley & Sons, Inc. Published 2023 by John Wiley & Sons, Inc.

Conversion

Canon/Old Testament/
   Jewish Scriptures

Faith vs. Rituals

Church

"Spirit"

Polemic/Rhetoric

The Problem of
   Anachronism

Creative Writing

After reading this chapter you will be able to:

- Recognize the complete integration of religion and society in the ancient world.
- Become familiar with the shared religious views and rituals that benefitted the communities of the Roman Empire.

Concepts and Terminology

Before we begin, there are several concepts and terms that are utilized throughout the book. Listing them at the beginning helps to avoid repetition in each chapter.

Religion

In the modern world, one's identity is often categorized by a specific religion (Jewish, Christian, Muslim, Hindu, etc.). What we mean by this word is a "system of belief" that includes concepts, rituals, law and social codes. But in the ancient world, the concept of religion as a separate category did not exist in the sense that we understand it today. In fact, there was no word for religion in ancient Greek or Hebrew. The modern term, which came into use in the seventeenth century, derived from the Latin root, *religio*, sometimes translated as "those things that tie or bind one to the gods".

All ancient peoples believed in the total integration of the **divine** (the gods, the powers in the heavens and under the earth), with humans and everyday life. If you stopped someone on the street and asked them what religion they practiced, they would have no idea what you were talking about. Instead, the question should be, "What customs do you live by?" The typical response would be, "The customs of our ancestors". These customs were what identified people as **ethnic groups**, with a common ancestor, history, homeland, language, rituals, and mythology. All these elements were handed down by the gods and provided the basis for the governing authorities, the social construction of gender roles, and appropriate law-codes of behavior.

All ethnic groups shared common ideas and rituals concerning the divine, but there was no one authority to turn to; a concept such as the Vatican did not exist. If you had questions, you could consult a member of the **priesthood** (specialized experts), and you may receive different answers from different individuals. **Sacred Scriptures** varied from group to group and region to region. The closest concept such as our Bible was found in the works of Homer, *The Iliad* and *The Odyssey*. Everyone in the Mediterranean Basin learned these stories, which included tales of constant interaction with the gods. Romans elevated their **foundation myths** as sacred (Romulus and Remus) as later told in Virgil's *Aenead* (first century BCE).

Polytheism and Monotheism

Polytheism (the belief in multiple deities), or sometimes **pantheism** (the belief in all powers) is always juxtaposed to **monotheism** (the belief in one god) understood as its polar opposite. However, the terms are problematic because they are modern. No one in the ancient world would identify with being a "polytheist". More importantly, there was no such concept as "ancient monotheism". *All ancient people were polytheists, including the Jews.*

In Western culture, monotheism specifically refers to the God of the Bible—the God of Judaism, Christianity, and Islam. This is demonstrated by the fact that this God is always written with a capital "G". It designates the God of Israel above all other gods, and assumes an element of faith. The God of Israel was simply one among the many thousands of deities that populated the universe. This text will continue to utilize the capitalization of God to differentiate this deity.

Ancient cultures viewed the universe on three levels: the heavens (the abode of the gods); the earth (the abode of humans); and the underworld, often referred to as "the land of the dead". Gods could transcend, or travel around all three. Many groups had the concept of a **high god**, or a "king of the gods" who ruled over diverse gradients of divine powers. Lower divinities were called *daemons*, but eventually were seen as evil, and hence the popular word "demons". Gods as well as demons could possess people. In the latter case, this was an ancient explanation of mental health issues and physical disabilities. There were many **exorcists**, or experts on expelling demons from people.

Like their neighbors, ancient Jews conceived of a hierarchy of powers in heaven: "sons of God" (Genesis 6), angels, archangels (the messengers from God who communicated God's will), cherubim, and seraphim. Jews also recognized the existence of demons, and introduced the concept of a fallen angel who eventually became Satan, the Devil.

The foundational story for the idea that Jews were monotheistic was when Moses received the commandments of God on Mt. Sinai: "I am the Lord your God … You shall have no other gods before me". The Hebrew could be better understood as "no other gods *beside* me." This does not indicate that other gods do not exist; it is a commandment that the Jews were not to **worship** any other gods. We combine "worship" with "belief" and "veneration", but *worship in the ancient world always meant sacrifices.* Jews could pray to angels and other powers in heaven, but they were only to offer sacrifices (animals, vegetables, libations) to the God of Israel. This commandment was one of the major differences between Jews and all other traditional ethnic cults.

The Jewish texts consistently refer to the existence of the gods of the nations (ethnic groups): Deuteronomy 6:14 "Do not follow other gods"; 29:18 "to serve the gods of those nations"; 32:43 "Praise O heavens, his people, worship him all you gods!"; Isaiah 36:20 "who among all of the gods of these nations have saved their nations?"; and Psalm 821 "God presides in the great assembly; he renders judgment among the gods". In the story of the Jews' Exodus from Egypt, God battled against the gods of Egypt to demonstrate who controls nature. This makes little sense if their existence was not recognized: "...I will bring judgment on all the gods of Egypt" (Exodus 12:12).

While Jews only offered sacrifices to the God of Israel, they shared a common conviction that all the gods should be respected; it was perilous to anger the other gods. Exodus 22:28 ordered the Jews never to revile the gods of the other nations. Early Christians accepted these levels of powers in heaven (and Hell) and the Apostle Paul often referred to the existence of the gods of the other nations in his letters. He berated "these powers" (*archons*) for interfering with his missions. Modern historians continue to debate the origins of a concept of "one god" in ancient Judaism. One theory placed it during the period when the Israelites adopted the Canaanite concept of the high god, El, into their views of Yahweh. Another theory claims that it was late, after the Babylonian captivity, adopting the high god, Marduk, in variations of Yahweh.

Religion and Society

The most dominating theme of all ancient cultures was that of fertility—fertility of crops, herds, and people. Wihtout fertility, the clan/tribe did not survive. Thus, the gods were portrayed as male with a female consort or goddess. These pairs mated and produced offspring. (Judaism did not have this concept; the God of Israel had no consort.) "As in the heavens, so on earth"; ancient societies mirrored the heavenly realm by making the **family** the basic social unit. The family was an extended household which included parents, inlaws, children, slaves (and ex-slaves), business clients, and dead ancestors.

The way in which the family was promoted and validated was through extra-familial elements of society that were common to all regions of the Mediterranean basin. One's social class defined the parameters of status and rank, while **honor and shame** established the codes of ideal behavior for both individuals and the community. Honor was not just a private goal of an individual, but a public acknowledgment of one's worth or value to the community. A person with honor was one who adhered to social codes and conventions, and respected the gods. This trait was crucially important for one's public persona, or one's dignity and status in the community.

The **patron/client** system (how things got done) provided the network for relationships necessary for the common good, including relationships between humans and the gods. These extra-familial elements became encoded in the self-perception of all classes and levels of society, both free and slave, in social morals, and in one's relationship with the divine (cult). The upper classes had a religious duty to help the lower, and in return, the lower classes supplied food and crafts. Such obligations were given to the gods (through prayer and sacrifice) with the expectation that the gods would reciprocate with benefits to the person and the community.

Social Class

When we think of class in the modern world, we automatically think of economics: upper, middle, and lower classes. In the ancient world, economics was an important element of the social classes, but not necessarily the most important part;

blood trumped wealth. Our image of the upper and middle classes will usually include education, just as it did in the ancient world (although levels of education differed). But in ancient society slaves also had opportunities for education.

At the top of the social order was the aristocracy ("rule of the excellent") where governing power resided in a small, privileged class who claimed descent from ancient, founding families. It was the bloodline that endowed nobility. Another class of males was equivalent to our middle or business class, where they engaged in manufacturing, trade, and banking. They could not claim the same kind of ancestry as the aristocracy, but they could and did accumulate wealth. Inter-marriage was permissable among the classes, with the tacit understanding that one should always "marry-up" to a higher class.

Slavery

Slavery in ancient Greece and Rome was not the same institution experienced in the ante-bellum South in the United States. Slavery was common throughout the ancient world, but it was not confined to one ethnic group or class; it consisted of all cultures and economic classes. Some educated Greeks sold themselves into slavery to work as *pedagogues* or tutors, and could thereby advance themselves. The beginning of the institution of slavery most likely began with war captives.

Manumission, the freeing of slaves, could occur if either the master paid over the price of the slave, or by the slave if he had saved enough money to buy his freedom. Particularly in Rome, domestic and commercial slaves were paid a minimum wage or sometimes given the management of a piece of property (*peculium*) that could be accumulated against their eventual manumission. Many slave owners, particularly businessmen, freed slaves and then set them up in business, where the freedman still retained a client's obligation to his former master. In Greece, freedom did not include the right of citizenship, but in Rome citizenship was conferred with manumission. Roman freedmen could not hold public office or priesthoods, but they could vote, and their children were free citizens. The possibility of manumission (and change of social status) is one of the great differences between slavery in the ancient world and the ante-bellum South.

Mirrored as class levels in society, there were classes of slaves. At the top were the household slaves (tutors, hairdressers, maids, cooks) and at the bottom, prisoners of war, rebellious slaves, and convicted criminals. These latter were the ones punished with having to work in the tin, silver and copper mines of the provinces or row the galleys of the commerical ships.

Myth

We often use the word **myth** to automatically designate "something false". In the study of religion, myths are ways in which people understand experiences with the divine, through stories, images, and metaphors. By their very nature, myths are not subject to verification. Myths are multivalent, meaning they are subject to many different interpretations. Myths help to create a worldview to explain origins (where did we come from?) but more importantly, they help to validate the social order of the *contemporary* world. Myths function to explain the ideals and institutions of society, gender roles, and law-codes.

All religions have "origin myths", set in primordial time that explain the beginning of the cosmos, gods, human beings, and sacred sites. The first eleven chapters of the book of Genesis are often described as "myth" in the sense that they explain origins. Myths utilize **etiologies** or explanations (e.g., the beginning of agriculture). Many of the towns and cities in the Mediterranean Basin had **foundation myths,** claiming a god or hero as their original ancestor.

Myths can be understood literally or as **allegory**, applied most often by the schools of philosophy and educated writers. They read myth as containing symbols that went beyond the basics to promote ideals or universals. Stories in the Bible were allegorically interpreted over the centuries by both Jewish and Christian writers.

Acts of Worship/Rituals

Temples were the homes of the gods on earth and were deemed **sacred space**. Unlike our modern places of worship, almost all the activity took place out of doors. This is where the **altar** was located, and people congregated around it. Because this was sacred space, one had to be in a state of **ritual purity** to enter and participate. "Ritual purity" is a state of being. Experiences of daily life, such as sexual intercourse and child-birth, rendered a person impure or "unclean" for a temporary amount of time before one could enter sacred space. These elements involved semen and blood, the two sources of life that were given by the gods and these moments were recognized as a suspension of normal activity. Another was the problem of **corpse contamination**. The dead ejected a miasma that was toxic, and had to be eliminated through certain rituals and time. Most purity rituals involved "washings", but the concept is not necessarily related to hygiene.

Overseeing all aspects of worship were **priests** and **priestesses**. Their function was to ensure that worship was done correctly (according to the ancestral traditions). Some communities had a priest elevated above others, the **high-priest**. Unlike modern clergy, the priesthoods were not charged with caring for the souls of the congregation. Their first loyalty was caring for the god/goddess. A major difference with the priesthoods in the ancient world is that with few exceptions, they were part-time jobs. Priests and priestesses served in rotation (sometimes a week, sometimes a month). When they were finished with their term of service, they went back to their normal jobs or businesses. Conferring of a priesthood and the title were sought-out advantages for the ancients. Not only did this activity command respect, but it was an important element for one's resume (the memory of a person), described on their funeral monuments.

Priests and priestesses oversaw the **rituals** (Latin, *ritus*, "doing things") that included **sacrifices**, **prayers**, and **hymns** (prayers sung to music). The most important element of these rituals was that of sacrifices. Sacrifices were crucial to maintaining the balance between gods and humans. These were communal events directed to the welfare and prosperity of the group. Sacrifices had to be something of value, which in the ancient world was most often meat. Priests sacrificed sheep, goats, pigs, oxen, fowl, and wheat cakes if you could not afford an animal. Thousands of Temples had daily sacrifices. A portion of the animal was divided among the priests, and then the rest was distributed to the people. This is likely the only time that the poor were able to eat meat.

Another element of rituals was specific to marking heightened stages in life: birth, puberty, marriage, death. The modern term for these occasions, which were all celebrated through religious rituals, is **rites of passage** (some of which became the later Catholic **sacraments**).

Cult

We typically apply the term **cult** negatively to religious ideas that differ radically from the majority. In the ancient world, *cultus* (Latin, *colere*, "care or cultivate") was a broad term for everything that was involved in the care and maintenance of the gods. This referred to the sacrificial knives, incense burners, and other implements of the rituals. *It did not indicate theology or spiritual differences.* In this text, we use "native" or "ethnic cults" as a category. Then as now criticism of someone else's "cult" occurred often. We encounter this specifically in Christian criticism of Judaism and the native cults.

In modern sociological studies of religion, cult is part of an evolutionary process. There is a basic "mother religion", but some members decide that reforms are needed. This becomes a **sect** within that system. Sects maintain the original concepts, but with updated reforms. (Think of the thousands of different denominations in modern Protestantism.) Later, the reformers may decide that more changes are needed, or new interpretations applied, and is deemed a cult. Ultimately, the group can break with the original mother religion as an independent faction. Christianity began as a sect within Judaism, became a cult in the Roman Empire, and eventually evolved into an independent religion.

Official Cults

Every village, town, and city in the Roman Empire had dozens of temples and shrines to both the **Olympian gods** as well as local gods. The government supported the worship of these gods, and added the state cults of Rome (the **Capitoline Trinity** of **Jupiter**, **Juno**, and **Minerva**). The first Emperor, Augustus, instituted the **Imperial Cult**, to honor the royal family (see Chapter IV on Martyrdom). Participants had the freedom to join in the worship and festivals of all these deities in a concept known as **religious pluralism**. In other words, worshipping multiple deities was not understood as a conflict or contradiction.

Voluntary Cults: The "Mysteries"

Running parallel to the official cults of the Empire, was the option to participate in voluntary religious practices, usually limited to a group who had to undergo **initiation**. There was a public side to this worship, but initiates were able to gain secret knowledge. This knowledge took the form of how to achieve benefits in this world as well as the afterlife. They took a vow never to reveal the secrets, and thus, these practices were deemed the **Mysteries**. What these cults had in common was an emphasis on fertility, in the cycles of birth and re-birth. Many scholars have proposed the theory that Christianity modeled itself upon these various Mystery cults.

The most popular and Empire-wide cults were:

1. The Mysteries at Eleusis and Athens of the cult of **Demeter**. The festivals re-enacted her search for her daughter, Persephone, who had been abducted by Hades. Demeter was the goddess of grain and the seasons. During the search, the earth wilted and nothing grew (winter), but upon the reunion with her daughter, the crops arose again (spring and summer).

2. The cult of **Dionysius**, the god of fertility, the vine, and wine-making. The Cult of Dionysus was associated with the origins of drama and dance, and his festivals coincided with the presentation of plays in Athens and elsewhere. Apparently the wine-drinking led to a relaxation of the social conventions; both women and slaves were welcome to attend. The rituals also incorporated the ability to go into a trance, "letting-go" as it were and experiencing an out-of-body freedom. This was known as **catharsis**. The festivals became quite raucous at times, and became a target of Christian criticism. The original Greek word for "ritual" was *orgia*, **orgy**. This term became the most popular negative Christian description of all native cults, claiming polemic charges of sexual freedom at those festivals.

3. **Magna Mater** (The Great Mother, Cybele). This was an ancient religious cult, most likely originating from Anatolia (central Turkey) and introduced in Rome during the second Punic War (218–201 BCE). The cult re-enacted the myth of Cybele (a grain goddess) and Attis, her lover, a devotee, who went into an ecstatic trance (who was made "mad" by the goddess) and castrated himself. Cybele's priests went into a trance-like state and castrated themselves in imitation of this devotion. Every year in Rome, the Megalesian games were celebrated by her eunuch priests and other initiates, dancing through the streets in ecstasy and self-flagellation.

4. The Cult of **Mithras**. Mithras was a Persian sun god who was eventually adopted by Rome, particularly by the legions. They had various degrees of initiation, somewhat like modern orders of the Masons. They met in underground chambers (*mithraea*) for communal meals and celebrated the death and re-birth of Mithras. Many of these chambers have been excavated throughout the Roman Empire. In late antiquity, the spread of this cult was one of the most competitive in relation to Christianity.

Religious Festivals

Throughout the Roman Empire, **religious festivals** were community events, either to honor a specific god or goddess or to honor a founding deity of the community. These festivals were also coordinated with **calendars,** or the marking of **sacred time** as well as the agricultural cycles. Festivals could last from one or two days to a week. Religious festivals consisted of three elements: sacrifices, drama, and games.

The many sacrifices throughout the city during festival time resulted in leftover quantities of meat and cakes, which were then distributed to the public. The myths of the gods were reenacted in plays during the same week. Athletic contests were added, the most popular of which were the chariot races. The combined events were labeled *ludi*, "games". All these simultaneous events drew people into the city from the countryside. At the same time, they were occassions to honor **magistrates** (the governing personnel who paid for the games), and served as propaganda venues in the Empire.

Divination: Astrology, Oracles, Magicians

The way in which humans communicated with the gods, and the gods with humans, is generally described as **divination**. This was done through **astrologers, seers, oracles, prophets, augurs, haruspexes, wonder-workers**, and **necromancers**. Astrology (the study of the nature and power of the stars/planets) flourished, as the stars controlled people born under their influence. While many did not take this seriously, nevertheless, "just in case," people often consulted experts who allegedly understood these powers. Knowing the time of one's birth, these experts consulted "star-charts", to determine which powers were dominant in your life.

Seers, oracles, and prophets went into an ecstatic trance and were "possessed" by a deity. The speech of the god was often in an unknown language, so a priest was usally required to translate. "Oracle" was the term for both the person as well as a place. There were hundreds of oracles sites throughout the Mediterranean Basin. One of the most famous oracles in the ancient world was the oracle at Delphi, controlled by the god Apollo. For the most part, oracles were consulted to determine if a decision that was already made "pleased the god". The **Prophets of Israel** were the Jewish version of oracles. When they spoke, it was the words of the God of Israel that were uttered.

Augurs in Rome adopted the ancient Etrucan methods of studying lightning and the flights of birds to determine good and bad omens. Haruspexes (also influenced by Etruscan rituals) were experts in examining the entrails of a sacrificial animal. If the entrails were bad or diseased, another animal had to replace it.

Wonder-workers were popular throughout the Empire. These were men (and sometimes women) who claimed special gifts that were granted by a god or goddess in relation to performing miracles. The result was physical cures for cripples, diseases, and the mentally ill. A common belief was that these problems were caused by demon-possession. Wonder-workers were expert **exorcists**, or those who "drove out" demons. Jesus of Nazareth fitted this traditional mold of a wonder-worker and exorcist.

Necromancers were experts in communicating with both the powers of the underworld (the land of the dead) as well as the ability to conjure up the dead. Unfortunately, in the Western tradition, wonder-workers and necromancers became grouped together under the term, "magicians". The term derived from Persian court astrologers, deemed *magi* (as in the visitors at the nativity in Matthew). Because of their knowledge of the universe and astrology, it was believed that they were experts in being able to manipulate nature, for good or for ill. Thus our modern descriptions of "white" and "black" magic. This has influenced histories of the ancient world by assuming that "magic" was a unique and separate category.

When scholars describe these specific rituals, they use terms such as "spells" and "incantations". But these "spells" and "incantations" were simply the same as prayers and hymns applied in all the rituals. The difference was in the fact that they often appealed to the powers of the underworld. These were known as the **cthonic** deities who required special rituals and sacrifices (black animals instead of white). There is a misconception that the powers of the underworld were all evil (influenced by later conceptions of Satan, the Devil). For example, Hecate was a benificent goddess whose role was to accompany dead souls to a blessed afterlife. Through Christian polemic, these practices were deemed "superstition," and these deities were demonized. Hecate became the "witch" of medieval Halloween practices.

Ancient Concepts of the Afterlife

Approximately 100,000 years ago, people began burying the dead with tools, weapons, decorated artifacts, and jars of food. Most scholars agree that these practices demonstrated a belief that there was another form of existence after death; the grave items would be useful. Generally, a belief in an afterlife refers to specific beliefs that a person continues to exist in some form, either in a disembodied personal essence (soul) or a combination of soul with a new or reconstituted physical body. A belief in an afterlife also assumes a location for this existence outside the realm of earthly life. In connecting the ancient world to the modern, we find belief in an afterlife and funeral rituals to be one of the most conservative elements in history, changing very little over the centuries.

We do not know exactly when or why, but it apparently became difficult to believe that the human person (and personality) could simply be annihilated. In dreams, the dead appeared alive. The idea began to emerge that the dead still existed in some form, and that the dead resided in a separate place. Often deemed the netherworld or the underworld, this place was located under the earth and originally it was a neutral place—neither good nor bad.

The ancient Mesopotamians developed a pessimistic view of death and the underworld. In one of their myths, they claimed that the gods created death in order to control humans and control the population of the earth. In *Irkalla*, their "land of no return", the dead suffered in agony, eating clay, and were eternally thirsty. Because they did exist, the dead could find ways to return to earth and either harm or help the living. Therefore, the dead spirits had to be placated with food and drink offerings.

In ancient Egypt, death was viewed more optimistically as another phase of the life cycle of birth, death, and re-birth. In the Old Kingdom (2600–2100 BCE) only the Pharaoh had access to an afterlife due to his nature as a living manifestation of divinity. By the Middle Kingdom (ca. 2000–1700 BCE) an afterlife was available to anyone who could afford the process (with mummification, funeral rites and ritual texts). This period also saw an increase in the popularity of the Osiris cult, particularly in his role as Lord and Judge of the Dead.

The emphasis on Osiris as Judge of the Dead was directly related to a new type of literature in the Middle Kingdom known collectively as **Admonition Texts**. Immediately preceding the Middle Kingdom, Egypt suffered a series of catastrophes, which may have included foreign invasion, plague, famine, and civil wars. Admonition texts were most often addressed by a father to a son and upheld the moral values of society. The child was admonished to lead a good and pious life and to avoid the pitfalls of evil deeds. Connected now to the Negative Confessions in Osiris' Hall of Judgment, one's deeds (and sins) in this life determined the type of existence in the next life. In these texts, we have some of the earliest indications that views of the afterlife reflect a social and historical context with elements of social justice.

It appears that there was a human need to believe that one's life matters, either now or later, and that the imbalances of justice in this life would eventually be reconciled in the next one. Codes of acceptable social behavior and social justice went hand-in-hand with the evolution of detailed elements of the afterlife. The idea that good people are rewarded, and evil people are punished after death remains ingrained in the Western tradition.

Ancient Judaism

Jewish views of the afterlife evolved over time and in reaction to historical events. Initially, *She'ol* (the land of the dead) was a neutral area where all the dead resided. Heaven remained the domain of God and his angelic beings. Views began to change with the destruction of Jerusalem and Solomon's Temple in 586 BCE. The Prophets of Israel had claimed that God would intervene one more time in human history, and Israel would be restored to her former glory. At that time, a new kingdom would arise, a utopia-like Eden on earth, God's original plan. Included in this dynamic is a general resurrection of all the dead who would be judged.

During the period of exile and then Persian and Greek rule, Jews adopted the concept of the soul that was separate from the body. During the Greek and Roman occupations of Judea, apocalyptic literature detailed the glories of the rewards for righteousness and the tortures for the wicked in the afterlife.

Ancient Greece and Rome

The Greek underworld, or the place of the dead, was named after the Lord of the Underworld, the god **Hades**. The son of Cronus and Rhea, Hades was not the god of death (that was Thanatos), nor was he the equivalent of the Devil in the Western tradition. In Greek mythology Hades referred to both the place of the dead beneath the earth as well as places on the Western horizon. Although he was not an evil deity, nevertheless he was feared by humans as they feared the cruel inevitability of death. There were many cult sites in Greece and Italy that served as entrances to the underworld.

Hermes Psychopompus (guider of souls) led the dead to the river Styx which was the boundary marker for Hades. Hermes handed over the dead to Charon, the Ferryman. He ushered the dead into boats to cross the river for which he charged a fee. This consisted of a coin (*obolus*) that was placed in the mouth of the dead to ensure that Charon would take them across. If they did not cross (if they did not have the fee), they would remain in the liminal area between death and life, condemned to wander for eternity. Charon also served as a guardian to ensure that no one ever escaped from Hades except gods and heroes.

The dead were consigned to four areas, appropriate to the life of the person. The Elysian Fields was the place for heroes and great men. The Asphodel Fields held ordinary souls who did not commit any major crimes, but who also did not achieve fame and glory. The Fields of Punishment contained mythological characters who committed crimes or sacrilege against the gods. Tartarus, the lowest pits of Hades, was reserved for those we would call "the damned".

Greek and Roman Funerals

Once a person died there was a process involved which the survivors (family) were required to complete through rituals that would stabilize the flux or liminal state caused by death. There were three stages involved: (1) dying itself; (2) being dead but not yet disposed of; and (3) completion of the burial rites. Ideally, before dying a man should settle his affairs (by making a will), commit one's children (if young) to the care of others, and make the proper prayers for a safe passage to Hades. The soul left the body at the moment of death and sometimes lingered near the body. The son or the next of kin closed the eyes and placed the coin in the mouth for Charon.

The second stage required the laying out of the body (*prothesis*). Women washed the body and dressed it in a shroud or tunic. Soldiers were covered with their military cloak and if the deceased was a young, newly married woman, she was dressed in her wedding clothes. The dead body was displayed in the house where family and friends could pay their respects. Funeral lamentations were sung in both the home and the funeral procession.

The third stage, completion of the burial rites, included the funeral procession (*ekphora*) and the inhumation or cremation. Funeral processions were public events because they were important for the honor and status of the surviving family. They were so important that from the time of Solon's reforms (sixth century BCE) to the Imperial era in Rome, there was consistent legislation to limit the amount of money spent on funerals. Public display and feasts could be interpreted as currying favor with the voters. However, funerals for military heroes and some public figures continued to be lavish affairs in recognition of their service to the community.

The lamentations and demonstrations of grief that accompanied the procession were understood as a catharsis in its meaning of purification or cleansing of the emotions. The funeral oration, or the eulogy (*epitaphios logos*), if a notable figure, would be given in the public square and was considered the height of Greek oratory.

In ancient Greece, no priests or religious personnel were directly included in the funeral rites, although priests were available for consultation. At the cemetery the body was placed upon a pyre (cremation) or laid in the grave. Food offerings were brought and burned as a sacrifice in a nearby trench. Libations were poured on the pyre and wine was used to quench the ashes after the body was cremated. The bone fragments and ashes were then collected and placed in an urn which was buried in a grave. This was followed by a funeral feast either at graveside or at the house which was prepared by women.

Rome absorbed views of the afterlife and funeral rituals from the indigenous Italian tribes, the Etruscans and the Greek colonies in Magna Graecia. One of the major differences between Greek and Roman funerals is that Rome had what we would call a funeral industry that was subject to state regulation, much like our modern equivalent of funeral homes. The business of death was under the auspices of both the state and the goddess *Venus Libitina*. *Libitina* may be Italian or Etruscan in origin, combining the aspects of a fertility and love goddess with a deity of the underworld. This aspect of the goddess Venus made sense to Romans because life and death were part of the never-ending cycle of existence. *Venus Libitina* symbolized the cessation of the life-force.

The *libitinarii* were trained priests who handled all aspects of death and funerals. *Libitinarii* were the first to be summoned to a dead body so that the necessary rituals could be performed to eliminate the danger. During the Republic one section of the Esquiline Hill was a public cemetery for the lower classes who could not afford a more expensive burial. Foreigners with no family, the very poor and slaves were buried collectively in grave-pits or *puticuli*. Dead animal carcasses from the streets were also dumped into these pits. The *puticuli* were kept open for easy access and public slaves most likely used lime to try to help stench the smell.

Both Greece and Rome established special religious holidays dedicated to dead ancestors, when it was believed that the dead roamed the earth during certain times of the year. Rituals evolved to both appease them (honor them), as well as rituals for sending them back to Hades.

Funeral Games

Funeral games were designed to honor and appease the dead and ensure a successful journey to the afterlife. Funeral games honored both the gods and ancestors and were combined with athletic contests. The model was taken from Homer's description of the funeral games that Achilles gave in honor of his friend Patroculus (the *Iliad*). Some of the earliest funeral games originated at Olympus and were performed every four years (**the Olympic Games**). The Etruscans (an ancient tribal people in Italy) developed specific funeral games that were ultimately adopted by Rome as **Gladiatorial Games**.

Gentiles and Pagans (Problematic Terms)

Thousands of native cults and religious associations dotted the landscape. One word cannot represent them all. What we have in the Bible is the Jewish point of view that identified themselves over and against all others. Translations of Bibles in English are somewhat tricky. In the Jewish Scriptures, all non-Jews are collectively identified as "the (other) nations", from the Hebrew, *goy* or *goyim* (plural). Depending upon the context of the passage, this term is sometimes translated as "stranger" or "foreigner".

In the New Testament, the word for "nations" is *ethnos*, referring to different ethnic communities. Through late Middle English (and through the King James Bible), the common translation became **Gentile** from the Latin *gens*, family or clan, for both *goy* and *ethnos*. "Gentile" simply means someone who was not Jewish and eventually someone who was not Christian.

However, a more popular term arose when Christians began to dominate and rule the Roman Empire. In the late fourth century *paganus*, **pagan**, became a derogatory term for people in the hinterlands who had not converted to Christianity (equivalent to "hillbillies," or the uneducated). Many of the native cults focused on nature and fertility rituals. In the second century, the Church Fathers demonized these people, applying scathing reviews of their lifestyle and behavior that are still conjured up when we see the word "pagan". This includes sexual orgies, drinking, and sometimes Satan worship. In this text "native" or "ethnic" cult is the term of choice, although you will find "pagan" in many of the Suggested Readings.

The inheritance of Biblical texts in Western culture provided the raw material for criticism of the native cults, beginning with the books of the Prophets. These writers continually railed against the worship of other gods as **idolatry** (the worship of icons, or images). Christians utilized these Prophetic texts in their literature, which contributed to the overall negative view of all non-Christians. The Prophets equated idolatry with "sexual immorality" and this became a dominant theme of Christian writers.

Conversion

Conversion means moving from one religious system to another. This word often appears in histories of ancient Judaism and early Christianity. People who participated in ethnic cults had the freedom to belong to several religious associations. They did not convert to another group by doing so. Ancient religion was in the blood; you were born into it as part of your clan or tribe. Conversion in the ancient world meant a change in lifestyle (one's daily "customs"). Greeks and Romans who wanted to become a Jew fully converted in this sense.

The most famous convert in history was the Apostle Paul, and his "conversion on the road to Damascus". However, this is a misnomer; at the time there was no Christian religious system to convert to. Paul himself described it as a "call" in the manner of the Prophets of Israel who were called by God for a specific mission.

Canon/Old Testament/Jewish Scriptures

You will often see the texts of the Bible referred to as the **canon** of Jewish texts and the four gospels as the **canonical gospels**. In Greek "canon" was a system of measurement. Applied in this sense canon refers to those books that were "measured" in later decisions taken to determine which books would be listed as sacred scripture. The Jewish books (the first half of the Christian Bible) were canonized ca. 200 CE under the auspices of a Rabbi known as Judah the Prince. The documents that became the New Testament, the gospels, and the letters of Paul took several centuries to reach agreement on the canon and only began to be considered in a formal list under Constantine I (325 CE).

The designation "Old Testament" is a familiar one for the Jewish books. However, it is a Christian invention that is derogatory in nature. **Testament** is a later word for the older term of **covenant**. "Covenant" simply meant a contract between you and your people and your god(s). Christians in the second century began claiming that the older covenants with Israel were no longer valid and were replaced by the "new covenant" through Jesus. This idea is known today as **supersessionism** (that Judaism was superseded by Christianity), and still resonates as an element of modern anti-Semitism).

Naming the older books the "Old Testament" implies a judgment call. For Jews, these texts are not "old" in the sense that they are no longer valid. They remain at the center of Jewish belief and life. This textbook will use the term, **Jewish Scriptures** or "the Scriptures", when referring to the various books of this collection. Some texts refer to the New Testament as the "Christian Scriptures", but "New Testament" is the earlier descriptor. In the first century when Christian texts referred to "the Scriptures", it was the Jewish Scriptures that they had in mind.

Mark, Matthew, Luke, and John are consistently designed the "canonical gospels". This is out of place, as there was no concept of "canon" for these gospels in the first century. Between the first and third centuries there were dozens of other gospels that narrated different details and different interpretations of the teachings of Jesus. In the second century, the Church Fathers began a process of declaring which of these gospels contained "correct belief" (**orthodoxy**) and which were **heretical** (from the Greek, *haíresis* "a school of thought"). The term "canonical gospels" is relative to the later decision that included only these four gospels in the New Testament.

Faith vs. Rituals

Any text that examines the Bible, and especially the New Testament, will encounter the English word "**faith**" in translation. However, it was only in the eighteenth century that "faith" was used to describe "belief" in a religious system, particularly in teachings on individual salvation. At the same time, the word faith also came to mean belief in something despite evidence to the contrary. But the ancients did not often articulate their ideas as belief or faith as we understand it. "Faith" (derived from the Greek word, *pistis*) originally meant "loyalty," in this case loyalty to a set of shared concepts and rituals involved in worship of a god or gods.

The great concern in the ancient world was to carry out rituals involved in the various native cults correctly. In ancient Rome, if a priest or augur stumbled over the words, he had to begin again. Several books in the Jewish Scriptures describe the correct way in which to perform the rituals of the Temple cult in Jerusalem.

Beginning with the New Testament, this focus on the rituals of non-Christians became a negative, derogatory way in which to attack both Jews and the native cults. Hence the modern concept that the Jews were "legalistic", and were only concerned with "the letter of the Law". The idea that native cults lacked "spirituality" (Christians had faith, pagans had rituals) still finds its biased way into many books on the early history of Christianity.

Church

In the New Testament, and particularly in the letters of Paul, you will encounter the word "church". It is translated from the Greek *ecclesia*, which means "assembly". The first missionaries apparently modeled their communities on the administrative structure of older Greek city-states and Roman towns, where the term referred to the assembly of free citizens who made up local government. In relation to the new groups of the followers of Jesus, a better translation would be "community". Translating this as "church" conjures up images of church buildings and institutional hierarchy. Both were part of later Christian evolution. In the earlier communities there were no church buildings; people met in each other's houses.

"Spirit"

Often mentioned in association with church activities, **spirit** is understood to be "the spirit of God" or "the spirit of Christ" (in Paul's letters) and not the third element of the later concept of "The Trinity" (fourth century CE). This is the spirit of God that breathed life into Adam and "possessed the Prophets of Israel". This is the spirit that came upon Jesus in the gospels at his baptism (the symbol of the dove) so that he was able to perform miracles and forgive sins. Christian English Bibles, reading back later Trinitarian concepts, always translate this with capitals, "Holy Spirit".

Polemic/Rhetoric

Polemic is a verbal or written attack against an opponent, either real or imagined. **Rhetoric** is the art of persuasion, often calling upon figures of speech and stereotypes, and designed to convince an audience of one's arguments or point of view. (We are familiar with these terms in relation to contemporary politics and charges of "fake news" from both sides.)

Polemic and rhetoric are literary devices applied by all writers in the ancient world. In polemical writings, opponents may be named or constructed in what is known as "a straw man". "Straw man" is the idea that the opponent's arguments (as reported by the writer) are always shown to be wrong and thus defeated. Throughout the Jewish Scriptures and the New Testament, we have numerous examples of these literary devices. It was a favorite device of Jewish Prophets against idolatry and the gospels' portraits of the Pharisees and the Sadducees and anyone who opposed Jesus. Christian writers continued to utilize these devices in their arguments against opponents. *But polemic and rhetoric are not historical evidence.*

The Problem of Anachronism

What is **anachronism**? It is placing something out of its own time and place, usually to a later time or place. The best way to understand this is the example of what are known as "gaffes" in Hollywood movies. It is like watching a movie that takes place in the 1970s but where people are using cellphones.

Anachronism is the bane of all historians. This is because we are modern humans. It is difficult to set aside our own experiences and knowledge so that we can be entirely objective. We expect objectivity from historians, but it is virtually impossible. All historians must decide what they think is important, and so you have immediate subjectivity in the selection. Knowing the end of a story always influences the past. For example, it is very difficult to write a history of World War II and ignore how it ended.

Historians of ancient Christianity do not escape this problem. Interpreting the literature of this period is quite a challenge. *We* know that these texts became the basis of a new, independent religion. *But the writers at the time did not know this.* Complicating our reconstructions is the fact that historians and theologians have 2000 years of Christian theology that is so often "read back" into the texts.

As a historian of ancient Christianity (I also research and teach the religions of Egypt, Greece, and Rome), I face the same struggles as other historians. I have attempted in every chapter to try and avoid such pitfalls where I can. I will often insert a modern analogy, simply to help with the reading and the reconstruction of early Christianity. You will be able to distinguish an analogy from anachronism.

Creative Writing

Modern analyses of Biblical literature are sometimes offensive to readers in their descriptions of ancient texts. Many historians conclude that a story was "made up", but this is the way in which ancient writers went about their craft.

Historians such as Herodotus, Polybius, and Livy, for example, were aware of "manuals" that provided the rules. You were expected to "make up speeches." In a speech by a general before the troops were sent into battle, no one "took notes". Moses was alone when he received the commandments on Mt. Sinai. Instead, the writer created a speech that highlighted the known characteristics of a general or a leader. He was then judged on how well the speech fit the character and the occasion. Both the writers/editors of the Jewish Scriptures as well as the New Testament utilized this device. This is especially true in the hundreds of speeches in Luke's Acts of the Apostles.

Perhaps a better way in which to explain this type of writing is found in the modern category known as "creative nonfiction". Creative nonfiction portrays real people and events, but with material added for dramatic effect. Creative nonfiction is employed by poets, playwrights, and screenwriters. In film biographies, speeches are added to highlight the meaning behind an event or to indicate what the person was thinking. We have the same process in ancient literature.

For brief history of the Roman Empire, see **Appendix I.**

Summary

- The Roman Empire contained hundreds of native cults that originated with ancestral traditions.
- Religion and society were fully integrated into everyday life to achieve the survival of each community.

Suggestions for Further Reading

Denova, Rebecca I. 2019. *The Religions of Greece and Rome*. Wiley-Backwell. This textbook surveys and compares the origins and practice of the religions of Greece and Rome.

Mikalson, Jon D. 2009. *Ancient Greek Religion*. Wiley-Blackwell. Mikalson includes analysis of Greek myths and literature in the practical applications of Greek religion.

Warrior, Valerie M. 2006. *Roman Religion*. Cambridge University Press. This is an anthology of the literature and mythology of Roman religion.

THE HISTORY OF ISRAEL

The Story of Israel

Who Wrote the Jewish Scriptures?

Genesis 1–11

Abraham

The Sacrifice

Joseph and His Brothers

The Book of Exodus

Did the Exodus Happen?

Leviticus

Purity/Impurity

Numbers and Deuteronomy

The Historical Books: Joshua, Judges, 1 & 2 Samuel, 1 & 2 Kings

1 & 2 Samuel

The Rise of Kingship and David

The Split into Two Kingdoms

Varieties of Early Christianity: The Formation of the Western Christian Tradition, First Edition. Rebecca I. Denova.
© 2023 John Wiley & Sons, Inc. Published 2023 by John Wiley & Sons, Inc.

22   The History of Israel

Disaster Strikes

The Babylonian Empire

Persia

The Diaspora

The Role of the Prophets

A New Hope

A Paradigmatic Shift and A New Disaster

Antiochus Epiphanes IV (Syria, 216 BCE–154 BCE)

The Maccabee Revolt

Jewish Sectarianism

Apocalyptic Eschatology

Pompey and the Rule of Rome

The Herodians

Direct Rule of Judea by Rome

The Jewish Revolt Against Rome (66–73 CE)

Flavius Josephus (36 CE–100 CE)

Josephus and Scholarship

The Destruction of the Temple and Jerusalem

The Importance of the Jewish War against Rome

After reading this chapter you will be able to:

- Become familiar with the history of ancient Israel as presented in the Jewish Scriptures.
- Understand the historical elements that contributed to Jewish and later Christian identity.

The Story of Israel

In the ancient world, "antiquity" gave you respect. Greeks and Romans considered Jews "eccentric" and "anti-social" (they did not join in the festivals) but were given respect because they had ancient roots. Like other native cults, the Jews claimed ancestral traditions. By the first century those traditions were incorporated into two umbrella references: the Scriptures; and the **Law of Moses**. The letters of Paul and the gospels assume a grounding in this literature, so we begin with a review of that history. The entire history of Israel cannot be told in one chapter (it would take another textbook, but reading the text is encouraged). The emphasis in this chapter is on those events and concepts that are quoted and repeated in the New Testament. In this way, you will see the connections applied by the writers.

Who Wrote the Jewish Scriptures?

The first five books (Genesis, Exodus, Leviticus, Numbers, Deuteronomy) are referred to as the **Pentateuch** (Greek, *penta*, "five"). Tradition claimed that Moses wrote them down and passed them on to his general, Joshua to take into Canaan.

The Jewish Scriptures consist of many and varied sources: myth, hymns, prayers, oracles, and historical narratives. The assumption is that the stories began as oral tradition and were passed down over several generations. But we also know that as the centuries passed and as Israel experienced a long history which included many momentous events as well as disasters, these oral stories were edited with updated material. The additions always reflect the "meaning" of the older narratives, updated to explain contemporary events.

Bible scholars in the seventeenth and eighteenth centuries began noticing that the Jewish Scriptures were very confusing. Sometimes there are two (and sometimes three) versions of the same event, but with differences—two creation stories, two flood stories. Or sometimes you will read a story, and then the passage jumps back and starts again. Scholars began trying to identify the various sources and came up with the "Documentary Hypothesis" for the way in which the

Jewish Scriptures were eventually written down (see Box II.1). The consensus is that older, oral traditions were first written down in the period of the exile (from ca. 600 BCE) where the various sources labeled JEPD were finally brought together.

Box II.1   The documentary hypothesis

"The Documentary Hypothesis", or the Graf–Wellhausen Hypothesis in honor of the two German scholars who worked on this theory, helps to explain the sources behind the stories in the Jewish Scriptures. It remains a theory, and modern Biblical scholars continue to update the original as well as argue specifics parts of it.

This theory claims that different stories, as well as different names and descriptions of God, arose from different "sources". We do not know who wrote these stories but "sources" in this sense indicates a "writer or community behind a text". These communities were understood to have specific ideologies that became encoded.

J = Yahweh, the Hebrew letter for God (in German J is pronounced as Y). The J also stands for "Judah" the southern tribes in and around Jerusalem. These sources often present God in anthropomorphic terms, e.g. "the hand of god", and refer to him as "lord".

E = *Elohim*, an ancient regional name for "gods", when God is also deemed "God almighty". E reflects the northern tribes of one of the sons of Joseph, Ephraim. E's portraits of God are more of an abstract deity.

P = Priestly, is a way in which to categorize the details of blood lineage (the "begats"), sacrifices, ritual purity, and worship.

D = D stands for the Deuteronomist, a term for the final editing process for the collection of the books.

Many scholars believe that J and E were the first to be combined and written down ca. 600 BCE.

Because the final version was not set down until ca. 600 BCE, I have often suggested that it is easier to read through all the books first, find out "how it ends", and then go back and read them again. This time you will be able to see the way in which later material was inserted into the older stories. For example, some of the later editors were against the rise of kingship in Israel (blaming this for the disasters that occurred). You will see their criticism of it in certain earlier stories. Identifying "sources" in a similar process is applied by New Testament scholars.

The opening stories of creation in Genesis ("In the beginning …") are not the oldest traditions. In fact, the first story of creation is "Priestly" and was most likely composed ca. 600 BCE. It takes time to get used to reading the Scriptures in this light. Figure II.1 is the recognized timeline for this "history" of Israel, in line with each book. See Figure II.2 for Map of Ancient Israel with the Later Settlement of the Tribes.

The years in the timeline are approximate and are drawn from scholarly estimates of the archaeological and literary evidence that we have. This schematic can also change, depending upon new excavations and theories. From 0 to about 800 BCE, archaeological evidence is sparse, restricted to sites that may reflect older place-names. Scholars look to the "stories" to determine a timeframe, based upon the cultural and religious elements described in the various

24   The History of Israel

Year(s) BCE	(Before the Common Era)
Creation; Genesis	0
Abraham and other Patriarchs; Genesis	1800 BCE
Moses and the Exodus; Exodus, Leviticus, Numbers, Deuteronomy	1300 BCE
Joshua and the taking of Canaan; Joshua, Judges	1200 BCE
David, Solomon and the United Monarchy; 1 & 2 Samuel; 1 Kings	1000 BCE
Division of the Kingdom: Israel (north), Judea (south); 2 Kings; Chronicles	980 BCE
Books of the Prophets; Amos, Hosea	800 BCE
1st Isaiah	735 BCE
The Assyrian Invasion; the fall of Israel; the ten tribes are disbursed	722 BCE
Josiah's reform and Jeremiah; joining of J and E traditions in the first composition of the texts	600 BCE
Destruction of Solomon's Temple; Jews taken to Babylon (period of the Exile)	586 BCE
2nd Isaiah	550 BCE
Cyrus of Persia	539 BCE
Return from Captivity	515 BCE
Restoration of Jerusalem and the Temple (Second Temple); Nehemiah, Ezra	440 BCE
Alexander the Great	330 BCE
Jewish Revolt against Antiochus Epiphanes (Books of the Maccabees; Daniel)	167 BCE
Pompey the Great conquers Jerusalem for Rome	63 BCE
Herod the Great as King of the Jews	37 BCE
Octavian (Augustus) as the first Emperor	27 BCE
Death of Herod	4 BCE

Figure II.1 Biblical time line for the history of Israel.

(These last four dates do not have literature in the Jewish Scriptures but are important for the timeline of the first century.)

books. For example, the stories of Abraham in Genesis fit known aspects of nomad culture in the region ca. 1800 BCE. Placing Moses ca. 1300 reflects elements of the New Kingdom in Egypt. In historical terms, recent excavations have uncovered seals and pottery with some names from the texts in the Jerusalem area. Earlier characters—Adam, Noah, Abraham, Moses—have yet to be historically confirmed.

Figure II.2 Map of ancient Israel with the later settlement of the tribes. Bible Study. Biblestudy.org

Genesis 1–11

The first eleven chapters of Genesis are referred to as myth, in that they function like all ancient myths to narrate the creation of the universe, the first humans, and gender roles. There are two creation stories, P and J, with J containing the more familiar story of Adam and Eve. These creation stories are also polemical, in that they include what is most likely criticism against some neighbors. Ancient Mesopotamia had an older creation myth, *The Enuma Elish*, that claimed that the gods were capricious and chaotic. Humans were created simply as servants to appease these gods with sacrifices.

In contrast to the Mesopotamians, the creation stories in Genesis continually show their God creating in an orderly fashion. Each time that God created something, the text says, "it is good". For these writers, God did not create evil, it was the fault of humans. That is the purpose of the story of Adam and Eve. Adam and Eve's disobedience brought death, the greatest evil, into the world.

The following chapters begin a list of the descendants from the first couple. After Cain killed Abel and was expelled from Eden, Adam and Eve had another son, Seth. When God punished the earth for the rise of evil (through the first blood-letting by Cain), the new line of Seth produced Noah, a "righteous man" who built the ark to save his family and various animals from the flood. (Flood stories were common, especially in the area between the Tigris and Euphrates river. One of the oldest of the stories is the Mesopotamian/Babylonian *Epic of Gilgamesh*.)

After the flood, Noah's sons begin the "list of nations" (Chapter 10) who repopulate the earth. These are the **begats**, scattered throughout Genesis, that trace bloodlines (genealogies). The "tower of Babel" story explains the many languages of the earth.

Abraham

The fundamental purpose of Genesis begins in Chapter 12, in a story known as "the call of Abraham". "Abram" and his wife "Sarai" live near the head of the Persian Gulf. They will later have name changes, to Abraham, and Sarai to Sarah. Name changes in the Bible usually signal a change of worldview.

Abram heard a voice from the God of Israel telling him to take all his family and clans and move to the land of **Canaan**, where God will make him the father of a "great nation". This is what the name "Abraham" means. He was promised that his descendants will be "as numerous as the stars or the sands of the sea". Canaan is the older name for what became the Phoenician Empire, today, Lebanon, parts of Syria, and Israel. This is known as the **Covenant with Abraham**. Covenants were essentially a "contract" between the divine and humans, spelling out what was expected of each. Abraham and his descendants were to be loyal to this God in return for his protection and granting them prosperity. Abraham was thus the ancestor who is the founder of the Jewish nation.

Abraham immediately obeyed, as he did in everything and so became a symbol of faithfulness throughout the history of Israel (and the New Testament). He took his group north and stopped at Haran (in modern day Iraq), where some relatives decided to settle. He then went on to Canaan where he and his flocks and clans prospered.

If you have ever had a literature class, you may have heard of a literary device known as "plot tension". Plot tension is what motivates the characters of a story and moves the plot along. The plot tension in the story of Abraham begins with this promise of God. Abraham and Sarah are old, and Sarah is barren. The rest of the book of Genesis centers on the problem—how is God going to fulfill his promise of "a nation", descendants", for a couple who are old and have no children? (see Box II.2).

Box II.2   Fertility and barren women in the Bible

A fundamental concern of all ancient cultures was that of fertility—fertility of crops, herds, and people. All native cults therefore had pairs of gods and goddesses (the goddess as consort). The ancients did not fully understand the reproduction cycle, but they knew that it took "two to tango". Without fertility, the clan did not survive. Jews however, did not present their God with a consort. The God of Israel "speaks", and brings about creation. (This is not unique. One of the older creation myths of Egypt has the god Ptah creating this way as well.) God's first commandment for humans was "Be fruitful and multiply".

Throughout the Jewish Scriptures, many women are deemed "barren". This is not because they had "sinned". It is a literary device for having their God involved in fertility, by way of divine intervention. Many of these women who are barren receive an **annunciation** (either from God or from an angel) telling them that they will eventually become mothers. The annunciation text always predicts that the son (it is always a son) will be a great person or be an instrument of God's divine will.

Sarah told Abraham to "go into her Egyptian slave, Hagar". "Go into her" is a euphemism for sexual intercourse. Abraham agreed to this, an ancient version of surrogate motherhood. Slaves in the ancient world were the property of their masters and had no rights of their own. Once Hagar is pregnant, the child is legally the child of Abraham and Sarah. By doing this, Abraham did not commit adultery. As a slave, Hagar was the property of Abraham (see Box II.3).

Box II.3   Marriage and sexual intercourse in the Jewish Scriptures

In most ancient cultures, women were the literal property of men (ancient Egypt was an exception in some details). When a daughter was born, she was first the property of her father who then made a "marriage contract" for her and her husband. When a girl married (right after puberty), she moved away from her father's house into the house of her husband. The marriage contract served as a legal transference of property (the girl) from her father's house to her husband's.

The Jewish Scriptures command that only men could initiate a divorce. This was a practical function, as the husband now controlled all communal property (such as flocks that were part of a woman's dowry). Only the husband could make a division of the property in the case of divorce.

Most ancient cultures, including Israel, had laws against adultery, which was technically, "the violation of another man's property". In the Jewish Scriptures (at least on the books), such a violation earned the extreme punishment—death by stoning for both the man and the woman. Why such a high penalty? The ancients had no test for DNA (paternity), but they were very concerned about keeping the clan and tribal bloodlines pure. This concern is what originally gave rise in the ancient Middle East, Greece, Rome, and the Islam to the veiling of women (having women cover their heads and faces) when they left the house and keeping them sheltered and away from the eyes of strange men. There could be absolutely no doubt about paternity.

The other end of the spectrum are the prostitutes (of which there are many in the Jewish Scriptures). Prostitution was *not* a sin in ancient Israel! Again, think property/contract law. Prostitutes were never parties to a legal contract, so sex with a prostitute did not violate anyone's property. Surprisingly, there are many stories of "righteous prostitutes" in the Jewish Scriptures who are more loyal to the God of Israel than Jewish men.

While prostitution was not a sin in the Jewish Scriptures, nevertheless, they were at the lower end of the social ladder and considered threats to the group. This is because of the limited medical knowledge of the ancients. They did not know that semen regenerates; they thought that men had a very limited supply. In this case, you should be using your semen to "be fruitful and multiply" within your own family/clan, and not "wasting it" on prostitutes.

Hagar became pregnant with Ismael. Ismael was not the "son of the promise", but Hagar was told that he would also become "a great nation". Ismael became the ancestor of the Arabs.

Genesis 17 contains another covenant. It repeats the promise to Abraham but now commands a "sign" of this covenant, **circumcision**. Circumcision is the removal of the loose foreskin of the penis. Jews were not the only ones to practice this; ancient Egyptians did as well as Arabs through the descent from Abraham. But why practice it at all? Many people assume that it was a hygienic measure, but most ancients did not understand such diseases and germs (although Egyptian doctors may be the exception).

What we can know about circumcision is the way it *functioned*. Our idea of "underwear" is quite modern; the great majority of the ancients wore nothing. If you wanted to identify a "Jew" you simply lifted the tunic. Circumcision was a permanent, physical marker for communal identity of this nation.

The Sacrifice

Sarah eventually had a son named Isaac. Surprisingly, God then ordered Abraham to take "the son whom he loves" up to Mt. Moriah and sacrifice him. (In the Islamic Qur'an, the claim is made that it was really Ismael, his first-born, whom "he loved", so the story was changed to reflect this.) Abraham obeyed, but at the last minute, an angel "stayed his hand".

Scholars and theologians have debated this story for centuries. Was this Israel's story about forbidding human sacrifice? Some ancient cultures did practice this, most often with prisoners of war. Without being able to fully comprehend the story, nevertheless it functions as a demonstration of the faithfulness of Abraham.

Once Isaac was born, the rest of the book of Genesis narrates the stories of his descendants, starting with Isaac's son, **Jacob**. Jacob is important for two reasons: (1) his "struggle" with God results in a new name for Jacob, that of "Israel" ("he who struggled with God") and (2) his twelve sons (through Leah, Rachel, and some slave women) became the **Twelve Tribes of Israel**.

Joseph and His Brothers

The story of Joseph serves as the rationale for why the sons of Jacob end up in Egypt. Joseph is a dream interpreter who is not very discreet. He related his dream to his brothers, that they were all standing around him and bowing. They sold him to a slave caravan going to Egypt. However, Joseph prospered there and became the Vizier (prime minister). When there was a famine in Canaan and the brothers came to Egypt to seek food, Joseph hid his identity for a while but ultimately told them to bring the clan to Egypt. By the end of the book of Genesis, the descendants of Abraham were multiplying rapidly. This "fulfills" the first promise of God (for descendants). However, they were in the wrong place according to the covenant.

The Book of Exodus

The Book of Exodus (from the Greek, "going out", "leaving") began by claiming that the **Hebrews** (another word for the Israelites in this book) lived for 450 years in Egypt and prospered in the Delta region. But a Pharaoh arose "who did not know Joseph", meaning that he knew nothing about the older relationship. The Delta region in Egypt was situated in the northeastern area of Egypt, and periodically saw "Asiatics" (the Egyptian derogatory term for these nomads) settle here whenever there was famine in their own lands. Because of the Nile, Egypt always had food. But if you are an efficient ruler, you do not want foreigners on your eastern flank. This new Pharaoh decided to enslave the Hebrews and set them to work on his grain cities. (The Hebrews did not build the pyramids.) Exodus does not name the Pharaoh, but the grain cities of Pithom-Rameses mentioned here connected the tradition to Rameses II, the most famous of the New Kingdom pharaohs.

To control the number of the Hebrews, Pharaoh ordered the midwives to kill every son born to them. Of course, they do not do this (but you are going to see this story again in Matthew's gospel). One of the babies was hidden by his mother by floating him in a small boat down the Nile. He was picked up by Pharaoh's daughter (who was barren) and raised in the Egyptian royal court. This baby was **Moses**. When Moses was an adult, he saw an Egyptian overseer beating a Hebrew slave and he killed the overseer. He had to flee Egypt and ended up at an oasis in the Sinai. Moses rescued some women shepherds here (one of them, Zipporah, became his wife) and he settled down to become a shepherd.

One day there was a strange event up on a mountain—a bush was on fire, but it did not burn up. When he went to investigate, he was given a revelation by God. God told him that he was sending him back to Egypt to tell pharaoh to "let my people go". When Moses asked God his name, he responded with "I am who I am". Not very enlightening, but this is when the four Hebrew letters for the consonants became the sacred name of God, **Yahweh**. Moses protested that he is not a good speaker, but God told him that his brother, **Aaron**, could do the talking. Aaron became the first high-priest of Israel.

And then an interesting line—at the end of this, God told Moses that he would "harden Pharaoh's heart" so that he will *not* let them go. This is a plot device to set the story up for the battle known the "ten plagues" of Egypt. These all involve nature, as a duel between the God of Israel and the gods of Egypt— which of these powers controls the universe?

After a series of natural disasters, the final plague was formalized in both story and ritual. Moses told the Hebrews to sacrifice a lamb, put its blood on their door lintels, and stay inside that night. The "angel of death" was going to "pass over" Egypt and kill the first-born of all Egyptians. The blood on the door lintels would protect the Hebrews. This became one of the most important of Jewish holidays—**Passover**. The text said they were to re-enact and tell this story every year.

Pharaoh's first-born died and so he relented. The Hebrews left Egypt, taking much loot and gold with them, but then Pharaoh changed his mind and went after them with the army. There was a race to the crossing of the Red Sea. When Moses got there he "parted the waters of the Red Sea" (a divine miracle), so that the Hebrews could cross over. When the chariots arrived, the water receded, and the army was drowned. Moses and the Hebrews ended up at the mountain where God told him to bring them.

Did the Exodus Happen?

There has been a recent flurry of books and documentaries on the problem of the historicity of the Exodus story. Egypt has been the focus of archaeological excavations for the past 200 years. No direct evidence of a group of Hebrews living in Egypt has ever been found. On the other hand, why would a group "create" a story that their ancestors were enslaved? There are hundreds of Egyptian concepts and religious elements in the Jewish Scriptures. However,

The History of Israel   31

those could have been absorbed when Egypt conquered and ruled Canaan during the New Kingdom (1300 BCE). Archaeologists have found several Egyptian artifacts in various excavations in Israel; trade was a connecting element between the two cultures. Whether historical or not, the narrative was foundational for the later history of Israel as well as elements in the New Testament.

Moses went back up the mountain to find out what God wanted them to do next. This is when he received "the commandments". No, despite the tradition, it is not "ten"—he received 613 commandments. Everyone assumes ten because that became the iconography of court rooms, synagogues, churches, and other art (where Moses is shown carrying two stone tablets). It is also because later Christians reduced the list of commandments to "ten", as the only ones that Christians must follow (see Chapter VIII).

The first ten commandments are highlighted at the beginning not because they are "universal", but because they are different from the rest. They are short because there is no atonement or no "fixing" these commandments once they are broken. The ones that follow are what we call "case law", meaning that they are "fixable". If you violate any of these others (the 603) you can atone or fix it with a sacrifice or a ritual.

What Moses brought down from the mountain is essentially *the constitution for the nation of Israel*. It outlined how they were to look, how they were to eat, how they were to settle legal problems, how they were to worship. In this sense, they were to be "set apart", and to be "different from all the nations". They were to be a model of a righteous nation that the rest of the world would eventually follow.

This is the **covenant with Moses**, where the Jews claim that they were God's **chosen people**. Everything he brought down was incorporated into the next several books: Leviticus, Numbers and Deuteronomy. By tradition, Moses even brought down the blue-prints for Solomon's Temple that was built centuries later. The "tablets" were placed in a box, **the ark of the covenant**. This became a sacred vessel, which was later placed in the "holy of holies" in the Temple in Jerusalem (see Box II.4).

Box II.4   Connecting phrases in the Jewish Scriptures

One of the easiest ways in which to observe how the Scriptures were edited over time, is in repeated words and phrases. One example is the word "ark". We first encounter this word with the story of Noah building a boat to save his family and the animals from the flood. When Moses is sent down the Nile, he is in a small cradle of reeds. The tablets of the Law are placed in a wooden chest. However, the text uses the word "ark" for all three, a boat, a cradle, a chest. What all three have in common is that they are "vessels". The theology behind the use of this term, is that all three serve as "vessels of salvation". The editors do this deliberately so that when you see the word "ark" you were reminded of times when God did things to "save" Israel.

Moses was on the mountain "40 days and 40 nights". Down below, the Hebrews, thinking they were abandoned, talked Aaron into making them an idol, a "golden calf" (bull worship was popular in Egypt as a symbol of fertility). This was the function of all that loot they took from the temples of Egypt. When Moses came down and found them in idolatry, he threw the "tablets", smashing them, which caused an earthquake that swallowed up half of these sinners. (Moses went back up later and got another set of commandments.) The Hebrews were punished by "wandering in the wilderness for forty years". They are not lost all that time; God did not allow the generation who came out of Egypt to reach the promised land (Canaan) until they had died off. "Forty" is a generic term for a generation. With Genesis, the books that follow Exodus (Leviticus, Numbers, and Deuteronomy), along with Genesis, became **Torah**, "teaching", as in the teachings of Moses.

Leviticus

The book of Leviticus is named for the tribe of Moses and Aaron, the Levites. This book is often known as "the priest's manual", because it contains all the rules for the (later) sacrifices at the Temple in Jerusalem. Leviticus remains one of the hardest books to understand; as moderns we do not think in the same conceptual elements that are a major part of this book.

Leviticus defines the rules that will keep Israel "apart from the nations": circumcision, dietary laws, incest rules, Sabbath. Other cultures had some dietary restrictions, but Israel's was deemed "eccentric". In the ancient world: pork was one of the cheapest and most popular of meats. Pork is forbidden not because of trichinosis, but because their category is ambiguous; pigs have a divided hoof, but do not chew the cud (like cattle). The writers (and priests) did not like ambiguity; foods should fit the correct category. Fish are easier to understand in this sense. Fish had to be "true fish", with fins and scales. Shellfish (such as crabs) could also walk on land and so were outside of the definite category. Jews were also forbidden to eat meat "with the blood" (it had to be drained). When Jews began living in the cities throughout the Mediterranean Basin, they often had their own quarter. Most of the meat in the markets was left-over from sacrifices. Not only was it now "tainted" with idolatry, but the blood remained. Jews required their own butchers.

Purity/Impurity

A great concern of the book of Leviticus is that of "purity/impurity", and avoiding "contamination" from things that are not sacred and the other nations: "You must therefore be holy because I am holy" (Lev. 11:44). The way in which to "be holy", for Jews is through ritual purity. These concepts are most often translated as "pure/impure", "clean/unclean". Impurity can cause what is translated into English as "contagion". To move from the ritually impure state utilizes water rituals, and so most people assume that these elements are simply concerned with hygiene.

All ancient cultures had rituals of purity. *Ritual purity was a state of being.* It had meaning in relation to those things that were "sacred" and set apart from the "mundane". "Impurity" was not a "sin". Most of the issues were involved in everyday life: the birth of a child; menstruation; sexual intercourse; the death of a family member (corpse contamination). Women were deemed "unclean" as the result of childbirth and menstruation because it involved blood. Men who had sexual intercourse were "unclean" for a day. Blood and semen were the two sources of life and belonged to God. The time of being "unclean" was a designation for setting aside these special times from daily routines. In most cases, time (until sunset of the next day, etc.) and a sprinkling of water removed the impurity.

Perhaps one of the greatest misunderstandings of all this material in Leviticus is that *these prohibitions were only related to sacred space.* In other words, "pure/impurity" only was a concern if you were entering "sacred space", in this case the Temple in Jerusalem. It basically did not matter if you were in an "impure" state if you were not participating in the Temple rituals (time took care of it). The other great misunderstanding relates to non-Jews. *All the rules in Leviticus were never understood as universal for everyone, only Jews.* Surprisingly, a non-Jewish menstruating woman could make it into the Court of Women at the Temple complex, but not a menstruating Jewish woman.

Highlighting the elements of Leviticus is important because all this material is subject to debate in the gospels, Paul's letters, and later Christian writers.

Numbers and Deuteronomy

The book of Numbers is exactly that: the lists of the individual names of all the Jews who came out of Egypt. It also has several stories about the wanderings in the wilderness which included frequent rebellions against Moses. The food miracles of Moses in the wilderness provided the parallel for the later multiplication of food by the Prophets and Jesus in the gospels. Deuteronomy means "second law". It is a summary of the first four books and included Moses' "farewell speech" to the Israelites before he died. Moses told the Israelites that sometime in the future, God would send another "prophet like me; listen to him!" This became a basic element in the gospel descriptions of Jesus of Nazareth as this "new Moses".

The Historical Books: Joshua, Judges, 1 & 2 Samuel, 1 & 2 Kings

The next six books are referred to as "historical" books, but again, not in the sense that we understand history today. They are called this because the writers claimed that this was the history of the stories of the conquest of Canaan, the rise of kingship, and the division of the kingdoms of Israel into North and South. They are also understood as historical in the sense that we have external evidence for some of the events from neighboring cultures through archaeology and ancient inscriptions.

Joshua and Judges relate the problems of settling in the land of Canaan. These books describe the period when Israel was ruled by a **Tribal Confederation**. The ark of the covenant was kept in a shrine, **the Tent of Meeting**, which traveled to various tribal lands to avoid jealousy. Joshua and Judges contain violent battles and violations of God's commandments. As a punishment, God permitted Canaanite oppression. "Judges" were not court judges, but individuals raised up by God at various times to smite the Canaanites in return. By the end of Judges, the tribes have gone to war with each other. The book presents an overall demonstration of a downward spiral of violence. The reader is set-up for the next series of books, where King David will solve all the problems and unify the tribes.

1 & 2 Samuel

There are two books of Samuel because it is a big story. There was only so much room on ancient scrolls. The Books of Samuel were constructed from many different sources, the "cult sites" where the Ark rested from time to time. The sources from these cult sites relate two important innovations in the history of Israel: the rise of **Prophets** and the rise of **Kingship**. Prophets, "spokespersons for God" functioned the same as other ancient oracles.

Like the native cult equivalent, some Prophets entered a trance-like state and were then possessed by "the spirit of God". Others received a "revelation", in being "called by God". In both cases this special status was what enabled the Prophets to work miracles. Some of the stories of the Prophets are included in larger books (Elijah and Elisha in the book of Kings) while others have their own (Isaiah, Jeremiah, Ezekiel). English Bibles have made it easy to distinguish the speech in these books. When it is God speaking, the text introduces it with "Thus says the lord", and then the speech is written and indented like poetry.

The Rise of Kingship and David

According to the book of Samuel, the **Philistines** (otherwise known from ancient literature as "the sea peoples") who invaded and settled in Canaan, could not be repulsed through a Tribal Confederation. Israel asked for a king and Samuel warned them of "the ways of a king" (recruiting armies and taking women into the palace as servants). God appointed **Saul** who turned out to be a bad king, making every mistake possible. Samuel (in his role as a Prophet) then went to the house of Jesse of the tribe of Judah in Bethlehem and found his youngest son, **David**. When Samuel poured oil over his head, this was "anointing" or the Hebrew, *meshiach*, **messiah** in English, "the anointed one".

David is known as the one of the greatest kings of Israel, and his rule as "the golden age" of a **United Monarchy**, uniting the tribes under one central system. He captured the city of Jerusalem and made it the capitol. The great irony is that David was a sinner. He committed adultery with his neighbor's wife, Bathsheba, who became pregnant and David murdered her husband, Uriah the Hittite. As their punishment, the baby was stillborn. David had plans to bring the Ark of the Covenant into Jerusalem and build a permanent "house" for God. Nathan, who was now the Prophet of the court, told David he will not do this, but that God will "build a house for David." This is the **Davidic Covenant**. God will establish a "dynasty" of David's descendants, among whom there would always be a descendant of David who would rule over Israel. David and Bathsheba had a second son, **Solomon**, who built the Temple in Jerusalem.

Solomon became famous for both his wisdom and his wealth. However, reading beyond those stories, he was ultimately condemned in the Scriptures. Kings were expected to have many wives as political alliances, including neighboring kingdoms. But Solomon's "sin" was permitting each of the foreign wives to erect temples and shrines to their own gods, allowing idolatry in Jerusalem. Solomon also conscripted labor from the tribes to build the Temple and his other projects, which appeared to parallel "Pharaoh".

The Split into Two Kingdoms

After Solomon's death, ten of the tribes petitioned his son to stop the conscription, but he refused. In response, these ten tribes, under the leadership of a man named Jeroboam, seceded and settled in northern Israel. Two of the tribes, Benjamin and Judah, remained in the south.

For the next several centuries, the **Northern Kingdom of Israel (10)**, and the **Southern Kingdom of Judah (2)**, sometimes joined together to fight foreign invaders but also fought each other. The rest of the book of kings is like a report card, narrating the reigns of all the kings in both the North and South and evaluating their rule. The common theme is that most were condemned for not ridding the land of Israel of idolatry. The books of the Prophets are interspersed with this material; the role of the king was to keep Israel obedient to God's commandments, while the role of the Prophet was to keep an eye on the king.

Disaster Strikes

In a period of empire-building, the **Assyrians** (the inheritors of ancient parts of Mesopotamia) moved west and conquered the Northern Kingdom of Israel in 722 BCE. Jerusalem was also under siege but held out. Refugees from the North fled to Jerusalem (with their traditions), and this is when we may have had the combination of the J and E sources first written down.

The Assyrians had a distinct "foreign policy". If you want to ensure that there is no future rebellion in a conquered territory, then the solution is to switch whole populations. The Assyrians moved their own people into the North (and the area known as the Galilee) and moved out many of the ten tribes of Israel who had settled there. Where did they end up? This is a great historical mystery, and they remain known as "the Ten Lost Tribes of Israel" (they are "lost" to history).

The Babylonian Empire

Assyria was conquered by the Neo-Babylonian Empire. The **Babylonians** succeeded in conquering the Southern Kingdom of Judah. For a time, it was ruled as a puppet state, but the Jewish ruler rebelled, and Babylon destroyed the city and Solomon's Temple in 587 BCE. The Babylonians had the same kind of foreign policy as the Assyrians. However, they were not interested in removing everyone—they only wanted the elite—the aristocrats (the rich), the scribes, the priests, and the merchants. They left the farmers and the poor in Judah. This elite was carried off into captivity to the city of Babylon, their capitol city. This period became known as **the Exile**, as the Jews were now exiled from their promised land. As an indication of this disaster, there is an entire book in the Jewish Scriptures, the Book of Lamentation—fully devoted to laments over the fall of Jerusalem and the Temple.

Stories of life in exile are found in the books of **Daniel** and **Esther**. They relate episodes of persecution against the Jews (usually by jealous court officials) and become the later basis of the concept of "pogrom". The story of how the Jewish Queen Esther saved her people, resulted in the later holiday of **Purim**.

Persia

Movement again—this time it is the rise of the **Persian Empire. Cyrus the Great** (ca. 600–530 BCE), conquered the Babylonians. He ruled over an Empire that began in the Fertile Crescent and reached all the way to India and which contained hundreds of various ethnic cults. He managed to organize them by having a "Satrap" (governor) rule in the different areas. He promoted the state religion of **Zoroastrianism**, but also had a policy of tolerance for all other gods and cults. He inherited the exiled Jews in Babylon, but they prospered under Cyrus. In 539 he issued an edict to the **Jews** (*Yehudi*, "those from Judah"). He gave them money to return to Jerusalem to rebuild the city and the Temple. The Jews who migrated back to Jerusalem were under the auspices of two priests, Nehemiah and Ezra who supervised the rebuilding.

The Second Temple was completed ca. 450 BCE. Persia was basically interested in the collection of tribute (taxes). There were no more kings, and this may have been when the position of high-priest and the priests in the Temple

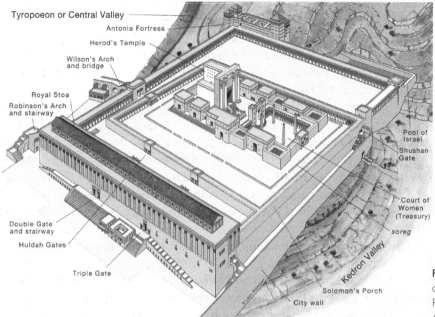

Figure II.3 Schematic of the Second Temple. Ritmeyer Archaeological Design.

became elevated. The everyday running of the city was now supervised along with the Temple cult. This period is referred to in all the scholarly literature with the descriptor of **The Second Temple** period, and the changes that occur as **Second Temple Judaism (450 BCE–70 CE)**. These terms are used throughout the rest of the book (see Figure II.3).

The Diaspora

Jews prospered under Persian rule, so that many decided to stay there. Jewish communities abroad became known as the **Diaspora** ("dispersion"). It reflected populations of Jews who settled outside the land of Israel. Reasons for living outside the land were initially as prisoners of war, but also the conditions of trade and craftsmen. Then as now, Israel was roughly the size of New Jersey, so that re-settlement may also have been a solution to population increases.

The Role of the Prophets

Israel had suffered two national disasters under the Assyrians and the Babylonians. The result was a major theological crisis: if God had covenants with Israel, if the Israelites were his chosen people, then what did this mean? Were the gods of the Assyrians and the Babylonians mightier than the God of

Israel? Like the writers of Genesis, the Prophets were not going to blame God for evil. Instead, they claimed the disasters were brought on by the sins of the people. The great sin was idolatry and neglect of the commandments. God remained the greatest God in the universe, but he utilized the gods (the powers) of the Assyrians and the Babylonians to punish and discipline Israel (as you would a wayward child).

In page after page of the books of the Prophets, they railed against the sins of Israel. Amos and Hosea critiqued the Northern Kingdom for its rich life-style and neglect of widows and orphans. (The books of the Prophets remain important resources for contemporary interpretation because of their teachings on social justice.) Isaiah was the Prophet of record for the Assyrian invasion, but the text was expanded and updated over three different time periods and is one of the longest of the Prophetic books. Jeremiah was the Prophet of note for the Babylonian disaster.

The great sin of idolatry took center stage in the critique. Because these "idols" involved fertility deities they utilized marriage and sexual metaphors to describe Israel's sins: "All Israel whored after the idols"; "God is the bridegroom and Israel the bride", but Israel committed adultery by "going after the other gods". In a particularly graphic passage in Jeremiah, he described Israel as "a harlot by the side of the road" … spreading her legs to any who came along.

These passages do not constitute historical proof that all Israel had sinned through idolatry and neglected the other commandments. This is an after-the-fact rationalization to find blame for the disasters. The polemics of the Prophets have a long shelf-life. They are quoted throughout the new Testament (Isaiah appears to be Paul's favorite) and later Christians turned to the same metaphors of sexuality in their critique of the dominant culture (see Chapter VI).

A New Hope

While the Prophets listed the sins of Israel, they simultaneously offered hope and encouragement ("you are suffering now but be patient"). Scattered throughout the books are "predictions" that God will intervene in human history one more time, "in the final days". Translated from the Greek, *eschaton*, the word provides scholars with the term, **eschatology**, "the study of things concerning the final days". Many of the books presented scenarios for God's final intervention, the goal of which is to restore Israel to its initial glory as originally planned by God. You will not find the term in the Scriptures, but scholars have constructed a rubric for all these ideas, **Jewish Restoration Theology** (see Box II.5).

> *Box II.5   Jewish Restoration Theology*
>
> Culling the material from the Prophets, scholars have listed the main events for "the final days" or the "end times" (sometimes referred to as God's "day of wrath.)"
>
> 1. God will recognize and "raise up" a messiah figure from the line of David to lead the people, and to lead the armies of God against the current oppressors.
> 2. Even during the days of the disasters, not everyone had sinned; there was always a small group of believers who remained faithful to God. This group became known as "the Righteous Remnant", who kept themselves pure.
> 3. Those faithful Jews living outside of the land "in exile" will be "gathered in" to return to Jerusalem and the land.
> 4. At this time some of "the nations", the Gentiles, will "turn" (repent) and worship the God of Israel.
> 5. There will be a final battle of Israel "against the nations". (God and Israel win.)
> 6. After the battle, there will be a "final judgment". This is when all the dead will "be raised" (the initial concepts of resurrection of the body) and judged. God will establish his kingdom (rule) on earth. The "wicked" will be annihilated in the place of the dead, *Gehenna*, with no memory of them. The "righteous" are rewarded with a "new Eden on earth", God's original plan.
> 7. God will build a new Jerusalem and a new Temple will descend from heaven.

The reason that is important to understand "Jewish Restoration Theology" is because by the first century, this "list" was abbreviated to one umbrella phrase: "the kingdom of God". When the gospels claimed that Jesus taught that "the kingdom of God was at hand," and that his ministry "fulfilled the Scriptures," this list of events was the fulfillment of what the Prophets had predicted.

A Paradigmatic Shift and A New Disaster

The Mediterranean Basin underwent a major cultural and social change beginning ca. 330 BCE. Alexander of Macedonia, later known as **Alexander the Great** (356 BCE–323 BCE), inherited the throne of his father, Phillip who had earlier conquered Greece. Macedonia (to the north) was culturally Greek and in fact, Aristotle was Alexander's tutor. In 490 BCE and again in 480 BCE, the Persians had crossed over the Hellespont and vied for dominance in Greece. In the first invasion, the Battle of Marathon, the Greeks beat them back. In the second invasion, at Thermopylae, the Greeks suffered defeat and the Persians sacked and burned Athens. Ultimately the Persians were defeated in a sea battle and driven out of the area.

When Alexander came to power, his great desire for revenge led him to invade Persia. After he conquered Persia, he invaded all of Asia (the former area of Anatolia, Turkey), Lebanon, Syria, Israel, Egypt and went on to Afghanistan and India (where he was finally turned back). Alexander was extremely proud of his Greek heritage. Everywhere he conquered, he introduced the Greek

Figure II.4 Alexander's empire (from Wikipedia).

language, government, philosophy, art, literature, and religious concepts. Greek became the *lingua franca* of the East which is why the New Testament is written in Greek. The eponymous founder of Greece was Hellas. Thus, the descriptors for this period are **Hellenism** and **Hellenistic Judaism** (see Figure II.4, Map of Alexander's Empire.

As the victor, Alexander had the right to impose his religious ideas upon conquered peoples, but he did not do this. Instead, what we have is **syncretism,** a concept indicative of the Hellenistic Age. It means the combining or merging of different religious and cultural ideas. Syncretism meant that people kept their older gods, but now layered them with the gods of Alexander. Entering a local temple, Alexander claimed that the ancient deity was actually a forerunner of Zeus; add a thunder-bolt in his hand, and both the old and new could be accommodated. The peoples of Alexander's Empire, if they wanted to get ahead, including the Jews, learned Greek. If you had leisure, the writings of the schools of Greek philosophy were available. New concepts and news ways of thinking were introduced to traditional Jewish ideas (see Box II.6).

Box II.6   Concepts of monism and dualism

The ancient concept of the universe's division into three areas, the heavens, the earth, and the underworld, were the mainstay of centuries of belief. The heavens were the domain of the gods. When humans died, they went to the place of the dead. The ancient concept of monism held that the human person consisted of "one" unit, the physical body and a personality. The ancients did not need Newton to explain gravity; heavy human bodies could not sit on a cloud.

This began to change, starting with the Persian state cult of Zoroaster (Zoroastrianism), the rise of the schools of Greek philosophy (ca. 600 BCE), and Alexander's introduction of Greek concepts throughout the East. The human person was now understood to consist of a physical body (matter) and an "essence" which was not physical, and thus not subject to decay at death, the soul (dualism). For philosophers (especially Plato), the care of the soul was much more important than the care of the body.

Having a part of a human being which was now ethereal and not subject to decay, is the period when the idea of dying and "going to heaven" first emerged.

The History of Israel   41

Alexander's death at such a young age (33) caused a crisis because he did not leave any legitimate heirs (sons). For the next few decades, his generals divided up and fought over the conquered territories. When the smoke cleared, two of his generals remained dominant in the region, Ptolemy (Egypt), and Seleucus (Syria). The first Ptolemy, Ptolemy Soter I, built the city of Alexandria with the famous Library complex, the Pharos Lighthouse (which became a "wonder" of the ancient world), and introduced a syncretistic god, Serapis, into Egyptian culture. He also built the tomb for Alexander in Alexandria which became a huge tourist attraction.

The Seleucids (Syria) and the Ptolemies (Egypt) would spend the next few hundred years fighting each other over hegemony, with Israel caught in the middle. Whoever was ruling at the time meant that a new high-priest was installed in the Temple in Jerusalem which essentially made the office a political football. The high-priest found it expedient to go along with whichever governing force was dominant at the time.

Every region in the Mediterranean Basin shared a common belief in the relationship between the king and the divine. Either the king was believed to be descended from a god and a mortal, or a manifestation of a god himself. (The God of Israel was an exception; their God did not procreate with humans.) When we think of Classical Greece (500's BCE), we think about Greek rational thought. However, Alexander's generals were also human. When they came to rule the areas of Alexander's conquests after his death, they liked what they saw. All these regions combined kingship with divinity— in Egypt, Pharaoh was a god on earth. And so, they adapted these ideas to their rule, utilizing age-old concepts to grant validity to themselves and their reigns.

Antiochus Epiphanes IV (Syria, 216 BCE–154 BCE)

A ruler of the Seleucid dynasty, Antiochus named himself, "Epiphanes". In modern terms, we utilize the concept of **epiphany**, as a metaphor for "enlightenment". In the ancient world, however, it literally meant, "a manifestation of the divine on earth".

In 167 BCE, Antiochus attempted to invade Egypt but was driven out. On his way home (through Jerusalem) and apparently in a bad mood, he then did something that no other ruler had done before. Antiochus forbids "the customs of the Jews" (in other words, he forbade their "religion"). All three previous Empires had conquered (Assyria, Babylon, Persia), but none had interfered with Jewish customs or rituals. Many Greeks, in their admiration for the physical attributes of the male body, considered circumcision a mutilation. Antiochus outlawed circumcision upon pain of death, slaughtered pigs on the altar at the Temple, and erected a statue to Zeus in the Holy of Holies.

The Maccabee Revolt

Antiochus sent soldiers to the villages to force them to "worship the Greek gods" (throwing a pinch of incense at the images, and perhaps an oath). In the village of Modeï'in in Galilee, a man by the name of Mattathias (of the family of the Hasmoneans), killed one of the Jews who was prepared to do this, and with a band of followers took to the hills to begin guerilla warfare. He had five sons, the eldest of whom was apparently known as "Judah the Hammer". "Hammer" in Greek is *maccabeus*, and thus the name of the revolt.

The story of the **Maccabee Revolt** (there are four books) did not make either the canon of the Jewish Scriptures or the New Testament. (Several of these books from the period are now placed "between the testaments" in modern study Bibles.) Nevertheless, the Maccabee literature is very important for understanding the period that leads into the first century. **1 Maccabees** related the battles, where each of the Hasmonean brothers took turns leading the rebels. Surprisingly, the Maccabees won and drove the Greeks out of Israel. Because Antiochus had defiled the Temple, a new altar was built followed by a dedication ceremony. This holiday eventually became **Hanukah**. (The legend of the miracle of the oil lamps burning for eight days is medieval.) Each of the sons took turns being "king", and resolved the problem of the position of high-priest as a political position, by combining the two offices.

2 Maccabees established the template for several innovations that became fundamental to Judaism, Christianity, and Islam. The second book detailed the torture of the Jews who refused to worship the Greek gods and who gave their lives for their beliefs. We find the details in the story of Hannah, a mother who had to watch her seven sons being tortured and executed.

The sons all refused to commit idolatry. The term **martyr** is introduced for the first time, which means "witness". Not as a witness who saw something, but as a witness in court—someone who is "testifying to the truth". Before each son died, he made a speech, claiming that he was dying for "the sins of the nation". The nation *must* have sinned, or God would not have let the Greeks oppress them, another form of divine discipline. Their deaths are understood as sacrifice to God as an **atonement** (a covering over or fixing a violation).

They were happy to die for their beliefs, they said, because they know their God will "raise them up", *anastasis* in Greek, **resurrection** in English. This is the origin of the reward for martyrdom, instantly being taken into the presence of God in heaven (both body and soul). It is also the first time that the word/concept of resurrection appeared in ancient Jewish literature.

By the first century, there was some precedent for this idea, in that Enoch, Elijah, and Moses were understood to be taken to heaven without physical death. By the first century legends and stories emerged that claimed that all the Prophets of Israel had died as "martyrs" and now resided in Heaven (see Box II.7).

Box II.7   Hell and heaven

The idea of what would become Hell in the Western tradition was older than the concept of Heaven as a place for the dead. Heaven was reserved as the place of God's throne and his heavenly attendants. All ancient people referred to "the land of the dead" with various names, such as "the underworld", or "the netherworld". The original Jewish concept was *she'ol*, the place for all the dead, both good and bad.

One of Israel's evil kings, Manasseh, had set up a shrine to the Moabite god, Molech, who required human sacrifice above the valley of Himnon. Down below, constant fires were kept burning to receive the victims. After his downfall, in the Second Temple period, this became the city dump. Like all dumpsites, periodically flames would burst through. From the word Himnon, this became Gehenna, now understood as the place in the underworld for the wicked dead. The wicked are annihilated in the fire, meaning that there is no memory of them in Israel.

Ancient Egypt had developed the idea of reward and punishment in the afterlife in the Middle Kingdom (2000 BCE). It was the ancient Egyptian concept of justice; what you did in life would affect your afterlife. If justice was not achieved in this world, it still awaited in the next. This idea was absorbed by the Greeks and Romans, where they began constructing details of reward and punishment in different sections of their land of the dead, Hades. The Greeks also had "hero cults", men whose great deeds sent them to be "among the gods" when they died. This idea influenced the concept of martyrdom. Over the centuries, all these ideas were absorbed into detailed aspects of the Christian afterlife.

Jewish Sectarianism

The term, **sectarianism** is a sociological/religious process. All major religions have an original, "mother" religion. At some point over time, some members of a religious community begin to believe that some "reforms" (changes) are necessary. They form a sub-group, known as a "sect". At some point in the sect, there is a determination that the reforms are not enough, and questions arise concerning the "mother religion" itself. This group becomes a "cult" and eventually evolves with new ideas that differ from the original concepts. The classic case is Christianity: originally a sect within Judaism, which became a cult in the Roman Empire, and finally a new, independent religion.

It is during this period that we have our earliest literature on the emergence of Jewish sects. So many Jews were apparently unhappy with the rule of the Maccabees (Hasmoneans). Tradition claimed that a king of Israel had to be descended from the tribe of Judah and King David; they were not. By this period another tradition claimed that the high-priest had to be able trace his ancestry at least as far back to the last righteous high-priest under Solomon, Zadock. The Hasmoneans could not. Under the Hasmoneans we see the emergence of Jewish sects that will influence descriptions in the later New Testament: Pharisees, Sadducees, Essenes, Zealots (see Box II.8).

> *Box II.8 Jewish sects in the second temple period*
>
> Pharisees surfaced as a religious/political party. They were concerned that all Jews should live according to the precepts of priests found in Leviticus. They also validated their ideas on a concept known as "oral law", or teachings of Moses that had been handed down to their ancestors, but not found in the Scriptures.
>
> The Sadducees derive from the term, Zadok and oversaw the maintenance and rituals in the Temple. They rejected ideas of an "oral law", following only what was found in the Scriptures. They were often seen as collaborators with Rome, in that they did not want to give Rome an excuse to stop the Temple services.
>
> The Essenes were a group of Jews who rejected Hasmonean leadership and moved to the community of Qumran, near the Dead Sea to await God's final intervention. It is through the documents of their library that we have their apocalyptic worldview.
>
> The Zealots looked back to the days of the Maccabee Revolt, claiming that just as God did then, God would help to overthrow Rome. They convinced other Jews to become involved in the **Jewish Revolt against Rome (66–73 CE)**. Among their group were the Sicarii ("dagger men") who attacked and executed any Jews who cooperated with the oppressor.
>
> Jewish sects agreed on the basics: the covenant with Abraham, and the Law of Moses. Problems arose in disagreements over ways in which to join and live in the greater cosmopolitan world of Hellenism, and yet still maintain a distinct Jewish identity. How far could Jews bend and still be "different from the nations?" The first Christian communities are understood as another sect of Judaism. As Christian communities evolved, we will continue to described them as "sects" within Christianity.

Apocalyptic Eschatology

The Essenes rejected Hasmonean rule and the way in which the Temple was run by the Hasmoneans. As there were no longer traditional Prophets in Israel, they utilized **seers**, or men who went into a trace and had an "out-of-body" experience. The experience always included a "tour of heaven", where they were shown signs of the "final days". Written in the name of a known figure as someone who had already been transferred to heaven (a popular one being Enoch), many of the secrets were written in symbolic code.

Apocalyptic ("hidden things revealed") texts were subversive literature that critiqued the current regime. Thus, they are written in coded language, and utilized symbols that only the community could understand. There is now a separate discipline of scholars who study the Dead Sea Scrolls in detail, and the concepts are referred to as **apocalyptic eschatology**, "the study of hidden things revealed concerning the final days".

The apocalyptic literature reveals a certain mind-set. The writers of the scrolls maintained all the elements that were included in the books of the Prophets concerning the "final days" (several scrolls of Isaiah were found at Qumran), but their thinking was now polarized. Where the Prophets had claimed that the final battle was between Israel and the nations, now that event would take place between all the powers of good and evil in the universe. Whereas the Prophets emphasized "turning back" through repentance, the Essenes claimed that repentance was no longer possible. The world was divided between the "sons of light" and the "sons of darkness"; who had already been determined by God.

For the Essenes, anyone who did not agree with them were the enemy, including other Jews. The scrolls contain some of our earliest literature that highlights "the personification of evil in the other". For the Essenes, these people were literally "agents of the Devil" (see Excursus I: The Origins and Evolution of Satan).

Pompey and the Rule of Rome

The Hasmoneans were in charge for about a hundred years. As Rome expanded, they sent the general Pompey Magnus to the East to settle some client kings who had aligned with the king of Pontus (on the Black Sea), Mithridates IV, who had conquered Asia Province. Pompey successfully conquered Mithridates and reorganized the area as individual client-kingdoms of Rome. He initially was going to let things stand in Jerusalem, but two brothers were fighting over the position of high-priest. When he could not get them to compromise, he laid siege to Jerusalem and conquered it in 63 BCE.

The Herodians

Rome had no interest in Israel except as a buffer-state against the Parthian Empire in the East (the inheritors of Persia). While Pompey was there, he used the services of a tribal chief from the area near the south of the Dead Sea, Idumea (originally Edom), by the name of Antipater. He and his son, **Herod the Great** committed to keep things "quiet" in Israel and became client-rulers for Rome. Herod was deemed "great" because of his building projects. He renovated the Temple and Temple Mount area, where you can still see the remains of his work today.

The **Herodians** (the umbrella term for this family in the New Testament) became embroiled in the civil wars that broke out after the assassination of Julius Caesar. Antipater's son Herod was called to Rome with others to report on conditions in the Eastern Empire. As a reward for his service, he was granted the title, "king of the Jews". Herod the Great became one of the most hated kings in Jewish history, often accused of "not really being a Jew" because he worked for Rome. Surprisingly, we know more about him than any other person in the ancient world. He had a court scribe, Nicolas of Damascus, who wrote a twenty-volume history of Herod. It has not survived, but much of it is quoted by a later Jewish historian (see below).

Herod the Great was infamous for his paranoia, that everyone was out to usurp him from the throne. However, is it paranoia, when, in fact there were so many out to get him? He had one of his wives, Mariamne (a Hasmonean princess) and her sons executed because he discovered a plot.

Direct Rule of Judea by Rome

Upon the death of Herod the Great (4 BCE), his territory was divided among four of his sons (the **Tetrarchy**). The confusion in the New Testament is that the writers simply refer to "Herod", and assume the reader knows which one. The city of Jerusalem was initially assigned to a son who was such a bad leader that the Jews sent a delegation to Rome to ask Augustus *not* to appoint another son after his death. Ruling Jerusalem was always a problem because of the civil disturbances that usually arose during the major festivals in the city; Jewish charismatic leaders often went there to agitate for the overthrow of Rome. In the year 6 CE, Judea (and Jerusalem) became a senatorial province of Rome, being ruled directly with a procurator, the most famous of which was Pontius Pilate.

The Jewish Revolt Against Rome (66–73 CE)

Rome's typical response to Jewish "fire-brands" was to send a "swat team", to take out the leaders and his followers and restore law and order against such mobs. As these leaders were promoting "the kingdom of God" on earth, such actions were treason—there was only one "kingdom" now, that of Rome. Throughout the 30's, 40's, and 50's Rome sent a series of corrupt and inept procurators. By the year 66, the Zealots attacked the Temple and took it over (slaughtering the priests) and convinced other Jews to formally rebel against Rome.

Flavius Josephus (36 CE–100 CE)

We know all about the rebellion against Rome because we have the rarity of an eyewitness. **Flavius Josephus** was from a priestly family. When the war broke out he was in Rome where he was negotiating for the release of some political hostages. Returning to Judea, he was made the commander in charge of Jewish forces in the Galilee and the North. The Roman general in the North was **Vespasian** (later to become Emperor after the death of Nero).

Things weren't going well for the Jews. Vespasian laid siege to a hill-top town in the Galilee, Jotopata. Josephus and the other defenders were holed up in a cave when they decided on a suicide pact, rather than be enslaved by Rome. One by one, they took turns helping to run swords into each other. It came down to Josephus and one other man. It was at this point that Josephus decided this was not a good plan and convinced the other man to surrender with him.

Vespasian determined that the prisoners should be executed. Josephus spoke up: "Don't you know that all Jews are endowed with prophecy? I predict that you will be the next Emperor of Rome". Vespasian (as a typical Roman who knew that you should take such things seriously), decided to let him live (just in case he was right). Vespasian had taken his son **Titus** with him. Josephus and Titus became not only best friends, but Josephus became their "Jewish expert" and a military adviser for the Roman siege against Jerusalem.

Why did Josephus switch sides? As he later explained, he claimed that the God of Israel was now on the side of Rome. He blamed the Zealots for getting everyone involved in the rebellion and that Roman victories were a sign of God's punishment against the rebellious Jews. After the war, Josephus was granted Roman citizenship and was given Vespasian's old house in Rome. There he had access to Roman archives and the libraries and began a career as an historian.

Josephus and Scholarship

Josephus looms large in the field of both ancient Jewish Studies and New Testament Studies because of the phenomenon of his writings. He wrote a seven-volume book, *The Jewish War*, a twenty-volume history of the Jews (*The Antiquities*), an apologetic work, *Against Apion* on Jewish–Pagan relations, and a biography to explain why he switched sides. *The Jewish War* is now one of those classics that you can find in any bookstore. In one of these odd quirks of history, all his writings were preserved by Christians. That is because he had a passage describing John the Baptist, the death of Jesus's brother James, and a controversial passage on Jesus himself. Josephus's rhetorical passages on the evil of the Zealots also became standard Christian polemic against the Jews as a whole.

Without Josephus, we would know very little about the history of the Jews in the first century (as well as events pertaining to the Julio-Claudians in Rome). The problem, however, is a constant debate in how far you can trust Josephus. In Josephus' history of the Jews, he was presenting Judaism in its best light, as an attempt to convince his now Roman audience that most Jews are loyal to Rome. (It was only the misguided Zealots who caused all the problems.) His writings are constantly assessed considering the context and circumstances.

The Destruction of the Temple and Jerusalem

After the Galilee was subdued, Vespasian left for Rome to challenge some other generals for the position of Emperor after the death of Nero. His son Titus took over the war. Titus moved south and in 68 CE destroyed the Essene community at Qumran. He then laid siege to Jerusalem. In *The Jewish War*, Josephus described the horrible conditions in the city for lack of food and diseases. Throughout the siege, Josephus rode daily around the walls outside and pleaded with the Jews to surrender, but to no avail.

Titus broke into the city from the north and proceeded to slaughter the Jews who were left. When he attacked the Temple area, a fire broke out resulting in the destruction of the entire complex. Josephus claimed that this was an accident, that Titus had never intended to destroy the Temple. But it was now gone. (In the ruins of the Temple Mount in the Old City, you can still see some of the pillars and the platform walls from this period.)

Some of the Zealots escaped the city and took over a Herodian fortress near the Dead Sea, **Masada**. Josephus related that after three years of a siege, the Jews decided on a suicide pact. When Roman armies broke through the fortifications, they were greeted by the silence of 960 bodies, laid out with the stores of food to show that they could have held out longer. Today, "Masada shall never fall again", is a rallying political/religious concept in modern Israel.

The Importance of the Jewish War against Rome

When Jerusalem was under siege, a Pharisee by the name of **Johanan ben Zakkai**, escaped the city in a coffin and negotiated with Titus. Claiming that he and his group were not rebels, he received permission for them to establish a school at **Yavne** (a town along the coast). At Yavne he taught the importance of prayer to replace sacrifices which were not possible after the destruction of the Temple. This is the beginning of what is later deemed **Rabbinical Judaism** ("rabbi" means teacher). These teachings became incorporated into the **Talmud** (the collective commentaries of Rabbis over the centuries). Rabbinical Judaism remains the practice of modern Jews.

What were Christians doing during the revolt against Rome? We have very little direct evidence about either the involvement of Christians during this time or their reactions to it. There is a tradition that the Christians of Jerusalem left the city and settled across the Jordan in the town of Pella to wait out the war. Later narratives will insist that Christians were never part of a rebellion against Rome. With the Temple and Jerusalem in ruins, the focus of Christian missionaries were the cities of the Roman Empire.

More importantly, the Jewish Revolt against Rome is the immediate historical context for our first gospel, Mark. As you read Mark you should constantly keep this context in mind as it helps to explain so many of the elements and details of Mark's narrative. At the same time, you will recognize this history of Israel as the gospels consistently refer to it in their arguments concerning Jesus of Nazareth.

Summary

- The history of Israel in the Scriptures provides the basic history of the foundation of the nation of the Jews.
- The Scriptures outline the elements of Jewish and later Christian identity.

Suggestions for Further Reading

Friedman, Richard. 2019. *Who Wrote the Bible?*. Simon and Schuster. Friedman surveys (and critiques) the "The Documentary Hypothesis".

Josephus, Flavius. 1984. *The Jewish War*. Penguin Classics.

Thonemann, Peter. 2018. *The Hellenistic Age: A Very Short Introduction*. Oxford University Press. Thonemann outlines the evolution and changing concepts of religious ideas in the Hellenistic period.

Vandercam, James C. 2000. *An Introduction to Early Judaism*. Eerdmans. This text outlines both the history and the interpreted history of the Jewish traditions.

EXCURSUS I
THE ORIGINS AND EVOLUTION OF SATAN, THE DEVIL

How Did Evil Come into the World?

Ha-Satan and The Book of Job

Zoroastrianism

The Dead Sea Scrolls

The New Testament

The "Harrowing of Hell"

Satan, the Devil, became a major character in the Western traditions of Judaism, Christianity, and Islam. Surprisingly, the concept was a late construction in the ancient world. This totally evil being, as one who opposes all of God's creation, does not appear as such in the Jewish Scriptures. The formal name, *ha-Satan*, comes from the Hebrew for "the opposer" or "the adversary", and in Greek, *diaolos* ("slanderer, accuser") the Devil. As a separate being, he began to emerge from theological reflections in ancient Judaism and the state religion of Zoroastrianism during the Persian Achaemenid Empire (ca. 550 BCE).

How Did Evil Come into the World?

Evil has always existed. Humans encountered natural disasters (earthquakes, floods), wars with pillage and rape, diseases, plagues, infant mortality, man-made evil such as murders and theft, and of course, death. The modern analysis of understanding the existence of evil is known as **Theodicy**: if God is good, why does evil exist; if God is all-powerful, why does he *let* it exist? The major world religions all have elements that address this problem.

As the ancients constructed their religious systems, the existence of evil had to be explained and rationalized. Creation myths often designated a high god or a king of the gods, who controlled everything including the other gods as well as nature. In this capacity, they were responsible for both good and evil. The term to describe this ability is **omnipotence** (all-powerful). In Deuteronomy 28, God declared that he controlled both prosperity and suffering.

Many creation myths addressed how and why evil arose. The opening chapters of Genesis relate the source of evil in the Jewish Scriptures. God (and all his creation) was described as "good"; the God of Israel did not create anything evil. It was the fault of the first humans, Adam and Eve, and their sin of disobedience that permitted evil to enter the world. This disobedience led to human struggles to produce food and pain in childbirth. The most severe punishment was the loss of their mortality. As their descendants, therefore we all die.

Ancient cultures (including the Jews) projected their own experiences upon their conceptions of the divine. Kings had courts of nobles and advisers and so "divine courts" were described with higher and lower officials. In Judaism, the higher beings became **angels**, while the lower ones were *daemons* (in Greek). The lower ones were originally neutral but became blamed for evil over time, the demons.

Excursus I The Origins and Evolution of Satan, the Devil   53

Ha-Satan and The Book of Job

The Book of Job (ca. 600 BCE) was one of the earliest texts to address the problem of theodicy. The book opens with the angels apparently reporting to God. Among them is the angel *ha-Satan*, whose function was to travel the world placing "obstacles" (the meaning of his name, "adversary") in front of humans, requiring them to make a choice (good or evil). In this role, we can say that he acted as God's prosecuting attorney. Reporting back to God, he mentioned God's servant Job, who had prospered. But, of course, he said, this is because God granted Job so much favor.

God ordered *ha-Satan* to test Job: destroy all his prosperity, everything except his life. God was sure that Job would not turn away from him. Job's children were killed, his crops and herds destroyed, and he suffered horrible diseases. Job's friends came to comfort him and convince him that he must have sinned because God is a God of justice. Throughout, Job insisted that he never sinned; God had unfairly punished him. Frustrated, Job called on God to explain, and a voice from the whirlwind admonished him: "Where were you when I laid the earth's foundation?" (Job 38:4). In other words: "How dare you (a mere mortal) question me?" Job was humbled and conceded the prerogatives and power of God.

Ha-Satan appeared rarely in the Jewish scriptures. In the few references to *ha-Satan*, he opposed humans, not God. Originally, in Eden, the serpent served this function, offering a choice to Adam and Eve. Throughout most of the books of the Prophets, evil was blamed on the people's sin of idolatry. God was still in control of all things.

Zoroastrianism

When Jerusalem was conquered and destroyed by the Neo-Babylonian Empire (587 BCE), some Jews were taken into captivity in Babylon. Cyrus the Great then conquered the Babylonians in 550 BCE and established the Persian Empire. The state cult of Persia was Zoroastrianism, founded by the prophet Zoroaster. In this system, evil was the polar opposite of good. A pure, good being, Ahura Mazda ("Wise Lord") was the source of everything, and at the polar end was *druj*, chaos. *Druj* became personified as Angra Mainyu ("false", "deception"), also known as Ahriman. The heavens, the earth, and all humans fell within this polarized range. Oppositional struggle occurs continually on every level. If you have ever seen cartoons with an angel on one shoulder and a devil on this other, this is the source of that idea.

Cyrus the Persian permitted the Jews to return to Jerusalem (539 BCE), although some stayed. They took many elements of ancient Persian religion with them. This is when the angels of the Jewish Scriptures now had wings. They merged the personification of chaos with earlier views of *ha-Satan*. Now he was just Satan, and the Jews began assigning all evil to Satan instead of God.

The Dead Sea Scrolls

In the writings of the Jewish sect of Essenes who settled at Qumran (ca. 150 BCE), we have our first literature that created a method known as "the personification of evil". The sectarian literature equated Satan not only with evil but specifically with anyone or any group not in agreement with their own views, including other Jews. According to their texts, God had created two spirits in humans: "the way of light and the way of darkness". The demons were now under the control of Satan; he sent them to possess those in darkness to commit evil. The Essenes applied symbolic names to Satan and his agents: *Belial* (Hebrew for "worthless") who will lead the "sons of darkness" against those of light in the final battle (*The War Scroll*). As with the angels and archangels in heaven, we now have hierarchy and different functions in Satan's court. *Beelzebub* was one of the seven princes of Hell and derived from an ancient Canaanite god who was known for getting rid of flies (carriers of disease). Thus, *Beelzebub*, "Lord of the Flies".

Various apocalyptic texts were among the scrolls at Qumran. The *Books of Enoch* filled in more details about the "sons of God" in Genesis 6. They were condemned for mating with human women and teaching humankind metallurgy and magic. They were punished by being tossed out of heaven and chained in the abyss (the Jewish concept of *She'ol*, the land of the dead) for eternity. The fallen angels now joined the ranks of the Devil.

In another text, *Jubilees*, more Devil lore was added. Satan's name here is *Mastema* (which means "hated" or "hostility"). We learn that *Mastema* wanted to be higher than God and rebelled. He and his fellow angels were tossed down into the bottomless pit. God wanted to destroy all the demons after the flood, but *Mastema* asked God to let him have a tenth of them to continue to plague men because "the evil of the sons of men is great" (10:8). With God's permission, *Mastema* became the tempter who was written back into earlier stories. In the text known as *Jubilees*, it was *Mastema* who was permitted to test Abraham with the binding of Isaac. In other words, God's omnipotence remains intact; Satan could not do his work without God's permission.

That God would permit an evil being to continue his work in the world remains a Gordian knot in terms of understanding because the text does not explain *why* God continued to let him live and have influence. The best way in which to understand it is an after-the-fact rationalization based upon the reality of the existence of evil. At least this claim kept God in charge of both "good and evil". In the Islamic tradition, we have the same story: God (Allah) grants *Iblis* (the Devil) his wish to continue to tempt humans.

The New Testament

In the letters of Paul and the gospels, we have a polarized view that Satan is now "the ruler of this world". This is expressed in a letter written by one of Paul's disciples: "Put on the full armor of God, so that you can take your stand against the Devil's schemes. For our struggle is not against flesh and blood, but against the rulers, against the authorities, against the powers of this dark world and against the spiritual forces of evil in the heavenly realms" (Ephesians 6:11–12).

Paul often referred to the demons as the agents of Satan who interfered with his mission. Writing from prison, Paul explained that he could not visit his community "because Satan hindered us" (1 Thessalonians 2:17–18). Paul's inner struggles were expressed in what can be understood as a form of possession: "And to keep me from being too elated ... a thorn was given me in the flesh, a messenger of Satan, to harass me" (2 Corinthians 12:7–9). Paul never revealed if the "thorn" was a physical impediment or a metaphor. But Paul saw this as God's ability to control Satan to test him. His familiar phrase, that believers now live "in Christ", referred to Christ's protection against the influence of Satan's demons and agents in the universe.

The Devil also looms large in the first gospel, Mark (ca. 70 CE). Mark utilized a common stereotype to describe the ministry of Jesus, that of a **charismatic exorcist** who both preached and performed miracles throughout the Roman Empire. "Charismatic" (Greek, "gifts") is the claim that their abilities were a "gift from the gods". An exorcist was someone who drove out demons. By the first century, physical and mental disabilities and diseases were understood as possession by demons. Mark emphasized the ministry as a battle between Jesus and the current rule of the Devil on earth.

> At once the Spirit sent him out into the wilderness and he was in the wilderness forty days, being tempted by Satan. He was with the wild animals, and angels attended him (Mark 1:12–13).

It is interesting that Mark did not have to explain the character of Satan; he assumed his readers knew. Both Matthew and Luke expanded this scene (Matthew 4:1–11; Luke 4:1–13). Satan, in his role as the tempter, presented Jesus with three temptations, but Jesus always knows the correct response from scripture. It is significant that Jesus does not dispute Satan's claim to control the "kingdoms of this world".

While Mark's disciples are often confused over the identity of Jesus, all the demons know him and recognize his superiority. In Mark 5:1–13, the collective name of the demons being driven out by Jesus is "Legion" (which may be Mark's not too subtle view of the Roman army). Mark and the others presented the opponents of Jesus as under the influence of Satan. In Luke and John, Satan "entered into Judas" to betray Jesus (Luke 22:3). The culmination of blame for the death of Jesus reached its heights in John 8:42. In John's gospel, the Jews can never achieve salvation because they are children of their "true father, the Devil".

The Book of Revelation (ca. 90–100 CE) by John of Patmos is an apocalyptic vision of when God would intervene in human affairs in the final days and punish Rome for its persecution against Christians. He included the claim that Satan was chained in the pits of Hell so that he relied upon his agents for his work. The principal agent is referred to as "the beast" and the "deceiver"; the term "anti-Christ" is not in Revelation, but in the three Johannine letters. The deceiver will appear as someone good and gather a world following. You will know his followers by the sign of "666" that they carry.

In one of John's visions, he referenced Isaiah 14, a polemic against the king of Babylon. Isaiah castigated the king who titled himself "day-star" for his hubris of thinking he was divine: "How you have fallen from heaven, morning star, son of the dawn!" When Jerome translated the Hebrew scriptures into Latin in the fourth century CE, he knew that the Romans named their morning star **Lucifer** and translated the passage as such. Lucifer became the most popular name for the Devil in the Middle Ages.

Throughout most of the book of Revelation, Satan remained chained in the pit. At the end of Christ's 1000-year reign on earth, Satan will be released for the final battle. The irony is found in the image of Christ "as a lamb" who nevertheless defeats this monster, described as "the dragon". He will be tossed into the "lake of fire", the Dead Sea (Rev. 20:1–5).

The "Harrowing of Hell"

In the Acts of the Apostles, Luke claimed that Hades (*she'ol*) could not hold the crucified Christ (2:27). In 1 Peter 3, Jesus "made proclamation to the imprisoned spirits who disobeyed long ago" and 4:6 "the gospel was preached even to those who are now dead".

While his body was in the grave, Jesus traveled to Hell where he battled Satan for the souls of the righteous. When the stone was rolled back, these righteous souls came with him (Adam, Noah, Moses, Plato, and Aristotle). The idea that Christ "descended into Hell [and] on the third day, he arose again" became embedded in the fourth-century CE **Nicene Creed**. By the early Middle Ages, the story was known as the **Harrowing of Hell**. The expression "to harry" meant a raid or incursion, such as the Viking raids. (See Chapter IX for the "Gospel of Peter" which details these events.)

Christian leaders in the second century CE adopted the method of the personification of evil against Jews, women, heretics, and all things pagan. The native cults believed that the gods resided in their temples, but Christians labeled them as agents of Satan. It was also in the second century CE that both Christians and Jews—the early Rabbis—applied new understandings to the story of the fall. This is when the serpent became fully identified as the Devil in disguise and Eve took on more significance as the primary sinner in Eden (who could not resist the temptation of the Devil).

The religious traditions of Europe (the Celts, Druidism, and Teutons) added other characteristics. The Celts had a horned god of the west, Cernunnos, in charge of fertility. The daughter of Loki had a dual role in fertility as well as rule over the dead, and her name, Hel, became incorporated to the place, Hell.

With animal characteristics, Lucifer and his demons had the ability to change shape, and so a constant watch was necessary. One could trick Lucifer and repel him with signs of the cross, holy water, the rosary, and communion wafers. Based upon feudal relationships, the concept of a pact arose in selling your soul to Lucifer in return for prosperity (the famous story of Faust). Only the intervention of Mary, the mother of Christ, could break the pact. This is when exorcism rituals were developed that are still taught to certain Catholic and Anglican priests.

Dante Alighieri's (1265–1321 CE) *Inferno* depicted Satan as a three-faced monster in the lowest section of Hell (ice, the furthest from the light) with giant bat-wings. For Dante, the greatest sin was betrayal, and Satan consumes Brutus, Cassius, and, of course, Judas, for eternity.

Suggestion for Further Reading

Pagels, Elaine. 1996. *The Origin of Satan: How Christians Demonized Jews, Pagans, and Heretics*. Vintage. Pagels traces the history of Satan and particularly the way in which Christianity utilized the existence of Satan to represent opposing concepts.

EXCURSUS II
INTRODUCTION TO THE GOSPELS

The Story of Jesus of Nazareth in the Canonical Gospels

The Crucifixion of Jesus

Summary of the Gospels

The Gospel of Mark (ca. 69/70 CE)

The Gospel of Matthew (85 CE?)

The Gospel of Luke and the Acts of the Apostles (95 CE?)

The Gospel of John (100 CE?)

Problems Faced by the Writers of the Gospels

The "Hero" of Their Story Is Dead

Where are the Jews?

Where is "The Kingdom of God?"

The Parousia

Excursus II Introduction to the Gospels

The Relationship among the Gospels

The Priority of Mark

Matthew and Luke: The "Q" Source

Additional Sources for Matthew and Luke

Sources for Mark

Names and Titles of Jesus in the New Testament

Analyzing the Gospels

The Passion Narrative/ Historical Anomalies

The Second Temple Complex

"The Last Supper"

The Arrest

The Jewish Trial(s)

The Real Pontius Pilate?

The Release of Barabbas

The Crucifixion of Jesus

Jesus Died Too Soon

Joseph of Arimathea

How Long Was Jesus in the Tomb?

What Really Happened?

Judas?

What about the Disciples?

The Legacy of the Trial and Crucifixion of Jesus

Gospel derives from an Anglo-Saxon word, "good story", or "good news". This was derived from the Greek word **evangelist**, a "herald or bringer of news". The gospels were announcing the "good news" brought by Jesus of Nazareth, that the "kingdom of God" foretold by the Prophets was imminent.

The Story of Jesus of Nazareth in the Canonical Gospels

The only sources for the life of Jesus of Nazareth are in the canonical gospels of Mark, Matthew, Luke, and John. We have no contemporary, eyewitness testimony of his teaching or actions, and there are no Jewish or Roman records that refer to him at the time. This is a synopsis of the events reported in the four gospels:

Sometime during the 20's of the Common Era, an itinerant preacher, in the style of the Prophets of ancient Israel, began addressing crowds in his native area, mainly the Galilee region of Northern Israel. He may have been in the circle attached to a character known as John, the Baptist, who was symbolically "dunking" people in the Jordan river after they had repented of their sins. Jesus apparently took up the same message after John's death. His basic message was, "Repent, for the Kingdom of God is at hand!" What he meant by this was that God would soon intervene one last time in history and restore the nation of Israel, who would now live in an ideal kingdom, on earth, as God originally intended before the fall in the Garden of Eden. It appears from the first three gospels that his favorite method of instruction was what is known as a parable, or a short, pithy story containing both simple elements, as well as higher abstract concepts in some cases.

He was also noted for miracles: healing, raising people from the dead (generally children), exorcisms, or the removal of "demons", and food miracles (such as the multiplying of the loaves and fishes). He gathered disciples (students, followers) around him, in the symbolic number of "twelve" (reflecting the Twelve Tribes of Israel). While drawing the countryside to his message, Mark reported a constant harassment and persecution by specific groups of Jews, namely the Pharisees and the scribes, and eventually the Sadducees. In the gospels, the Pharisees consistently accused Jesus of "violating the Law of Moses", while the writers specifically deny that he challenged the customs of the Jews—he offered what is understood as the "true interpretation" of Moses and the traditions associated with it.

Excursus II Introduction to the Gospels   61

In Mark, Matthew, and Luke, Jesus spent most of his time moving around the Galilee, and then he made a final trip to the city of Jerusalem during the holiday of Passover (when all Jews were supposed to try and make a pilgrimage to that city). In John, Jesus made several trips to Jerusalem throughout the ministry.

When Jesus entered the city before Passover, the crowds used palm branches to welcome him, and proclaimed him the "messiah", or "anointed one", from the line of David, and hence, a "political" element to the title, as "King of the Jews". This entry is the basis for the Christian observance of "Palm Sunday", a week before Easter. Jesus went to the outer court of the Temple and drove out the men who were selling animals for the sacrifices, as well as the men in charge of money-changing tables, claiming, "My house shall be a house of prayer for all the nations, but you have made it a den of thieves". According to Mark, it is this incident that directly led to the death of Jesus.

Jesus and his disciples celebrated a Passover meal on Thursday evening (Mark, Matthew, Luke), or a simple meal on Wednesday evening (John), where the tradition of the ritual known as the "last supper" took place. This became the basis for the Christian celebration of the "eucharist", or communion meal. Jesus, for the third or fourth time, predicted his own death, but claimed that he would overcome it, as the kingdom takes over. After dinner, he and his followers went over to the Mt. of Olives, to an olive oil press area, known as Gethsemane and Jesus prayed that God would release him from the upcoming torture and death. The gospels do not record any answer from God, but Jesus accepted his fate.

One of the disciples, Judas, betrayed Jesus by telling the priests/temple captains/and or Romans (depending upon which gospel you are reading) where he would be that evening and Jesus was arrested (see Box II.9).

Box II.9   Who was Judas Iscariot?

"Even my close friend, someone I trusted, one who shared my bread, has turned against me" (Psalm 41:9). The story of Judas appears first in Mark's gospel; we can find no earlier evidence of a story of betrayal or this individual. Paul did not know of a betrayal story by Judas Iscariot. When he listed the resurrection appearances of Jesus to the Corinthians, he said, "… He (Jesus) appeared to Cephas (Peter) and then to the twelve" (1. Cor. 15:5). Would Judas have been honored with a resurrection appearance if he had betrayed Jesus? In 1 Cor. 11:23, when Paul related the eucharistic formula, he began with, "… on the night when he was handed over …". Every English Bible translates "handed-over" as "betrayed". The Greek word here simply means "handed over to the authorities". The translation into "betrayed" is automatically read back into this because the story of Judas is thoroughly embedded in the Western tradition.

There is a scriptural parallel to the story of Judas in the story of Ahitophel, a courtier of David during Absalom's rebellion: "Let me choose twelve thousand men, and I will set out and pursue David tonight. I will come upon him when he is weary and discouraged and throw him into a panic; and all the people with him will flee. I will strike down the king only. You seek the life of only one man, and all the people will be at peace" (2 Samuel 17:1–4). David had sought refuge on the Mt. of Olives, weeping. "Judas" could represent the Jewish leadership.

Both Matthew and Luke narrate a story of Judas' suicide. Matthew said he hung himself (as Ahitophel did), while Luke said he threw himself off a cliff. The sources for these details remain unknown.

Jesus was either taken to a meeting of the whole Jewish city council (the Sanhedrin, or parts of it), or to the high-priest's house (John). A very confusing trial follows, where the charges are not clear (and there is variation in the number of trials and their location). Finally, in Mark, the high-priest asks Jesus if he is "the Blessed One" (meaning the "messiah"). Jesus, reticent up until this moment in Mark, answered that he is "the Son of Man", whom some apocalyptic traditions described as the final judge of mankind in the "final days". At this, the high-priest claimed that he committed blasphemy, and he was condemned to death.

Taken before the Roman magistrate in Jerusalem, Pontius Pilate, Pilate declared Jesus innocent, but gave into the Jews' demand for execution.

The Crucifixion of Jesus

All four gospels relate the crucifixion of Jesus and his death. As it was the evening before Sabbath, there was a rush to get him buried. A rich man, **Joseph of Arimathea**, already had his family tomb prepared and that is where Jesus was buried. The women could not finish the proper burial rituals, which is why they visit the tomb on Sunday morning after the Sabbath. This was when the women discovered it empty and were told by an angel, that Jesus had "risen from the dead".

Summary of the Gospels

The four gospels that now constitute the New Testament originally had no names attached to them. In the second century, a group of Christian leaders retrospectively titled **Church Fathers** provided names with the opening line of, "the gospel according to …".

The Gospel of Mark (ca. 69/70 CE)

Mark is the earliest of the gospels, where he portrayed Jesus as a traditional, "apocalyptic Prophet". It was named after a character of John Mark from the Acts of the Apostles, who allegedly followed Peter to Rome. Aware that Galilean fishermen would not be educated in Greek, the Church Fathers claimed that Peter dictated the story to Mark. Written 40 years after the death of Jesus, the historical context for Mark's gospel is the Jewish Revolt against Rome (63–70). Although narrating events that took place in the 20's–30's, there are hints throughout the gospel of the impending destruction of the Temple in Jerusalem. Mark created the template for the constant harassment of Jesus by the Jews.

The Gospel of Matthew (85 CE?)

Matthew's gospel received its name from the fact that the tax-collector called by Jesus is named Matthew (Mark and Luke name him Levi). The Church Fathers claimed that this writer provided his own identity in this version.

Matthew's community was most likely settled in the Galilee. He increased the vitriol against the Jews, perhaps because the remnants of the Pharisees who survived the destruction of Jerusalem also settled there. Matthew's Jesus constantly rails against his followers doing things the way "they" do, in contrast to the new community. Matthew's gospel portrayed Jesus as "the new Moses", the Prophet who was predicted by Moses himself. It is aligned with five teaching panels (the "five books of Moses"). Only Jesus and his followers know the true meaning of the commandments (the **Sermon on the Mount**).

The Gospel of Luke and the Acts of the Apostles (95 CE?)

These two texts are the longest in the New Testament. Luke's Jesus emphasizes the elements of social justice from the Prophets, more than any other gospel. His sequel, The Acts of the Apostles, narrated what happened to the movement after the death of Jesus and the beginning of Christian missions. The second half is devoted to the missionary journeys of Paul.

The Church Fathers were aware that there was no disciple named Luke. However, because he related the stories of Paul's missions, they consulted some of Paul's letters. Paul mentioned a "traveling companion" named Luke, and thus the name.

The Gospel of John (100 CE?)

In both structure and the portrait of Jesus, John's gospel is vastly different from the other three. The first three presented Jesus as a Prophet of Israel. John portrayed him more in line with a Greek philosopher. John utilized the concept of *logos* into Christianity, that Jesus was the divine manifestation of the philosophical concept of rationality. Translated as "word", it was the claim that Jesus was a manifestation of God on earth. This became the Christian concept of **Incarnation** (from the Latin *carnate*, "embodied with flesh".

Throughout this gospel there a reference to "a beloved disciple". At the end of the first century, there were stories that one of Jesus' disciples, John, was a major figure in Ephesus. They claimed that this John was the brother of James, two of the first disciples to be called. Hence, "John" became the traditional narrator of this gospel.

Problems Faced by the Writers of the Gospels

All four gospel writers had several problematic issues they had to address. If they wanted credibility, they were compelled to provide some explanations:

The "Hero" of Their Story Is Dead

By the first century, the tradition that the messiah would arise from the tribe of Judah as an avatar of David assumed David-like activity—leading the armies of Israel against the enemies of God and the nation. But a dead messiah cannot be of much help to the Jews. At the same time, Jesus of Nazareth died by crucifixion, which was the Roman punishment reserved for treason.

An early Christian utilized the passages of Isaiah's "suffering servant" as a precursor to Christ. Hence, Mark's description of the crucifixion of Jesus incorporates many of these Prophetic elements ("He was pierced for our transgressions"). And of course, a simpler way of refuting the problem of a dead messiah was found in the proclamation that Jesus was not dead but resurrected.

Where are the Jews?

One of the most problematic issues faced by the gospel writers was a problem that apparently emerged in the first communities. If Jesus was the messiah of Israel, where were all the Jews? Why did not most of the Jews at the time believe that Jesus of Nazareth was the messiah? By the time Mark wrote his gospel, it is likely that the Gentiles (non-Jews) outnumbered Jews in the first communities.

Mark's gospel set the tone for explaining this, in his "conflict dialogues" between Jesus and his opponents (the Pharisees, scribes, Herodians, and lawyers). Mark was at pains to distinguish his Jews from those who were involved in the current rebellion against Rome. Mark therefore placed the blame for the death of Jesus on these oppositional Jews, despite the fact of crucifixion. The followers of Jesus had to live in the Roman Empire, and so Mark had to remove any signs of treason among his group. Mark claimed that Jesus himself kept "salvation" from the Jews, knowing it would go to the Gentiles (see Mark 4). Matthew presented the same stories of opposition to Jesus but framing it within the Prophetic tradition that only a "righteous remnant" (of true believers among the Jews) would be saved. By the time that we get to the gospel of John, the writer claimed that neither God nor Jesus ever intended to "save" the Jews because they are descended from the Devil (John 8:42).

Where is "The Kingdom of God?"

The ministry of Jesus of Nazareth proclaimed that the "kingdom of God was at hand." If that was true, then where was it? In that list of what the Prophets claimed would happen in the "final days", Christians could check off only three items: (1) God had raised up a messiah from the line of David (Jesus). This was the function of the nativity stories of Matthew and Luke, with Jesus born in Bethlehem, David's city. (2) God had recognized a "righteous remnant" (the followers of Jesus), and (3) some Gentiles now "turned and worshipped the God of Israel". The rest, including the "in-gathering of the exiles", the final battle, the final judgment, and God's reign on earth did not happen during Jesus's lifetime. This message of Jesus became problematic as time passed and the kingdom did not appear.

The Parousia

Again, an early, unknown Christian solved this problem with a concept that became known as the *parousia* ("second appearance"). Jesus was coming back in "the final days". In this second appearance, all the items predicted by the Prophets would take place: the final battle, the final judgment. In the interim, the followers of Jesus were to live proleptically, *as if* the "kingdom" were already here. This became the basis of what eventually constituted the law-codes and standards of behavior in the Christian communities (the Church).

The Relationship among the Gospels

The way in which the gospels related to each other is known by the scholarly rubric, the **Synoptic Problem**. "Synoptic" ("seen together") is the term for Mark, Matthew, and Luke, as these three have similar structures and teachings (John is different). The problem is figuring out who was first, who borrowed what, and how and why changes were made over the decades.

The Priority of Mark

The consensus places Mark as the earliest of the gospels, although there are still some who challenge this conclusion. Almost all of Mark's story appears in Matthew and Luke. When Mark's details appear in those two, they are often verbatim from Mark and between each other. If you or I were translating something

66   Excursus II Introduction to the Gospels

from the Greek, it would most likely be similar, but not verbatim. This convinces scholars that Matthew and Luke had a *written* copy of Mark in front of them.

Matthew and Luke: The "Q" Source

Matthew and Luke both added additional teachings, stories, and events not found in Mark. Some of these additional teachings and stories in Matthew and Luke also appear verbatim in the Greek. So again, scholars concluded that Matthew and Luke had a *second written* source. Unlike the text of Mark, this second written source has not survived independently. German scholars worked on it, and so they named it the **Q source**, after the German word, "quelle", ("source"). The Q Source consists largely of teachings in the ministry, with no narrative concerning the trial and crucifixion. In Matthew and Luke, many of these additional teachings are found in what is labeled, "the Sermon on the Mount" which is absent in Mark.

Additional Sources for Matthew and Luke

This is like peeling the layers of an onion. In addition to Mark and "Q", both Matthew and Luke have additional stories that are not found in either of those sources. For instance, some of Matthew's teachings are found nowhere else and some of Luke's parables are unique to Luke (such as "The Parable of the Prodigal Son"). We cannot determine where they obtained these additional stories, so scholars simply label them "**M**" and "**L**".

The schematic for the sources

Mark	Matthew	Luke	John
Oral	Mark, Q, M	Mark, Q, L	Mark? Matthew/Luke?
Tradition?			John's unique concepts

Sources for Mark

While we have Matthew and Luke re-writing Mark, the problem remains the great mystery of where Mark obtained his sources. Between Paul's letters (50's and 60's) and Mark's gospel, details about the traditions of Jesus are scarce. There is a teaching manual, *The Didache* ("teaching") that probably dates from the first century. It is rather like an early Christian catechism, listing the proper way to perform the early rituals. But it does not contain stories of Jesus or the ministry.

An older theory was that Mark utilized "oral tradition", that there must have been early stories about Jesus, his ministry, and his death. In fact, the first commentaries on Mark speculated that the death and resurrection were the earliest levels, and then Mark provided "a very long introduction," the ministry. That theory no longer holds among scholars and the writer known as Mark is recognized as a major contributor to this gospel.

The theory of "oral tradition" is problematic because we cannot find such stories prior to Mark. The earliest sources for the historical Jesus are the letters of Paul. Paul never met Jesus. He only encountered him in a vision (when he was already in heaven). By his own admission, Paul made two trips to Jerusalem and met twice with Peter and James. One could only wish that Paul had fully interviewed them concerning historical details, but that was not Paul's interest.

Paul has an almost verbatim ritual formula for the Eucharist ("the last supper") that is found in Mark. This tells us that both the formula and the ritual (of meeting in "remembrance of Jesus") were very early. According to Paul, Jesus was crucified by "the rulers of this world", meaning the governing authorities. But he cited no stories of multiple trials by the Sanhedrin or a trial by Pilate. Nor did he cite an "empty tomb" tradition.

If other "oral traditions" existed, it is odd that we find so little in Paul. He cited no parables (or even that Jesus taught in parables), no miracles of Jesus, no stories of his ministry. Almost all of Paul's references to the sufferings, death, and resurrection of Jesus are framed within the traditions of the Prophets and the "fulfillment of the end times", often utilizing metaphors for the events (see 1 Corinthians. 15).

Several New Testament scholars have argued that the reason some of the details are missing in Paul's letters is because Paul most likely told stories of the ministry and miracles when he arrived in each city. The letters only addressed specific issues in the communities after Paul has moved on, so there was no reason to refer to these traditions. This is an argument from silence.

Names and Titles of Jesus in the New Testament

The gospels were written decades after the lifetime of Jesus (from 70 to ca. 100 CE). However, there was no central authority to organize all the claims concerning Jesus; everyone added their own understanding and concepts. Some of the titles are connected to concepts of Biblical and Second Temple Judaism, while others appear to be borrowed from native cults. The various titles include: Emmanuel ("God is with us"); messiah ("anointed one"); Christ; "lord" ("master, *kyrios* in Greek"); "son of God" (denotes a personal relationship with God and a term often applied to the Prophets of Israel); "son of David" (the messianic lineage from David); "son of man" (the end-time judge after the final battle); "lamb of God" (John's metaphor for Jesus as the sacrificial lamb); *logos* ("word" in Greek).

68   Excursus II Introduction to the Gospels

By the time we get to the gospels, *all* these titles were applied to Jesus throughout the texts. The challenge for historians is to decide which of these titles (if any) were applied during the lifetime of Jesus and even which titles Jesus may have claimed for himself. It is always best to consider a name or title within the context of a specific passage.

Analyzing the Gospels

In the past 200 years, a scholarly discipline arose in what is known as "the Quest for the Historical Jesus". This quest sought both to locate Jesus within his historical context (a Jew of the first century), but also served as methodology to attempt to distinguish what we can know about him absolutely, given the lateness and individual concerns of each gospel over time. Without knowing the sources for Mark, how can we know that a saying of Jesus was his, and not Mark (or a pre-Markan source)?

Scholars have developed criteria for the analysis of a saying of Jesus (the *logia*): (1) language; (2) coherence; (3) multiple-attestation; (4) dissimilarity. The gospels are written in Greek. But the tradition posits Jesus speaking the local language, Aramaic (the language of the Assyrian and later Seleucid Empires). If you translate a saying into Aramaic, and it works (not just word for word, but syntax, grammar, etc.), it does not prove that Jesus said it, but can be placed in a column of "probable sayings". If it does not work at all, then it gets eliminated.

However, this criterion is currently being re-evaluated. In the 1970s, at the excavations of the Galilean city of Sepphoris, archaeologists discovered "mixed" communities of Jews and Gentiles. It was located on a nearby hill to Nazareth, which never grew beyond a small village. If Jesus worked as a "carpenter" (Mark), then simply to ply his trade he would have had to travel to these towns and cities. As such, there is the probability that he would have to know at least "street Greek" (*koine*) to do business.

Coherence applies to any saying or tradition that is similar to one that has already been accepted or verified, but more importantly, coheres to the world of Second Temple Judaism in the 20's and 30's. For example, John opens with a complicated and esoteric reference to Christ as *logos*, the philosophical principle of rationality, who "became flesh". Would an audience of Galilean peasants gathered around him understand or relate to such a concept?

Multiple-attestation is the most often misunderstood. Because a saying or an event occurs in all four gospels, does not provide historicity; the other three used Mark as the first source. The criterion applies to a saying or event found *outside* the gospel traditions (the letters of Paul; Jewish or Roman records). These are rare in the New Testament, but when we have them, they are considered "gems". Two examples: Mark claimed that Jesus taught against divorce. In Paul's letters (in the 50's), he was aware of this early tradition, citing it as a "teaching of the Lord". The other example is that Paul's repeating the "words of the Last Supper" in his letter to the Corinthians, is almost verbatim with Mark. Again, this does not prove that Jesus said these words, but that they are a very early tradition.

Dissimilarity is the most complicated. It was a theory that anything that Jesus taught that "went against the Judaism of his day" *must* be historical on the premise that this was why "Jesus came into the world". At the same time, anything he said or taught that went against the later formation of the Churches *must* have been before the creation of that institution. Both theories remain speculative due to the absence of clear elements on both sides during this period. Currently, dissimilarity is most often utilized to analyze those sayings or teachings that are now classified as "embarrassment".

"Embarrassment" refers to traditions that were problematic but were so well-known in the tradition that believers were "stuck with them". Again, two examples: the crucifixion of Jesus as a traitor to Rome. As Paul stated, this was a "scandal" for both Jews and Gentiles, which required detailed explanation (and thus, "the fulfillment of Scripture"). The second example: Jesus was baptized by John the Baptist. All four gospel writers are compelled to include the story with their individual "explanations" of it. There may have been a very early tradition that Jesus first came from the circle around John. (And what to do with Mark's line that Jesus came to John to have "his sins forgiven?") The evidence of the gospels (and Acts) demonstrates that the followers of John may have outnumbered the followers of Jesus in the first decades. The gospel versions always portray John as inferior to Jesus.

The Passion Narrative/Historical Anomalies

Mark established the template for what became known as **the Passion Narrative** in all four gospels. This was the chronology from when Jesus entered Jerusalem, to his death and established the later Easter liturgy.

There are several historical anomalies in the trial and crucifixion. The problem is not so much the added details (writers were expected to do that), but some of the details are contradictory. The story as written contains elements that are problematic. It is often difficult to separate the events from the way in which the events were framed "according to the Scriptures". Did an event happen and then someone found an appropriate "prediction" in Scripture? Or the reverse—were the Scriptures studied and then an event "created" to demonstrate "fulfillment?"

After a ministry in the Galilee, Mark's Jesus traveled to Jericho and then Bethany on his way to Jerusalem. Jesus told his disciples where to find an ass which he mounted and rode into the city ("fulfilling" the Prophet Zechariah, "your king shall come to you, mounted on an ass"). The people welcomed him by waving palm branches and spreading their cloaks on the ground before him. They shouted, "Blessed is the coming kingdom of our ancestor David!"

We cannot confirm that this was on a "Sunday" but all Jews came to Jerusalem early because of the prohibition of not being able to participate in the Passover festival if you had "corpse contamination" (being near a dead body anytime during the year). The contamination could only be removed through "sprinklings" every few days with special vats of water in the Temple complex.

The next day, Jesus entered the Temple area and "drove out those who were selling and those who were buying in the Temple, and he overturned the tables of the money-changers and the seats of those who sold doves, and he would not allow anyone to carry anything through the Temple. He was teaching, and saying, 'Is it not written, my house shall be called a house of prayer for all the nations? But you have made it a den of thieves'" (Mark 11:15–17).

This is an incredibly powerful scene in Mark that remains a fundamental element in Jewish–Christian relations. For Christians, it summarizes "what was wrong with Judaism". It is important in Mark's narrative because he claimed that it was this incident that led to the death of Jesus by the Jews. It is also the rationale for Mark and later gospel claims that such corruption led to the destruction of the Temple by Rome.

The Second Temple Complex

First, an understanding of the way in which the Temple functioned in the first century is important. Like all temples in the ancient world, the basis of sacrifices were mostly animals. The temples owned farms outside the cities for raising such animals, but the Jews had a requirement that they be "without blemish". The southern end of the Temple Mount had an area known as "Solomon's porch", an arcade structure where animals could be purchased. This was a convenience for pilgrims. If you were coming into the city for one of the pilgrimage festivals, you would not risk "blemish" by dragging your animal long distances. This area was next to the "court of the Gentiles"; non-Jews could and did make sacrifices at the Temple.

Where this temple differed from others was the presence of the "money-changers". Jews banned "images"; coins carried in purses had images of Emperors and sometimes gods. At the same time, Jewish men contributed a "half-shekel", "temple tax" each year for the upkeep of the Temple. This could only be paid in a specific kind of half-shekel available at the entrance. Outside of Mark, we have no absolute evidence that either the animal-sellers or the money-changers were "cheating people". This conviction arises from this scene of "over-turning", as well as the quote implying a "den of thieves".

This is where we must recognize that Mark's statements were consistently with references to the Prophets. The quote is combined from both Isaiah and Jeremiah. We always focus on the wrong word "thieves" instead of the entire phrase. What is a "den of thieves?" Thieves do not steal from each other in their den. Rather a "den of thieves" is a "safe haven" where they distribute their loot

Excursus II Introduction to the Gospels   71

away from the authorities. Both Isaiah and Jeremiah criticized Jews for the assumption that the Temple was a "safe haven" where they could perform the sacrifices, thinking that would save them from "the coming judgment". Without true repentance, the sacrifices meant nothing. But neither Isaiah nor Jeremiah ever suggested that the sacrifices and rituals should stop.

One suggestion is Mark's context of the Jewish Revolt and the destruction of the Temple. The word he used for "thieves", is *lestes*. *Lestes* meant "bandit", but in the sense of a revolutionary bandit (such as Robin Hood). This was a term charged against the Zealots with their attacks on Roman convoys leading up to the Revolt. The Zealots attacked the Temple and slaughtered several priests, taking it over for their base of operations. Mark could have applied it meaning that these *lestes* had defiled the Temple. New Testaments translate the word as "thieves", but their crime was not theft; the two "thieves" next to Jesus on the cross were there because crucifixion was the Roman punishment for *lestes*, rebels (traitors).

In the last fifty years or so, scholars have been re-thinking the "Temple Incident". Did Jesus really do this, or was it a creation of Mark? If he did it, what did he mean by it? These speculations often go hand in hand with speculations of Jesus' motives and psychology. Those scholars who believe he did it, claim that, seeing himself in line with the Prophets of Israel, this was a very "prophetic" gesture. Jeremiah used to go through the same area of the Temple, smashing pots everywhere to signify the coming Babylonian destruction. Could this be a symbolic gesture as part of the "predictions" of the coming destruction of the Temple and Jerusalem by Rome?

Other scholars are skeptical. Throughout the ministry, neither the priesthood nor Rome are issues. At some point Mark must get Jesus to the attention of both. The story of the entrance into the city is always described as the "triumphal entrance", because that is exactly what Mark described. At the entrance of a king (and now Emperors), people lined up on the roads leading into a city, waving branches and laying down cloaks.

During the pilgrimage festivals in Jerusalem, thousands of Jews and others made their way here, camping out on the hills around the city. But pilgrimage festivals were also the best opportunity for charismatic leaders to whip up these crowds, either petitioning God to bring on "the final days", or to chastise Rome. At every festival, the Roman ruler left Caesarea and moved himself and a legion into the **Antonia Fortress** which was at the upper left corner of the Temple Mount. Soldiers stood around the top of the Temple columns watching for disturbances below.

The narrative is quite a mess here in terms of common sense. If Jesus had entered the city as the redeemer king (the reference to David), would not the legions have noticed? If he had disrupted the Temple sacrifices, would not both the legions and the priests have noticed? The legions and the priests were duty-bound to keep an eye out for "trouble-makers". On the other hand, given the size of the Temple Mount (three soccer fields), perhaps no one noticed what may have taken place only in the outer court of the Gentiles?

Complicating the episode, Mark and the gospels claim that Jesus came back for several days and "taught" in the Temple. Would the priests have let him back in? Would the legions? Narratively, these stories of teachings (and more parables) fill in the time from the entrance into the city until the first night of Passover.

"The Last Supper"

In Mark, Matthew, and Luke, "The Last Supper" is the first night of Passover. John's gospel has a major change. Instead of Thursday, he moved the scene to Wednesday evening. An important element to recognize is that Jews counted the "day" from sunset to sunset. The "day of preparation" mentioned in the gospels refers to the day-time hours before the first evening of Passover when the priests in rotation slaughtered the thousands of lambs required for the pilgrims in Jerusalem. John's gospel had already introduced Jesus with John the Baptist proclaiming, "Behold the lamb of God". This was one of John's many metaphors to indicate that Jesus would die as a sacrifice. John changed the meal to Wednesday evening, so that the next day, "the day of preparation", would see Jesus "sacrificed" on the cross while the lambs were being slaughtered in the Temple. Hence, there was no Passover meal in John's story. He replaced it with a foot-washing scene as an indication of "service".

The historical problem concerns the claim that Jesus was arrested and tried on the first night of Passover. Passover was (and remains) one of the holiest of the Jewish religious festivals. Would the entire Sanhedrin, including the high-priest, get up from their family tables to put a Galilean peasant on trial? Jewish tradition forbade trials both at night or during a religious festival. Even more problematic, Matthew claimed that the high-priests and others stood at the base of the cross "mocking Jesus". Roman traitors were crucified at "the killing-fields", the execution sites which lined the roads going into the city. Passover was celebrated for a week. Would the high-priest risk "corpse contamination" for the rest of the holiday? He could not carry out his functions if he did so. If the Sanhedrin really believed that Jesus was a threat, they could have contained him in a holding cell until the end of the festival.

The Arrest

According to the gospels, there are variations in who arrested Jesus: "the chief priests, scribes, and elders" (Mark); "chief priests and elders of the people" (Matthew); the "temple guards" (Luke); a Roman auxiliary (John). An auxiliary meant locals who had joined the legions, numbering six hundred men. In the interim, we learned that Judas offered to lead the Jewish authorities to where

Jesus could be arrested that night in secret "as they were afraid of the crowds". Judas betrayed Jesus with a kiss ("*Well meant are the wounds of a friend that afflicts, but profuse are the kisses of an enemy*", Proverbs 27:6). The disciples reacted with swords, cut off the ear of a slave, but Jesus restored the wound. The disciples, in a panic, scattered and abandoned Jesus to his fate, "fulfilling" what Jesus had predicted.

The Jewish Trial(s)

Again, variation and confusion in the Synoptic gospels as to where Jesus was taken for his trial: before the entire council, the Sanhedrin, "the chief priests, scribes, and elders" (Mark); the high-priest's house (Luke, John). The other confusion is the number of trials: one at night (Mark, Matthew); one at night, one in the morning (Luke); in front of the former high-priest, Ananias (John); in front of the high-priest Caiaphas (John, again). Luke included a separate trial in front of Herod Antipas (in town for Passover), as Pilate recognized that Jesus was from Herod's territory (the Galilee), and not Judea.

The denouement is reached in Mark's gospel when Jesus was before the council. Mark said that the witnesses "did not agree" on the charges that Jesus threatened the Temple. Jewish Law stated that if the witnesses did not agree, charges should be thrown out. This is Mark's claim that the trial was "illegal". Mark loved irony. When the high-priest declared that Jesus committed "blasphemy", the reader would see the point. Of all Jews, the high-priest should have recognized who Jesus was. In other words, Mark claimed that the high-priest lied. "Blasphemy" in Judaism consisted of abusing the name of God (taken in an oath) and idolatry. The other anomaly is that if the entire Sanhedrin had condemned him, *the Jewish punishment for blasphemy was stoning.* Everyone knew that Jesus had been crucified and not stoned. The narrative plot (and the historical crucifixion) *required* the Jewish leaders to hand him over to Rome.

The Real Pontius Pilate?

Chronologies of Jesus place his death between 26 and 36 CE, as this is when Pontius Pilate served in Judea during the reign of Tiberius. We cannot confirm that Jesus died at Passover. The proof-text for this is always taken from Paul, 1 Corinthians 5:7 "Get rid of the old yeast, so that you may be a new unleavened batch, as you really are. For Christ, our paschal (Passover) lamb has been sacrificed". Rather than proof that Jesus died at Passover, the context of the passage in Paul is that of "sexual immorality" in the group. He applied the analogy of the yeast (leaven) removal at Passover to indicate that the group should get rid of the offender. The analogy is similar but is not proof for the time of year.

74   Excursus II Introduction to the Gospels

If it was during Passover (or any other festival), Pilate would have been in town with the legions to ensure law and order. We know about Pilate from the writings of Philo of Alexandria (writing in the 30's and 40's) and Flavius Josephus (a witness to the Jewish Revolt). Both listed Pilate's abuses of power in Judea. According to these writers Pilate upset the Jews by carrying "images" into Jerusalem (the standards of the legions with portraits of the Emperor on the top). He stole money from the Temple treasury to build an aqueduct. He apparently hated being there so much that at one point he ordered his legions to dress in civilian clothes and go through the crowds of pilgrims stabbing them. However, this material is not without problems. Both these authors argued that any problems between Jews and non-Jews in the cities, and any problems with the "mobs" in Jerusalem were always the result of corrupt and incompetent Roman administrations and not the Jews themselves.

We cannot confirm it, but Philo claimed that Pilate was recalled to Rome in the year 36 to stand trial for mismanagement in the province. One of the charges was that he did not permit trials for Roman citizens. All Roman citizens had the right to a fair trial (due process). If he abused this for citizens, would he bother with a "trial" for a non-citizen peasant such as Jesus? Beginning with Mark, the gospels presented Pilate as a weak ruler who was bullied by the Jewish leaders into condemning Jesus.

The Release of Barabbas

Mark claimed that Pilate had a habit of releasing a prisoner at the Passover festival. The name of the prisoner was Barabbas", an Aramaic name that means "son of the father". Barabbas "was in prison with the rebels who had committed murder during the insurrection". Mark ironically had the Jews cry out for the release of the *wrong* "son of the father" (the reader knows who the *true* "son of the father" is). Narratively, the story is a mess. Is this the same crowd who welcomed Jesus into the city a few days earlier as their deliverer? The same crowd that the priests feared would riot so that they had to arrest Jesus in secret at night? Mark provides no details as to the identity of this group or why they turned against Jesus. In all the research that has been done on Pilate, there is no evidence that he had a habit of "releasing a prisoner" at Passover.

The most important element of the presentation of Pilate is that he declared Jesus "innocent" (three times in Luke). Matthew had Pilate wash his hands of the affair and claimed the Jews had turned Jesus over out of jealousy. Matthew increased the vitriol by adding, "The people as a whole" said, "His blood be on us and on our children" (Matthew 27:25). What Matthew meant by the quote was related to the destruction of the Temple, "on our children," the next generation after the death of Jesus. Matthew did not have the Holocaust in mind, but unfortunately, the quote was cited through the centuries and into the modern era to justify the murder of Jews.

"Innocent" of what? The manner of his death, as a traitor to Rome. The followers of Jesus had to undo this "scandal of the cross". The best way was to have a Roman magistrate declare Jesus innocent of rebellion. By implication, his followers were innocent of this charge as well (unlike the other Jews in the Revolt against Rome). Throughout the book of the Acts of the Apostles, every time that Paul is arrested "for stirring up by the crowds", it is because the jealous Jews "turned him over" to the magistrate. The writer, Luke, had Roman magistrates in Acts deem Paul "innocent" of civil disorder.

The Crucifixion of Jesus

There is no doubt that Mark (and the others) were witnesses to crucifixions by Rome (but not necessarily witnesses to *this* crucifixion). Many details that we know about Roman crucifixion are included. Prisoners were flogged first and then carried the cross-beam (not the entire cross, they were too heavy). Soldiers had the authority to force a by-stander to carry the beam when the prisoner flagged (Simon of Cyrene). The "gall and vinegar" on a sponge was to stimulate the victim when he fainted. Mark incorporated Psalms of lament and the "suffering servant" passages from the book of Isaiah. The "casting lots for the clothes" is from Psalm 22:18. The allusions demonstrate that all of this was "predicted" in the Scriptures. Crowds of Jews at the cross, mocking Jesus, is historically unreliable. Why would Jews serve as "cheerleaders" for Rome? Most Jews, seeing this along the road, most likely would turn their heads away, grieving for one more victim of Roman oppression.

Jesus Died Too Soon

Romans crucified victims along the roads leading into cities where they served as propaganda for the Empire—this is what happens when you rebel against Rome. They attempted to keep the victim alive as long as possible (hence, the vinegar stimulants) to demonstrate how rebels would suffer extreme torture. (Despite later Christian art, nails were not placed in the palms, as the weight of the body would cause a rip in the flesh. The nails were placed where the ulna meets the wrist-bone instead.)

The average time of survival was approximately anywhere from three to five days. The cause of death is a combination of not being able to lift yourself up enough to breath (asphyxiation), as well as loss of blood, pain, and trauma. Jesus died within three hours. John's gospel, perhaps with a better understanding of the process, claimed that when sunset arrived, the soldiers "broke the legs of the victims" (which would relieve support and speed up the process of asphyxiation). This is when a soldier pierced the side of Jesus. Later Christians emphasized the *stigmata* ("scars") of Jesus as "the five wounds".

Joseph of Arimathea

When Rome punished criminals, they wanted it to last for eternity; crucifixion victims were denied funeral rituals. Such victims were left on the cross until the vultures got to them and then their bones were thrown to feral dogs. The narrative function of Joseph was to ensure that this did not happen to Jesus. ("Resurrection" implied the resurrection of the whole body.)

Being a "rich man" is an allusion to Isaiah 53:9, after the death of God's "suffering servant:" "They made his grave with the wicked and his tomb with the rich, although he had done no violence, and there was no deceit in his mouth". On the other hand, Roman magistrates were notorious for accepting bribes. John's gospel filled out this detail when he said that Joseph asked Pilate for the body (John 19:38).

The archaeological record sheds some light on this. To date, only one skeleton of a crucifixion victim has been recovered from the first century Judea. It is significant that it was found in a wealthy family tomb near Jerusalem. Recently archaeologists working in Roman Britain have found another victim, but no details yet of his status.

How Long Was Jesus in the Tomb?

The tradition had Jesus in the tomb "for three days". Yet, if counting sunset to sunset (Friday evening to Sunday morning), it was only one day and a morning. Nevertheless, the gospels all have references to "three days" in the predictions. Matthew used the analogy of Jonah and the whale. Matthew also alluded to the Prophet Hosea: "He will raise us up on the third day".

This element involved Jewish views on the afterlife. There were no medical examiners as such in the ancient world. The family was duty-bound to visit a tomb for at least three days to make sure someone was truly dead and not in a coma. On the fourth day, the tomb was sealed. It was at this point that Jews believed that the physical body began to decay. Claiming resurrection from the dead for Jesus meant that it had to be "three" and not "four". (Jesus could not emerge with what would have been "corpse contamination".)

What Really Happened?

We may never be able to answer that question with certainty. We can attempt a reconstruction of probable events through everything we know concerning the rule of Rome in the provinces, various issues debated among Jews at the time, and the charged elements that were "in the air" in hopes for God's final intervention.

If Jesus went to Jerusalem for Passover, some followers most likely went as well, and he probably picked up several more in the city. *If* the pilgrims welcomed him as a messiah figure (either with palms or even just shouting), this would have alerted the legions and the priests to a potential "trouble-maker". The combination of Jesus preaching a "kingdom" that was not Rome's with a crowd of followers at festival time is most likely what got him executed as a rebel.

If Jesus tried to disrupt the services in the Temple, the priesthood, in prior arrangement with the Roman procurator, would have immediately turned him over. This would be the extent of any involvement in the death of Jesus by the Jewish leadership—not a long-running plot to kill him from the beginning of the ministry (as in Mark). The level of polemic by the Pharisees against the Sadducees survives in some of the earlier Rabbinic writings. But as far as we know, no one was ever condemned to death over the differences. If "handed over", this would be followed by immediate crucifixion by Rome. One of the reasons that the Jews eventually revolted against Rome was the practice of Rome crucifying thousands of Jews, particularly during the festivals.

There was no series of Jewish "trials" on the first night of Passover or the following morning. The holiday would preclude any of this action described in the gospels; hence no "trial" before Pilate.

Judas?

We cannot verify a betrayal by Judas. His story is so embedded in scriptural references that it remains difficult to sort out probable events. But one suggestion is that "Judas" is personified as "the Jews" who rejected (and according to Mark), betrayed Jesus. For the disciples and his other followers, the shock of the death of Jesus must have been enormously traumatic. How to explain the death of this man who had been the focus of all their hopes? They did what all Jews had done for centuries; they turned to the Scriptures for an answer.

What about the Disciples?

Mark said that when Jesus was arrested, the disciples "abandoned him and fled". It fits into one of the "embarrassment" criteria applied to the early tradition. It may have been so well known, that it had to be included. However, no one after Mark attempted to "clean this up", in any sense of softening it or explaining it. The standard action by Rome was rounding up the followers of a charismatic leader as well. So, were they "in hiding?"

Within twenty years after the death of Jesus, his followers (especially Peter and James) led the community in Jerusalem. We know this because Paul visited them there. Luke related stories of persecution of the followers in the city (particularly during the reign of Herod Agrippa I (in the 40's). But both Paul and Luke described a major meeting of the missionaries in Jerusalem, perhaps ca. the year 49 CE. Another procurator? Different times? This issue remains a conundrum.

The Legacy of the Trial and Crucifixion of Jesus

While analysis of the gospels continues with theologians and historians (with hundreds of new books and articles every year), nevertheless, when it comes to the trial and crucifixion, many still report it as "what really happened". That the "Jews killed Christ" remains embedded in the Christian tradition. It remains a unique "historical" claim. Rome persecuted Christians in the arenas, but modern Italian descendants are never "blamed" for this 2000 years later.

The New Testament theologian and scholar, John Dominic Crossan, has claimed that blaming the Jews for the death of Jesus is "the longest lie in history" (*Who Killed Jesus?*). Exploring the historicity of this story does not challenge "faith". The teachings of Jesus are foundational in and of themselves, without the necessity for assigning blame.

Suggestions for Further Reading

Crossan, John Dominic. 1996. *Who Killed Jesus? Exposing the Roots of Anti-Semitism in the Gospel Story of the Death of Jesus*. HarperOne. Crossan distinguishes the teaching of Jesus from symbolic (and non-literal) "actions" of Jesus.

Denova, Rebecca I. 2021. *Origins of Christianity and the New Testament*. Wiley-Blackwell. This is an introductory textbook that details the individual gospels and the letters of Paul.

Fredriksen, Paula. 2000. *From Jesus to Christ: The Origins of the New Testament Images of Jesus*. Yale University Press. The gospels and Paul's letters from the points of view of the different portrayals of Christ in each.

the leadership remains in the hands of the "twelve", from the base in Jerusalem (central to Luke's theology). According to the Prophets, salvation comes from Jerusalem, so the twelve are there in leadership positions.

From here on out, the narrative focused on the missionary activity of Paul and issues as they arose in the communities. Acts 9 related that Paul went to the high-priest to obtain "arrest warrants" for the believers in Damascus. (This is highly improbable; the high-priest had no authority in another province.) This is when Paul had a vision of the risen Christ. Luke claimed that Paul was "struck blind on the road to Damascus", and heard a voice asking, "Saul, Saul, why do you persecute me?" His Hebrew name Saul, now changed to Paul, was commissioned to go to the Gentiles, to "turn them from darkness to light". He moved on to Damascus where believers in the community healed his blindness (literally and spiritually), and he joined the community. The second half of Acts details his journeys to various cities in the Eastern Roman Empire.

The Mission to the Gentiles

Acts 10 represented a major turning point in Acts, and as such is quite an elaborate story. In Caesarea, Cornelius was "a centurion of the Italian Cohort … a devout man who feared God with all his household". In a vision, he was told to send for Peter (who was in Joppa), and Peter had a simultaneous vision of a huge sheet lowered from the sky containing "four-footed creatures, reptiles, and birds of the air". He was told to "get up, kill, and eat". Three times Peter refused, but finally was told, "What God has made clean, you must not call profane". Peter arrived, baptized Cornelius and his household, and "the holy spirit fell upon all who heard the word". The group then "spoke in tongues". The importance of this moment is emphasized when Luke had Peter repeat the entire story to those in Jerusalem.

Most scholars read this narrative in line with Mark's claim that *Jesus declared all foods clean*, and involved the dietary laws of Judaism. The traditional understanding of the story was that an innovation was introduced so that Jewish–Christians and Gentile–Christians could now eat together in what is coined as **table fellowship**, by introducing "universalism" which was absent in Judaism. However, Jews and Gentiles could and did share meals; in the mingling of crowded cities regular socializing at meals was normal. Everyone knew the rules. If you invited your Jewish neighbor to a meal, you did not serve pork. The significance of this event was again found in the "fulfillment" concept of salvation for the Gentiles in "the final days", who would now be joined to believing Jews (see Box III.1).

84 The Origins of Christianity

Box III.1   The "God-fearers of Acts"

Luke applied a variety of terms to describe levels of interest in Judaism on the part of Gentiles: "devote"; "pious"; and "God-fearing". God-fearing meant respect for the God of Israel. Jews had lived in the cities of the Empire for centuries and had established synagogues, or "places of assembly" for their communities. Synagogues were not sacred space, so there was no bar to anyone participating or joining in the community festivals. The synagogues were closer to modern-day community centers, where Jews could gather to study Torah, and receive charity.

For centuries, Luke was somewhat accused of inventing the "God-fearers" as a unique category. No letters or writings of "God-fearers" have survived. However, in 1976, in the site of the archaeological excavations at the Turkish city of Aphrodisias, an inscribed pillar was unearthed. There is a list of names of Jewish donors who funded an addition of a soup kitchen, followed by a list designated as "God-fearers", non-Jewish notables in the city who also donated to the building. We know some of these names because they appear on other public buildings and temples in the city.

"God-fearers" could participate in both worlds; they did not have to convert to Judaism to participate in that community. What drew Gentiles to the synagogues? It was most likely a combination of factors such as intellectual interest, admiration for Jewish ethics, and sometimes ordinary political propaganda when you were running for office.

It is within this juncture of Jewish and Gentile communities that the Christian message was most likely first proclaimed.

Acts 15: The Meeting in Jerusalem

As the missionaries took the message to the synagogues of the Empire, to their surprise non-God-fearing types of Gentiles wanted to join the movement. In other words, people who had no prior relationship with Judaism, the "pagans". With no central authority established, the debate centered on whether these Gentiles should become Jews first. It was decided that everyone should come to Jerusalem to meet concerning this matter. Acts 15 described what became known as the first **Apostolic Council**. Everyone reported their stories of Gentiles "turning" and "receiving the spirit". James, the brother of Jesus, summarized the meeting by quoting the Prophet Amos where the inclusion of Gentiles had always been God's divine plan. His decision for the Gentiles was that "We should not trouble the Gentiles who are turning to God, but we should write to them to abstain only from things polluted by idols and from fornication and from whatever has been strangled, and from blood".

Gentiles did not have to undergo circumcision. They must, however, avoid eating meat that has been sacrificed to the gods, meat that has been found in the wild without the proper treatment and meat with blood in it. The "fornication" is actually "illicit sexual unions", meaning that these Gentiles should perhaps follow Jewish incest laws rather than Greco-Roman codes. Jews were commanded to follow "ritual purity", but Gentiles "who dwelt with Jews" (foreigners) had to only maintain a concept known as "morality purity". These were two distinct concepts in ancient Judaism. By the first century, Jews had created "vice-lists" of what they saw as items leading to negative life-styles and social conventions in Gentile culture that involved idolatry and thus led to immoral life-styles. These were the elements cited by James.

With hindsight, the meeting was understood as the establishment of the institution of the Church; this form of **Gentile–Christianity** evolved into what became a separate, independent religion by the second century. *But within the context of Luke–Acts, this is not an innovation.* It follows precisely the predictions of the Prophets. When Isaiah, Jeremiah, Amos and others claimed that some Gentiles would turn to God, *they remained ethnic Gentiles.* Gentiles were never subject to the command of circumcision. Luke emphasized this ideological point in that what resulted was a two-tiered community: believing Jews and some "saved" Gentiles, who consistently maintained their separate, ethnic status.

Luke was the first to call these new believers "Christians" (followers of Christ). However, the word only appears once more (in a speech by Paul before a Roman magistrate). His preferred term is "brothers", and "followers of the way". In other words, Luke was not promoting the concept of a new religion; his new believers remained within the promises of the Prophets of Israel.

The Ordeals and Trials of Paul in Acts

The trials and tribulations of Paul in Acts are narrative parallels to the harassment of Jesus, Peter and the disciples in Jerusalem, and Stephen, all arrested with "false charges". Paul went to Jerusalem to offer his "collection" (donations from the Gentile members of his communities). While there, James claimed that it was rumored that Paul taught against the Law of Moses. He allegedly brought some Gentiles into the Temple with him which alarmed the Jews.

Historically, Gentiles could enter in the outer courts; this is a literary device to set up Paul's arrest and subsequent trials. When a Roman tribune tried to arrest him, Paul claimed that he was a "citizen of Tarsus (Cilicia)" and was given permission to address the crowd. This began a series of three "defense speeches" (to the people, the Sanhedrin, and Roman magistrates), where the details varied depending upon the rhetorical needs of the audience. All Roman citizens had the right to appeal to the Emperor. Acts ended with Paul under house arrest in Rome, waiting to appeal to Nero Caesar.

The Legacy of the Acts of the Apostles

Luke applied many literary devices in his narration of the missions of Paul. A typological theme for Luke was that of "rejected Prophet". Prophets were often rejected because of their charges against the sins of Israel. Luke portrayed Paul in this light, hence the many stories of his rejection by Jews in the synagogues.

Despite the decisions of the Apostolic Council, we know from Paul's letters that tension continued between **Jewish–Christians** (those who still claimed that Gentiles had to convert) and Gentile–Christians (those who accepted James' decision). As we will learn from the writings of the second-century Church Fathers, the details of Acts were utilized to argue the "fact" of Jewish persecution. However, we have yet to uncover historical evidence for Jewish persecution per se. The problem involved a family feud *within* the communities, and not Christianity vs. Judaism per se, but "Jewish–Christians" vs. "Gentile–Christians."

The Polemic of the Gospels and the Acts of the Apostles

The polemic of the gospels and Acts utilized standard literary forms to distinguish one point of view from another, a method applied by all writers in antiquity (and beyond). The Pharisees were noted for their daily adherence to the Law of Moses that went above and beyond the practices of other Jews. As such, they became the foil in oppositional debates between Jesus and the current system. But the timing of their writing is important, written within the context of the destruction of the Second Temple.

"Telescoping" the ministry of Jesus (in the 20's and 30's), to the Jewish Revolt against Rome, created a "cause and effect" to explain the failure of the Revolt. In other words, the criticism of the priesthood and the Temple cult was drawn from Israel's *past, as the cult was no longer viable.* The historical problem remains debatable in determining reconstructions of Jewish–Christian relations after the year 70 CE and the centuries that followed. In other words, it is methodologically incorrect to recreate ancient "Judaism" in this period from the writings of Christians alone. As we will see in Chapter VIII, Christian writers in the second century continued to critique Jews and Judaism by turning to their past "Scriptures", to assign blame.

Paul: Apostle to the Gentiles

Paul was an educated Diaspora Jew, a member of the party of the Pharisees, who experienced a revelation of the resurrected Jesus. In this vision, Jesus commissioned him to be the "Apostle (herald) to the Gentiles". After this experience, he traveled widely throughout the eastern Roman Empire, spreading the "good news" that Jesus would soon return from heaven and usher in the reign of God ("the kingdom"). Paul was not establishing a new religion; he believed that his generation was the last before the "end time" when this age and the universe would be literally "transformed".

In the New Testament, we have fourteen letters traditionally assigned to him, but the scholarly consensus now recognizes that of the fourteen, seven were written by

Paul: 1 Thessalonians, Galatians, Philemon, Philippians, 1 & 2 Corinthians, and Romans. Ephesians and Colossians remain debatable among some scholars. The other letters were most likely written by disciples of Paul's, using his name to carry authority.

We understand these letters to be "circumstantial". They were never intended as systematic theology, or as treatises on Christianity. In other words, the letters are responses to specific problems and circumstances as they arose in his communities. Paul spent time in cities establishing a group and then moved on. He received letters and sometimes reports from these groups with more detailed questions or advice on how to settle conflicts. Unfortunately, when Paul's letters were saved and circulated (some at least by the 90's), the original letters from the communities were not preserved. The reconstruction of the original problems can only be determined by Paul's responses.

Paul was proud of being a Jewish Pharisee, a member of the tribe of Benjamin. He claimed that when it came to "the Law", he was more "zealous" and knew more about the Law than anyone else. For the most part in his letters, the "Law" at issue was "the Law of Moses". In English translations of his letters, a capital "L" is used for the Law of Moses to distinguish it from when Paul discussed universal, civil, or natural law.

Known as the most famous "convert" in history, Paul did not undergo conversion. Conversion assumes changing from one religious system to another. At the time, there was no Christian system for him to convert to. Paul himself was ambiguous when it came to his self-identity: "When among the Gentiles, I acted as a Gentile, and when among the Jews, I acted as Jew; I was all things to all men". This does not help to resolve the issue. It is better to follow what he says, in that he was "called". This is the tradition of the way in which the Prophets of Israel were called to their individual missions.

What happened to Paul? "For I want you to know brothers that the gospel that was proclaimed by me is not of human origin; for I did not receive it from a human source, nor was I taught it, but I received it through a revelation of Jesus Christ" (Galatians 1:11–12). This claim was crucial for Paul in terms of his authority. Everyone knew that he was never one of the inner circle, so a directive straight from Jesus was the way in which Paul argued that he had as much authority as the other Apostles. There was an early tradition that an apostle had to be a witness of the resurrection of Jesus. Through his vision, Paul could claim the same experience. It is also crucially important in unraveling Paul's views of the Law of Moses when it comes to his recruitment area.

Paul's Eschatology

When reading Paul's letters, it is apparent that what eventually became Christian teaching is embedded in his arguments. However, it is important to remember that in the context of Paul's missions, he worked within a limited time-frame. Jesus had taught the imminence of "the kingdom of God"

The Origins of Christianity

roughly twenty years before. For Paul, it was still to be manifest, although "the time is short". He incorporated the concept of the *parousia*, that Jesus would return and then the entire universe would be transformed; all social conventions would be upended. Paul saw himself and his fellow believers as the last generation of the old order.

Paul and the Law of Moses

In Christian tradition, Paul is either credited or blamed for the eventual separation of Christianity from Judaism. On that topic, there are more books written about Paul than Jesus. Paul was interpreted over the centuries by the second century Church Fathers, by Augustine of Hippo, and in the middle ages, by Martin Luther. In the last few decades, there has been a new scholarly endeavor known as "The New Perspective on Paul". This involves the attempt to analyze what Paul wrote without the hindsight of later Christian theology. The new perspective is enhanced by more recent studies of Second Temple Judaism and the literature of various Jewish sects.

Paul's job, as he saw it, was to bring salvation to the Gentiles. Almost everything he wrote about the Law of Moses was related to this. The physical, identity-markers of the Law of Moses was never understood to be applied to the Gentiles in Israelite tradition, so Gentiles need not be subject to circumcision, dietary laws, or Sabbath regulations. These three are the focus, as they are physical rituals that keep communities separated, and Paul sought to break down these barriers between Jews and Gentiles.

Paul was adamant about the topic. One of the reasons is that it was probably what he experienced. When these Gentiles were baptized, Paul most likely observed some manifestation of the "spirit" take place (such as "speaking in tongues", the room shaking, prophecy, and healing). He was convinced that if God chose to validate them in this way, how can they not be included?

But Paul had a problem. As a Pharisee, the Law of Moses held great meaning for him. Why would God create the Law but then not expect all humans to follow it? This is where Paul sometimes painted himself into a corner. He could never say that the Law was *not* good, but when it came to the Gentiles, the rituals of Moses were not required. He said that the Law served as a *pedagogus*. A "pedagogus" was a tutor, a guide, most often a slave, who accompanied young boys to school, and offered classes in the home. In other words, the Law served as a "guide" to "define sin", for if we did not know what sin was, how could we choose? But now Christ is the *telos* of the Law. Some Bibles translate this as "the end of the Law", but more accurately, it means "the goal of the Law". But again, Paul most likely wrote this only in relation to Gentile inclusion, and not the whole of Judaism itself.

The Origins of Christianity   89

"Faith vs. Works of the Law"

One of the most famous (and complicated) teachings of Paul was his claim: "There is no longer Jew or Greek, slave or free, male or female; for all of you are one in Christ" (Galatians 3:28). How does this community exist together? Gentiles are "saved" on the basis of "faith" and not "works of the Law". Ever since Paul wrote that line, Christians have interpreted it to mean a full rejection of the Law of Moses (a full rejection of Judaism). But that is not what Paul meant. His "works of the Law" only referred to the physical identity markers of Judaism: circumcision, dietary laws, and Sabbath observance. However, once they were admitted, they had to follow all the rest of the precepts of Moses and the life-style and ethics of Judaism. It is difficult to imagine that Paul would allow his Gentiles to continue in idolatry, a *Jewish* commandment. Throughout his letters, Jewish believers in Christ were to continue to live under the Law of Moses with the exception of identity-markers.

"Justified by Faith"

"Faith" as understood in the modern world is defined as a strong belief in something based upon spiritual apprehension rather than proof. It also assumes a transformative experience of a person. Always translated as "faith" in Paul's letters, the Greek word was *pistis*, "loyalty". What Paul meant was loyalty to the teachings of Christ (and Paul).

"Justified" was one of those Greek words that had several meanings. In English Bibles, it is sometimes translated as "justified", and sometimes as "righteoused", to be declared "righteous". To understand what Paul meant by "righteoused by faith", we need to look back to an early letter, 1 Thessalonians and jump ahead to his letter to the Romans where the concept was more fully explained.

The concept of "salvation" occurs throughout Paul's letters. But what were we being "saved" from? The standard Christian response was that we are being saved from "sin", that "Jesus died for our sins", or that "Jesus took on the sins of the world". The concept is not found in the gospels, but only projected into the story. But if Jesus "died for our sins", why is sin still present in the world?

We do not know whether Paul created an innovation in the understanding of the death of Jesus or if he inherited it from an earlier Christian. Paul was a God-centered Pharisee, meaning that everything that happened in the universe was according to God's will and divine plan. As Jesus had died, then God must have sent him into the world for that purpose. Why would God do such a thing?

Paul worked this out in what would become the doctrine of **atonement**, or the doctrine to explain not only why Jesus died, but how his death transformed believers. Romans 5 contains an analogy of "first man, last man", between Adam

90   The Origins of Christianity

and Jesus. Adam, the first man, sinned and brought death into the world. Or, as Paul said, "The wages of sin is death". As we are all descended from Adam, we all die. Jesus, the "last man", through his sacrificial death brought "eternal life" to those who believe.

Jesus did not die for "our sins", but for the *punishment of our sins*. This was what he "took on" so that future believers would escape the punishment of death as inherited from Adam. When Paul said that the Gentiles would be justified by their loyalty, the equivalent concept is "acquitted" (as in a trial). *They would now be acquitted as no longer having to be punished with death.*

Paul's community at Thessalonica had written to him in some confusion. Some members of the community had died before the return of Christ. Paul wrote back:

> Brothers, we do not want you to be uninformed about those who sleep in death, so that you do not grieve like the rest of mankind, who have no hope. For we believe that Jesus died and rose again, and so we believe that God will bring with Jesus those who have fallen asleep in him. According to the Lord's word, we tell you that we who are still alive, who are left until the coming of the Lord, will certainly not precede those who have fallen asleep. For the Lord himself will come down from heaven, with a loud command, with the voice of the archangel and with the trumpet call of God, and the dead in Christ will rise first. After that, we who are still alive and are left will be caught up together with them in the clouds to meet the Lord in the air. And so, we will be with the Lord forever. Therefore encourage one another with these words.
>
> (1 Thessalonians 13–18)

Paul believed that when Jesus returned, he and his fellow believers would still be alive. They would be transformed into "spiritual bodies", "imperishable" so that they could join with Jesus (1 Corinthians 15). As the decades passed and Christ did not return, the concept was adjusted; believers were still now subject to physical death, but their faith would assure a continuing afterlife in heaven.

The "Judaizers" of Galatians

Paul was outraged that "others" had come to the Galatians preaching a "different gospel"; he referred to these others as **Judaizers**, meaning those who advocated Jewish conversion for the non-Jews first. For centuries the Judaizers were interpreted as fellow Jews in the synagogue communities. In reality, the Judaizers were not Jews per se, but fellow Christians who nevertheless claimed that members had to become Jews first. In other words, this was an in-house, family feud in the communities, and not the differences between two distinct communities.

The Judaizers may in fact, have been Gentile–Christians. If so, why would Gentile–Christians now demand that they undergo conversion and become formally Jews? This may have had something to do with the time-frame and the delay of "the kingdom". The meeting in Jerusalem to decide the issue of Gentile inclusion is usually located ca. 49 to 50. In Acts, Peter's meeting with Cornelius and his "God-fearers" was accepted by those in Jerusalem very early. Why does the issue keep causing tension? One theory holds that perhaps some Gentile-Christians thought they had made an error by not becoming Jews first. By doing so, it would help speed up the return of Christ.

Paul is not worried about the time in the same way. With his own experience, he decided that when his Gentiles "turned" to the God of Israel, this was a sign of the "final days". While utilizing the same list of events as found in the Prophets (Jewish Restoration Theology), Paul "tweaked" the events. He claimed that "some Gentiles turning to God" would precede the "in-gathering of (the Jewish) exiles". If Paul appears to sound arrogant at times, his saw his role as "Apostle to the Gentiles" as the lynch-pin upon which the universe awaited the transformation. Only when he had completed this work among the Gentiles, would everything else then fall into place. The manifestation of "the kingdom" waited upon Paul himself to complete his work.

The Inheritors of Abraham's Promise

To argue that Gentiles were never intended to follow the Law of Moses, Paul provided the rationale by utilizing the story of Abraham in Genesis 12. With both the name ("father of nations") and the promise, Paul claimed that Gentiles were included in this original covenant ("nations" in Greek, "*ethnos*", is what is translated as "Gentiles"). Genesis 12 was the basic text as it preceded Genesis 17 when circumcision was later added as part of the covenant. It also preceded the Law of Moses.

At the same time, Paul utilized a concept found in Roman culture, that of adoption. Roman fathers who had not produced sons quite often adopted a male from another family. This resulted in full, legal status of the new member as a son who could now inherit. Gentile-believers were now "grafted onto" Israel, as "sons by adoption". For Paul, Jews and Gentiles now made up "eschatological Israel", the combination of Jews and Gentiles (as Gentiles) that would populate the coming "kingdom".

The Ordeals of Paul

In 2 Corinthians, Paul complained about not getting the same respect as the other apostles: "Are they servants of Christ? I am speaking like I am out of my mind, but I am so much more: in harder labor, in more imprisonments, in worse beatings, in frequent danger of death. Five times I received from the Jews the forty lashes minus one. Three times I was beaten with rods, once I was stoned, three times I was shipwrecked. I spent a night and a day in the open sea ..." (2 Cor. 11:24–25).

92   The Origins of Christianity

Many theories on Paul's ordeals have been offered over the centuries. These are based upon reconstructions of the history of Jewish–Christian relations culled from a combination of Paul's letters, the stories in Acts, and the anti-Jewish polemics of the Church Fathers in the second century (see Box III.2).

Box III.2   Synagogues, native cults, and the first Christians

Even without the stories in Acts, from the level of polemic in his Paul's description of his opponents, it is apparent that tensions ran high in the earliest communities. Some of the theories to explain this tension include the following:

1. Christians taught against and denounced the Law of Moses. This is a simplistic way to account for the tension but is blatantly false. Christians incorporated the Law of Moses into their teaching, albeit with different interpretations of the Scriptures that fitted their new understanding of the role of Christ.
2. Christians were stirring people up with "messianic fervor". In the decades leading up to the Jewish Revolt against Rome, preaching a "kingdom" that was not Rome could be interpreted as a threat to the peace of Jewish communities vis-à-vis Rome. In *The Twelve Caesars*, the Roman historian Seutonius wrote: "Since the Jews constantly made disturbances at the instigation of Chrestus, Claudius expelled them from Rome" (Claudius, xxv). "Chrestus" is understood to be "Christ". This expulsion of the Jews from Rome (ca. 48 to 49?) is also mentioned in the Acts of the Apostles, where Paul met Priscilla and Aquilla in Corinth, recently expelled from Rome. A similar expulsion had been done under Tiberius in ca. 19 CE. Such expulsions were not directed against Jews per se, but against the plethora of "eastern cults" (wonder-workers and "charlatans" who congregated in the Forum to sell their wares.
3. Christians and Jews were in hard-fought competition for the "souls" of those Gentiles who were hanging out at the synagogues, and Jews saw the Christians as a threat to their recruitment areas. But Judaism was not a missionary religion.

The "forty lashes minus one," was a method of discipline in the synagogues (they stopped at thirty-nine to avoid a possible miscount). Before his vision, Paul fully admitted to "persecuting" the followers of Christ. But he never explained *why* or *how*, although it may have been in the form of "lashings". The historical problem is that Jews had no authority to issue this discipline outside of the community. If you did not agree with it, you simply could "vote with your feet", walk away. The fact that Paul "took this punishment" indicates that he still perceived himself as a Jew and subject to Jewish authority.

"Stoning" is a Jewish punishment for several violations, including breaking the Sabbath, cursing god, idolatry, encouraging others in idolatry, and some cases of rape. This one reference by Paul does not include any details. Stoning was done until the person died of blunt trauma. Obviously, Paul survived if he was stoned. Or. it may have been a case where he was chased out of town with people throwing rocks at him? Another option is that it could be rhetorical. When Paul tried to explain the Christian belief in the resurrection of the dead in 1 Corinthians, he said: "If I fought wild beasts in Ephesus with no more than human hopes, what have I gained? If the dead are not raised, 'Let us eat and drink for tomorrow we die'" (15:32).

The reference to "wild beasts" is in relation to the Roman *Venatio* shows. Trained *Beastiarii* ("beast men") re-enacted animal hunts in the amphitheaters and arenas. Rome took advantage of these animals (lions, panthers, bears) to execute convicted criminals. The problem, however, is that a person did not usually survive "the beasts". Or, should we understand this as symbolic or even rhetorical? Were the "wild beasts" of Ephesus opponents of Paul? In philosophical circles, "wild beasts" was a euphemism for "the passions".

"Three times I was beaten with rods" refers to Roman punishment. Rods were used to beat the back and the back of the legs for offenses of Roman law. Here we have another problem between Luke's Paul and Paul himself. In Acts, Luke had Paul declare himself a Roman citizen to the centurion in Jerusalem after he is arrested for inciting a riot at the Temple. But Roman citizens could not be beaten without a trial first ("due process"). Paul himself never claimed to be a Roman citizen, and hence the "rods". But he also never provided the details of why he received this punishment. A few letters were written "from prison", but without detail.

Speculation

The most likely explanation for the "rods" and imprisonment, may have been Paul's preaching against idolatry in the public forums. For Gentiles, the claim that Jesus was a god who came down to earth and then re-joined the divine would be an easy idea—many of their traditional gods had done so and often—no problem with that. The hardest part for these Gentiles would be limiting "worship" only to God and Christ but ceasing all their traditional rituals and sacrifices to the other gods. This upended millennia of religious and cultural traditions in the cities. It would have been considered a threat, in the potential "angering of the gods", and against the prosperity of the Empire.

But why would Paul be disciplined with lashes, or even kicked out of a synagogue (as Luke reports)? There is nothing in the "good news", the gospel message that God would soon intervene and establish his kingdom that violates anything in Jewish Law. Claiming to be the "messiah" did not violate Judaism in any way.

We have no idea what the disciples experienced with their claim of the resurrection of Jesus. No one wrote anything down at the time. However, most scholars agree that they experienced *something*—either physical or spiritual (his "presence" was with them), or perhaps a "vision" like Paul's? The claim that Jesus was resurrected from the dead and was now in heaven was very early. Believers turned to the Scriptures and sought precedents for such a claim.

By the first century, it was believed that many of the patriarchs (Noah, Abraham, Jacob, Moses) and Prophets were in heaven, as well as the Maccabee martyrs and others who had died for their faith. This "exalted" status for patriarchs and heroes could be one way in which early Christians understood what happened to Jesus. The initial claim of an "empty tomb" in Mark was subsequently added with the claim of exaltation to heaven. As the heavens were crowded with these exalted figures, angels, and archangels, placing Jesus in heaven would not necessarily be considered all that radical in Judaism.

Paul contains a confusing combination about Jesus: Jesus was both a divine pre-existent figure (present at creation and helping God with creation) and someone "... descended from David according to the flesh, born of a woman ... and declared to be son of God with power ... by resurrection from the dead" (Romans 3). If Paul and the early Christians had simply claimed that Jesus was now in heaven but would return to lead God's armies in the final eschatological battle, that would fit in with many Jewish views in Second Temple Judaism. However, they did this in a proleptic sense, not just having Jesus important at the end, but at the beginning—present and involved in creation—the two things that were essential to the identity of the God of Israel.

In Second Temple Judaism, one could petition angels in prayer, "venerate" them, and call upon them as mediators (especially in the Jewish magic formulas we have). However, no one could "worship" angels where worship entailed sacrifices—that was reserved for God alone. The Second Temple literature that discusses angels always has them standing before God in the role as servants—they never share his throne.

An early hymn recited by Paul is found in Phil. 2:9–11:

> (Jesus) Who, being in the very nature God, did not consider equality with God something to be used to his own advantage; rather, he made himself nothing by taking the very nature of a servant, being made in human likeness. And being found in appearance as a man, he humbled himself by becoming obedient to death—even death on a cross! Therefore, God also highly exalted him and gave him the name that is above every name, so that at the name of Jesus every knee should bend, in heaven and on earth and under the earth, and every tongue should confess that Jesus Christ is Lord, to the glory of God the father.

The "name that is above every name" is the Tetragrammaton (YHWH) the name of God. "That every knee should bend" meant "worship", in an age-old concept of "bowing down" before images of various gods. How could Paul, a Pharisee, hold such a view?

This hymn to Christ is already formalized which may be an indication of something that he may have learned from another believer. Phil. 2:9–11 is essentially an exegesis (an interpretation) of Isaiah 45;52–53, where the "suffering servant" passages are almost identical with Phil. 2:9–11. The "suffering servant" humbles himself in obedience, suffers, and dies, only to be "exalted" above all others by God, and placed side by side with God on the heavenly throne.

As Paul said, the suffering and death of Jesus was a "stumbling block" for both Jews and Gentiles. If Jesus was equivalent to God, how could he be crucified? Paul's favorite prophet to cite was Isaiah: "Thus says the exalted and lofty one who inhabits eternity, whose name is holy: 'I will dwell in the high and holy place, and also with those who are crushed and lowly in spirit ...'" (57:15).

This idea was also an identity marker of Jews for their God—that he is *selfless*, manifesting himself and acting in history for the salvation of Israel. In the books of the Prophets and especially in Isaiah, in the "final days" God would manifest himself one more time and reveal himself to *all the nations*, who could now share in the salvation of Israel.

The Christian innovation here was to interpret these passages to understand that the suffering servant was in reality God himself—who humbled himself to be manifested in the earthly Jesus of Nazareth. Paul continued to honor God as God, but now added Jesus as "Lord". This can be quite confusing in his letters because the one word in Greek for "lord" *kyrios*, can mean the God of Israel or a title for a master or magistrate.

What did the Worship of Jesus Consist of?

When Paul said that all should worship Jesus, what did this mean? As far as we know, this worship consisted of hymns and prayers to Jesus, petitions to Jesus, baptizing in his name, healing and exorcisms in his name, "eucharistic meals" in his memory. We do not know much about baptizing in Judaism, but healing and exorcisms were to be done in the name of God. Including Jesus now in the ritual formulas and identifying him with the God of Israel may have been the main source of tension in the synagogue communities. This deification of Jesus differed radically from the concept of exalted patriarchs and Prophets in heaven. The deification of Jesus continues to be a significant difference between modern Jews and Christians.

"In Christ"

"There is therefore now no condemnation for those who are in Christ Jesus. For the law of the spirit of life in Christ Jesus has set you free from the law of sin and death" (Romans 8:1–2). Paul consistently referred to the communities either *living in Christ*, or *being in Christ*. Sometimes this is related to behavior or ethics, and at other times as a metaphorical understanding of sharing elements of Christ in their new lives. It can also be a literal understanding that the "spirit of Christ" was present in the community.

Paul pointed out that the Jews have the Law of Moses and the Gentiles have their law codes; each group understands the difference between good and evil. Why then do we still sin? If you recall the three-tiered universe (the heavens, the earth, and the underworld), the earth was understood to be influenced by the powers in the heavens, both good and evil. Paul referred to the evil influence as *being under the power of sin*. "Being in Christ" was a way in which the evil powers out there (the demons) can no longer affect believers. "Christ" is literally like a protective umbrella for the community.

Baptism for Paul

We know that baptism was one of the earliest rituals in the new communities. Paul demonstrated a "death to life" analogy when he wrote about baptism in relation to now "living in Christ":

> How can we who died to sin go on living it? Do you not know that all of us who have been baptized into Christ Jesus were baptized into his death? Therefore, we have been buried with him by baptism into death, so that, just as Christ was raised from the dead by the glory of the father, so we too might walk in newness of life. For if we have been united with him in a death like his, we will certainly be united with him in a resurrection like his ... the death he died, he died to sin ... but the life he lives he lives to God. So, you also must consider yourselves dead to sin and alive to God in Christ Jesus.
>
> (Romans 6:3–11)

Those who were being baptized stripped off their clothing, "went down" into the water (as going down into the tomb) and emerged as what Paul described as being "re-born". They put on a new white robe and were understood to be transformed in some way. Baptized individuals were no longer "under the power of sin".

What about the Jews?

In Paul's last letter to the Romans, we find one of the few times that he addressed his fellow Jews:

> I have great sorrow and unceasing anguish in my heart. For I could wish that I myself were accursed and cut off from Christ for the sake of my own people, my kindred according to the flesh. They are Israelites and to them belong the adoption, the glory, the covenants, the giving of the Law, the worship and the promises.
>
> (Romans 9:2–5)

"The worship" includes the elements of the sacrifices at the Temple in Jerusalem. Throughout his letters Paul has only positive things to say about the Temple as both the "presence of God on earth" and the place in which the commandments were actualized. But he then pointed out that not all Israelites in the flesh belong to Abraham, but only the children of the "promise":

"I ask then, has God rejected his people? By no means ... Have they stumbled so as to fall? By no means! But through their stumbling salvation has come to the Gentiles, so as to make Israel jealous". This was deliberate on God's part he wrote. Once the Jews see what has happened to the Gentiles, they will ultimately repent and accept the "good news" of Christ and believe. In the meantime, the Gentiles are not to gloat over their good fortune, as they are secondary. They were "grafted onto the original vine of Israel". "So that you may not claim to be wiser than you are brother, I want you to understand this mystery: a hardening has come upon part of Israel, until the full number of the Gentiles has come in. And so, all Israel will be saved, as it is written, 'Out of Zion will come the deliverer; he will banish ungodliness from Jacob and this is my covenant with them, when I take away their sins'" (Isaiah 59:20–21).

How long would it take? How many Gentiles constituted a "full number?" Paul did not indicate a time-frame nor any idea of a quota. But this was Paul's self-understanding of his role in salvation: the "kingdom" awaited Paul's crucial work among the Gentiles and then the Jews would come to believe.

The Death and Legacy of Paul

At the end of the letter to the Romans, Paul indicated some nervousness about his upcoming trip to Jerusalem. He was going there to bring the "collection" he had accumulated from his communities and hoped that it would be accepted. He saw this acceptance as the acceptance of his life's work.

Acts ended with Paul under house arrest in Rome, continuing his preaching. It is only in later, second-century narratives that we find legendary material of Paul's trial in Rome (with alleged letters between Paul and the Stoic philosopher, Seneca). After conviction, he was beheaded, and his body buried outside the walls of the city, on the road to Ostia, so that his grave would not become a shrine. Years later, this site would become the current basilica in Rome, "St. Paul's Outside-the-Walls". The Vatican has always claimed that his body rests in a sarcophagus within the church. In an early letter written by Bishop Clement in Rome (ca. 90's), he opened the letter by claiming that Rome was the city in which both Peter and Paul underwent martyrdom.

Historians and some critics of early Christianity have noted that Paul's claim that in the communities "there is neither Jew nor Greek, male nor female, slave nor free", was never manifest in the Churches. We only have the letters that survived where almost all of the discussion is the problem between "Jew and Greek" (Jewish–Christians and Gentile–Christians). Paul did elevate women (as apostles, teachers, healers, and prophets), most likely on his conviction that "male and female" would be reconstituted in the "kingdom". As we will see in Chapter VI, women leadership positions were greatly diminished in the second century. Christians continued to participate in the ownership of slaves and slave trade, which was not fully challenged until 1807 by English ministers.

Summary

- The "mission to the Gentiles" brought problems both within the synagogue communities as well as Greco-Roman culture.
- Paul's letters provided the basis for later Christian theology.

Suggestions for Further Reading

Denova, Rebecca I. 1995. *The Things Accomplished Among Us: Prophetic Tradition in the Structural Pattern of Luke-Acts*. Journal for the Study of the New Testament Supplement, Sheffield Press. This works examines the narrative structure and teachings of Luke's gospel and the Acts of the Apostles.

Fredriksen, Paula. 2019. *When Christians Were Jews: The First Generation*. Yale University Press. Fredriksen surveys what we can know about the first generations of Christians through the analysis of Paul's letters.

Sanders, E. P. 2001. *Paul: A Very Short Introduction*. Oxford University Press. Sanders focuses on Paul's relationship to the "Law of Moses," in both traditional Judaism and Paul's innovations.

MARTYRDOM

IV

- Collegia
- The Emergence of the Imperial Cult
- Augustus
- Tiberius, Caligula, Claudius, and Nero
- Domitian (83–96 CE)
- The Crime of Atheism
- John of Patmos and the Book of Revelation
- "The Noble Death"
- Socrates and Plato (469–399 BCE; 427–347 BCE)
- The Maccabee Martyrs
- Early Literature on the Persecution of Christians
- Pliny's Letter to Trajan
- Ignatius of Antioch and Martyrdom
- Martyrologies: Polycarp of Smyrna (ca. 151 CE)

Varieties of Early Christianity: The Formation of the Western Christian Tradition,
First Edition. Rebecca I. Denova.
© 2023 John Wiley & Sons, Inc. Published 2023 by John Wiley & Sons, Inc.

100 Martyrdom

The Passion of Perpetua and Felicity (203 CE)

The Roman Penal System

The Arenas/Gladiator Games

The Pattern of Roman Persecution

The Roman Empire Between 250 and 305 CE

Diocletian and the "Great Persecution"

Schisms in the Church

After reading this chapter you will be able to:

- Trace the persecution of Christians in the Roman Empire from the first century to the fourth century.
- Recognize the concept of martyrdom that remains a fundamental teaching in the Western traditions of Judaism, Christianity, and Islam.
- Survey the process of Christian trials and punishment in the Roman penal system.

A popular way to describe religion in the Roman Empire is the claim that Rome practiced "toleration of religion", where this term is often paired with *religio licta*, or the granting of "legality to religious beliefs". "Toleration" is a misnomer because it assumes an official policy. There was no official policy of toleration issued by Rome, either during the Republic or the early Empire. Rome simply followed the same tradition as everyone else from time immemorial— *all* the gods of different ethnic groups were acknowledged and respected. This included the gods of your enemy as well. Romans practiced *evocatio*, where gods of the enemy were invited to switch sides before a battle. Rome promised temples and worship if they did so.

While there were no official, government policies of toleration that does not mean that we have an ancient equivalent of "freedom of religion". People could not freely and openly disrespect the gods. **Impiety** (not showing respect for the gods) and **sacrilege** (damaging a sacred object or site) carried death sentences, as such actions threatened the prosperity of everyone.

But in certain circumstances, a few religious associations were *not* tolerated (in this sense meaning, "respected") such as the cult of Bacchus, the Druids, and Christians. In 186 BCE, the Senate banned the cult of Bacchus temporarily (the Roman version of Dionysus) because there were rumors that their secret rituals threatened "family values". Druids were priests of the Gauls and Celts and practiced human sacrifice (of slaves and war captives). The Druids helped organize the resistance to Roman conquest under Julius Caesar (60 BCE) and were ultimately defeated.

Collegia

The term *religio licta*, was coined by the Church Father Tertullian, in the second century CE, and was not an official policy per se. He utilized the term in his appeal to Rome for Christians to be granted permission as a *collegia*. *Collegia* referred to official trade guilds, burial clubs, and commercial associations. There were also *collegia* of pontiffs (the priesthoods of Rome).

All these groups met under the supervision of a god or goddess. There were regular, monthly meetings where members' dues paid for the food and drink.

However, these groups had to have the official sanction of the Roman Senate to be able to "assemble", rather like a license. The Senate (and provincial magistrates) could revoke a group's license, usually during times of political instability. This occurred quite often in the last stages of the Roman Republic; groups meeting (and drinking) in private had the potential to plot insurrection or treason. For three hundred years, Christian leaders appealed to the Roman government to be granted a license to assemble without success. It was only granted upon the conversion of the Emperor Constantine in 313 CE (see Chapter XI).

The Emergence of the Imperial Cult

Greece had created the practice of "hero cults", with the concept of **apotheosis**, or the deifying of individuals after their death. Their accomplishment of great deeds in life were rewarded with being "among the gods" after death (the Elysian Fields). The god Herakles/Hercules was a model. People made pilgrimages to the sites of the heroes' alleged tombs and were able to petition them for benefits. Rome was slow to borrow this idea, but it became a popular way to honor great generals such as Scipio Africanus, who defeated Hannibal in the Second Punic War (218–201 BCE). Common people began leaving flowers and mementoes at his grave.

Rome had been a Republic for centuries, but a series of civil wars in the first century BCE called for periodic "first citizens" to lead the country out of crisis. Julius Caesar made the bid for power (backing it up with military victories) but was assassinated in 44 BCE before he could rule for very long. Although a **Patrician** (upper-class) he was always popular with the common people (the **Plebeians** and lower ranks). When his funeral pyre was in Forum for the eulogy, the common people of Rome raided the public buildings for furniture, tossed it on and cremated him there. They continued to bring flowers and mementos to the site, as well as the site of his murder in Pompey's theatre (which someone still does in modern Rome).

Although married three times, Caesar left no legitimate son. In his will, he adopted his eighteen-year-old great-nephew, Octavianus as his legal heir. He not only inherited Caesar's wealth, but the loyalty of his legions. As the legal heir, Octavianus went to Rome to put on the funeral games for Caesar.

When a comet was seen for three nights running shortly after this, the people took it as a sign that Julius was "with the gods". Although most of the Senate hated and feared Caesar when he was alive, they gave in to popular demand, and officially "deified" the dead Julius; he was now officially among the gods, and could as such, be worshipped. This meant that Octavianus, as the legal son, could (and did) adopt the title, "son of (a) god". Temples were constructed to the now deified Julius.

Augustus

Everyone had expected Caesar to name his Master of the Horse, Marc Anthony (and his cousin), as his heir. Temporarily, Octavianus, and Anthony settled their differences in what is known was the "Second Triumvirate" along with Lepidus (43–32 BC). Anthony then made a bid for power in the East with Cleopatra, the Pharaoh of Egypt. These two were defeated by Octavianus in the sea battle of Actium in 31 BCE. Now the sole ruler of the Empire, Octavianus received the title **Augustus** ("esteemed one") from the Senate and centralized power in an Empire (27 BCE). An Empire meant consolidating all authority in one Emperor and one bureaucracy. Vestiges of a "Republic" were nominal; August chose the slate of candidates for the elections.

After the end of the civil wars the eastern client-kings petitioned Augustus to allow them to build temples and worship him. Kingship in the East had connotations of combining their rulers with divinity (such as the Ptolemaic Pharaohs in Egypt). At first insulted (Rome got rid of kings and did not "worship" their "magistrates") August recognized the fiscal and propaganda advantage of these temples, and so granted permission.

They were to set up a temple to the goddess **Roma** (the personification of all things Roman) and just include his statue in the same place. The people could petition the goddess for the prosperity of the Empire as a whole, and not just the Emperor. Augustus extended the Roman worship of the *Lares*, household deities that protected the family. He claimed that the *Lares* of his family could protect his *Pax Romana* ("the peace of Rome").

Figure IV.1 *Ara Pacis.* The "Altar of Peace" was dedicated in 13 BCE. It highlighted all the members of the Imperial Family.

Imperial temples were established throughout the Empire and included members of the family of Augustus and Livia, the "mother and father" of the system. In the provinces, the Imperial Cult was now understood as a way in which to "climb the ladder" in terms of status. The priesthoods of the Imperial Cult were sold to the highest bidders. When Augustus died, he was deified by the Senate. The precedent was established for the deification of emperors, but only after their death (see Figure IV.I).

Martyrdom 103

Tiberius, Caligula, Claudius, and Nero

Tiberius, abandoning his duties as Emperor toward the end of his reign (living on the island of Capri), had permitted the head of the Praetorians (Sejanus) to run a "reign of terror" against the Senate. Upon his death, he was not deified. His adopted heir, Caligula, who succeeded Tiberius, declared himself to be a "living god", and had the heads of the statues of the gods in Rome replaced with his own. In accordance with a violent reign, he was assassinated, and no one even hinted at deifying him. Claudius did not much bother with the idea, but after he conquered Britain, the citizens of Colchester declared him a god, and he permitted his "divinity" to be acclaimed on some of his statues in Rome.

Nero's reign was as bad as Caligula's, and ended with his suicide, followed by at least four generals trying to claim the throne (see Box IV.1).

Box IV.1   Nero and the persecution of Christians

The Emperor Nero did not think that the palace complex on the Palatine Hill in Rome was good enough for himself. He had plans to build what became "The Golden House" down near the Forum. In the year 64 CE a devastating fire broke out in the city. You may have seen cartoons or seen references to the idea that "Nero fiddled while Rome burned". (It has become a metaphor for doing nothing in a crisis.) It was not a "fiddle" or violin, but a lyre. The story was that he watched Rome burning from one of his villas on another hill while singing a poem that he had written on the fall of Troy.

The fact that the burned-out sections contained the worst slums of Rome, exactly where Nero intended to build his Golden House, gave rise to rumors that Nero had started the fire himself. According to the story, he was determined to get rid of the rumors and so found a scapegoat in the Christians of Rome. He rounded them up and then invited the displaced poor to a banquet in one of his amphitheaters that night. Lighting was provided by tying Christians to poles and setting them on fire. He brought caterers in, and then entertained the crowd by torturing Christians, both through animal hunts as well as crucifixions. Thus, Nero is listed as the first Roman to persecute the faith.

Historically, we have evidence for this fire in Rome through the ash layers under the modern city. However, we lack contemporary, eyewitness evidence for the story of Nero's persecution against Christians. The Roman historian Tacitus (56–120 CE) first wrote about it ca. 110. Clement, an early Bishop in Rome, wrote a letter to the Corinthian community in the 90's:

By reason of jealousy and envy the greatest and most righteous pillars of the Church were persecuted, and contended even unto death ... There was Peter who by reason of unrighteous jealousy endured not one not one but many labors, and thus having borne his testimony went to his appointed place of glory ... By reason of jealousy and strife Paul by his example pointed out the prize of patient endurance. After that he had been seven times in bonds, had been driven into exile, had been stoned, had preached in the East and in the West, he won the noble renown which was the reward of his faith, having taught righteousness unto the whole world and having reached the farthest bounds of the West; and when he had borne his testimony before the rulers, so he departed from the world and went unto the holy place, having been found a notable pattern of patient endurance.

(1 Clement 5:2–6)

Beginning in the second century, legendary stories added more details and claimed that both Peter and Paul died during Nero's persecution in Rome. The site of the amphitheater Nero used was on Vatican Hill. In the fourth century, a Christian basilica was built upon the site, St. Peter's. It should be noted that if Nero did this, it was an aberration. In the first century there was no official Roman government policy concerning Christians.

The winner was Vespasian, the first of a new dynasty, and one of a traditional Roman tax-collecting and military family, who had no interest in "Eastern ways". His son Titus followed him but died after only two years in office. Both were subsequently deified. This process of deification became institutionalized for (good) Emperors.

Domitian (83–96 CE)

Vespasian's second son, Domitian, renewed all the old policies that usually got Emperors killed. He quickly went through the treasury and was seeking means to gain income when he remembered the **Jewish Tax** that his father had ordered as reparations for the Jewish Revolt. Jews had historically volunteered a "half-shekel" for the maintenance of the Temple in Jerusalem. Vespasian mandated that they continue this donation after the Temple was destroyed, but now it should be sent to Rome. However, apparently, the collection of this Jewish Tax had been neglected in Rome and the provinces.

The Roman historian Suetonius (writing about 120) recalled that when he was a child in Domitian's court he saw soldiers dragging in an elderly Jew and pulled up his robe to see if he was Jewish. Raiding the tenements in Rome, the Praetorians would have encountered "Christians" who claimed that they did not owe a tax, because they were not Jews (not circumcised). This most likely confused Roman officials. These Christians worshipped the same God as the Jews, honored the Jewish Scriptures, but were not ethnic Jews.

Later historians claimed that Domitian ordered everyone to address him as "Lord and God". Within the historical context of his reign, however, it is difficult to evaluate this in terms of how it affected the Empire. But another way in which to increase revenue was a mandate that everyone should attend the Imperial temples and offer sacrifices. "Sacrifices" however were encouraged to be presented in the form of cash donations, and not necessarily the traditional animals. Like the Jews, Christians were forbidden to worship the traditional gods of the Empire, and that included the Imperial Cult. *This is most likely the major cause of the beginning of the persecution of Christians in the Empire.*

The Crime of Atheism

Refusal to participate in the state cults of the empire was **atheism** or "disrespect of the gods". As the gods were responsible for the prosperity of the Roman Empire, disbelief and nonparticipation were the ancient equivalents of treason. It meant that you did not want the Empire to prosper and threatened the stability of society by angering the gods. Treason, always and everywhere, resulted in the death penalty. This was the reason that Christians were executed in the arenas, with the phrase "Christians to the lions" (see Box IV.2; Figure IV.2).

Box IV.2 Early Graffiti

Figure IV.2 Early graffiti. Unknown Source / Wikimedia Commons / Public domain.

This graffiti is perhaps one of the earliest depictions of Christ. Known as the "Alexamenos graffito", it is a man with the head of an ass on a cross. The second man may be in the stance of offering prayer. The caption, written in crude letters, reads "ΑΛΕ ξΑΜΕΝΟC CEBETE ϑΕΟΝ", meaning "Alexamenos worshipping his God". It apparently mocked the idea of a "crucified god". The marble slab now resides in the Palatine Museum on Capitoline Hill in Rome.

The reference to donkey-worship comes from a story recounted by the Roman historian Tacitus, in which a group of Jews, expelled from Egypt, wandered through the desert, exhausted and dying of thirst, until they were led to water by a herd of wild asses. In turn, they started worshipping the animal that delivered them. Tertullian addressed the slander:

> You (non-Christians) say that our god is the head of an ass, but you in fact worship the ass in its entirety, not just the head. You throw in the patron god of donkeys and all the beasts of burden, cattle, and wild animals. You even worship their stables (a reference to the obsession of chariot races and horses). Perhaps this is your charge against us that in the midst of all these indiscriminate animal lovers, we save our devotion for asses alone.

The Jews were a special case. When Julius had returned from settling the civil wars in the East, he granted the Jews exemption from the state and traditional cults of Rome. Julius had always utilized Jewish mercenaries in his armies. Antipater and his son Herod had relieved and rescued Caesar when he was under siege in Alexandria. This was their reward. Out of all the native cults in the empire, Jews could continue practicing their "ancestral customs" (their religion). The "converts", the now "Gentile–Christians" were caught in this bind. They had to cease their former life in idolatry, but, being uncircumcised, they could not utilize the same exemption offered to the Jews of the Roman Empire.

John of Patmos and the Book of Revelation

The reign of Domitian is most likely the historical context for the one apocalyptic book that eventually made it into the New Testament: "The *Apokalypsis* ('Unveiling') of Unseen Realities", known as the **Book of Revelation**. In a series of visions written by John, who was in exile on the island of Patmos, the book combined the apocalyptic views of Ezekiel and Daniel. The concept replicates traditional ideas of the Prophetic "final days", including all the violent "tribulations" that will occur first. The Christ of Revelation is the messiah of popular expectation, a conquering warrior-king who will return to slay all the enemies of the faithful. The overall purpose of the book was to indicate God's revenge against the Roman Empire for the persecution of Christians.

As a typical apocalypse, the book views the world as thoroughly corrupt. Rome is depicted as "the great whore of Babylon", who rides on a seven-headed beast. Only God's (and Christ's) final intervention will bring about justice. As subversive literature, it is written in code, through symbols, metaphors, and irony. Although portrayed as a lamb, Christ nevertheless will ultimately war with and defeat "the dragon", Satan and his agents.

The book opens with seven letters, written to communities in Asia Province (Turkey). Some are praised for their faithfulness in relation to persecution, while others are reviled for loss of faithfulness or their misconstrued practices. In one of the more interesting letters, John reviles those who belong to **the synagogue of Satan**. Scholars debate what he meant by this. It could mean that some of the Christians were claiming to be Jews to avoid persecution. Or, it could be a reference to what became a Christian charge that Jews were "ratting out" Christians to the government, just as they did in the gospel stories of Jesus.

As Christians began dying, they borrowed concepts from both the dominant culture on "voluntary death", and stories of the Jewish martyrs of the Maccabee Revolt.

Martyrdom 107

"The Noble Death"

The act of voluntary death (suicide) was never condemned in the ancient world, but the reason for the death was one that had to be honorable and necessary. Referred to as "the noble death", the models were initially drawn from Home's *Iliad*, in the stories of the deaths of Achilles and Ajax. Achilles's mother had told him that if he went to the war in Troy, he would die, but be remembered forever. He chose to go. Ajax fought over the inheritance of Achilles' armor, lost, and fell on his sword in shame. The concept was analyzed and taught in various schools of philosophy.

Socrates and Plato (469–399 BCE; 427–347 BCE)

The death of Socrates became the exemplar for voluntary death. We should welcome death in order to attain "the greatest blessings"; "come after me as quickly as you can". The body and material existence are impediments to the philosophical pursuit of truth. But we are possessions of the gods: we can only voluntarily cease our life through *anangke*, necessity, or divine compulsion— wait for a "sign". Socrates had been condemned to death by the Athenian Assembly. Refusing to take his friends' advice to escape, he "drank the hemlock", as a demonstration that he and he alone controlled his fate. In writing about the teachings of Socrates, Plato (in *Phaedo* and *Laws*) articulated the rationale for a voluntary death. It must always be for an honorable reason, or to reverse public shame.

The Maccabee Martyrs

Christians absorbed the story of the Maccabee martyrs, with the introduction of the idea that anyone who died for their beliefs was automatically rewarded with instantly being in the presence of God. These Christians were now designated "martyrs", "witnesses", and their deaths as a testimony to the power of their convictions.

"If any man would come after me, let him deny himself and take up his cross and follow me. For whoever would save his life will lose it; and whoever loses his life for my sake and the gospel's will save it" (Mark 8:34–35). Early in the Christian tradition, the template was set for believers to act "in imitation of Christ". Jesus' death and suffering, as well as the martyrdom of Stephen (Acts 9) set the parameters.

Apparently, Paul struggled with the idea:

> For me, to live is Christ and to die is gain. Yet, which I shall choose I cannot tell. I am hard pressed between the two. My strong desire is to depart and be with Christ, for that is better. But to remain in the flesh is more necessary on your account. Convinced of this, I shall remain and continue with you all, for your progress and joy in the faith, so that in me you may have ample cause to glory in Christ Jesus, because of my coming to you again.
>
> (Phil. 1:21–26)

Early Literature on the Persecution of Christians

Pliny's Letter to Trajan

In the province of Bithynia (along the Southern coast of the Black Sea), Pliny the Younger (the nephew of Pliny the Elder) was governor and wrote to the Emperor Trajan (ca. 110–113) to ask his advice on how to handle matters in the province. He said that he had not been present at a **Christian trial** before and wanted the Emperor to condone how he handled it. Historically, this is our first written evidence for such a thing as a "Christian trial".

Pliny began by telling the Emperor that participation in the local and Imperial temples had fallen off. Apparently, this was blamed on Christians. Some "anonymous" tips were received, and Christians were arrested. These Christians were also meeting in *collegia* that had not been authorized by Rome. Of the several interesting points in the letter, there was a description that is rather fascinating. Pliny reported that after the initial questioning, some men said that they had tried being Christians but had abandoned it several years ago. That group was released. He also tortured two women slaves who were deaconesses. Slave testimony was only permissible under torture. All he learned from their testimony was that they met weekly (on Sundays) to sing hymns to their "Lord".

For the rest of the Christians, Pliny said that he brought in several images of gods, as well as a bust of the Emperor, and required that they "honor" them. This involved offering a pinch of incense at the effigies with perhaps a loyalty oath of some kind. When they refused, he had them executed. He also added that he would have executed them anyway, simply for their "stubbornness". This "worship" was never to the Emperor alone, but in conjunction with the Capitoline trinity of Jupiter, Minerva, and Juno, and the Imperial cult.

Trajan wrote back that the way Pliny handled the situation was fine, but that he should not arrest anyone simply on "anonymous" tips. This meant that officially he was *not* to "seek out Christians" unless they deliberately did something that had to be brought to the attention of the government.

Ignatius of Antioch and Martyrdom

Our next evidence comes from six preserved letters of a Christian bishop, Ignatius of Antioch (written ca. 110). His letters addressed the sacraments, the role of bishops, and his martyrdom. We do not have the details of how and why he was arrested, but while he was on his way to Rome accompanied by Praetorian guards for his execution, he wrote letters to Christian communities. The presence of Praetorians, the bodyguards of the Imperial household, are fascinating hints to his high-status. One of the common elements in all these letters was his pleading for other Christians not to try and rescue him when he stopped in their cities, as he joyfully anticipated being "torn by beasts" for the "sake of Christ".

Throughout the letters, Ignatius continually discussed his coming sacrifice as the way in which all Christians should demonstrate their faith. His excruciating details about "floggings" and being annihilated by the beasts created the way in which Christians can reverse the present oppression. By physical torture and humiliation (just like Jesus), the irony is that while Rome saw this as punishment, the result for Christians was "triumph over the forces of evil". Through their sacrifice, they are unified with Christ.

In the second century, Bishop Tertullian encouraged martyrdom. In addressing Roman Emperors: "Nothing matters to us in this age, but to escape from it with all speed" (*Apology* 41.5). Death should be sought out as an *autoapotheosis*, as "a shortcut to immortality". "Who does not join us, and joining us, does not wish to suffer, that he may purchase for himself the whole grace of God, that he may win full pardon from God by paying his own blood for it? For all sins are forgiven to a deed like this. That is why, on being sentenced by you, at that moment we render you thanks ... We are condemned by you, we are acquitted by God" (*Apology* 50, 15–16). Tertullian also claimed that Christian martyrs were the "seed", in terms of recruitment. Gentile audiences were awed and impressed by their courage in the face of death.

Martyrologies: Polycarp of Smyrna (ca. 151 CE)

One of our first detailed descriptions of a Christian martyr is the story of Bishop Polycarp of Smyrna (Asia Province). The story of the trial and death of a martyr became a unique type of literature, a **martyrology**. Martyrologies follow the same pattern. We rarely have the details of how or why a Christian was arrested. They begin in the course of the trial and follow through to the condemnation and execution.

Beginning with the martyrdom of Polycarp, the template for the trials was based upon the sufferings and death of Jesus as the traditional first martyr. We are told that the arrest and trial of Polycarp took place on "good Friday", and where the Jews in the city were the ones who stirred up the crowds and petitioned for his death. There is even a Jew named Herod in the crowd. The victim then has the opportunity for a series of speeches outlining his innocence (comparable to the speeches of the Maccabee brothers).

Over the next few centuries, more details were added to these stories in the narration of various miracles that took place throughout their trials and death. In Polycarp's case, condemned to be burned at the stake, they had to stab him to death: "At length the lawless men, seeing that his body could not be consumed by the fire, commanded an executioner to go up and stab him with a dagger, and when he did this, there came out a dove, and much blood, so that the fire was quenched and all the crowd marveled that there was such a difference between the unbelievers and the elect" (Chapter 16).

The Passion of Perpetua and Felicity (203 CE)

One of the most popular of the martyrologies was "The Passion of Perpetua and Felicity" (which retained its popularity throughout the Middle Ages). Vibia Perpetua was a converted Roman matron in Carthage, North Africa, who was arrested along with a slave woman from the Christian community, Felicity.

In an alleged "prison diary" that was kept, we learn that Perpetua's father (still a Gentile), came to the prison to plead with her not to die "for the sake of her child". She had recently given birth to a son (no mention of the husband or father). She refused, as she determined that it was more important to die for her faith. Perpetua then had a series of visions where she met two former, dead bishops from her community, who addressed resolutions to the contemporary problems in the group. (Such visions always addressed local issues.) When she was taken to the arena, the executioner, awed by her "piety" and "bravery", had trouble killing her. Perpetua "guided his hand" to complete the deed.

The slave Felicity arrived in the prison in the last stages of her pregnancy. Her greatest fear was that her execution would be delayed; Rome did not execute pregnant women. To her relief, she gave birth in the cell, and then immediately ran to her death, "naked", and "dripping milk from her breasts", joyously embracing her fate. We are told that the crowd was in awe of such devotion. These two women were promoted as ideal versions of "true Christian women" where the willingness to die for the faith upended the traditional concepts of family and procreation in their gender roles (see Box IV.3).

Box IV.3   Virgin Martyrs

Although both Perpetua and Felicity were mothers, as the centuries passed, more and more of the martyrologies highlighted a concept known as "virgin martyrs". They all follow the same pattern, as exemplified in the stories of Agnes and Catherine of Alexandria. Both were members of the nobility, and either the Emperor (or his son), or a magistrate falls in love, but as Christians they refuse all attempts at seduction. Roman law forbade the execution of a virgin; virgin girls had to be raped in their cells first.

But miracles always intervened. The men who attempted to rape Agnes were immediately struck blind. Other stories often narrated that lionesses would refuse to attack the women, so that other means had to be taken to execute them. When they tried to burn her at the stake, the flames did not light. She was finally beheaded. Another martyr, Agatha, was famous for having her breasts cut off (symbolic of rejection of motherhood), so that she was rolled naked over hot coals.

As a young girl, Catherine of Alexandria committed herself to a mystical marriage with Christ, shunning traditional marriage. When the Emperor Maxentius permitted her to plea against the persecutions, he called in philosophers and orators for a debate, but the result was that they all converted to Christianity. She was condemned to be tied to a torture device, a "breaking wheel", but it broke. She was ultimately beheaded. For the importance of the state of virginity for Christians, see Chapter VI.

The Roman Penal System

Rome did not have an established institution for convicted felons such as we have now. Crimes such as theft or fraud were punished with fines. There were no "life sentences" where criminals were housed and fed. The system was created according to class and status. Upper-class Romans, even if they were convicted of murder, were given the option of "time to depart". This meant time to get their affairs in order and chose a place of exile. They were forbidden to live anywhere within 500 miles of Rome. Under some of the Emperors, those convicted of treason were decapitated, considered "a quick end". The lower classes did not have an option to leave. They were publicly executed in the arenas for the higher crimes.

Anyone condemned to the arena was placed in a "holding cell", where they awaited the next round of *ludi* "the games". The games were offered in combination with religious festivals and plays throughout the city. The games also featured chariot races, the most popular athletic element of the Mediterranean. As people came in from the countryside and jammed the arenas, this was a good time to demonstrate "law and order" under the Empire by executing criminals.

The Arenas/Gladiator Games

Early in the Republic, Rome adopted the ancient Etruscan practice of "funeral games". At death, two of the person's slaves were selected to fight at the funeral. The one who died would accompany his master on the journey through the afterlife. Roman expanded upon the idea and created large Gladiator schools to specifically train men for this purpose. The term came from the *gladius*, the short sword of the legions.

Gladiator bouts were held immediately following the death of an individual, although in later years Romans could offer them several years after a relative's death. We also know that funeral games in the "Etruscan style" were held collectively by the Senate as early as the First Punic War in the third century BCE. They were conducted either to honor those killed in battle and as expiation to the gods, or perhaps to serve as a demonstration of martial skill despite defeats by the Carthaginians. This combination of both private and public (state-sponsored) aspects of gladiator games dominated the late Republic and early Empire.

The funeral aspect of gladiator games began to change as Rome conquered nearby territories and expanded throughout the Mediterranean; gladiator games began to be incorporated into the national ethos. Gladiators were dressed in armor of the enemies of Rome—Samnites, Thracians, and Gauls. The bouts were moral lessons of the virtues of courage, martial skill, and above all, dying well. By 105 BCE, individually sponsored gladiator games were combined with the regular *ludi* or religious festivals of the city. Under the Empire they remained individually funded but were also pledged as an offering for the well-being of the Emperor.

Gladiator schools were expensive undertakings and several years of training were required to produce skilled fighters. Not all gladiators died in the combats and if a fighter survived twenty-five bouts, he would be granted his freedom. The crowd appreciated their skills and many gladiators became famous sporting figures, although they remained at the lower end of the social scale as all gladiators were slaves. The schools were populated with slaves, prisoners of war, and criminals. However, free men who were in debt often sold themselves into slavery to join a gladiator school. Many retired gladiators signed back up to work as *lanistas* or trainers and in the late Republic hired themselves out as bodyguards or bouncers.

Munus means "duty or obligation" (involving munificence) that the nobility owed in service to the community. In relation to gladiator games, *munus* not only meant the duty of honoring the ancestral dead, but the largesse involved in paying for public games. Eventually, *munera sine missione* (fighting without release) came to designate gladiator games where sometimes up to a hundred combatants fought to the death. Given the expense, this kind of largesse was not common. It did impress the crowds so that sponsoring a gladiator *munera* became an element of propaganda for private individuals running for office. Voters would always remember magnificent games of a man who was working himself up the ladder to eventually obtain the highest office of consul.

However, gladiators were not wasted on fighting common criminals; this would be a poor showing against untrained opponents. Despite tradition (and Hollywood versions) they did not fight against Christians in the arenas.

A secondary element of gladiator games was the **venatio** or the animal hunts. Animals were collected from all the provinces of the Empire (sometimes to extinction) and transported to the cities for arena shows. **Bestiarii**, or animal men, were trained in gladiator schools to stage elaborate hunt scenes in the arenas with re-creations of their home territory (sand and palm trees from North Africa). Although this element was not the original concept of funeral games, it quickly became a convenient vehicle for the execution of state criminals. The presence of wild animals (lions, panthers, bears) were now utilized as "state executioners". Convicts were either part of the hunt or left to be hunted down by the animals alone. In the more elaborate shows, "fatal charades" were enacted using prisoners, reproducing stories from mythology with living actors who died on stage (see Figure IV.3).

Despite the propaganda and entertainment elements of the gladiator and *bestiarii* games, they remained under the traditional auspices of religion. All of the games began with the necessary sacrifices and prayers to the gods, and images of the gods were paraded in floats around the arena. The executions conveyed the traditional values of Roman tradition, in that law and order was being upheld through the will of the gods. During the execution of prisoners, the statues of the gods surrounding the colonnades of the arena were covered lest they be offended by the convict's crimes.

Rome also wanted to make sure that convicted criminals were punished for eternity. No criminal was permitted to have the proper "funeral rites". In Rome, dead criminals were simply tossed into the Tiber River. This meant that a criminal remained in the liminal state (not being permitted to cross the river Styx), condemned to be a ghost. However, we do know that some Christian women in the second century were able to bribe magistrates and collected the bones of the martyrs for burial in the **catacombs** (see Box IV.4).

Figure IV.3 Venatio games.
Source: Rached Msadek / Wikimedia Commons.

> *Box IV.4 The catacombs of Rome*
>
> The catacombs (Latin "near the tombs", or "near the quarry") were underground burial chambers. They were carved from the soft tufa stone in and around Rome. Due to corpse contamination, burials were not permitted within the city walls; catacombs were found on family estates and along the major highways leading into the city. The tombs were layered (somewhat like a modern parking garage) and thus also accommodated land shortage as Rome grew in population.
>
> The traditional Roman burial practice was cremation. But by the second century CE (for reasons unknown), interment became more popular. The bodies were wrapped in linen shrouds and placed in a carved niche. This was then plastered over, and if affordable, decorated and sculpted in traditional afterlife symbols and scenes. The catacombs included open, atrium-like chambers where the family could meet on the anniversary of the death. It was only in the Middle Ages, when the catacombs were re-discovered, that Christian pilgrims began building altars in the chambers for conducting "mass". Modern Christian pilgrims can apply for special masses in the catacombs, which are now under the authority of the Vatican (see Figure IV.4)
>
>
>
> **Figure IV.4** The catacomb of Pricilla.

A fascinating element of the catacombs was the combination of many symbols, adopted by Jews, Gentiles, and Christians. Both Jews and Christians portrayed scenes of "Jonah and the whale", and "Daniel in the lion's den". The catacombs have our earliest iconography of Jesus, often shown as a young man, not bearded, holding a lamb on his shoulders. In Christian tradition, this is Jesus as "the good shepherd". However, it was borrowed from a Greco-Roman art piece. We also have Jesus with a "magician's wand" in the raising of Lazarus

Figure IV.5 A picture of the "good shepherd" that was adopted for Jesus. Unknown Source / Wikimedia Commons / Public domain.

(who is bound as an Egyptian-like mummy). See Figures IV.5 and IV.6. In common with Jews, Christians utilized the story of Daniel in the lions' Den as expressions of God's "salvation" (see Figure IV.7).

There are also pictures of shared meals. However, scholars debate if this was a depiction of a typical Roman meal at a funeral, or the earliest version of the "Last Supper" (see Figure IV.8).

The Pattern of Roman Persecution

Traditional histories of Christian martyrs (as well as Christian liturgy) list "thousands" of Christian martyrs. However, there is little historical evidence for vast numbers of Christians dying in the arenas. Over the course of 300 years, we only have some evidence for the persecution of Christians perhaps seven to eight times, and usually only in the provinces. This is because persecution was directly related to a crisis.

Whenever there was famine, drought, an earthquake, plague, or a disaster on a border because of an invading army, this was when Rome paid attention to Christians.

Figure IV.6 "The raising of Lazarus". André Held /AKG Images.

Figure IV.7 Daniel in the Lions' Den. *Source:* Early Church History.

Figure IV.8 Funeral meal or Eucharist? Unknown Source / Wikimedia Commons / Public domain.

Trying to find the blame for a disaster, the Christians became targets because they "angered the gods". But when times were normal and prosperous, Rome really did not care what the Christians were doing or preaching if they did not "foment rebellion" or interfere with established social conventions.

Everyone knew who the Christians were; they did not have to "go into hiding", and they did not assemble in their catacombs to perform "mass". In very crowded tenements, it was obvious during the dozens of religious festivals each year who did not attend (especially when the festivals gave out free food). The Prefect of Rome (rather like a chief of police) was the only one who could grant permission for burial in the catacombs, so he had records of the Christians in Rome (see Figure IV.9).

Date: 64: Emperor Nero (alleged)

Nature and Extent of Persecution: This took place only in Rome. Christians were made scapegoats and accused of setting the great fire of Rome. Sadistic measures included burning Christians alive to illuminate Nero's banquet in his garden-villa on Vatican Hill.

Notable Martyrs: Peter, Paul

Date: 90–96

Emperor Domitian

Nature and Extent of Persecution: This was capricious and sporadic, centered in Rome and Asia Province. Christians were also persecuted for refusal to offer incense to the genius of the Emperor.

Notable Martyrs: John of Patmos

Date: 98–117

Emperor Trajan

Nature and Extent of Persecution: Evidence of "Christian trials" in Bithynia. Christians were to be executed when found, but not sought out deliberately.

Emperor Hadrian

Nature and Extent of Persecution: Christians were grouped together with some Jews in Cyrene who were planning rebellion. Policies of Trajan continued. Any who brought false witnesses against Christians were to be punished.

Notable Martyr: Telesphorus

Date: 161–180

Emperor Marcus Aurelius

Nature and Extent of Persecution: Emperor was a Stoic who opposed Christianity on philosophical grounds. Christians were blamed for natural disasters. Bishop Irenaeus (as a witness) related the persecution in Lyon, France.

Figure IV.9 Roman persecution of Christians.

Notable Martyrs: Justin Martyr (Rome), Blandina (France)

Date: 202–211

Emperor Septimius Severus

Nature and Extent of Persecution: Conversion to both Judaism and Christianity was forbidden. It is at this time that citizenship is offered to everyone within the Roman Empire. One's status was scrutinized in an effort to determine tax rolls.

Notable Martyrs: Leonidas, Irenaeus, Perpetua and Felicity (Carthage)

Date: 235–236

Emperor Maximinus the Thracian

Nature and Extent of Persecution: Christian clergy were ordered to be executed. Christians were opposed because they had supported the Emperor's predecessor, whom Maximinus had assassinated.

Notable Martyrs: Ursula, Hippolytus

Date: 251

Emperor Decius

Nature and Extent of Persecution: The Empire was beset by several disasters. This was the first Empire-wide edict that affected Christians. Offering of incense to the gods of Rome was demanded of everyone.

Notable Martyrs: Fabianus, Alexander of Jerusalem

Date: 257–260

Emperor Valerian

Nature and Extent of Persecution: Christians' property was confiscated, and Christians were prohibited right of assembly.

Notable Martyrs: Bishop Origen, Cyprian, Sixtus II

Date: 303–311

Emperor Diocletian

Nature and Extent of Persecution: The worst persecution of all—Churches were destroyed, and scriptures burned. All civil rights of Christians were suspended and sacrifice to the gods was required.

Figure IV.9 (Con't)   Notable Martyrs: Mauritius, Alban

The Roman Empire Between 250 and 305 CE

Surprisingly, there was no official, Empire-wide Roman policy against Christians per se until the latter part of the third century. Between 250 and 300, the Roman Empire experienced a series of crises: famine, drought, inflation, various plagues, and invading armies along the borders. Generals often took advantage of these opportunities to stage coups in the field or when the Emperor was busy elsewhere. This period saw the installation of twenty-five Emperors, of whom only three died in their beds. Depending upon local conditions, actions against Christians occurred sporadically.

In 251 CE, the Emperor **Decius** was facing the same problems. To appease the gods, he mandated that everyone should make sacrifices at the both the Imperial and traditional Temples. In doing so, one had to obtain a "receipt" that they had been there. (There was quite a black market for "fake" receipts.) This was not specifically directed to the Christians, but they were identified by their refusal to carry out the mandate. When things went back to normal, the persecution was ignored temporarily. In fact, one or two of these competing generals issued temporary "edicts", declaring Christianity a "permitted assembly". This however, was done in the hope of recruitment for their armies. (Christians were present in the legions since the second century. Others however, were known pacifists.)

Aurelian was Emperor between 270 and 275 CE and made some progress in restoring the Empire both through military victories as well as putting down some internal revolts. (You can still see the Aurelian walls in the city of Rome.) Most likely in an effort for unity, he promoted the cult of **Sol Invictus** ("the unconquered sun"), originally the main deity of the Palmyra Empire (which he conquered in 273), derived from the god Mithras. The propaganda read, "One god, One Emperor, One Empire."

Diocletian and the "Great Persecution"

The Emperor **Diocletian** (reigned 284–305 CE) spent several years stabilizing the borders, the currency, and trade. Now covering thousands of miles (and various cultures) he reformed Roman rule by creating what was known as the **Tetrarchy** ("the rule of four"). The Empire was divided between an Emperor of the East and one of the West, with subservient rulers beneath them (a "Caesar" and an "Augusti").

Upon his return, in celebrating his victories with sacrifices to the traditional gods, the examination of the entrails failed three times (a bad omen). We can only speculate, but perhaps one of the priests opined that it may have been the fault of "those Christians".

During the period of all these crises and occasional coups many magistrates and local leaders had to do their military duty. Traditionally, these were the social and cultural "benefactors", those who had sponsored and paid for the religious festivals and community needs. It appears that Christians were able slowly to elevate their status in this period. Christians now stepped in to fulfil these roles, especially with their Jewish heritage of community charity and care of the sick. Diocletian was apparently appalled at the number of Christians serving in the Imperial bureaucracy. This is when we find that some of the richer Christians had begun building their own church buildings.

Diocletian consulted the oracle of Apollo at Didyma for advice. The oracle allegedly responded that the "impious on earth interfered with the god's ability to advise". Diocletian's court advisers told him that the "impious" could only mean the Christians.

On February 23, 303, Diocletian ordered the newly built church at Nicomedia (Turkey) to be destroyed. Publishing an "edict against the Christians", he attacked senior clergy and Christian property and forbid Christians to assemble. Again, Christians had to prove their loyalty by sacrificing to the traditional gods. An additional element was the order that the clergy must "hand-over" their sacred scriptures for burning and destruction. Christians lost all rights to petition in the courts, and Christian senators, veterans and soldiers were deprived of their rank and pensions. Christian Imperial freedmen in the bureaucracy were enslaved again. At the same time, he oppressed a Persian Christian sect, Manichaeism, which had been spread from the Eastern Empire (see Chapter VII).

Known as the "great persecution" for the Empire-wide attack on all classes of Christians, it appears that this edict was not popular with most of the non-Christians. Numbers are difficult to verify, but more Christians suffered in prisons and through torture than those who were executed. Becoming ill, Diocletian then took the unprecedented step of abdication, retiring to the Dalmatian coast in 306, until his death in 311 CE.

Schisms in the Church

Surprisingly, Christian martyrdom was not popular with all Christians, particularly the Bishops. This was the result of two problems. For the first, Bishops were writing to magistrates and Emperors in their appeals to stop the persecution. As part of their arguments, they highlighted what good citizens Christians were. But some Christians were deliberately attacking and trashing native shrines, in the "hope of martyrdom". Addressing this problem, Bishop Clement of Alexandria upheld Socrates' criteria of first "hearing a divine call:" "He who presents himself before the judgment-seat becomes guilty of his own death. And such is also the case with him who does not avoid persecution, but out of daring presents himself for capture. Such a person ... becomes an accomplice in the crime of the persecutor. And if he also uses provocation, he is wholly guilty, challenging the wild beast (*Stromateis* 4.77.1).

The second problem was the role and function of the Bishop. By the second century, Bishops had developed the unique position of being able to "forgive sins on earth" (see Chapter X). However, if a Christian was sitting in a holding cell, scheduled to be executed the next day, other members of the community often flocked to the cells to receive "forgiveness". The impending martyr was going to be "in heaven" shortly, and in a better position to intercede for one's soul. Some Bishops viewed the martyrs as competition for their unique authority.

But the most lasting problem among the Christians was that both the persecutions of Decius and Diocletian led to severe **schism** (a divisive split between parties or factions). On both occasions, the problem was that some Christians, including Bishops, obeyed the edicts by sacrificing to the gods. Under Diocletian, some clergy did, in fact, hand-over the sacred scriptures. When the persecution ceased temporarily, Christians debated how to treat these people. What should be done with a "lapsed" Bishop?

The churches were literally divided over the problem. Half counseled forgiveness, but the rest demanded removal from office and condemnation to Hell. Bishops were responsible for baptisms and marriages among other things. Did this mean that the Christians who had been baptized or married by a lapsed Bishop had to repeat the sacraments? We will see how Constantine resolved this issue after his conversion in Chapter XI.

Summary

- Christians in the Roman Empire were persecuted for the crime of atheism which was equivalent to treason.
- The victims of persecution were framed within concepts of "the noble death", the Maccabee concept of the reward for martyrdom and the suffering and death of Chris.
- Christian persecution was sporadic and dependent upon various crises in the Roman Empire.

Suggestions for Further Reading

Barnes, Timothy D. 1982. *The New Empire of Diocletian and Constantine*. Cambridge University Press. While surveying martyrdom, Barnes also includes the subsequent changes between Diocletian and Constantine.

MacMullen, Ramsay. 1984. *Christianizing the Roman Empire*. Yale University Press. MacMullen utilizes specific examples of persecution in the various cities of the Empire.

Moss, Candida R. 2013. *The Myth of Persecution: How Early Christians Invented a Story of Martyrdom*. HarperOne. Somewhat controversial, Moss claims that contemporary evidence of martyrdom is scare; most of our information only became detailed in the later legends.

EXCURSUS III
THE CHURCH FATHERS

The Methods of the Church Fathers

In the formation of Christianity as a religion, most of our literature comes from the writings of a group retrospectively entitled "the Church Fathers" of the first to the fourth centuries. As Christianity evolved and became institutionalized, these writers were deemed experts in their views and later honored as "doctors of the church". Their writings include responses to the critiques of Christianity from the dominant culture as well as debates among the various Christian communities. This literature contributed to what eventually became Christian **dogma**, or the official teachings and beliefs of the Church. The term, "fathers" is reflected in the study of this literature, a sub-discipline in Christian history, known as "Patristics" or **Patristic Literature**.

Within the group are the **Apostolic Fathers**, those theologians who lived and wrote in the first and second centuries CE and are distinguished by the claim that some of them may have known (and learned from) the original twelve Apostles. Among the Apostolic Fathers are Clement of Rome, Ignatius of Antioch, Polycarp of Smyrna, and Papias of Hierapolis.

These writers are sometimes designated the "Greek Fathers", because they utilized both the *lingua franca* of the Eastern Empire as well as the writings and terminology of the Greek schools of philosophy. Among the more important of the Greek Fathers were Justin Martyr, Irenaeus of Lyons, Clement of Alexandria, Origen of Caesarea, Athanasius of Alexandria, the Cappadocian Fathers (Basil of Caesarea, Gregory of Nyssa, and Gregory of Nazianzus). From this same period, we have Bishop Tertullian, who was the first to write in Latin, but utilized Greek concepts.

The Methods of the Church Fathers

As we will learn, the Church Fathers in each of their historical contexts addressed multiple issues and utilized various literary devices in their arguments. Scholars have classified the literature in three main areas:

1. **Apologies. Apologia**, "apology" is not "being sorry for something", but a style of writing that defines and explains a topic. In this sense, we have letters and treatises addressed to Roman Emperors and magistrates trying to explain why Christians should not be persecuted. At the same time, they utilized this method to respond to Roman writers and philosophers who criticized Christianity as a "false philosophy".

2. *Adversos* **Literature**. *Adversos* meant "adversary". *Adversos* Literature is the term we apply to the Christian writings that were directed against Jews and Judaism. Christians were being charged with creating a "new religion" (always denounced by conservative Romans). The Jews were exempted from mandatory participation in the state and Imperial cults. Christians wanted the same exemption, arguing that their beliefs were "ancient"

because they were "*verus Israel*", the "true Jews" of a "new covenant" established by the God of Israel. This is when the Jewish Scriptures were incorporated as "the Old Testament", using allegory to claim that the Prophets had "predicted" everything about Christ. This literature became formative in the eventual separation of Christianity from Judaism.

3. **Heresiologists**. A heresiologist is now defined as "an expert in the study of heresy." These writings contain the Christian Fathers' innovative doctrine of **orthodoxy** vs. **heresy**. "Orthodoxy" meant "correct belief". The word "heresy" was derived from the Greek term for a school of philosophy, *haeresis*. In the ancient world, an authoritative concept of "correct belief" did not exist. The Church Fathers declared that anyone who did not agree with their concepts and rituals, are guilty of "incorrect belief and actions" and thus, "heresy". It is important to remember however, that Orthodoxy/ Heresy are simply two sides of the same coin. Some people see themselves as "heretics" (and are proud of it). However, as a "heretic", you think that you have the "correct thinking") It all depends upon who is slinging the mud.

4. And finally, not necessarily a method, but a process: the **personification of evil** in all areas relating to heretics, Jews, pagans, and women. This idea was first articulated in the Jewish sect of Essenes at Qumran, where they claimed that any Jews who did not agree with their teachings were "agents of the Devil", driven by demons into sin. The Church Fathers adopted the same polemic for what they deemed "their opponents".

To study the writings of the Church Fathers, scholars utilize the separate categories outlined above. However, the various methodologies and styles of writing continually overlap. In the next three Chapters, we will explore their roles as apologists, the creation of *Adversos* literature, and heresiologists. There were many writers in this period, but throughout the next few chapters we will highlight the works of the second-century Church Fathers: Justin Martyr (100–165 CE), Irenaeus (130–202 CE), Clement of Alexandria (150–215 CE), and Tertullian (155–220). We will explore the Latin Fathers in Chapter XIII.

CLASSICAL CULTURE (PAIDEIA)

Philosophy and Religion

Common Views of Philosophy/The Philosophical Universe

Plato, Socrates and Platonism (428–348 BCE)

Stoicism

Epicurus and Epicureanism

Epicures

Philosophical Criticism

Galen (129–216 CE)

The Church Fathers' Response: The Doctrine of the *Logos*

Philo of Alexandria (20 BCE–40 CE)

The Church Fathers and the Doctrine of the *Logos*

Justin Martyr

Resurrection of the Dead?

Tertullian (155–220 CE)

Irenaeus (130–202 CE)

Varieties of Early Christianity: The Formation of the Western Christian Tradition,
First Edition. Rebecca I. Denova.
© 2023 John Wiley & Sons, Inc. Published 2023 by John Wiley & Sons, Inc.

128   Classical Culture (*Paideia*)

**Clement of Alexandria
(150–215 ce)**

**Philosophy, Not the Queen
of the Sciences, but as the
Handmaid of Theology**

The Creation of Dogma

**Religion, Philosophy, and the
Common People**

After reading this chapter you will be able to:

- Understand the connection between traditional religious concepts and the schools of philosophy.
- Recognize that schools of philosophy taught different ways of thinking about the divine, which nevertheless validated some conventional beliefs and practices.
- Trace the philosophical elements adopted by Christian writers.

According to tradition, a new way of thinking and looking at the world arose in and around the city of Miletus in Anatolia in the seventh century BCE. This new way of thinking was known as philosophy, or "love of wisdom". Philosophy was an attempt to understand humans and their place in the universe by applying reasoned analysis to a body of observable phenomena. The Greek term, *paideia*, meant "education" or "learning", and referred to classical Greek and Hellenistic training in gymnastics, grammar, rhetoric, music, mathematics, geography, natural history, and philosophy.

Philosophy and Religion

By the fifth century BCE, almost all the various schools were represented in Athens, which became famous for intellectual pursuits of higher knowledge. Such pursuits were most often limited to the upper classes; it required money and leisure time for education, assets that the working and lower classes did not possess.

Philosophy was categorized by "schools of thought" (*haeresis*) that formed communities of disciples (students) around a revered master and his teachings. Each had its distinctive way of life, practices and worldview. As schools proliferated, rivalries and competition developed. Many aspiring philosophers depended upon fees (tuition) for their livelihood, fees that fathers were expected to pay for an education for their sons. Philosophers hawked their skills and benefits of their teaching in the agoras and forums of cities and towns. After the death of their founder, they wrote treatises on his life and teachings, passing this down to subsequent generations. They had rivalries and conversion stories. Philosophy even had its "holy men" and martyrs.

The modern concept of philosophy revolves around a secular pursuit of rationality and metaphysics, or the first principles of being, knowing, cause, time, and space. Modern schools trace their origins to the major philosophers of the ancient world. There is an inherent admiration for these thinkers because of what appears to be their critique of traditional religion and abuses of the political order at times. Philosophers wrote treatises on moral guidelines and ethics.

Classical Culture (*Paideia*)   129

This concern with ethics is the way in which we still tend to distinguish schools of philosophy from popular religion, as the traditional cults did not produce an equivalent type of literature. Because ancient philosophers often criticized the masses for their acceptance of fabulous myths and simple thinking, we tend to identify with these thinkers rather than those who practiced the native cults. This modern view still dominates the way in which we distinguish ancient philosophy from ancient religion. But philosophy and religion were not distinct or separate categories of thought (or living) in the ancient world. What they shared was a worldview that offered practical guidance on "the best way to live one's life", and achieve a good afterlife.

A few of the schools criticized popular religion and practices by disdaining the more fabulous elements of myth, such as fantastic monsters and talking animals. They attacked the anthropomorphism of the gods and their immoral behavior, their anger, jealousy, and vengeance. But most philosophers were not atheists (disbelieving in the gods) as we understand the concept today. It is more appropriate to understand them as redefining and re-imaging the divine, than doing away with these powers altogether. There was no official canon or center of authority to reject. Rather, they proposed what should be proper attitudes during sacrifices and that poets and writers should describe more elevated views of the gods.

The method by which ancient philosophers often described the universe as well as traditional myths was that of **allegory**. Allegory is a literary device that posits hidden meanings through symbolic figures, actions, images, and events, usually to provide a spiritual, moral or political interpretation. The device of allegory offers a way in which a text can be open to more interpretations than traditionally understood. Teaching how to live the best life included how to understand one's place in the universe and in the natural world. Philosophical schools included the study of mathematics, physics, biology (ancient doctors studied in the schools that focused on medicine), cosmology (the origin and development of the universe), astronomy, geography and some of the natural sciences.

Common Views of Philosophy/The Philosophical Universe

The schools emphasized *philia* (love) and *koinonia* (fellowship). There were often rules and practices regarding admission, retention of membership, and advancement. Many schools observed communal meals, often in memory of their founder. Through allegory, philosophers promoted the concept of *ascesis* "discipline", in the manner of athletic training so that excessive physical urges of the body did not control one's life. This did not result in rejection of the dominant society, but in the proper way in which to deal with the exigencies of life.

As in the native cults, philosophical views of the universe shared the understanding that the "heavens" contained multiple powers, in gradients of divinity. But they emphasized the existence of a "high god", "the One", as the unique source of all being. The idea of the One, variously named "the highest good"; "the ultimate"; or "the most perfect"; defined god as an abstract consisting of pure essence and removed from the rest of the universe that consisted of physical matter. In other words, the One did not manifest itself in human form on earth, walk around visiting people or places, and certainly did not mate with humans. This belief in a "high god" became known as **philosophical monotheism**.

When Rome conquered and absorbed Greek culture, three of the most influential schools of philosophy were Platonism, Stoicism, and Epicureanism.

Plato, Socrates and Platonism (428–348 BCE)

Founder of the Academy in Athens, Plato is one of the most important philosophers in Western history. He was a pupil of Socrates, whose teachings were conveyed through the writings of Plato. Socrates was known for the dialectic method of reasoning. This was a dialogue with arguments and counter-arguments to arrive at the truth of a proposition or known belief. These works not only influenced the Greek world, but they continued to influence learning throughout the Roman Empire, including Christian philosophy.

According to Plato, the material world was not the real world but a copy of the forms which existed in the abstract. For example, if you are sitting at a desk in a classroom, you can see and feel the desk with all its physical properties. If there were no desks in the room and you were asked to go and find a desk, you would know exactly what it was. "Desk" or the "idea of desk", exists independently of the physical form. This positing of two different realms later led to debates on whether the realms work in harmony or are opposed to each other.

God, the "highest good", "the ultimate reality", for Plato, did not create the physical universe of matter. To think so would be to admit that god was imperfect because the physical world was imperfect. Matter brought fallacy, discord, and the decay of all things. Humans consisted of soma (body), nous (mind), and psyche (soul).

God is immutable, not subject to change, and change was inherent in creation. God is the highest power, but there were other levels of divinity. Rather than being created by god, these other powers emanated from god. Today we understand light as part of an electromagnetic spectrum that occurs in wavelengths. For ancient philosophers, the idea of emanation from the mind of god was analogous to the light from a candle or the sun. You could see it, but it was not physical. One of the emanations from god was termed the *demiurge*, a subordinate power that became responsible for the physical creation of matter.

While god did not directly create the material universe, nevertheless Plato kept god connected to the physical world through the idea of the *logos*, or the principle of reason. Sometimes translated as "word", the *logos* imbued the physical universe with rationality. (How did trees know to grow "up?" How did dogs know how to bark?") This rationality was present in the soul. Like everything else, the soul was an ideal which existed first on the divine level but was then manifest in the body. Plato had Socrates claim that the soul was trapped in a body until reason helped it to escape. The soul took on rewards and punishments in the afterlife.

Stoicism

Zeno of Citium (334–262 BCE) is credited with founding the school of Stoic philosophy, named after the *stoa* (an open colonnade) where he taught in Athens. For Stoics, deeds and behavior were what mattered, not particularly thoughts, and all behavior had to be in harmony with reason and nature. Because the universe was subject to natural laws, one must accept everything that happens with equanimity. All existence in the universe is material; Stoics rejected the idea that things exist in the abstract independently.

This material universe is known as god or nature, through which reason is active upon passive matter. All creation has substance, qualities, and exists in relation to other objects (space and time). The universe is one that is energized by divine reason known as the *logos spermatikos* which orders things according to laws (cause and effect). This "world-soul" is found in all objects, humans, animals, and plants. Souls are immortal by nature, and at death can unify with the world-soul. The world-soul has a goal in that eventually all creation will cease to exist in a fiery inferno and begin again.

Humans have access to divine reason through their intellect, recognizing that there is a divine plan, often deemed Fate, which the good Stoic learns to accept; it cannot be changed by anything that we think or do. This acceptance is accomplished through a disciplined life-style of never letting the emotions rule one's life, or *apatheia*. In modern jargon, a Stoic was to "grin and bear it", being impervious to both pain and pleasure. One exercised one's freedom of will in relation to nature or fate. A Stoic sought wisdom (understanding the true nature of the universe), courage, patience and justice. Evil arises from human ignorance.

Epicurus and Epicureanism

Epicurus (341–270 BCE) founded a school of philosophy that has unfortunately lent it concepts and name to a way of life that is often misunderstood. Today we use the word epicure, for someone with discriminating taste in food and drink, but it is also used to imply someone who is devoted to sensual pleasure of any kind.

Epicurus claimed that philosophy should teach humans how to obtain a happy, serene life in both *ataraxia* (freedom from fear) and *agonia* (the absence of pain). Good and evil are manifest in the world as pleasure and pain. Death sees the end of both the body and soul and therefore it should not be feared. This school of philosophy was the first officially to admit and welcome women and slaves.

Epicurus was an atomist in his belief of how the universe worked. His idea of freedom from fear included any fear from the gods. The gods did exist as powers, but they took no interest in human affairs. There was no concept of reward or punishment in this world or the next. However, traditional beliefs concerning the gods were useful in their positive elements, in demonstrating how to enjoy the pleasurable things in life.

Epicurus did not advocate pleasure at any price because any overindulgence led to pain and suffering. Anger and destruction against one's neighbor did not bring a tranquil life; in the end suffering from such behavior would enter the cycle again. Seeking the absence of pain would lead to tranquility. Epicureans advocated the avoidance of participating in politics, as politics was full of corruption and the abuse of power. However, laws and behavioral codes are necessary for society to live in harmony.

Epicures

Rather than through literature, it was in the life-style of some upper-class Romans that the term, **epicure**, became associated with the views of Epicurean thought, on the mistaken assumption that Epicurus taught indulgence. Individual upper-class Romans became famous for their excessiveness in exotic food and drink which became an element of this legacy. One of the most important ways in which to establish contacts (for business, politics, etc.) was through dinner invitations. Dinner became the height of socialization, with traditional structures (who got to sit where) and menus. As Rome expanded through conquest, new food and drink was introduced for those who could afford them, with exotic ingredients and spices culled from all the provinces.

This extravagant life-style remains the image we have of ancient Rome through art, novels, movies, and television series. It should be emphasized that only the very rich could afford such luxuries. At the same time, the indulgences of the rich do not necessarily reveal the absence of traditional religious and philosophical views or beliefs.

Philosophical Criticism

The Church Fathers of the second century, while writing their apologies to Emperors and magistrates, utilized their learning in the schools of philosophy to address two charges against Christians: (1) Christianity was a new religion;

and (2) various philosophers critiqued the movement as flawed, or incomplete philosophy. At the same time, the epicure life-style was condemned as the embodiment of Christian "sin" and misuses of the body.

Roman culture and particularly the Senate were what we can describe as very conservative in their worldviews and religious beliefs. The *mos maiorum*, the "customs of our ancestors", was an unwritten code that governed religion, behavior and social classes, that were present in private, political, and military life. Anything new that affected their life was viewed with suspicion, especially new religious ideas.

You may have heard the expression "all roads lead to Rome". The down-side was that many claimed that this also permitted cults and what was deemed "outrageous" beliefs to set-up in the city as well. This was addressed collectively in what was termed "Eastern cults", especially those with "wonder-workers" and astrologers. Roman law (the Twelve Tables) had historically banned practices that would be categorized under **magic**. Magic rituals and potions that were directed to harm a person or group, or to upend social conventions, were regularly denounced. Periodically, the Senate drove away all these "charlatans" from the forum and advised people against their fraudulent claims.

One of the ways in which the Church Fathers argued that they were not "new" was to locate Christianity within the cognitive frame of the basic teaching of the philosophical understanding of the universe. Two philosophers, Celsus and Galen, had written critiques of Christianity.

Celsus (175–177 CE) was a second century Greek philosopher and an early opponent of Christianity. His only surviving work, *Doctrine* or *Discourse*, is found in quotations and references to it by a later Christian Bishop, Origen (the *Contra Celsum*, 248 CE). We have few details about his life, but it most likely reflects training in the Platonic school with Stoic ideals.

We classify Celsus as a conservative, upholding the age-old traditions of Greco-Roman customs and beliefs. As a philosopher, he also derided the anthropomorphism of myths, and any belief that the stories should be taken literally. But what makes Celsus so fascinating is that he apparently took the time to research and study both the Jewish Scriptures as well as Christian history and writings and interviewed Christians. He referred to an earlier anti-Christian polemic by an unknown Jewish writer (whom Origen called "Celsus' Jew"). No fan of Judaism, Celsus nevertheless applied Jewish arguments when it came to Christianity. His conclusion was that Christianity was both new and foreign.

Celsus began with the claim that, "There is an ancient doctrine (*archaios logos*) which has existed from the beginning, which has always been maintained by the wisest nations and cities and wise men". But he blamed Moses for the Jewish corruption of this idea: "The goatherds and shepherds who followed Moses as their leader were deluded by clumsy deceits into thinking that there was only one god, [and] without any rational cause ... these goatherds and shepherds abandoned the worship of many gods". Deluded by the Jews, Christians similarly "wall themselves off and break away from the rest of mankind".

Jews in the ancient world had always received a grudging respect because of their antiquity. However, non-Jews viewed them as "misanthropists" ("a dislike or hatred of the human species") because they never participated in the broader culture of religious festivals and beliefs. The term was now applied to Christians, for their same refusal to participate in the dominant culture.

Celsus repeated an alleged Jewish rumor that Jesus' father was a Roman solider, Pantera, who raped Mary. The miracles of Jesus were simply the age-old "tricks" of wonder-workers and charlatans. In fact, Jesus utilized the tools of sorcery to perform them. As to the belief in the resurrection of the dead, Celsus called it absurd; the evidence of what happens to a dead body belies any such claim.

It is to Celsus that we owe a common tradition that Christians only preached to the lower classes. "Christians only appeal to the vulgar and ignorant, refusing to debate with wise men". Taking advantage of these weaknesses, Christians also teach children to disrespect their parents and to reject family traditions. In this capacity, Celsus viewed Christian teaching as the greatest threat in that it upended both sacred traditions and social conventions. In other words, Christianity proposed a radical life-style that could only be detrimental to the Empire.

Galen (129–216 CE)

Aelius Galenus of Pergamum was a Greek physician, surgeon and philosopher whose works continued to influence anatomy, physiology, pathology, psychotherapy, and pharmacology well into the Middle Ages and beyond. In his research, he studied the bodies of dead gladiators and was eventually hired by several gladiator schools in Rome. He was elevated to the position of physician of the Imperial family.

Galen also appears to know much about both Judaism and Christianity, and in his remarks, pairs them in his combined references to "Moses and Christ". On the negative side, he faulted both Judaism and Christianity with "flawed philosophy", but had positive opinions on the asceticism of Christians which led to a healthy life-style.

Jews and Christians share the common conviction that human beings have been fashioned by a provident creator in some sense, either nature, demiurge, or god. But "Moses and Christ" have eliminated a crucial step in the process:

> This is the point at which my teaching and that of Plato and the others amongst the Greeks who have correctly handled theories about nature, differs from that of Moses. For him it suffices for god to have willed material to be arranged and straightway it was arranged, because Moses held everything to be possible for god, even if he should wish to make a horse or ox out of ashes. We, however, do not hold this, saying rather that some things are impossible by nature, and that god does not attempt these at all but chooses from amongst the creative possibilities what is best to be done.

What is missing in the opening passages of Genesis is both a logical reason *why* God began creation, and *how* he did so—creation can only be accomplished with matter, but there is no reference to pre-existent matter in the text. Galen claimed that both Jews and Christians accepted this by elevating "faith" over "reason", a flaw which he also found in other philosophical schools. Jews and Christians adhere through loyalty and obedience to doctrines that have not been proven. Centuries later, other Christian writers took on Galen's criticism in what became known as the doctrine of "*ex nihilo*" creation—creation "from nothing". God indeed created matter out of nothing, as this is what distinguished the God of Israel from all others.

The Church Fathers' Response: The Doctrine of the *Logos*

With the conquests of Alexander and the Hellenization of the Middle East, some Jews reacted with writings against the Greeks, and Greeks responded. We can describe this as an ancient form of "culture clash". Jewish writers accused Greeks of usurping all their ideas from Moses, while Greeks claimed that the "writings of Moses" simply plagiarized Plato. The arguments involved which provided the greater benefits to humans and society.

Philo of Alexandria (20 BCE–40 CE)

In the city of Alexandria in the first century BCE, a Jewish philosopher named Philo left several treatises that attempted to reconcile the two cultures. Alexandria had a large community of Jews, but local problems had arisen with the non-Jewish citizens, often in the form of riots. This was typical behavior in Ptolemaic Egypt. He also was a member of an "Embassy to Gaius" (the Emperor Gaius Caesar Augustus Germanicus, known as Caligula), traveling to Rome to argue for Jewish rights within the city.

Philo utilized the device of allegory to harmonize Torah with Greek philosophy (*On the Life of Moses*, *On the Jews*, and *On the Contemplative Life*). The revelations of God (through Moses and the Prophets) are not only "the truth", but the source of "all truth". Characters and events in the Jewish Scriptures represent universal human experience. Adam symbolizes "the mind", Eve "the senses", and Noah, a "stage of righteousness".

Mirroring the schools of philosophy, for Philo, God is a transcendent being without physicality or emotions and exists beyond time and space. As such, God uses mediators to govern the world, the chief of which is *logos*, his "first-born son". *Logos* functions as the mind of the Eternal and is therefore imperishable. *Logos* is not created but entrusted with power. *Logos* is distinct from the physical world yet also pervades the world and binds it to God. Philo then declared that just as *logos* functions in the philosophical schools, so *Moses*

Classical Culture (*Paideia*)

served as the logos for the Jews, rationally ordering and structuring their worldview and behavior. In fact, Moses was "the summit of philosophy" who was the source for all Greek philosophers and law-givers.

An interesting note to his teaching however, included the limits of allegory. In describing the dietary distinctions of Jews, he demonstrated that such distinctions were symbolic of human behavior. Moses protected the health of the Jews by these restrictions:

> Moses has forbidden with all his might all animals, whether of the land, or of the water, or that fly through the air, which are most fleshy and fat, and calculated to excite treacherous pleasure, well knowing that such, attracting as with a bait that most slavish of all the outward senses, namely, taste, produce insatiability, an incurable evil to both souls and bodies, for insatiability produces indigestion, which is the origin and source of all diseases and weaknesses. "Peaceful birds", that only eat pulses, are permitted, but "violent" birds that attack other animals could engender violence in humans.

But recognizing the dietary laws as symbolic of instruction in virtue and proper conduct, did not eliminate those laws in practice. Some Jews in Alexandria took his teaching to mean that they no longer had to follow dietary laws. Philo admonished them for this misunderstanding; as Jews they were required to literally follow all the teachings of Moses.

The Church Fathers and the Doctrine of the *Logos*

Educated in various schools of philosophy, the Church Fathers accepted the Platonic view of the universe and agreed with it. Through their apologies, they explained Christianity with the shared terminology and concepts of philosophical training, arguing that Christianity "also teaches philosophy" in the same manner. This is not a new religion or a new philosophy, but the correct interpretation of Plato and others:

1. The "one high-god", "the pure essence" of Plato was in fact, the God of Israel.
2. As in the philosophical concept, God "emanated" the *logos*, which was in the form of the pre-existent Christ.
3. Taking on the form of physicality, God himself became manifest in this body. After the resurrection, Christ returned to heaven and was reunited with God.

Justin Martyr

In his apologies, Justin Martyr defended Christianity as a rational philosophy, which like the schools, also taught its followers morality and right-behavior. Christians also honor the divine principle of rationality in the *logos*. Where

Classical Culture (*Paideia*)   137

schools have gone astray is in their ignorance that Christ was the *logos* of their teaching. In this sense, the schools of philosophy were incomplete and only taught a partial truth. Christianity corrects and completes the true nature of the *logos*. But anyone who believed in and taught the true principles of rationality, were in fact "pre-Christians", even if they lived before Christ.

For Justin, Christ as *logos* is the mediating agent who works on God's behalf: "But God's son, who alone is called son in the proper sense, the *logos*, who before all the things which were made, was both with him and was begotten when at the beginning he made and ordered all things through him". He compared it to mythological views of Athena, which claimed that "Athena arose as the first thought".

Justin argued against the persecution of Christians simply for the name:

> For of philosophy, too, some assume the name and the garb who do nothing worthy of their profession; and you are well aware, that those of the ancients whose opinions and teachings were quite diverse, are yet all called by the one name of philosophers. And of these some taught atheism; and the poets who have flourished among you raise a laugh out of the uncleanness of Jupiter with his own children. And those who now adopt such instruction are not restrained by you; but, on the contrary, you bestow prizes and honors upon those who euphoniously insult the gods.

Christian teachings concerning Christ are no different from Greco-Roman traditions about the gods:

> And when we say also that the Word, who is the first-birth of God, was produced without sexual union, and that he, Jesus Christ, our Teacher, was crucified and died, and rose again, and ascended into heaven, we propound nothing different from what you believe regarding those whom you esteem sons of Jupiter. For you know how many sons your esteemed writers ascribed to Jupiter: Mercury, the interpreting word and … Aesculapius, who, though he was a great physician, was struck by a thunderbolt and so ascended to heaven … And what of the Emperors who die among yourselves, whom you deem worthy of deification, and in whose behalf you produce someone who swears he has seen the burning Caesar rise to heaven from the funeral pyre?

Justin then presented a long speech on what has led other philosophers astray. Greco-Roman religions, philosophy, and society have been imbued with "evil demons". Though educated, philosophers especially, were fooled into believing in the existence and beneficence of these "gods". The demons are apparent in the immorality of society (citing several abuses). This was particularly true in the social convention of exposing unwanted children.

> Our doctrines, then, appear to be greater than all human teaching; because Christ, who appeared for our sakes, became the whole rational being, both body, and reason, and soul. For whatever either lawgivers or philosophers uttered well, they elaborated by finding and contemplating some part of the Word. But since they did not know the whole of the Word, which is Christ, they often contradicted themselves. And those who by human birth were more ancient than

Christ, when they attempted to consider and prove things by reason, were brought before the tribunals as impious persons and busybodies. And Socrates, who was more zealous in this direction than all of them, was accused of the very same crimes as ourselves. For they said that he was introducing new divinities and did not consider those to be gods whom the state recognized. But he cast out from the state both Homer and the rest of the poets, and taught men to reject the wicked demons and those who did the things which the poets related; and he exhorted them to become acquainted with the God who was to them unknown.

Justin argued against the charge of atheism, by not only pointing out that Christians were good citizens, but by citing the gospel material that Christ did not teach civil disobedience: "Render to Caesar what is Caesar's and to God what is God's". Criticism of Christians assumes that they are urging a human kingdom, but it is a kingdom of God's future reign.

Plato was aware of "the truth", but it became misinterpreted by the schools of philosophy. Plato's description of creation was "borrowed" from Moses, that God, having altered matter which was shapeless, made the world. Plato himself had "predicted" the death of Jesus on the cross from a story of Moses: "In the *Timaeus*, Plato said that he (God) placed him (the *logos*) crosswise in the universe. When the Israelites in the wilderness were overtaken by serpents, Moses took brass and made it into the figure of a cross to dispel the serpents".

Resurrection of the Dead?

Plato confirmed the immortality of the soul and reward and punishment after death:

> And Plato, in like manner, used to say that Rhadamanthus and Minos would punish the wicked who came before them; and we say that the same thing will be done, but at the hand of Christ, and upon the wicked in the same bodies united again to their spirits which are now to undergo everlasting punishment; and not only, as Plato said, for a period of a thousand years. And if anyone say that this is incredible or impossible, this error of ours is one which concerns ourselves only, and no other person, so long as you cannot convict us of doing any harm.

Justin cited witnesses to the resurrection from the gospels, where the effect was profound. In addition, resurrection can be understood with the analogy of natural cycles (the seasons of death and re-birth).

Justin pointed out that everyone believes in the process of procreation, although no one has ever witnessed exactly how the semen infuses life. The same for bodily resurrection; because no one has witnessed it does not mean that it is false. In summation, Justin argued for understanding Christianity on the same level as the schools of philosophy:

For while we say that all things have been produced and arranged into a world by God, we shall seem to utter the doctrine of Plato; and while we say that there will be a burning up of all, we shall seem to utter the doctrine of the Stoics: and while we affirm that the souls of the wicked, being endowed with sensation even after death, are punished, and that those of the good being delivered from punishment spend a blessed existence, we shall seem to say the same things as the poets and philosophers.

Tertullian (155–220 CE)

Tertullian of Carthage (North Africa) wrote extensively on Christianity and was one of the first to write in Latin. He perceived his conversion to Christianity as a radical break with tradition: "Christians are made, not born". He wrote treatises against Gentiles, Judaism, immorality, and heretics. Although trained in philosophy, Tertullian cited no writers, most likely because he disapproved of all of them. In contrast to viewing philosophy as a "forerunner" of Christ, he claimed that philosophy was in fact, the basis for the views of Christian heretics. Nevertheless, his views were influenced by the same philosophical concepts and terminology.

The soul, or spirit, was not preexistent as Plato taught. It was created new in the individual. What makes the soul "sinful" is its bondage to Satan. When Satan is renounced through baptism, the soul calls upon God and passes into a healthy state. Once in this state, a good Christian should practice discipline and not being polluted by attending the theater or the amphitheaters.

Tertullian's *logos* doctrine included the idea of an inherent, invisible force in baptized Christians. As the *logos* had always been present in God, Christ as *logos*, is now manifest in Christians: "When you think, there is a second person within you". This "second person" (*persona*) became the basis for Tertullian's early concept of what evolved into the doctrine of "the Trinity" (see Chapter X.)

Irenaeus (130–202 CE)

A Greek Christian, Irenaeus became Bishop of Lugdumum (now Lyon, France). During a persecution under the Emperor Marcus Aurelius, Irenaeus later described their sufferings and torture. Irenaeus is more famous for his monumental work, *Adversus Haereses* ("Against Heresies" (see Chapter VI). In demonstrating the errors of the heretics, Irenaeus adopted Justin Martyr's concept of the unity of the *logos* with God.

Irenaeus declared heretics as those who had completely adopted Plato's universe into their teachings. Plato explained the one god as emanating "archons", "powers", and the demiurge, who had created the material universe. While Irenaeus did not contribute anything new to *logos* doctrine, he

140 Classical Culture (*Paideia*)

nevertheless railed against those who separated "creation from the Creator". Such separation also promoted a separation between God and Christ.

God deliberately designed the world as a difficult place so that humans can make moral decisions. Christ was created before the world, because God knew he would be needed for salvation. Salvation occurs through Christ's incarnation, which conveys incorruptibility on humanity. Human nature is joined to God's nature in Christ and so humans can achieve victory over sin.

Clement of Alexandria (150–215 CE)

Titus Flavius Clemens was a Christian theologian and philosopher who taught at the Catechetical School of Alexandria. Alexandria had several schools of philosophy, and Christians established the same structure to disseminate Christian teachings. Clement grew up in a Gentile household and apparently was familiar with Greek religious concepts as well as the Mysteries. He traveled extensively through Greece, Asia Province, Palestine, and Egypt. Having decided that native cults contributed to moral corruption, he converted to Christianity. Clement soon achieved a reputation for utilizing Plato and Stoicism into his teachings. His three-surviving works are: The *Protrepticus* ("Exhortation"), the *Paedagogus* ("Tutor"), and the *Stromata* ("Miscellanies").

The *Protrepticus* was an appeal to Gentiles to become Christians. As such, it was similar to what we would now call an anthropological approach. He explained native religion as occurring in seven stages. At first, humans believed that the sun, moon, and stars were deities. With the development of agriculture, powers were assigned to the products and deified (Demeter and Dionysus). Humans then began deifying heroes and other humans. The "idols" are simply wood and stone, illusions of false belief.

The *Paedagogus* presented Christ as the teacher of all humans. In parallel to Plato's *Republic* (4.441), he divided life into three elements: character, actions, and passions. He also cited Homer over sixty times for models of honorable men; humans should imitate Christ in their behavior. Sin is involuntary, and thus irrational. God's guiding humans away from sin is evidence of his love of humankind. In contrast to other Church Fathers, Clement argued for what we could term "equality of the sexes", in that women are also saved on the same basis of faith as men. He wrote of several inspirational Biblical and Classical women as models. Clement promoted moderation in all things; table manners, eating, drinking, excessive body adornments, and make-up. Both promiscuity and sexual abstinence are unnatural, disrupting the goal of procreation.

In the *Stromata*, Clement claimed that philosophy for Greeks functioned in the same way in which the Law of Moses functioned for Jews. He also argued for the primacy of Moses' influence on the Greeks. He discussed martyrdom, claiming that Christians should not seek it; this vitiates God's gift of life. Martyrdom can be achieved by those who practice good deeds, not just the

Classical Culture (*Paideia*) 141

profession of one's faith. In what almost appears to parallel modern discourse, Clement wrote a treatise, *Who is the Rich Man Who is Saved?* where he argued that the rich can be saved through charity and good works.

Philosophy, Not the Queen of the Sciences, but as the Handmaid of Theology

One of the more famous phrases by Clement was in understanding the purpose of philosophy in relation to religious beliefs:

> Before the advent of the Lord, philosophy was necessary to the Greeks for righteousness. And now it becomes conducive to piety; being a king of preparatory training to those who attain to faith through demonstration. Perchance, too, philosophy was given to the Greek directly and primarily until the Lord should call the Greeks. For this was as a schoolmaster to bring the Hellenic mind, as the law, the Hebrews, "to Christ". Philosophy, therefore was a preparation, paving the way for him who is perfected in Christ ... For what was bestowed on each generation advantageously is a preliminary training for the word of the Lord.

In other words, philosophy served as a "hand-maiden", a servant whose concepts and terminology could prepare a Christian to eventually understand the "true philosophy" of the world. This concept became invaluable in the Middle Ages in the writings of the Scholastics (*ancella theologiae*), such as Thomas Aquinas, and later political theorists such as John Locke.

Another text, known as *The Octavius of the Minucius Felix* (ca. 197 CE), is often misunderstood as a standard polemic against Christianity. It is a dialogue between two friends, discussing "what people think about Christians". It contains an infamous charge that Christian initiation involved the candidate killing a non-Christian baby (disguised in flour). At the end of the ceremony, trained dogs pulled down the lamps and everyone groped their nearest neighbor in an "orgy of sex". This text however, was written by a Christian, most likely as satire on the Mystery cults. We cannot confirm that most people thought that this was what went on in a Christian assembly.

The Creation of Dogma

The second century Church Fathers' response to criticism eventually became Christian dogma, or a set of beliefs that is accepted by members of a group without being questioned or doubted. Utilizing traditional philosophical discourse became the best way to counter criticism by placing Christianity within the parameters of both philosophy and society:

1. Christians are not atheists. Plato himself believed in an unseen god. All truth found in philosophy anticipates Christianity and is brought together by it.

Classical Culture (*Paideia*)

2. Christians do not worship a criminal. Jesus's trial violated Jewish law.
3. Christianity is not new but has been in preparation for all eternity; Moses antedated the Greek philosophers.
4. Christians are patriots. They obey all the laws that do not violate conscience.
5. Christianity does not lead to the destruction of society (a "counter-culture"). Natural calamities are the result of God's judgment against the evil of false worship.

Religion, Philosophy, and the Common People

How many of the views of philosophers on the gods and religion influenced the views of common Greeks and Romans? Scholars estimate the level of literacy in the ancient world anywhere from 1–5% which was restricted to the upper classes. However, it is better to calculate this statistic by comparing "educated" to "literate". "Educated" would be the level of study and reflection in the schools of philosophy. But for what we would term the middle and lower classes, the bankers, businessmen, and craftsmen, some level of literacy in both numbers and letters would be required simply to do business. Common sense tells us that the evidence of the proliferation of graffiti on ancient walls was done with the expectation that people could read it.

For the majority, ancient life was experienced through the interaction of social connections and the public venues of villages, towns, and cities. The moral tone set by philosophers could be experienced simply by strolling through the agora or forum on any given day. There were frequent speeches by magistrates and candidates for office who had been trained in philosophical schools for oratory devices. Law courts (then and now) were sources of public entertainment. Many philosophical schools were on display in the theaters, where playwrights integrated views on the gods, philosophy, politics, and moral conduct. There was also the most common form of communication, gossip, where ideas perhaps heard in the streets could be bandied about. Without a body of literature, we simply do not have enough information to judge the impact of philosophical attitudes on the religious views of average people, Gentile or Christian.

Summary

- Ancient Religions and schools of philosophy shared many concepts and traditions concerning the relationship between humans and the divine.
- While presenting different views of the divine, philosophers nevertheless validated contemporary practices and social conventions.
- In response to criticism, Christian writers utilized the worldviews and terminology of the philosophical schools to create Christian dogma.

Classical Culture (*Paideia*) | 43

Suggestions for Further Reading

Ehrman, Bart D. 2014. *After the New Testament: 100–300 C.E.: A Reader in Early Christianity*, 2nd edn. Oxford University Press. This is an anthology with explanations and excerpts of the writings of the Church Fathers.

Eshleman, Kendra. 2020. *The Social World of Intellectuals in the Roman Empire: Sophists, Philosophers, and Christians*. Cambridge University Press. This work highlights the intellectual world of upper-class Christians.

GRECO-ROMAN VIEWS ON LIFE, SEX AND MARRIAGE: CHRISTIAN "INNOVATIONS"

VI

Human Sexuality and Gender Roles in the Roman Empire

Philosophical Views

Human Sexual Intercourse

Gendered Roles

Homosexuality in the Ancient World

The Books of the Prophets

Christian Views of Native Life-Styles

The Church Fathers Views on Human Sexuality

"The Octavius of Marcus Minucius Felix"

Human Intercourse as a "Sin"

"Lust as a Necessary Evil"

Radical Christians

Celibacy and Chastity

"Where Did All This Madness Come From?"

Varieties of Early Christianity: The Formation of the Western Christian Tradition, First Edition. Rebecca I. Denova.
© 2023 John Wiley & Sons, Inc. Published 2023 by John Wiley & Sons, Inc.

After reading this chapter you will be able to:

- Understand the importance of fertility in ancient cultures and religious concepts.
- Analyze the transformation of human sexuality and society by Christian leaders.

While adopting the concepts and terminology of the schools of philosophy, the second-century Church Fathers also argued that Christianity was the "most perfect philosophy" in relation to daily life, gender, and social conventions. They utilized the books of the Prophets, and their own experiences with contemporary society.

Human Sexuality and Gender Roles in the Roman Empire

It is important to recognize that ancient attitudes and views of the body were directly related to the community. In a world of harsh conditions, short life-expectancy, devastating natural disasters (floods, famines), high infant mortality rates, and constant wars, the eons-old concept of fertility remained crucially important.

The village, town, and city were the core of an individual's identity in the ancient world, with the understanding that the good of the community transcended the good of one person. The community had to survive, essentially through the procreation of new humans to replace those who had died. Behind the conviction that procreation was essential, lay the structure and order of society, particularly in the roles (and obligations) of gender. One's "sex" is the physical difference that one is born with; one's "gender" was a social construction which differentiated men and women and organized the role and duties of each in society. These roles and duties had been "handed down by the gods" (and thus understood as "religious duties") and codified under the laws of each culture.

Every man had a religious duty to marry and produce offspring, while every woman had increased pressure on her value of reproduction, virtually the only value she brought to society. Men could rule the city and go to war to defend it, but women had only one redeeming quality—the potential for bearing children. The importance of the dead, or the ancestors, played a role in the social structure as well, as they remained examples of virtue, in the unending struggle to convey the flow of life "from generation to generation". It was the "seed" of famous ancestors that could still convey status and rank in the community. A good example of this was in the election of magistrates. No matter how corrupt, no matter how many scandals, if a candidate for office had an ancestor who had made it all the way to the consulship, he was elected. The *potentia* (power) inherent in his semen elevated him above other candidates.

Then (as now) unwanted pregnancies became a social problem for various reasons. This was particularly a scandal involving children born through adultery and the association of shame conferred upon the husband of not being able to control his wife. Methods for dealing with unwanted pregnancy involved prophylactics (artificial tools for preventing pregnancy), surgery, drugs, potions (elixirs), and magic formulas. We have medical texts from Egypt describing formulas of paste to be applied to the vagina to thwart pregnancy. But the general attitude was one taken from the importance of fertility and the rights of the father.

Some philosophical views (such as the Pythagoreans, Diogenes, and some Stoics) discussed when a fetus became a "person". But socially, when a child was born, it was laid at the feet of the father who had the choice to pick it up and acknowledge the child as his. This is when we can say that "personhood" was legally conferred. The practice of infanticide (abandoning unwanted children on hillsides) is largely a myth. And "mythic" in the sense because this idea was rooted in the stories of various gods who were "abandoned" at birth, raised by someone else (usually shepherds) and ultimately recovered their standing and went on to great deeds. More commonly, unwanted children were left outside the house, where anyone could then "pick them up" and adopt them.

Philosophical Views

Gender roles were rationalized through the various schools of philosophy and their analysis of medical knowledge (medicine was a specialty of these schools). Philosophers explained the differences between male and female. Men had hot blood, while women had cold blood. "Hot" equated to "active", and "cold" equated to "passive". According to medical texts of the time, during the menstrual cycle, this cold blood, affected by the "vapors" of the womb (and liver), could rise to the brain, resulting in "hysteria" (the ancient concept of PMS, Pre-Menstrual Syndrome).

The womb was understood as an incubator, the sole function of which was to nurture the fetus until birth. It was believed that the physical traits of a person were contained solely in the semen. Women were cautioned to live healthily and passively during pregnancy as untoward behavior could affect the fetus. The philosopher Aristotle had claimed that the birth of a girl (rather than a son), resulted from "something going wrong in the womb". For Aristotle, the female was an incomplete, and unformed, male fetus.

But the activeness of men could not be given free rein, or the emotions would run amok and society would suffer from irrationality. The philosophical schools taught *apatheia*, not being ruled by the passions (urges) of the body or the emotions. Men had to be in control, never allowing the passions to take over and where both public and private behavior should be the basis of social harmony, peace, and goodwill.

A man's public honor was constructed by how well he performed his family, religious, and public duties. Being physically weaker (and thus inferior), women had to be monitored, controlled, and held to the proper codes of conduct. Any aggressive or irrational behavior or infidelity on their part would render shame to their husband's honor, demonstrating that he could not control his household.

Human Sexual Intercourse

The hot blood of men indicated their virility and their potency, and this was why they should rule and control society. Medically, the idea was promoted that periodic discharge of semen was the way in which male "heat" should be dispersed, rather than exploding in anger or violence. If men did not demonstrate this virility through intercourse, they risked becoming "soft", or powerless, in the sense of skating too close to the role of women. But overindulgence in intercourse was frowned upon. Not understanding that semen regenerates, one's semen should be directed to the procreation of the family and community.

Schools of philosophy transferred the concept of honor/shame into the physical act of human intercourse. Philosophers viewed this activity as the worst time when men risked "losing control", in the inevitable moment of orgasm. Various schools taught that during intercourse, one should concentrate on the "higher things", such as music, or the spheres of the universe, so that the passions of the body did not dominate the act. Intercourse should be conducted in a "passionless" state, and not the shameful dominance of purely physical urges of the body.

One of the ways in which philosophers cautioned against the "uncontrolled passions" was through the analogy of athletic training. In other words, you could learn to control your body through the same kind of training before athletic contests: not indulging in feasting, drinking, and sexual activity in moderation. The Greek term, *ascesis* "discipline", became the concept of **asceticism**, fighting against the indulgences of the body. The precepts of asceticism grew to become a fundamental concept for Christianity in the next several centuries.

Although biased against human intercourse, this does not mean that philosophers taught against marriage and sexuality; everyone was compelled to get married (and do their duty) to the community or the city-state (Socrates was married). Aristotle had taught that men had a "civic" duty to reproduce, for the benefit of the city-state. But they taught one marriage only, for the sole requirement of procreation, after which, such continuing "indulgence" was frowned upon.

Gendered Roles

Every member of the family had religious roles to fulfill, beginning with the father (the *paterfamilias* of the Roman family). The father's role as *paterfamilias* recognized his role in passing on the seed of the generations, and thus held a position of life or death over family members. Fathers were responsible for the daily religious rituals of the household (and the farm), and the religious education of their sons. Fathers maintained the funeral rituals for the ancestors. In addition, depending upon resources, the father was expected to join local cults and provided the money for community religious festivals and sacrifices.

Beyond their first religious obligation to procreate, mothers educated their children and especially their daughters in the skills of maintaining a household. With the emergence of the military conquests of Rome, men were often absent from their estates either fighting battles, or as magistrates in the provinces for several years. Women were expected to manage everything and became quite adept at this. Widows often inherited the businesses of their husbands. Thus, characters such as the Christian widow Lydia in the Acts of the Apostles had a large enough villa to open it for meetings of the community.

Young girls became women at puberty (12–14), ready to accept their role in the structured society they had learned to accept. Their fathers made a marriage contract for them and they moved into the husband's house. Young boys had a few more years to complete their military training, to explore the world, including its sexual nature. They then took their place as leaders of their household and community in service of the state. The ideal age was 25–30. This age difference resulted in the fact that a woman's older husband often died first. In this case, widows who could still bear children were under social pressure to re-marry and "do their duty".

"Virginity" was recognized as the state of the young, but never achieved the heightened status that it would under Christian leadership. Sexual abstinence was required for two to three days before priests and priestesses did their rotations in the temples, but then life went back to normal. The Vestal Virgins of Rome were famous precisely because they were not the norm. Young girls were recruited at the age of six to eight to devote thirty years of their lives to the maintenance of Vesta's hearth fire (a belief that this contributed to the prosperity of Rome). They could marry after their service was over. But the Vestals were never held up as the ideal state for all women; they did not personify a mythical pristine status to which all should return.

The importance of the family and procreation was enhanced in the early days of the Roman Empire when Augustus consolidated power in the office of Emperor. He was concerned that too many men in Rome were not performing their duties by getting married. He reformed the marriage laws and granted tax relief to those who married. At the same time, he limited a widow's status to eighteen months. If a widow did not find a second husband by then, he often literally found one for her.

Then as now, divorce was common in the Roman Empire, especially among the upper-class magistrates and senators. In moving up the ladder in ancient Rome ("the course of honor") connections and relations with powerful families helped to achieve status. Hence, when it appeared as if your current family connections were not helpful (through either scandal or simply the winds of political change) divorce and remarriage were the means in which to change alliances.

Homosexuality in the Ancient World

Unlike modern debates on homosexuality, same-sex marriages, and gender identification, in the ancient world there was no such concept as a "gay life-style".

In ancient Greek culture, men and women led separate lives. The Greek household was literally divided between male and female. When the husband entertained other men for dinner (known as a *symposium*), the only women present were the slave women and sometimes dancers and singers. A *hetaera*, an educated woman in the arts of entertainment, philosophy, and literature could be hired for the evening. These women could also be called upon for their sexual favors. As with female slaves, they were not contracted in legal marriages, so this was not adultery.

While inheriting many of the cultural traditions of Greece, women in ancient Rome appeared to have more freedom. They attended meals with their husbands, even when there were male guests. However, in the classic *triclinium* ("dining room") men reclined on the couches while women sat on chairs facing them. They were expected to speak only when spoken to, and to leave the room when the after-dinner drinking began.

In both cultures, this social distancing meant that close relationships developed only with other males. In Greece, the most important relationship was between an older man, a mentor, and a younger boy, past puberty, but in the interim stage before adulthood. The role of the mentor was to educate the boy in the arts of governance and the social rules, so that the next generation could take over. Although never required, such relationships could entail the emotions and physical, sexual contact.

There were rules: no one publicly admitted to performing sodomy, defined as "anal penetration". No shame was applied to the man doing the penetrating, but to the recipient. To agree to this activity conjured up a weakness, succumbing to the role of women whose job was restricted to being on the "receiving end" of penetration. Rather, sexual activity among men was to be done "face to face," with the use of the hands or orally (see Figure VI.1).

Figure VI.1 From Symposium scene, tomb of the diver. Miguel Hermoso Cuesta / Wikimedia Commons / CC BY-SA.

But once the boy had achieved adult status, the relationship ended. The now adult boy was to marry and procreate for the good of the community. An older male who continued to "chase" his young charge was mocked and derided by society. Our modern term, pedophilia, derives from the Greek *paidós* "child", and *philía* "friendly love" or "friendship". But the purchase of prepubescent boys for sexual activity was a crime in ancient Greece.

In their superior views, Romans derided such "Greek practices"; "As Romans, we do the penetrating, we do not get penetrated". (Thus, our Latin word, *vagina*, the "sheath to house a sword".) Roman mockery did not indicate that these practices did not exist. Roman society had some famous men who were rumored to "indulge the Greek practice", but never openly. Cicero's friend and correspondent, Titus Pomponius Atticus (101–32 BCE), was married with children, but everyone knew that he made yearly trips to Athens, where he could live a different life-style.

There is scant evidence for lesbian relationships in ancient society. We only have references to the famous female poet Sappho (630–570 BCE), who allegedly ran a school for young girls on the island of Lesbos (and hence, the modern term). She left several poems with sometimes quite graphic descriptions of her love for one of her students. Ultimately "lesbianism" became the term for sexual relations between women.

The Jewish condemnation of homosexual relationships begins with the story of the destruction of the cities of Sodom and Gomorrah in the book of Genesis. However, the text is not quite clear as to what the actual sin of Sodom was (the root of "sodomy"). When the men of Sodom want Lot to send out the visiting angels so that "we may go into them," (sexual intercourse), it could either be the sin of sodomy or the violation of the sacred concept of never violating the rules of hospitality, even among strangers.

A more definite concept is found in the book of Leviticus. Leviticus distinguishes between common sins and "abominations". An abomination was a sin for which there was no atonement or rectifying the violation. In the books of the Prophets, abominations resulted in Jews being exiled from the land: "If a man lies with a male as with a woman, both have committed an abomination; they shall surely be put to death; their blood is upon them" (Leviticus 20:13). The abomination of "a male as with a woman", is driven by the waste or spilling of semen (the source of life) that could not result in procreation (the first commandment of God). Lesbianism is not mentioned because it did not involve semen.

The Books of the Prophets

The Prophets of Israel had explained that God permitted foreign nations to conquer Israel in the past because Israel permitted idolatry to continue in the land. Idolatry involved fertility deities, so the Prophets utilized metaphors of marriage (and adultery) in their descriptions. Such worship led to "sexual immortality" (Greek, *pornea*, "illicit sexual unions") and the source of our modern word, pornography. Originally denoting degrees of kinship for incest codes, the Prophets expanded the idea to critique native and non-Jewish life-styles. In their view, idolatry led to "sexual immorality" which led to death (the violence of the conquests). In all English Bibles, the word *pornea* is translated as "fornication". This was derived from the Latin *forne* "arches". It was a reference for the way in which street prostitutes practiced their trade, standing up, "under the arches" along the streets.

Christian Views of Native Life-Styles

After the Greek conquest, some Jews created "vice-lists" to critique the now dominant Greek culture. We find a typical "vice-list" in Paul's first letter to the Corinthians: "Or do you not know that wrongdoers will not inherit the kingdom of God? Do not be deceived: Neither the sexually immoral nor idolaters nor adulterers nor men who have sex with men nor thieves nor the greedy nor drunkards nor slanderers nor swindlers will inherit the kingdom of God" (1 Corinthians 6:9–10).

The only time that women were specifically mentioned in relation to sinful behavior is in Paul's letter to the Romans: "Because of this (idolatry), God gave them over to shameful lusts. Even their women exchanged natural sexual relations for unnatural ones. In the same way the men also abandoned natural relations with women and were inflamed with lust for one another. Men committed shameful acts with other men and received in themselves the due penalty for their error" (Romans 1:26–27). Some interpreters claim that the "unnatural sexual acts" of women referred to bestiality, but there is no detail in this passage.

In one of the letters written by a follower of Paul (1 Timothy, ca. 85 CE), we have: "We also know that the law is made not for the righteous but for law-breakers and rebels, the ungodly and sinful, the unholy and irreligious, for those who kill their fathers or mothers, for murderers, for the sexually immoral, for those practicing homosexuality, for slave traders and liars and perjurers—and for whatever else is contrary to the sound doctrine" (1 Timothy 1:9–10).

The gospels record no specific teachings of Jesus on human sexuality. However, it appears that he upheld the traditional Jewish importance of marriage and procreation: "But at the beginning of creation God 'made them male and female. For this reason, a man will leave his father and mother and be united to his wife, and the two will become one flesh' … Therefore, what God has joined together, let no one separate" (Mark 10:9). The gospel claim that Jesus was against divorce (which Paul replicated), was not against divorce per se (Moses had permitted it), but the issue of remarriage. In the first century, remarriage was discouraged by Paul and the earliest Christians because of the imminence of the kingdom, when all social conventions (marriage and gender roles) would no longer apply.

The Church Fathers Views on Human Sexuality

In Justin Martyr's attempt to stop the persecution of Christians, he compared the life-style of the dominant culture to those of Christians. The "sexual immorality" of Gentiles was the fault of the "fallen angels" who now acted as demons, the agents of the Devil.

An earlier Jewish apocalyptic text, 1 Enoch, had elaborated upon the story found in Genesis 6:

> When human beings began to increase in number on the earth and daughters were born to the sons of God [angels] saw that the daughters of humans were beautiful, and they married any of them they chose … The Nephilim were on the earth in those days—and also afterward—when the sons of God went to the daughters of humans and had children by them. They were the heroes of old, men of renown (giants).

1 Enoch claimed that these angels were banished to the lowest pits of *she'ol* (Hell), for not only crossing the threshold between humans and divine, but because they introduced the art of metallurgy into the world (the creation of weapons and the coining of money). Although trapped in Hell, they nevertheless sent their agents, demons, into the world to wreak havoc. According to Justin, these demons had settled into shrines and temples, and fooled Gentiles into believing that they were benevolent. All but Christians were caught up through their magic arts and their temptations into sexual deviation and sins.

"The Octavius of Marcus Minucius Felix"

A second century manuscript has survived known as "The Octavius of Marcus Minucius Felix". In the popular form of a dialogue between two friends (the other is Caecilius), it contains Christian views of the dominant culture as well as what is purported to be Gentile views of Christians. "Rome, in ignorant antipathy, delighted with its own fables, has brought ridiculous traditions ... silly and impious, in that most ancient of men have venerated their kings, their illustrious generals, and inventors of arts, because of their remarkable deeds, making them gods" (Chapter 20).

In attacking the "Mysteries:"

> And if you reconsider the rites of these gods, how many things are laughable, and how many also pitiable! Naked people run about in the raw winter; some walk bonneted, and carry around old bucklers, or beat drums, or lead their gods a-begging through the streets ... Some sacred places are crowned by a woman having one husband, some by a woman with many; and she who can reckon up most adulteries is sought after with most religious zeal. What! Would not a man who makes libations of his own blood, and supplicates (his god) by his own wounds, be better if he were altogether profane, than religious in such a way is this? And he whose shameful parts are cut off, how greatly does he wrong God in seeking to propitiate him in this manner! since, if God wished for eunuchs, he could bring them as such into existence, and would not make them so afterwards.

On Rome's adoption of the native cults of goddesses (Diana and Isis): "And where are adulteries better arranged by the priests than among the very altars and shrines? Where are more panderings debated, or more acts of violence concerted? Finally, burning lust is more frequently gratified in the little chambers of the keepers of the temple, than in the brothels themselves".

In agreement with Justin: "Demons lurk under the statues and images, they animate the fibers of the entrails, direct the flights of birds, govern the lots, pour forth oracles involved in false responses. These things are not from God".

One of the more famous passages was protesting the absurdity of the alleged charges against Christians in their meetings. Christian initiates were required to kill a Gentile baby (hidden in a loaf of bread) and drink its blood. Dogs, leashed to the lamp stands, were trained to pull them over so that the room was in complete darkness. Then:

> Everyone grabbed the nearest partner for unbridled sex. In this way, Christians were accused of the most awful level of incest, mothers with sons. The story about Christians drinking the blood of an infant that they have cruelly murdered "is a barefaced calumny". But the Gentiles, both cruelly expose their children newly born and before they are born [and] destroy them by a cruel abortion. Christians are neither allowed to see nor to hear of manslaughter.

(Chapter 30)

Scholars debate if, in fact, such rumors were rampant at the time. One theory is that the text was a satire of the various rumors that outsiders had concerning the "Mysteries". Especially in the female Mysteries, many men assumed drinking and rampant sex. Justin's response to such charges was "not to dignify them with a reply". He said that all you had to do was study the life-style of Christians to realize that this was all a lie.

Human Intercourse as a "Sin"

Paul's letters named several women in his ministry: apostles, prophets, healers, teachers, fellow-workers. He also wrote that the other apostles traveled with their wives. The most likely reason for this elevation of women was related to Paul's belief in the impending kingdom. Upon Christ's return, all social conventions and gender roles would be "transformed". A hundred years later, the role of women in the Churches was greatly diminished.

As educated men, the Church Fathers adopted the views of the schools of philosophy in the act of human intercourse. They promoted the bias against "losing control of the passions" in this physical act. At the same time, they added a Christian innovation to human sexuality—sexual intercourse was now a "sin".

The evolution of this concept was rooted in the dominant culture of misogynistic views of women. Misogynism is defined as "a hatred or prejudice against women". As women were weaker than men, their only source of power was in their arts of sexual seduction of men. This was their way of gaining control and dominance. Many writings described their clothes, hair, make-up, jewelry, and "sexual ways of walking", all utilized to evoke the weakness of men. In Greek culture, these aspects of women were emphasized in the myth of the creation of the first woman, Pandora ("all gifts", as in receiving "all gifts from the gods"). Zeus apparently thought that men disrespected him and were not offering the best parts of the sacrifices for his edification. Zeus created the first woman, Pandora, solely to punish men.

By the second century, both the Jewish Rabbis and Christians contributed their own ideas on the "wiles of women" by utilizing their own story of Creation. Genesis recounted the way in which evil entered the world (the greatest evil, death), through the sin of disobedience by Adam and Eve. Originally, the character of the serpent served as a mere plot device to explain why Adam and Eve sinned. The serpent was now reinterpreted to be Satan, the Devil.

The second century saw the earliest Christian iconography of this being. **Pan** was an ancient fertility deity of the forests, who was half-man, half-goat. Utilizing this image is when the Devil acquired his hooves and horns. As a fertility deity, Pan consistently attempted to seduce nymphs (lower, nature divinities). Pan shared characteristics with another fertility deity, Priapus. Both pictures and statues of Pan and Priapus were popular in homes and gardens.

In their aspect of fertility, both were portrayed with huge, erect phalluses. Along with carved penises above doorways (such as those found at Pompeii), both were symbols of "good luck" (fertility).

The "fall" in Genesis was now explained that (with his huge phallus) the Devil seduced Eve. Learning from him she then turned and used her wiles to seduce Adam. Yes, God's first commandment had been "to be fruitful and multiply", but originally, it was to be done without seduction, without involving the "passions". What Eve introduced with the passions was now deemed "lust". Lust was declared a sin. (Augustine would add additional details to this concept in his creation of "Original Sin", see Chapter XIII.)

The second century Bishop of Carthage, Tertullian (115–220 CE) upheld this demonization of all women through the first woman:

> And do you not know that you are Eve? God's sentence hangs still over all your sex and his punishment weighs down upon you. You are the devil's gateway; you are she who first violated the forbidden tree and broke the law of God. It was you who coaxed your way around him whom the Devil had not the force to attack. With what ease you shattered that image of God: Man! Because of the death you merited, even the Son of God had to die.
>
> (*On the Apparel of Women*, Chapter 1)

A heavy burden to bear.

"Lust as a Necessary Evil"

But without procreation, the Christian movement could not grow and flourish. God had permitted this necessary evil as the means in which to spread "the word" throughout the Empire. Philosophical medical knowledge absorbed from the schools was now utilized by the Church Fathers to define the proper way in which Christians should perform human intercourse. It was believed that women could only get pregnant in one position: man, on top, woman on the bottom, in her capacity as the receiving end for the womb as incubator.

This position became the official teaching of the Churches. Christians were to practice sexual intercourse in this position only, for the sole purpose of having children. If sexual intercourse was performed in any other position, including times of infertility within the menstrual cycle, this indicated that your purpose was directed solely for "lust", violating God's original plan, and thus a sin. If a Christian woman did not produce offspring after several years of marriage, she was declared barren, and all sexual activity had to stop. The same applied after women reached menopause.

During the age of exploration, missionaries from Europe were sent to the indigenous people of Asia, Africa, and the Americas. Part of their ministry was to undo what they saw as rampant sexuality, and so the proper position that they taught became known as "the missionary position".

Radical Christians

While some Christian communities promoted "restraint" (in Latin, "continence") in sexual behavior, others were more radical in their views. From the beginning of Jesus' ministry, Christians believed that the "rulers of this world" (those various powers in the heavens) were aligned with the Devil. People were in bondage to sin. This is what caused all the current pain and suffering. The "kingdom" would rectify all of this, but perhaps Christians could motivate the reign of God on earth by eliminating all this evil *now*. This could be achieved through more rigorous asceticism in diet, the elimination of drinking, celibacy, and life-long chastity. These ideas were promoted through the writings of Tatian and a group known as the **Encratites**.

Located throughout Asia Province and Syria, "Encratite" meant "self-controlled". They forbade eating meat (it led to an animal nature in humans) and drinking wine (drunkenness led to sexual immortality). One of the goals was to "undo the works of women". Since Eden, women and sexual intercourse were held captive to Satan. Accepting philosophical discourse that we should strive for mind over matter, disciplining the body became the tool to salvation in the here and now. The body could be liberated from Satan only through the total annihilation of the human sexual drive itself.

Encratities were ultimately declared heretical in the latter fourth century (they did not accept the writings of Paul). But their teachings contributed to the overall trend of Christian views that it is the body (and what you do with it) that "gives rise to sin". Hence much of the Christian literature of the period presents an almost obsessive reflection on the uses and abuses of the body.

Celibacy and Chastity

The second century saw the emergence of what became Church hierarchy. Church leaders were recognized as **Bishops** ("overseers", see Chapter X). But in a community where everyone was equal, at least in theory, why should the community listen to a Bishop? This is when life-long **celibacy** and **chastity** were adopted for the clergy. Celibacy was defined as not entering into a legal, marriage contract, and chastity meant never indulging in human sexuality.

Both Judaism and the native cults had a concept of temporary chastity, in that purity was required for certain rituals. The Christian adoption of celibacy and chastity was now construed as a "living sacrifice"; a Bishop gave up a normal life (marriage and children) to devote himself to the Church. This achieved an aura of sanctity for Church leaders which elevated the clergy above the rest of the community. Extra daughters were to be devoted to the Church (in "cradle to grave virginity") and widows should not re-marry and devote their lives to good works.

It would take several centuries (and several Council meetings) to finalize Catholic clerical celibacy into Canon Law. One of the earliest references was the

Council of Elvia (Spain, 306): "Bishops, presbyters, deacons, and others with a position in the ministry are to abstain completely from sexual intercourse with their wives and from the procreation of children. If anyone disobeys, he shall be removed from the clerical office" (Canon 33). Emperor Justinian I (530) declared that any such marriages were null and void, and the offspring illegitimate.

The First Lateran Council (1123) forbade any association by priests, deacons, and monks with concubines or women who were not relatives (mothers and aunts). In the medieval period, scandals arose from clerics appointing illegitimate sons to the clergy (such as the Borgia Pope Alexander VI who made his son, Cesare, a Cardinal). Celibate clergy became officially canonized in the Catholic Church under Pope Benedict XV in 1917.

"Where Did All This Madness Come From?"

The Jewish and Gentile reaction to this Christian teaching was one of confusion. Human sexuality in the ancient world was never understood as a sin. Along with creation, human intercourse was "a gift from the gods", to renew each generation, and something to be enjoyed. Rather than denying human sexuality, the greater concern was the degree of kinship permitted in the act (incest-codes). Along with human intercourse, the divine gifts of introducing the "hunt", the arts of agriculture (and wine-making) were created for the benefit of humans. To reject such gifts was an insult to the gods.

Summary

- The importance of fertility dictated the construction of gender and gender roles in ancient cultures.
- Christian leaders transformed the relation between "body and society" in their interpretations of human sexuality and gender.

Suggestions for Further Reading

Brown, Peter. 2008. *The Body and Society: Men, Women, and Sexual Renunciation in Early Christianity*. Columbia University Press. Brown surveys the various teachings from the earliest communities to the evolution of Monasticism, emphasizing the relationship between one's sexual identity with that of larger society.

Harper, Kyle. 2016. *From Shame to Sin: The Christian Transformation of Sexual Morality in Late Antiquity*. Harvard University Press. Harper's study builds upon Brown, but with more in-depth coverage of the philosophical and intellectual debates.

THE CHALLENGE OF GNOSTICISM, "WISDOM, FALSELY SO-CALLED"

VII

Gnostic/Agnostic

The Nag Hammadi Library

What Is Gnosticism?

Theology

God Undoes the "Fall," by Emanating the *Logos*, Christ

Allegory

That "Zen Moment"

The Invention of Doctrinal Orthodoxy/Heresy

Why Were the Gnostics Condemned as Heretics?

The Apostolic Tradition

Monism and Dualism

Gnostic Rituals

The Bridal Chamber

Gnostic Gospels

The Gospel of Judas

Marcion of Sinope (85–160 CE)

Varieties of Early Christianity: The Formation of the Western Christian Tradition,
First Edition. Rebecca I. Denova.
© 2023 John Wiley & Sons, Inc. Published 2023 by John Wiley & Sons, Inc.

160 The Challenge of Gnosticism, "Wisdom, Falsely So-Called"

The Antitheses

Marcion's Scriptures

The Formation of the New Testament Canon

The Demise of the Gnostics

Modern Gnosticism

After reading this chapter you will be able to:

- Explore the rise of alternate views of Christianity.
- Understand the unique worldview of the Gnostic Christians.
- Trace the formation of the innovation of Orthodoxy, vs. Heresy.

Much of the second century Church was occupied with what we term, "family feuds". In addition to responding to criticism from the dominant culture, Christians were embroiled in debates over correct beliefs and practices by the many different Christian communities in the Empire. There was no central authority to determine these matters; various writers and Bishops vied for dominance in relation to other communities with their individual views.

Beginning in the second century, we become aware of groups of Christians who are collectively categorized under the umbrella term, **Gnostics**. "*Gnosis*" meant "knowledge" in Greek. These Christians claimed to have "secret knowledge" about the nature of the universe, the nature of Christ, and what his appearance on earth meant to believers.

Gnostic/Agnostic

We use the term, "agnostic", to describe someone who "knows something is out there" (in relation to the divine) but is not sure exactly what. The original word was coined by an eighteenth century minister, who, claimed that he was "agnostic", meaning, in its original sense, "*not* a gnostic—not one of those people"). Aldous Huxley coined "agnosticism" in his novels on the basis that all knowledge must be based on reason. The psychologist Carl Jung utilized Gnostic concepts found in medieval alchemy for his theory of archetypes. Modern interest in Gnostics was revived when Dan Brown published his novel, *The Da Vinci Code* in 2003, where he utilized Gnostic teachings in his claim that Jesus and Mary Magdalene were married and produced the royal line of Merovingians in France. The evidence for this theory was found in Da Vinci's painting of the "Last Supper", among others.

The Nag Hammadi Library

The Church Fathers wrote volumes against the Gnostics, in their role as "heresiologists" (writings against heresy). They often quoted from Gnostic writings, but scholars were skeptical—the Church Fathers were voracious in their criticism. How could we be sure that their quotations were accurate?

The Challenge of Gnosticism, "Wisdom, Falsely So-Called" 161

In 1945, two brothers were digging nitrate in the Egyptian desert (good for fertilizer) near the town of Nag Hammadi in Upper Egypt. Their shovel hit a large jar filled with **codices** (early books). They took them to a man they knew who was active in the black market antiquities business. There were thirteen books containing treatises, gospels, and Gnostic myths. They are collected in one volume (now available in any bookstore, Amazon, the Internet) with the title, **The Nag Hammadi Library**. As it turns out, the Church Fathers did a fair job of copying. We now have the complete texts for a better analysis each document.

What Is Gnosticism?

Gnosticism combined concepts from Eastern religions which were incorporated in the Hellenistic period of Alexander. As such, it is often referred to "dualism", in its portrayal of polarity: the struggle between God and the world, the soul and the body, good and evil, and a longing for redemption and immortality. There were some forms of Jewish Gnosticism, and other world religions incorporate shared concepts (Zoroastrianism, Hinduism, and Buddhism).

Gnostic Christians utilized the same training in philosophical schools to articulate their beliefs, following the precepts of Plato. Where they differed from the other apologists, was in restoring Plato's concept of the "Demi-Urge", which other Christians had simply removed.

Christian Gnosticism is the belief that human beings contain a piece of God (the highest good, a "divine spark") within themselves, which has fallen from the immaterial world into the bodies of humans. All physical matter is subject to decay, rotting, and death. Those bodies and the material world, created by an inferior being (the Demi-Urge), are therefore evil. Trapped in the material world, but ignorant of its status, the pieces of God require knowledge (*gnosis*) to inform them of their true status. That knowledge must come from *outside* the material world, and the agent who brings it is the savior or redeemer. The function of Gnostic myth is to explain the present condition of humans, alienated from the true God.

Gnostic concepts mirror a modern school of philosophy known as Existentialism ("How and why do we exist?"). Gnostics asked and answered such questions as: "Who am I?" "Where did I come from?" "What is the meaning of life?" "Why am I here?" "What is my true self?"

Theology

Gnostics promoted concepts of radical dualism that govern the universe. This was polarized as the soul/spark against "the flesh", light from darkness. God, who does not create, originally emanated *archons* (powers), like the light from

Theos – the highest God – Mind (Greek, *nous*) – the ultimate Good

(characterized as perfect and unchangeable), having nothing to do with creation]

_____Emanation_____

The *Pleroma*, or Heavenly Realm

(Characterized as being active, and thus changeable)

Inhabited initially by pairs of Archons, as well as Sophia (Wisdom) and

the Demi-urge (who is responsible for creation)

Some systems will add divinities, angels, demons and layers of heavens

_____"Fall"_____

The physical universe and the material world

(Everything below this line is subject to change, imperfect,

corruptible, decaying, and generally, evil)

Figure VII.1 Schematic for Gnosticism.

the sun, seen, but not physical. One of the archons, **Sophia** ("wisdom") in a moment of weakness, produced the Demi-Urge, who then created a physical universe (including humans). In philosophical thought, the *logos* ("word") was the principle of rationality that connected the highest god to the material world (see Figure VII.1).

God Undoes the "Fall," by Emanating the *Logos*, Christ

Some systems claimed a mythic "pre-Adam and Eve", before their manifestation as humans in Eden. This was the sight of the original fall. The fall was construed as the direct result of creation. The Gnostic understanding of the sin of Adam and Eve was in the creation of gender. In keeping with the "oneness" of the eternal God, Gnostics promoted the idea of **androgyny**, or the original union of gender. After the fall, which separated them, the *logos*, the pre-existent Christ, came to earth in human appearance to teach us how to return to both this original androgyny and re-unite with God. God sent Christ to restore the original cosmos. When this is accomplished the rule of *Archons* will end.

Allegory

Like everyone else who was trained in philosophy, Gnostics utilized the literary device of allegory. But if one is not attuned to the allegorical symbols or meaning, many of the Gnostic writings appear incredibly esoteric and puzzling to the average reader. For example, abstract concepts were personified, such as "Error", and "Fear" as living realities.

Reading such texts, one gets the impression that they spent their lives in "ivory towers", contemplating the universe. But they *did* participate in the congregations to which they belonged. This may be the reason the Church Fathers felt so threatened by them. They had "study groups", but what they studied was the upper reaches of the universe where gradients of powers dwelt. When a Gnostic died, his spark/soul was released from his evil body, but then had to make the journey home. On the way, he/she had to know the "passwords" to get through and around the powers so that he/she wasn't distracted. Think of a lab-rat maze, or modern video games. Some systems claimed there were seven heavens while others claimed 365 levels.

That "Zen Moment"

But the initial impetus for gaining *gnosis* was not an intellectual pursuit. As the divine spark within humans had fallen asleep, it did not remember its origins. One had to be "awakened" to the presence of this "piece of God" within you. It mirrors Buddhism, when Buddha fasted and meditated under a tree and was "enlightened". The founder of the sect of Zen Buddhism (in China), allegedly meditated staring at a wall for nine years; suddenly, he was "enlightened" and the movement spread to Korea and Japan.

The Invention of Doctrinal Orthodoxy/Heresy

The Church Fathers reacted to Gnostic teachings by promoting the twin concepts of orthodoxy and heresy. Orthodoxy means "correct belief". Heresy was taken from the Greek word *haeresis* which meant a school of thought (philosophical schools), in this case, any views that disagreed with the Church Fathers. The words themselves were not actually new inventions; they were part of the shared terminology of philosophical schools. But Christians utilized them in defining Christian doctrine. With the thousands of different native cults in the Mediterranean Basin, there was no central authority that determined what people were "to believe". Beliefs and practices were localized in villages, towns, and cities, but where religious pluralism contributed to variations. **Orthopraxy,** or doing the rituals correctly (as taught through ancestral customs), dominated the practices. In other words, no one stopped people going into a temple and asked if they were "thinking" or "believing" correctly.

Irenaeus claimed that heresy arose from a character known as Simon Magus, or Simon the Sorcerer. The Acts of the Apostles 8:9–14 related a confrontation between Peter and Simon in Samaria. Seeing the manifestation of the spirit when the Samaritans were baptized, Simon asked Peter if he could buy this "magic trick." Outraged, Peter denied him. The later term, **simony**, derives from this story; simony is the attempt to buy one's way into heaven. (More details of Simon's life and adventures are found in Chapter IX.) It was Irenaeus who wrote that Gnostic thought was "wisdom, falsely so-called".

Why Were the Gnostics Condemned as Heretics?

There were variations in the schools of Gnostic thought. But we can summarize why the Church Fathers reacted so vehemently to Gnostic teachings:

1. Gnostics claimed that there were two gods above and beyond the material universe, the creator god, and the "god of pure essence and love". It was this higher god that was promoted by the Gnostics as being the true god.
2. The God of Israel. By the second century, Christianity was in the process of separating from Judaism. But most Christians retained the God of Israel and the teachings of the Jewish Scriptures. Gnostics agreed that the creator God in Genesis created the universe, but creation consisted of evil matter. In some Gnostic systems, the God of Israel was not only evil, but Satan himself. Thus, all the literal "commandments" of the God of Israel were deemed invalid.
3. Consisting of physical matter, the human body was evil. For most Gnostic systems, Jesus was *not* "incarnated" into a human body. They preached the concept known as **docetic**, or "appearance". Jesus only appeared in the form of a human so that he could communicate with us (somewhat like a modern hologram). If Christ never had a material body, the central pillars of Christianity, the crucifixion and the resurrection of the dead, appeared nullified.
4. Some Gnostic systems claimed that there were two manifestations, the "man", Jesus, who had a normal birth, and "Christ" (the manifestation of the *logos*). Recalling the story of Jesus' baptism in the gospels, the *logos* entered Jesus in the form of a dove. It was the man Jesus who was crucified; the "Christ" part had ascended before the execution.
5. Gnostics claimed that their teachings came directly from Jesus. In those scenes in the gospels when Jesus "takes the disciples aside" to better inform them, he also taught "secret things" that were passed down to them.
6. A Gnostic, after being "awakened", studied the heavens and learned the means to navigate the various layers. In this sense, Gnostics viewed

salvation as an individual matter. "Resurrection" for Gnostics meant the return of the divine spark to their original source, from which they had become alienated. It did not necessarily involve the rest of the community. In other words, salvation could not be achieved through "the cross", Church hierarchy or Church sacraments and rules.

7. To break the cycle of "divine sparks" being trapped in a physical body, the Gnostics were the first to advocate celibacy and chastity. For many of the Gnostic systems, the Church should only grow through recruitment and conversion. Androgyny for Gnostics was the primordial existence of "oneness", the true state of existence. The fall of Sophia destroyed this androgyny by producing what became gender. On the claim that the "divine spark" was trapped in an evil body, it was prohibited to produce more evil bodies.

8. In some Gnostic systems, but not all, there was a denial of the Christian concept of eschatology, or the future return of Christ to usher in "the kingdom of God". Many Gnostics condoned an interpretation of the teaching found in the gospels of Luke and John, "the kingdom is within you", an existential alteration of the inner person.

9. Once you successfully made it through the upper atmosphere, your spark, now "home", united with the godhead; in some systems the believer "became God".

--- The Apostolic Tradition

The Church Fathers countered Gnostic claims that Jesus had imparted "secret knowledge", with the same charge they had received from philosophers: Gnostics introduced something "new". They upheld the gospel traditions that Jesus taught "the twelve" (the original disciples), who then, in their missions, taught the correct beliefs to men whom the disciples appointed as the first bishops in each city. This became a concept known as the **Apostolic Tradition**. In their arguments, we have the earliest Christian literature on the subsequent lives and details of the disciples after the death of Jesus. We cannot historically confirm these details; by the second century these stories had been collected as legends (see Chapter IX).

> Let them produce the original records of their churches; let them unfold the roll of their bishops, running down in due succession from the beginning in such a manner that [that first bishop of theirs] shall be able to show for his ordination and predecessor some one of the apostles or of apostolic men—a man, moreover, who continued steadfast with the apostles. For this is the manner in which the apostolic churches transmit their registers: as the church of Smyrna, which records that Polycarp was placed therein by John; as also the church of Rome,

which makes Clement to have been ordained in like manner by Peter. In exactly the same way the other churches likewise exhibit (their several worthies), whom, as having been appointed to their episcopal places by apostles, they regard as transmitters of the apostolic seed.

Within Western Christian tradition, the charge that Gnosticism was something new that only arose in the second century remains pervasive. The Apostolic Tradition remains embedded in Christianity; it was the Gnostics who introduced "innovations". The historical problem is the absence of Gnostic literature in the first century. There is speculation that Paul may have encountered some of these thinkers in Corinth, but no real proof. Most of the Gnostic literature is from the second century, but that alone is not proof that the ideas did not exist earlier (see Box VII.1).

Box VII.1   Various Gnostic teachers and systems

Cerinthus. Cerinthus and his group were perhaps located in Ephesus toward the end of the first century. He was one of the first to distinguish between the man, "Jesus" and the "Christ" and that an exchange took place at baptism. These teachings may be the object of polemic in the first letter of John in the New Testament: "That which was from the beginning, which we have heard, which we have seen with our eyes, which we have looked at and our hands have touched—this we proclaim concerning the Word of life" (1 John 1).

Saturninus. He is mentioned as a disciple of another individual named Meander, perhaps a Jewish Gnostic. According to Saturninus, the physical world was created by seven angels, where one of them became the God of the Jews. In trying to recreate an "image of the supreme god", they failed and created humanity instead. Moved by mercy, the supreme god gave one of the angels, Christ, eternal substance and sent him into the world to liberate humans from matter. This school upheld sexual continence and dietary restrictions.

Carpocrates. Carpocrates taught in Alexandria (ca. 130 CE), where he combined elements of Neoplatonism. The material world was created by spirits who were inferior to the Father. Human souls existed before their birth and salvation is achieved only by recalling that existence. This concept was developed by Plato (Greek, *anamnesis* "remembrance") in *Phaedo* and *Meno*. The body with the senses, distracts us from remembering, but we can overcome this through catharsis ("cleansing", "purification") and applying our reason to reunite with our soul. Those who do not recall are condemned to a series of reincarnations. Jesus was human, but a perfect man, who recalled with perfect clarity and proclaimed the eternal realities that had been forgotten. Carpocrates' system, more so than others, was consistently maligned as being sexually immoral.

Basilides. Basilides also taught in Alexandria ca. 120–140 CE. He claimed to have known the disciple Matthias (the disciple who replaced Judas in Acts 2). The origin of all heavenly realities is the Father, from whom 365 beings emanated. One of these beings, the God of the Jews, chose a people and tried to establish its rule over the world, but other angels prevented him from doing so. As 364 "heavens" separate the angels from the Father, they were ignorant, and this ignorance led them to create an imperfect world. Christ was sent to eliminate this ignorance.

The school of Basilides was known for its "bait and switch" teaching on the crucifixion of Christ. Basilides did not deny the crucifixion; people witnessed it. However, he claimed that Simon of Cyrene, who helped to carry the cross in the gospels, was the one who was crucified. "Christ" had already left the body of "Jesus", and ascended before the event.

Valentinus. Valentinus taught first in Alexandria, moved to Rome, but may have been expelled from that city. He was apparently popular enough to almost be elected as a Bishop in Rome. Irenaeus claimed that he was the author of *The Gospel of Truth*, one of the most complicated and esoteric of the Gnostic Gospels:

The gospel of truth is joy to those who have received from the Father of truth the gift of knowing him by the power of the *Logos*, who has come from the Pleroma and who is in the thought and the mind of the Father; he it is who is called "the Savior", since that is the name of the work which he must do for the redemption of those who have not known the Father. For the name of the gospel is the manifestation of hope, since that is the discovery of those who seek him, because the All sought him from whom it had come forth. You see, the All had been inside of him, that illimitable, inconceivable one, who is better than every thought.

This ignorance of the Father brought about Terror and Fear. And Terror became dense like a fog, that no one was able to see. Because of this, Error became strong. But it worked on its hylic substance vainly, because it did not know the truth. It was in a fashioned form while it was preparing, in power and in beauty, the equivalent of truth. This then, was not a humiliation for him, that illimitable, inconceivable one. For they were as nothing, this Terror and this Forgetfulness and this figure of Falsehood, whereas this established truth is unchanging, unperturbed and completely beautiful.

It is in this document that we have a further development of the concept of *Sofia*, "wisdom" as an entity. The last of the archons to be emanated, Sofia, in "her passion", produced the Demi-Urge, without a mate. Described as an "abortion", this act created disorder in the Pleroma. The Father then emanated Christ to regain order. Christ freed Sofia from her passion and led her to repentance and it is "repentance that originated souls". The three elements, matter, soul, and spirit are still in the world, although the spirit, the "divine spark" of god remained unknown to the Demi-Urge. It is the rescue of this "divine spark" that is achieved through Christ at death.

Monism and Dualism

The conceptual shift in ancient thinking about the person in the Hellenistic period in the schools of philosophy (monism, one nature, dualism, two natures) is evident in several Gnostic teachings that positioned the person in relation to the physical universe. The more esoteric texts questioned reality itself. Radical systems attempted to reunite the person to their original position in the process of creation and redemption. An attempt to achieve this reunion is termed **mysticism**. Union with or absorption into the deity or absolute that is beyond the intellect can be achieved through contemplation and self-surrender (see Figure VII.2).

Ordinary Monism: Homer, Hesiod; most of the Jewish Scriptures

- body only, not an additional entity called "soul"
- body + personality (the "breath" of man)
- "this world" only for humans; the "other world" is the domain of the divine
- matter only, no immateriality (or no spirit)
- reality is based on the senses

Mild Dualism: Plato, Aristotle, Paul, most of the New Testament

- a second substance: in humans, the soul
- the soul is in harmony with the body (where "harmony" does not mean "identical"; although separate entities, the soul is dominate)
- the "other" world is in harmony with this one
- soul is superior, but still connected in harmony to the body

Radical Dualism: Most Gnostic systems; some of the New Testament; some interpretations of the Gospel of John

- difference is in the relationship between body and soul
- the soul is *opposed* to the body
- the "other" world is opposed to this world
- the soul seeks escape from the body and this world

Radical Monism:

A. Classical mysticism; Valentinian Gnosticism; Buddhism; some Hinduism (Vedantism)

- one substance, soul
- the other world *only*
- body (and material world) are illusions

B. More Radical Monism: Some Hinduism; Buddhism (Tantrism traditions)

- soul is identical to body
- this world is identical to "other" world
- existence is thus *undifferentiated.*

Figure VII.2 Concepts of Monism and Dualism.

We cannot determine if Gnostic teachings influenced later traditions. Examples are found in the writings of St. Catherine of Sienna (1347–1380) and St. Theresa of Avila, 1515–1582). Both described mystical unions with Christ ("uniting with the godhead"). Examples in other world religions are found in Hindu philosophy and the Islamic sect of Sufis.

Gnostic Rituals

The esoteric nature of Gnostic teachings often leads to two false assumptions: (1) that they separated themselves from the larger community; and (2) that they did not participate in rituals. Gnostics did not create separate communities or churches. We know that they participated in the ritual of baptism, and the eucharist (communion). But the ritual of eucharist involved a debate between some Gnostics and the mainstream; some Gnostics advocated that women could be eucharistic ministers.

The Bridal Chamber

A text named *The Exegesis of the Soul* describes a marriage rite between Christ as the bridegroom and the fallen soul of (wo)man, in a reunification that led to a blurring of the sexes and uniting with God/Christ. However, we cannot confirm if the ritual was understood as metaphor or literal. The text is quite graphic in its description, although graphic language need not indicate a literal demonstration. The Prophets of Israel also applied metaphors of marriage and sexual intercourse in their claim that idolatry produces sexual immorality. Irenaeus scathingly reported that the leader of a Gnostic school in Lyons named Marcus conducted ritual sex with numerous women who were seduced into joining "the cult". Or, was this a "spiritual marriage", where the language of intercourse was used to describe the union?

Unfortunately, as the Nag Hammadi library became more well-known, some scholars began describing some of the groups as "libertine". This was an unfortunate word taken from the literature of the Marquis de Sade during the period of the French Revolution, although first coined to describe the opponents of John Calvin in Geneva, Switzerland. A "libertine" came to mean a person without morals, particularly in relation to sexual freedom and behavior. Some Gnostic schools may have imitated the ancient philosophical precepts of the Cynics who deliberately flouted conventional behavior to demonstrate that they were not subject to man-made laws or codes. Hence, some Gnostic thinkers, viewing society as evil, may have deliberately overturned behavioral codes for the same reason. This issue continues to be debated by scholars.

Gnostic Gospels

Various sects of Gnostics produced their own gospels. They combined the traditional stories of the canonical gospels but added their own interpretations. Many of these gospels "filled in gaps" in the stories. We have explored *The Gospel of Truth*, but below are examples of others.

The Gospel of Philip

The Gospel of Philip continued the themes found in *The Gospel of Truth* but also included the compromise with the mainstream churches over the crucifixion of Christ. "Christ", in the manifestation of the *Logos*, entered the man Jesus at his baptism, and then left the body of Jesus at the cross, so that it was the man who was crucified. *The Gospel of Philip* is also famous for what became infamous in Dan Brown's *The DaVinci Code*—the relationship between Jesus and Mary Magdalene. This relationship has always been open to speculation, as the canonical gospels also grant her prominence in her presence at the tomb, receiving a solo appearance by Christ in the Gospel of John.

In *The Gospel of Philip*, the disciples are sitting around remembering Jesus. One of the disciples mentions that Jesus always had a special relationship with Mary, claiming that Jesus always greeted her "with a kiss on ..."—here the manuscript is frustratingly incomplete as there is literally a hole in the papyrus. This line may be significant, or it may simply refer to the fact that the early Christians (including the men) used to greet each other with a kiss on the lips.

Despite 1400 hundred years of tradition, and the constant portrayals by Hollywood, Mary Magdalene was never described as a prostitute in the gospels. She was not directly named a "disciple", although the Greek for "follower" could imply a similar meaning. Luke is the only one who provided the detail that she had "seven demons" driven out of her.

It was Pope Gregory I (540–604), who associated Mary Magdalene with two stories from the gospels (1) the "sinful" woman who anointed Jesus; and (2) the story of the "woman caught in adultery". Only found in later manuscripts of Luke and John, there is a story of a woman who was going to be stoned to death for adultery (not prostitution, as prostitution was not a sin). Jesus rescued her from the mob. In both manuscripts, the woman is not named. (The Eastern Orthodox Churches do not accept this identification of Mary Magdalene.)

The Gospel of Mary Magdalene

This text is incomplete, and the surviving copy begins in the middle. The disciples are at a loss of what to do now that their teacher is dead. One of the disciples asked Mary to convey any information she can offer, as it was recognized that Jesus "... always liked her best". Mary then related that she had a post-resurrection revelation from Jesus, who explained many of the Gnostic themes that we have already seen. Peter is upset by this, claiming that Jesus would not appear to a woman, but the other disciples berate him as being jealous—Peter never comes out as a hero in the Gnostic texts—most often he symbolizes the "earth-bound" material view of non-enlightened Christians.

The Gospel of Thomas

"These are the secret sayings which the living Jesus spoke, and which Didymos Judas Thomas wrote down. (1) And he said, 'Whoever finds the interpretation of these sayings will not experience death.'". (Didymus meant "twin" as the English translation of "Thomas".)

The Gospel of Thomas is quite different from traditional gospels in that there is no narrative account of the deeds of Jesus. It consists of 118 *logia*, sayings of Jesus, sometimes standing alone and sometimes embedded in short dialogues and parables. There are similar teachings from the canonical gospels, but there is no depiction of the trials and crucifixion, nor the final judgment of the Prophets. Many of the sayings are only imparted to Jesus' (metaphorical?) twin, Thomas, who appears to be the only one of the disciples who understands him.

Since its discovery, The *Gospel of Thomas* has become popular as the basis for the validity of a movement known as Liberation Theology. Liberation theology could be interpreted as an attempt to return to the gospel of the early church where Christianity is politically and culturally decentralized. Gustavo Gutierrez coined the term in his 1971 book, *A Theology of Liberation*, which criticized the Catholic Church in Latin America for its alliance with corrupt corporations and tyrannical governments and having lost the original gospel message that was addressed to the poor and the oppressed. At the heart of this message, Gutierrez emphasized a concept that it is at the heart of *The Gospel of Thomas*, "that the kingdom is within you". He interpreted this to mean that all people are potentially "Christs", a message that was condemned by the Catholic Church (and as fostering Marxist ideas in Latin America).

The *Gospel of Thomas* is also important for its concept of gender roles. Gnostics, because of their inclusion of women in their study groups, their advocacy for women eucharistic ministers, and their honoring the feminine concept of "Sofia", are often described as the forerunners of modern feminism. But consider *logia* 114: "Simon Peter said to them: 'Let Mary go out from our midst, for women are not worthy of life!' Jesus said.' See, I will draw her so as to make her male so that she also may become a living spirit like you males. For every woman who has become male will enter the Kingdom of heaven.'"

For Gnostics, the original fall took place in the Pleroma, when Sophia (feminine) created the Demi-Urge (masculine). What this *logion* indicates is that to undo the fall, women cannot be saved as "women"; the original androgyny must be restored by women rejecting the traditional roles of wives and mothers.

The Gospel of Judas

The *Gospel of Judas* created a sensation when it was published in 2006 by the National Geographic Society (when it was found in a private collection in a bank vault in Switzerland). It consists of conversations between Jesus and Judas Iscariot. In contrast to the canonical gospels, which paint Judas as a betrayer, this gospel portrayed Judas' actions resulting in obedience to instructions given him by Jesus. It asserts that the other disciples had not learned the true gospel, which Jesus only taught to Judas.

At the beginning of time, God created a group of angels and lower gods. Twelve angels were willed to "come into being [to] rule over chaos and the underworld". The angels of creation were tasked with creating a physical body for *Adamas*, which became known as the first man Adam. Gradually, humanity began to forget its divine origins and some of Adam's descendants (Cain and Abel) became embroiled in the world's first murder. Many humans came to think that the imperfect physical universe was the totality of creation, losing their knowledge of God and the imperishable realm.

Jesus was sent as the son of the true god, not of one of the lesser gods. His mission was to show that salvation lies in connecting god within man. Through embracing the internal god, man can then return to the divine realm.

Eleven of the disciples whom Jesus chose to spread his message misunderstood the central tenets of his teaching. They were obsessed with the physical world of the senses. The author says that they continued to practice religious animal sacrifice, which pleased the lower gods but did not help to foster a connection with the true god. They wrongly taught that those martyred in the name of Christ would be bodily resurrected. Martyrdom alone will not save you (it involves the physical body).

In contrast, Jesus is able to teach Judas the true meaning of his life, ministry, and death. Mankind can be divided into two races, or groups. Those who are furnished with the immortal soul, like Judas, can come to know the god within and enter the imperishable realm at death. Those who belong to the same generation of the other eleven disciples cannot enter the realm of god and will die both spiritually and physically. As practices that are intertwined with the physical world, animal sacrifice and a communion ceremony involving "cannibalism" (the consumption of Jesus' flesh and blood) are condemned as abhorrent. The other Gospels say that Jesus had to die in order to atone for the sins of humanity. The author of Judas expresses the view that this sort of substitutionary justice pleases the lower gods and angels. The true god is gracious and thus does not demand any sacrifice.

Jesus favors Judas above other disciples by saying, "Step away from the others and I shall tell you the mysteries of the kingdom", and "Look, you have been told everything. Lift up your eyes and look at the cloud and the light within it and the stars surrounding it. The star that leads the way is your star".

Before the discovery of *The Gospel of Judas*, those of us who work in this area already knew about it. Irenaeus described it and condemned it in his *Against All Heresies*. However, similar views of the role of Judas were presented in the 1971 rock opera by Andrew Lloyd Webber and Time Rice, *Jesus Christ Superstar*. Martin Scorsese created *The Last Temptation of Christ* in 1988, based on the 1955 novel by Nikos Kazantzakis, where Judas appears to be the favored companion of Jesus.

Marcion of Sinope (85–160 CE)

Sinope was in the province of Pontus, on the southern shore of the Black Sea. Marcion was the son of the Bishop of Sinope who was also a wealthy shipbuilder. Marcion was allegedly excommunicated by his father for his teachings.

His major work, *Antithesis* (in five books) is lost, but Irenaeus quoted from it. He was nicknamed the "wolf of Pontus" by Tertullian (*Adversus Marcionem*). He emigrated to Rome ca. 140 with his followers. He was rich enough to pay for their travel, room, and board. He also brought a donation to the church in Rome (140,000 sesterces) which was scorned by the Church Fathers. He was eventually excommunicated from Rome.

Unlike other Gnostics groups, who only founded "schools", Marcion founded his own church, with its own hierarchy of bishops, priests, and deacons, and with liturgies like those of the Roman Church. In this way he gained more followers than any other Gnostic teacher, so that ten years after his excommunication, Justin Martyr wrote that he "caused many of every nation to speak blasphemies". Some Marcionite communities existed up to the beginning of the Middle Ages, especially in Syria. Determined to avoid the "divine spark" being trapped in a body, Marcion's entire community was celibate.

He may have been influenced by a Syrian Gnostic named Cerdon who also came to Rome. He taught that the God of Israel is not the same as the Father of Jesus Christ. According to Irenaeus, Marcion taught that Jesus came "to do away with the Prophets and the Law and all the works of that God who made the world". Irenaeus claimed that Marcion asked Polycarp, Bishop of Smyrna, "Do you recognize me?" Polycarp answered, "I recognize you as the first-born of Satan".

In addition to similar Gnostic ideas, Marcion taught that Jesus's humanity and suffering were illusions. According to Marcion, Jesus was not born of the Virgin Mary; indeed, he was not born at all, but simply appeared suddenly in the synagogue of Capernaum. He retained the appearance of humanity until his death on the cross, by which he redeemed souls from the dominion of the creator. Marcion's view of the creator God of Israel differed from other Gnostic teachings, in that he was not necessarily an evil being from the beginning of time. He was however, a god of "justice". In other words, his sole function was to reward and punish humans. You may have heard a Christian phrase, "the God of Israel was a God of wrath", while the God of Christ "is a God of love". This is the source of that teaching.

The Antitheses

This work laid out his arguments for the inconsistencies between the "two gods", the God of Israel and the "higher" (true) God of Christ (the supreme god). He did this by quoting the Jewish Scriptures and then the parallel "anti-type" ("*Antitheses*") found in the gospels. "I am the Lord, and there is none else; I form the light, and create darkness; I make peace, and create evil ..." (Isaiah 45:6,7). But according to Jesus: "For an evil tree brings forth not good fruit; neither does a good tree bring forth evil fruit. For every tree is known by his own fruit" (Luke 6:43,44a). In other words, the God of Israel is responsible for evil. Christ, as "the good fruit" emerged from a different and benevolent God. One time when the Assyrians were marching on the northern Kingdom of Israel, "God smote them with blindness". "But what did our Lord do? He healed the blind".

The God of Israel is inconsistent, sometimes changing his mind (the story of the flood, regret at making Saul a king) and punishing the innocent as well as the guilty with national disasters against Israel. He is quick to anger, jealous of any other power (by his own admission). But Jesus taught forgiveness, even of our enemies (Matthew 5).

The Christ who in the days of Tiberius was, by a previously unknown god, revealed for the salvation of all nations, is a different being from he who was ordained by the creator God for the restoration of the Jewish state, and who is yet to come. The Creator's Christ is to be a warrior, a bearer of arms, and mighty in war. The Christ of the good God, who has come, is a far different being. In their ignorance, the Jews killed him as an enemy. The Jews' concept of "Christ" is selfishly only to rescue the Jews; the true Christ was appointed by the good God for the liberation of all humanity.

Marcion's Scriptures

Having dismissed the God of Israel in the role of salvation, Marcion uniquely taught the need for Christians to create their own "scriptures". He was a great admirer of Paul as the only one who had "understood the truth". Paul had described an "out-of-body journey to the heavens" in 2 Corinthians where he received the truth. Marcion claimed that he had ten letters of Paul, which should be the basis of Christian teaching. But in addition, he also claimed that the third gospel, Luke, was the only gospel that promoted a "God of love" above the creator God of Israel.

However, he rallied against the fact that "someone" had added the many references to the Prophets in Paul's letters (especially Isaiah) and Luke's references to both the Prophets and the history of Israel. He therefore "edited" out those sections. His "canon" consisted of these now shortened letters of Paul and the gospel of Luke (dismissing Mark, Matthew, and John). It must have been a very small edition.

The Formation of the New Testament Canon

The significance of Marcion's "scriptures" are found in the reaction of the Church Fathers. Between 140 and 200, the canonization of what became the New Testament evolved, largely in response to Gnostic teachings, but also in response to Marcion's proposed canon: "Marcion has ten letters of Paul? We have fourteen; Marcion has one gospel? We have four". They selected the four with the argument that these four were not only the earliest, but they claimed that they were read and used throughout the various communities.

It was during this period that the four were assigned their names ("This is the gospel according to …") and they proposed "background" traditions of the writers. "Besides", Irenaeus had written, "God only ever intended that there should be four, as in four cardinal points of the world", and the four seasons. The four gospels also shared the most important element of Christian teaching, the story of the suffering, trials, and crucifixion of Jesus. The fourth gospel of John, with its emphasis on Jesus as the *logos*, as a pre-existent Christ, is quite similar to Gnostic teaching. However, John also included the crucifixion as a physical, historical event.

In condemning the Gnostics' new teaching, the Church Fathers pointed out that Valentinus, Marcion and others were not even born when "the word" has been established by Christ. Paul should not be elevated over Peter, who was the first witness and "brought the word to Rome". Collectively, the Church Fathers claimed that such heretics should never be permitted to cite the Jewish Scriptures in any debate; they had misunderstood and abused them, leading people into doubt and sin.

The Demise of the Gnostics

The Church Fathers utilized a standard literary device, that of *damnatio memoriae*, not only condemning heretics to Hell, but the more important condemnation that there should be no "memory" of them. With no memory, this was equivalent to annihilation.

When Constantine converted in 312, he converted to the Christianity of the Church Fathers. Any dissent from their teachings was deemed heresy, and such texts were ordered to be destroyed. We think this is when someone (perhaps a monk?) buried the texts at Nag Hammadi. Heresy was now viewed as treason. Gnostics essentially "went underground", where some of their teachings emerged in the Middle Ages in the Balkans (the Waldensians) and southern France (the Albigensians). Their teachings were the motivation for the creation of the institution of **The Inquisition** by the Catholic Church in the twelfth century to "hunt out" such heretics.

Modern Gnosticism

The modern "re-discovery" of Gnostic concepts has now led to analyses of classical Western literature and drama, to determine if they may have been influenced by these ideas over the centuries. This is particularly done in relation to the continuing application of allegory. Some examples include: Dante's *Divine Comedy*, John Bunyan's *Pilgrim's Progress*, John Milton's *Paradise Lost*, William Golding's *Lord of the Flies*, George Orwell's *Animal Farm*, Herman Melville's *Moby Dick*, C.S. Lewis' *The Chronicles of Narnia*, and John Steinbeck's *Of Mice and Men*.

Some modern feminist and New-Age movements have focused on Gnostic writings of "the divine feminine" (Sophia) as a counter against the traditional misogynistic views of women in the Western tradition. And several modern Gnostic "churches" have been established.

But it is Hollywood that has promoted Gnostic concepts more than any other genre, in the current spate of science-fiction films. It began with Ridley Scott's 1982 ground-breaking *Blade Runner*. It was based upon a short story by Philip K. Dick, "Do Androids Dream of Electric Sheep?" The plot concerned the creation of perfect androids, who nevertheless began to develop human emotions because of memory implants in their systems. Their inventor is portrayed as "the creator god". The question remains, are androids real humans or illusions?

The Wachowski brothers' 1999 hit release, *The Matrix* and sequels), combined Gnostic Christianity and Buddhism to pose humanity's fundamental problem and its solution in terms of ignorance and enlightenment. Because of ignorance, people mistake the "material" world for something real, but they may "wake up" from this dream with help from a guide who teaches them their true nature.

Most of the movies take place in a post-apocalyptic world, where all previous social conventions and behavior become altered in the search for survival. In common with Gnostic thought, there is always a group or a person who serves as a "redeemer" figure, often an alien because redemption can only come from outside the material universe. The most recent attempt has been accomplished in James Cameron's *Avatar* (2009). Having depleted all the resources on earth, humans travel to the planet Pandora to establish new mines. At this point humans have developed the ability to project themselves into aliens, as avatars of the natives, resulting in a new view of reality. Sully, a marine, is the outsider who brings redemption to the tribes.

Summary

- The unique worldviews and views of the nature of Christ differed from mainstream Christian communities.
- The innovation of "orthodoxy" and "heresy" became standard ways in which to judge any divergent concepts and teachings.
- A direct result of Gnostic teaching resulted in the formation of the New Testament canon.

Suggestions for Further Reading

Internet: http://gnosis.org/naghamm/nhl.html. This Contains "The Gnostic Society Library" with Detailed Articles, Lectures, and Translations of the Gnostic Texts and Gospels.

Meyer, Marvin W. and Pagels, Elaine. 2009. *The Nag Hammadi Scriptures: The Revised and Updated Translation of Sacred Gnostic Texts*. HarperOne. This anthology surveys each of the Gnostic documents.

Pagels, Elaine. 1989. *The Gnostic Gospels*. Vintage. An international expert on Gnosticism, Pagels provides a readable explanation of both concepts and how it influenced the daily life of Gnostics.

FINDING AN IDENTITY AND SEPARATING FROM JUDAISM VIII

Adversos Literature

The Methods of the Church Fathers

Justin Martyr's *Dialogue with Trypho the Jew*

Emperor Hadrian (76–138 CE)

Christian Views on the War

Allegory

The Ten Commandments

The Result of Reading Jewish Scriptures as Allegory

Did the Jews Persecute Christians?

Varieties of Early Christianity: The Formation of the Western Christian Tradition,
First Edition. Rebecca I. Denova.
© 2023 John Wiley & Sons, Inc. Published 2023 by John Wiley & Sons, Inc.

Finding an Identity and Separating from Judaism

After reading this chapter you will be able to:

- Explore the background of how and when Christianity became an independent religion in the Roman Empire.
- Examine the incorporation of Jewish concepts that remained essential to Christianity.

From the very beginning Christian communities were faced with a compelling problem. As a Jewish movement, the primary concern was to spread the "good news" of the message of Jesus of Nazareth to other Jews. But during this initial process in the first century, something totally unexpected happened. When disciples and missionaries preached the message in cities and towns outside of Jerusalem, to their surprise, Gentiles were far more interested in this message than Jews.

At the same time, we could say that Christians were faced with what we would call a "theological crisis". If Christians had access to the "truth", why did not the Jews "believe?" The continuing existence of Jewish communities flew in the face of their "truth," and was viewed as a direct challenge to the Church (see Box VIII.1).

Box VIII.1   Jewish rejection of Christian Claims

There were many reasons why most Jews did not accept this new teaching:

1. In claiming that Jesus of Nazareth was the messiah ("anointed one") of Israel, Christian missionaries were faced with the problem that there were many and varied views of that individual and his function among Jews (both at home and abroad). The opinions ranged from a warrior-king like David, to a pre-existent angelic being overseeing judgment (1 Enoch).
2. Many Jews who did look for "deliverance" from a messiah figure, assumed that this would only happen in the "final days" and that his appearance would signal the final battle for the restoration of the nation of Israel. None of this happened during the lifetime of Jesus; God's reign on earth had not materialized. Many Pharisees promoted the idea of the "resurrection of the dead", but for all, not just one man.
3. Language involving "kingdom" was politically dangerous under Rome. While Rome was quite tolerant of various religious beliefs, anything that aroused the crowds in opposition to the rule of Rome was never tolerated. Many Jews may have understood the message of the Christian missionaries as one of politics and revolution and were averse to getting involved in anything of that nature. Jews had long-ago worked out ways in which to co-exist with occupying powers.
4. During the first century, many "messiah" claimants who called for God's intervention had come and gone, with none being successful, and many Jews may have seen this latest claim in the same light. The disaster of the Zealot revolt had destroyed Jerusalem and the Temple.
5. Some Jews may have been troubled about both the numbers and elevation of Gentiles in these new communities. Did this make them equal to Jews and as partners in the Covenant?
6. The exaltation of Christ sharing God's throne and the worship of Christ as a god remained offensive to many Jews.

Adversos Literature

Recall that the second century Church Fathers had responded to Roman philosophical criticism by claiming they were not "new" (foreign). At the same time, Christians were dying in the arenas of Rome. The Jews had been exempted from the Imperial and State cults during the rule of Julius Caesar as a reward for their service in his Eastern armies. The Church Fathers repeatedly petitioned Emperors and magistrates to offer the same exception to Christians. Why should Rome do this? Because, as Justin Martyr claimed, Christians were *verus Israel*, the "true Jews" of the covenant with Moses. The material proof of this claim? God had permitted Rome to destroy Jerusalem and the Temple.

Collectively, these writings are categorized under *Adversos* **Literature** (with *Adversos* meaning "adversary"), literature directed to Christian adversaries, the Jews. The very nature of the term claimed that as "adversaries", Jews often and violently persecuted Christians. These writings became the template for the eventual modern concept of **anti-Semitism**. "Anti-Jewish" views did not originate with Christianity; Gentiles considered Jews eccentric and anti-social. However, they respected their antiquity. Modern anti-Semitism eventually incorporated aspects of genetics, blood, and racial discrimination, but these were essentially not institutionalized until sixteenth century Spain and then Europe.

The Methods of the Church Fathers

The Church Fathers approached their arguments with two literary tools: scriptural exegesis (scriptural interpretation of specific passages) and allegory. Reviewing the history of Israel, they demonstrated that Christianity was not new; it had been formed in the mind of God from the very beginning. All the Prophets had predicted the emergence of Jesus with a new understanding of the old traditions. The reason that God had to send Christ was because Judaism, the rituals, the priesthood, and the Temple in Jerusalem had become incurably corrupt. As demonstrated in their own Scriptures, God had to constantly intervene and punish the Jews for their sins and disobedience.

Adversos literature is complicated and at times incredibly dense. The writers assume an audience that is thoroughly familiar with the history of Israel and Jewish literature. But even if the audience was not that familiar, *Adversos* literature is replete with extraordinarily long quotations from Genesis, Exodus, and the Prophets. At the same time, their devices of polemic and rhetoric cloud our ability to distinguish "argument" from historical people and events. In other words, how do we relate this literature to the reality of daily interactions between Jews and Christians on the ground? (see Box VIII.2).

Finding an Identity and Separating from Judaism

> **Box VIII.2 *The plurality of ethnic/religious identities***
>
> As we saw in Chapter I, ancient people identified with their ethnic group (common ancestors, language, geography, myths, customs). Jews had additional identity-markers of circumcision, dietary laws, and Sabbath observance. Native cults had no central authority that determined concepts or behavior as absolute. Jews did have their traditions and their Scriptures, but at the same time, Jewish groups differed in both interpretation and how to live out the dictates in relation to the dominant culture. Christianity had no central authority at this time; we have various Christian "sects" throughout the Empire.
>
> What is problematic in the *Adversos* literature is the application of collective language in the arguments. The references are simply "Jews", and "Christians" without distinction. This takes for granted what is referred to as "systematic theology", an agreement of how a religious system of belief functions for all participants. This is an anachronism; there was no agreed upon "system" that was held by all Jews or all Christians. We consistently use the terms, Judaism and Christianity, but various forms of "Judaisms" and "Christianities" would be more correct.
>
> We saw the variation in the section on Jewish sects in the first century (Pharisees, Sadducees, Qumran). There were others, including the distinctions between Samaritan Jews and those in Jerusalem. We also have "Jewish–Christians". The *Adversos* literature painted "the Jews" as one unified system, and thus their critique applied to all Jews everywhere in every city, and for all time.
>
> Most of the *Adversos* literature is from the Church Fathers attached to Rome (and what became the Western tradition). While there were distinct communities of Christians throughout the Empire, the authors promoted *their* "Christians" against all "Jews", as two universally-opposed systems of belief.

Justin Martyr's *Dialogue with Trypho the Jew*

The *Dialogue* is an alleged conversation between Justin and Trypho, a Jewish refugee who came to Rome after the end of the disaster of the failed **Bar Kokhba Revolt** (132–136 CE). Scholars often debate the historicity of both the person of Trypho as well as the conversation; ancient writers often created "a straw man" to which they could assign points of view, setting up their subsequent refutation of each view. Nevertheless, the *Dialogue* became a standard model of explicating what was wrong with Judaism, in that "Christianity" was sent by God to eliminate it.

After the failed Jewish Revolt of 66–73, with the destruction of the Second Temple in 70, the Roman authorities instituted some changes in the province. Instead of a procurator, they appointed a praetor as governor (a higher-level magistrate) and permanently installed a legion of Roman soldiers, the *X Fretensis*. During that Revolt, some surviving Pharisees settled at Yavne, along the coast, to provide spiritual guidance now that the Temple was gone. Many Jews accepted the status quo of Jewish–Roman relations, but others did not. During this period, the Temple complex (the Temple Mount) remained in ruins.

Emperor Hadrian (76–138 CE)

Traianus Hadrianus became Emperor in 117, inheriting Trajan's Empire. (He is now more famously known as the builder of Hadrian's Wall, between England and Scotland. He also refurbished the older Pantheon in Rome, built earlier by Marcus Agrippa, first century BCE.) It was during his reign that Jews led another major rebellion against Rome. It is known to history as the Bar Kokhba Revolt, a pseudonym for the name of the leader, Simon Bar Kosiba. "Bar Kohkba" meant "son of the star", and was taken from a passage in Numbers 24:17: "A star will come out of Jacob; a scepter will rise out of Israel", to crush Israel's enemies. This name was allegedly given to him by a prominent Rabbi at the time, Rabbi Akiva, who endorsed him as the expected "messiah" of the "final days".

There are many reasons for the revolt, but the surviving literature contains mixed and sometimes contradictory evidence. Legends were added in subsequent years which are difficult to separate from the original context. In 131, the governor of Judea, Tineius Rufus, performed a foundation ceremony to rename Jerusalem, now to be known as **Aelia Capitolina**. Aelia was the family name of Hadrian. An additional legion was sent in (*VI Ferrata*) to maintain order as the construction began for a temple on the previous site of the Jewish Temple (See Figure VIII.1).

The reverse depicts Hadrian as founder ploughing with bull and cow the *sulcus primigenius* (aboriginal furrow) that established the colony's *pomerium* (sacred boundary). The vexillum, or military standard, in the background represents the veteran status of the colony's new inhabitants. The legend, COL[ONIA] AEL[IA] KAPIT[OLINA] COND[ITA], translates "The founding of Colonia Aelia Capitolina".

This "plowing of the ground" re-enacted the founding of the city of Rome by Romulus, and his laying the *pomerium*, or what became "sacred space" within the city. Although in ruins, the Temple Mount was still considered sacred space to the Jews and they were outraged by this ceremony. There were rumors that

Figure VIII.1 Drawing of the reverse of a coin from Colonia Aelia Capitolina.

Hadrian intended to build a temple to Jupiter on this sacred site. The Prophet Jeremiah had predicted that a second Temple would be built 70 years after the Babylonian destruction (587 BCE). In anticipation, many Jews looked for the restoration of another Temple as the decades passed.

Hadrian was enamored with Greek culture and Greek cultural traditions. He was one of the first Emperors to wear longer hair and beard, in the manner of the portrayal of Greek gods and philosophers. He traveled to Greece and met a young Greek by the name of Antinous who joined the entourage allegedly as Hadrian's lover. Moving on to Egypt, while sailing down the Nile, Antinous fell overboard and drowned. In his grief, Hadrian instituted a cult with Antinous as a now resurrected god.

But traditionally, the major reason given for this second revolt was the claim that Hadrian had banned the rite of circumcision. As an admirer of Hellenistic culture, Hadrian would have agreed with many Greeks that circumcision was a "mutilation of the body". But it is difficult to locate if this ban was ordered before (and hence, the reason for the revolt) or once the revolt had begun. Our only evidence comes from a manuscript, the *Historia Augusta*, most likely written during the reigns of either Diocletian or Constantine I (fourth century CE). The critique of "genital mutilation" in this text may have been directed to some Roman denunciations of masters who castrated their slaves.

As with many ancient texts, casualties are difficult to verify. Cassius Dio (55–235 CE), reported in his later history that a Roman legion of 4000 was destroyed, and 58,000 Jews killed. Later Rabbinic stories related the tortures of captive Jewish martyrs, including Rabbi Akiva who was burned alive. Archaeological evidence supports many elements of the revolt; caves in the Dead Sea Area were utilized as bases for the rebels. They utilized the same guerilla tactics (and concepts) as applied in the Maccabee Revolt (167 BCE). Bar Kokhba minted coins with the "Era of the redemption of Israel".

Manuscript evidence of letters were excavated in the caves, some by Bar Kokhba himself (now housed in the Israeli Museum). Roman legions eventually lowered ropes and massacred the cave occupants. Bar Kokhba died in the siege of Beitar, a town south of Jerusalem. The Christian historian Eusebius later claimed that Bar Kokhba ruthlessly punished any Jew who refused to join, but also: "He severely punished the sect of the Christians with death by different means of torture for their refusal to fight against the Romans" (*Chronicon*).

In the aftermath of the revolt, Hadrian did build a temple to Jupiter (which included a statue of himself) and officially designated a new name to Judea, **Syria Palestina**, an older name for the region during the time of Syrian dominance. An insulting title for Jews, "Palestina" was the Latin for the Jews' historic enemy, the Philistines. (Thus, "Palestine", and "Palestinians" remain modern descriptors of the region and its native people.) More significantly, Jews were forbidden to enter the city except on one day of the year, *Tisha B'Av* (the ninth of August), the traditional date for the destruction of both Solomon's Temple and the Second Temple and a day of fasting and mourning.

With the ban against Jews, this is the period when Christian groups began flocking to the city, seeking out the "holy sites" associated with the gospels. One community, the Armenian Church, claims to have been one of the first to establish itself in the city. The Armenians maintain their own separate "quarter" in what is known today as the Old City of Jerusalem.

Rabbinic Judaism had also become a portable religion, where the center of Jewish life remained the synagogues. In both Persia and the Galilee, the beginnings of the **Talmud** were established (commentaries on Scripture) and "messianism" was de-emphasized after this revolt but remained a spiritual element of the future.

Christian Views on the War

In his dialogue with Trypho, Justin Martyr used the recent rebellion as the starting point to argue that Christians were "peace loving", and "good, patriotic citizens" of the Roman Empire. In contrast, one only need consult the Jewish Scriptures to see that the Jews, by their stubborn nature, had always been disobedient to authority, even to the commandments of God himself. The recent disobedience to authority was the final straw. Again, God had permitted Rome to win as another punishment for the Jews.

Justin's Trypho responds with a major complaint against Christians; they no longer follow the Law (of Moses) at all:

> Moreover, I am aware that your precepts in the so-called Gospel are so wonderful and so great, that I suspect no one can keep them; for I have carefully read them. But this is what we are most at a loss about: that you, professing to be pious, and supposing yourselves better than others, are not in any particular separated from them, and do not alter your mode of living from the nations, in that you observe no festivals or sabbaths, and do not have the rite of circumcision; and further, resting your hopes on a man that was crucified, you yet expect to obtain some good thing from God, while you do not obey His commandments.

Justin's response:

> There will be no other God, O Trypho, nor was there from eternity any other existing (I thus addressed him), but he who made and disposed all this universe. Nor do we think that there is one God for us, another for you, but that he alone is God who led your fathers out from Egypt with a strong hand and a high arm. Nor have we trusted in any other (for there is no other), but in him in whom you also have trusted, the God of Abraham, and of Isaac, and of Jacob. But we do not trust through Moses or through the law; for then we would do the same as yourselves … For the law promulgated on Horeb is now old and belongs to yourselves alone; but this is for all universally … Have you not read this which Isaiah says: "Hearken to me, my people; and you kings, give ear to me: for a law shall go forth from me, and my judgment shall be for a light to the nations". And by Jeremiah, concerning this same new covenant, God thus speaks: "Behold, the days come, that I will make a new covenant with the house of Israel and with the house of Judah".

Justin reminded Trypho that "Abraham" was deemed righteous and blessed before the law of circumcision was introduced.

Throughout the *Dialogue*, Justin went on to critique every aspect of Judaism and its subsequent "misunderstandings". For example, why did God command circumcision of the Jews? In God's foreknowledge, this was a physical marker so that all the world would know them and "drive them away for their evil deeds done to Christ and the Christians ... For other nations have not inflicted on us and on Christ this wrong to such an extent as you have ... You selected and sent out from Jerusalem chosen men through all the land to tell that a godless heresy of the Christians had sprung up, and to publish those things which all they who knew us not speak against us. So that you are the cause not only of your own unrighteousness, but in fact of that of all other men". Just as the Jews conspired against Christ, they continue to conspire against Christians through their lies.

Justin presented detailed arguments from the Scriptures and the books of the Prophets on the sins of the Jews, the many times that God had rescued them, but "Israel continued to sin". There was a long passage on why the "water rituals" of the Jews could not "wash away sin":

> But the cisterns which you have dug for yourselves are broken and profitless to you. For what is the use of that baptism which cleanses the flesh and body alone? But you have understood all things in a carnal sense, and you suppose it to be piety if you do such things, while your souls are filled with deceit, and, in short, with every wickedness.

True atonement . sacrifice of Christ. Unlike current rumors, Christians do not "drink blood", but recognize the power of the "the spirit" in the ritual of "the last supper". Like others before him, Justin included many of the items of the "suffering servant" passages of Isaiah that had already been adopted by Christians: "And he shall bear our sins; therefore, he shall inherit many, and shall divide the spoil of the strong, because his soul was delivered to death".

Trypho pointed out that "many are called Christians", but they eat meat offered to idols, live the same life-style, and sometimes contradict the teachings of Christ. Justin responded that these men (heretics) do so in "fulfillment" of the many times that Christ predicted that many "false prophets" would speak in his name ("men in sheep's clothing, but inwardly wolves"). Justin claimed that such heretical teachings only strengthened the resolve and true beliefs of Christ. He then named some of the Gnostic groups, as blasphemers, the cause of schisms.

Allegory

It is through the device of allegory that Justin made the most significant contribution to the formation of Christianity as a separate religion. Recall the Christian argument that Christianity was not new. Justin now demonstrated to

Trypho his "proof" for the antiquity of Christian belief, through applying allegory throughout the Scriptures and the books of the Prophets. There were figures of the things ("types") which pertain ("pointed to Christ").

> The mystery, then, of the lamb which God enjoined to be sacrificed as the Passover, was a type of Christ; with whose blood, in proportion to their faith in him, they anoint their houses, i.e., themselves, who believe on him ... knowing that the days will come, after the suffering of Christ, when even the place in Jerusalem shall be given over to your enemies, and all the offerings, in short, shall cease; and that lamb which was commanded to be wholly roasted was a symbol of the suffering of the cross which Christ would undergo. For the lamb, which is roasted, is roasted and dressed up in the form of the cross (the spits of wood).

The twelve bells attached to the robe of the high priest, "pointed to" the call of the twelve apostles, with Christ as "the eternal priest". Justin claimed that the "binding of Isaac", pointed to the "binding on the cross". Only this time, God accepted this "pure" sacrifice. When the Israelites battled various tribes in the wilderness on their way to Canaan, Moses would stand with his arms "raised up", and they would win. When he tired, and his arms fell, they would lose. This symbolized that "salvation" would be granted by the "raised arms of Christ" on the cross.

Trypho then said, "Tell me, shall those who lived according to the law given by Moses, live in the same manner with Jacob, Enoch, and Noah, but also join in the resurrection of the dead?" Justin replied, "Each shall be saved by his own righteousness ... those who are good ... shall be saved through this Christ ... by this dispensation, the serpent that sinned from the beginning, and the angels like him, may be destroyed, and that death may be condemned at the second coming of Christ himself".

But, Trypho asked again, "If a man who keeps the Law but is also convinced that Jesus is the Christ of God, and the judge of all, can he be saved?" Justin replied that their ritual observance "contributes nothing to righteousness". Abraham and his descendants and their wives lived before the Law of Moses. But Justin provided a compromise in that a Jewish believer can live as a Jew but must not be permitted to argue against or try to "turn back" other Christians.

Trypho argued a Jewish belief that the Prophet Elijah (who had been taken up to heaven) would return to earth to announce the Messiah. However, Elijah had not yet appeared. Justin narrated the same rationale as the gospels, that John the Baptist had fulfilled this role in announcing Jesus as the messiah.

The *Dialogue* then narrates the many times that the Jews believed that God descended and interacted with Jews on earth. According to Justin, it was not God who conversed with Moses from a burning bush, but the pre-existent form of Christ as the *logos. Everywhere in the Scriptures where one reads "God", it was always Christ in his pre-earthly manifestation in a body.* Thus, Christ pre-dated all of creation; this was what gave Christ his "equal standing" with God, and thus worthy of "worship".

Trypho's final argument: "You admitted to us that he (Christ) was both cir- cumcised, and observed the other legal ceremonies ordained by Moses". So did the patriarchs, said Justin, and they were deemed blessed because of it. But God gave these commandments because of the "hard-heartedness" of the Jews, that without them, they would sin even more. God also said that he would send a new dispensation which was manifest in Christ. Christ obeyed the command- ments because he was an obedient son, unlike the Jews.

Justin repeated a passage from the gospel of Matthew, that the Jews spread the rumor that the disciples "stole the body of Jesus", and claimed it as "resurrection from the dead". "Yet we do not hate you or those who, by your means, have con- ceived such prejudices against us; but we pray that even now all of you may repent and obtain mercy from God, the compassionate and long-suffering Father of all".

The Ten Commandments

The charge that Jews only understood everything literally and not "spiritually" most likely evolved from Jewish allegory of the Scriptures (such as Philo's) or from other unknown sources. It is in the second century that Christians reduced the original commandments at Sinai to ten.

Recall that Moses received 613 commandments at Sinai. Many of these com- mandments were directed to distinguish the Jews "from the nations", in worship, in appearance, behavior, and rituals. When Moses first received the command- ments, he went down from the mountain to find the Israelites in idolatry. He smashed the tablets, creating an earthquake that swallowed up many of the sin- ners. He later went back up and received a second set of tablets.

Christians were now obligated to follow the first ten because the 603 other commandments were given to the Jews as their punishment for idolatry. Arguments were added that the first ten were ordained by God as universal pre- cepts for all humans. Therefore, Jews who continued to follow the rest, "cutting themselves off from the rest of humanity", were deemed "hardened" against the original intentions of God as well as hardened against all people.

In addition to the writings of Justin, Irenaeus wrote a lengthy tract, *Demonstration (of Apostolic Teachings)* against the Jews. Tertullian wrote his *Adversus Judaeos* in a similar "dialogue" with a Jew. Both utilized the same arguments as Justin and incorporated allegorical understanding of the history of Israel.

The Result of Reading Jewish Scriptures as Allegory

If you have ever wondered why Christians consider both the "Old Testament" as well as the "New Testament" as "sacred scripture", it is the result of this application of allegory to provide "ancient roots" for Christian claims. In the ancient world, ancient traditions were respected. The Jewish Scriptures had a long history, so Christians argued that that history belonged to Christians. Jews should no longer be considered a legitimate (officially sanctioned group) because they remained entirely ignorant of how to interpret their sacred texts.

Thus, eventually, the entire "Bible" continued (and continues) to be utilized as "the proof from Scripture", for the "fulfillment" of Christian claims. In relation to Roman criticism, Christians maintained the "monotheism" of the Jews, that Jews could only worship the God of Israel. Rome had permitted the exemption of Jews from the state cults, and the purpose of most of this literature was to argue that Christians should be granted the same exception. Thus, the "true Jews" of God's covenant.

The Bar Kokhba Revolt can be understood as the "turning-point" in Jewish–Christian relations. Twice now, Jewish rebels had challenged Rome, only to be met with disaster. The *Adversos* literature consistently quoted Isaiah as "fulfilment": "Your sacred cities have become a wasteland; even Zion is a wasteland, Jerusalem a desolation. Our holy and glorious temple, where our ancestors praised you, has been burned with fire, and all that we treasured lies in ruins" (64:10–12). Through the *Adversos* literature, Christianity no longer could be viewed as just another "sect of Judaism". Without Jewish identity markers and their refusal to participate in the dominant religious culture (no idolatry), Christianity became a unique religious system in the Empire.

Did the Jews Persecute Christians?

Unfortunately, *Adversos* literature has a long and tragic influence on Jewish–Christian relations. These texts were consistently utilized for both later anti-Jewish legislation and the justification of the murder of Jews from late antiquity, through the Middle Ages and beyond. Charged with "deicide" (the killing of God), the combined Scriptures were presented as "proof" of their crimes.

The historical evidence for Jewish persecution of Christians continues to be debated among scholars. It begins with the *birkat haminim* "benediction against dissenters", which became incorporated as part of the *Shemoneh Esreh* ("Eighteen Benedictions") recited in daily prayer services in synagogues. The date is difficult to verify, with theories of an early response where "dissenters" were understood as Christians or articulated in later centuries. In premodern Europe, some Jewish communities designated Christians "apostates".

Beginning in the second century, Rabbis began formulating the *Mishnah* (an exposition of the "oral Law" passed from Moses to the Rabbis) and the *Halakah*, commentaries on the Scriptures. Over the centuries, these were combined for an entire collection known as *Talmud*, the foundation today of Jewish religious law. Often designated as *Yeshu* (an Aramaic vocalization) in these writings, Jesus was more often characterized as a sorcerer, who learned his tricks in Egypt.

But there were several individual Yeshuas; some of the texts placed him during the reign of the Hasmoneans, while others at the time of the Bar Kokhba revolt. The rumor that Jesus was the son of a Roman legionary was also repeated. In some of the texts, Yeshua is condemned for leading people into idolatry (the worship of Jesus as a god).

Justin Martyr mentioned seven times that "the Jews curse Christ" in their synagogues, which *may* be a reference to the *birkat haminim*). Tertullian mentioned that the Jewish pejorative epithet for Christians was *Nazareni* ("Nazarenes"). The other complication is that such descriptions could have been directed to various "Jewish–Christian" sects that survived into the sixth century. The later Christian fathers, Origen and Jerome, who both lived and worked in Israel (and consulted Rabbinic scholars) mentioned that "Jews anathematize Christ", but without details.

Another response was in reaction to the portrayal of a "false trail" or illegal activity of the Sanhedrin in the gospel traditions. Perhaps to correct this view:

> And it was taught: On the eve of the Passover Yeshua [the Nazarene] was hanged. For forty days before the execution took place a herald went forth and cried, "He is going forth to be stoned because he has practiced sorcery and enticed Israel to apostasy. Anyone who can say anything in his favor, let him come and plead on his behalf". And since nothing was brought forward in his favor, he was hanged on the eve of Passover.
>
> (*Babylonian Talmud. Sanhedrin* 43a)

Note the obvious contradiction between hanging and stoning.

The problem for the historian is distinguishing polemic from reality, on either side. Luke's story of Paul gaining arrest warrants from the Sanhedrin in Jerusalem to arrest Christians in Damascus (only found in Acts 9) remained a Christian conviction that Judaism collectively "persecuted Christians", which they claimed that contemporary Jews still attempted. We saw in the chapter on Martyrdom that some Christians accused Jews of collusion with the Roman government in "turning-over" Christians, just as they did Jesus. And the charge of "persecution" is often a response of a minority group in their perceptions of a dominant majority who oppose the smaller group. If Jews "denounced" Christians in their synagogues, there is no evidence that this led to either physical abuse or executions. Legally, Jews could not discipline anyone beyond their community. At the same time, as an illegal assembly at this time, Christians had no authority to do anything concerning alleged "persecution" by Jews.

The only historical conclusion we can derive from the *Adversos* literature is that many Christian leaders perceived the continuing existence of Jews and Judaism as both competition in the Empire as well as a threat to their convictions. As we will see in Chapter XI, the later Latin Fathers repeated the same anti-Jewish diatribes because apparently, Christians and Jews continued to mix and interact with each other in daily life and in sharing some religious festivals. In other words, despite the theological and intellectual denigrations of the Fathers, average Christians and Jews appeared to have no problem with "mixed communities".

Despite the *Adversos* literature, Rome was not convinced that Christians were "the true Jews"; Christians were not circumcised. It would take the conversion of Constantine I in 312 to provide Christians with legitimacy (see Chapter XI).

Modern, post-war Holocaust Studies attempt to analyze the roots of modern anti-Semitism. There has recently been a sub-group within the discipline that traces the origins of this tragedy. Various books, articles, and conferences designated "The Parting of the Ways", and "The Ways that Never Parted", not only trace the roots, but attempt to reconcile differences in Jewish–Christian theology and relations in the modern world.

Summary

- The official separation of Christianity from Judaism most likely occurred after the Bar Kokhba Rebellion.
- Christians retained the basic precepts of Judaism but recreated a "new understanding" of that history, as the "inheritors" of God's original covenant.

Suggestions for Further Reading

Fredriksen, Paula and Reinhartz, Adele. 2002. *Jesus, Judaism and Christian Anti-Judaism: Reading the New Testament after the Holocaust.* Westminster John Know Press. This is an anthology of attempts to trace the continuing concepts of Anti-Semitism from late antiquity into the modern world.

Gager, John G. 1983. *The Origins of Anti-Semitism: Attitudes toward Judaism in Pagan and Christian Antiquity.* Oxford University Press. In modern studies, this was one of the first major evaluations for understanding the tensions between Judaism and Christianity.

CHARISMATIC CHRISTIANITY
APOCRYPHA AND PSEUDEPIGRAPHA

Manuscript Traditions

Acts of the Apostles

The Nero Traditions in the Acts of Peter

The Acts of Paul and Thecla

Apocalypses

Varieties of Early Christianity: The Formation of the Western Christian Tradition,
First Edition. Rebecca I. Denova.
© 2023 John Wiley & Sons, Inc. Published 2023 by John Wiley & Sons, Inc.

After reading this chapter you will be able to:

- Explore early Christian literature that provided more details of the lives of Jesus, Mary and Joseph, and the Apostles.
- Appreciate the utilization of Greco-Roman literary devices in the stories of the first Christians.

Apochrypha are those books considered "outside the canon", meaning that they were not included when the New Testament became official under Constantine (after 325). Many of them were written from the end of the first century and beyond. **Pseudepigrapha**, "false writing", are those texts that are bluntly "forgeries". They were written or pretended to be written in the name of a past person, who was also considered to be someone "in the know". Jews had utilized this literary device, such as the apocalyptic texts that pretend to be written by Enoch, Moses, and Abraham. Because they were in heaven, they were sources of both traditional and "hidden secrets".

As we saw in the first Christian communities, Christian religious expression encompassed "ecstatic" behavior, such as "speaking in tongues", spirit possession resulting in "prophecy", and developed rules and regulations on bodily behavior. *Caris*, "gifts", were understood as gifts from "the spirit of God", and hence the term, "charismatic". People, being people, now wanted to know more details about the movement. Only Matthew and Luke provided the birth story of Jesus, but then moved directly to the ministry. What was his life like in the interim? How did Mary and Joseph meet? And, of particular fascination, what happened to the original Apostles after they left Jerusalem?

Beginning in the second century, stories and legends emerged that attempted to fill in all these details. In stories of the lives of the Apostles, the concept of charismatic gifts was utilized as the background for the ways in which they could perform miracles, such as healing, and miraculous "conversions". At the same time, the dominant culturecs stories of "great deeds" of ancient heroes were templates for the way in which similar "gifts from the gods" were now present in Christian "heroes", in the "spirit of Christ".

Manuscript Traditions

By the second century, the codex (the early form of "books") became popular and apparently were less cumbersome than scrolls, particularly for public reading. The manuscripts that have survived (in Syriac and Latin) often demonstrate attempts (by scribes?) to harmonize either contradictory material, or to clarify older traditions. Christians began using *nomina sacra*, or key words written in abbreviated form such as *theos, kyrios, Christos,* and the use of the *staurogram*, ⳨. This was the abbreviated letters that were applied as a reference to the crucifixion of Jesus. The texts often indicated pauses in the reading at important events, most likely for liturgical reasons. It could be noted that some of the manuscripts demonstrate less concern for high, literary skills and allegory, and more for "miraculous details". This could be an indication of the educational level of the majority of Christians in communities, or, simply a more preferred way of recounting the stories.

The Shepherd of Hermas

Originating in the second century, some Church Fathers argued for its inclusion, but it was subsequently dropped from the canon. It was in the *Codex Sinaiticus*, between the Acts of the Apostles and the Acts of Paul. Originally written in Rome in Greek, it was translated to local languages in many communities in the Eastern Empire. It contains a series of five visions and ten parables, utilizing allegory. The visions were granted to Hermas, a former slave: "He who bought me sold me to a certain Rhoda, who was at Rome. After many years I began to love her as a sister".

On the road to Cumae, he had a vision of Rhoda (now in heaven), who told him that she is now his "accuser" because of his previous "impure thoughts concerning her". He must repent and pray for himself and his house. He also had a vision of the Church as an old woman, helpless because of the sins of her children. Hermas must correct this. As he does, he has repeated visions of the old woman getting younger and younger, ultimately as a "glorious bride". The final visions revealed "the Angel of repentance", in the guise of a shepherd (and thus its title).

The angel delivered ten mandates on Christian ethics. It is the duty of a Christian husband to forgive and take back an adulterous wife; watch out for "false prophets" who only want to share the best seats with the presbyters ("overseers", bishops). The parables occur in visions. An earlier reference to the building of a tower now posited the Church as the tower, built with stones of the faithful.

Three ancient writers claimed that Hermas was the brother of Bishop Pius I, who led the Church at Rome between 140 and 155 (later declared a Pope). There may have various reasons for not including it in the official canon, but one Christian critic wrote: "Hermas wrote *The Shepard* very recently, in our times, in the city of Rome, while Bishop Pius, his brother, was occupying the chair of the Church. And therefore, it ought indeed to be read; but it cannot be read publicly to the people, positioned either among the Prophets, whose number is complete, or among the Apostles, for it is after their time". This may be a reference to the order of the early liturgy of the Church of readings in the Church (see Chapter X).

The Infancy Gospel of Thomas

What was Jesus like as a child? Did he know from the beginning that he was the messiah? *The Infancy Gospel of Thomas* answered those questions. The writer of this text remains unknown, but it was not the same "Thomas" who wrote the Gnostic "Gospel of Thomas". It was assigned to another "Thomas", an early missionary (see below). For many modern Christians, the child Jesus is not what they expect; this is a portrait of what we would now deem, "a super-brat".

In the ancient world (and sometimes in the modern), people believed that "great men" must have had an unusual birth and childhood, where they showed early signs of being a prodigy. (Hercules battling snakes in his cradle, tales of Augustus' mother being impregnated with "divinity" as examples.) We do this with modern biographies all the time—Mozart composing a symphony at the age of six—what were the signs that great men and women would grow up to be creative, to invent things, solve problems?

So, with the young Jesus. The text opened with Jesus playing in the mud (like all children), but then he fashioned the mud into birds which fly. So far, not bad. But when Jesus plays with the other boys on the street, he got mad and struck one dead. The parents come to Mary and Joseph with, "Can't you do something to control your child?" They try to find him a tutor, but of course, Jesus is shown to be smarter than all of them. (This involves Jesus "teaching" his tutor on the correct and allegorical way in which to understand the letters and numbering of the alphabet.)

One day a boy fell off a roof and died. Everyone blamed Jesus, so he then "resurrected" the boy from the dead (a preview of his later activity as an adult). This text does have a happy ending; Jesus went back and resurrected the first boy he struck down. The overall purpose of the text is to show the young Jesus (who has great power) learning eventually to control his gifts to be used for the "salvation of all humans" and not his own interests.

The Protoevangsselicum of James

This is the "back story" of Mary and Joseph. *Proto* "before", *evangelicum* "the good news", the title translates as "The Good News Before the Good News." This story eventually became absorbed into the traditional biographies of Mary and Joseph.

By the second century, Jesus was fully understood to be a "god", and/or God himself. As such, this divinity of Jesus led to the creation of an alteration in the status of his mother, Mary. This is where we learn the names of Mary's parents, Joachim and Anna, and that they lived near one of the gates in Jerusalem. (You can now visit the site in tours of the Old City.) Of course, they are old and barren (a typology from the Jewish Scriptures). Anna prayed for a child, and promised "to devote the child to God", if granted her wish. After Mary was weaned, in keeping her promise, Anna took the baby Mary to the Temple to be raised by the priests. What did Mary do all day? She wove tapestries and curtains for the Temple. Having Mary raised in the Temple kept her pure and isolated from all evil and outside influences.

However, when Mary reached the age of puberty, the priests had a problem: menstruating women were forbidden the inner sacred zones of the Temple. They decided to marry her off, but to whom? Someone came up with the idea of sponsoring a "contest" for the hand of Mary.

Many men applied, and they were lined up for the inspection by the priests. Some of them were farmers, holding their staves or walking sticks. One of the staves miraculously blossomed, which told the priests that this man was "chosen by God". This was the elderly Joseph. Have you ever wondered why nativity scenes always show Mary as a young girl, but Joseph has white hair and beard? This is the source. In other words, always showing Joseph as "an old man" indicates that there was never any sexual attraction between these two.

The text then moved on to the birth of Jesus. We learn that midwives were attending Mary. After the birth of Jesus, one of the midwives named Salome, had doubts about "the virgin birth". She forced her fist up through Mary's vagina, to the hymen, and discovered it was still "intact" even after the birth, and so she was convinced. But because she doubted, when she pulled her arm back out, it was horribly burned and scalded. She then placed her arm on the cradle of Jesus, and her arm was restored. (Renaissance artists, copying earlier Christian art, often depicted this story (see Figure XI.1).

The Brothers of Jesus?

The gospels (even Matthew and Luke who reported "the virgin birth") nevertheless all claimed that Jesus had brothers and sisters after his birth. In Mark 6:3, when Jesus returned to Nazareth, Mary, his brothers, and sisters are in the crowd. Only the brothers are named, "James and Joses and Judas and Simon".

Figure IX.1 The midwife bathing the infant Jesus, twelfth century fresco from Cappadocia.

Two of the names, James and Joses, appear again in Mark 15:40, where they are said to be the sons of a Mary, one of the women watching the crucifixion. We can only verify the historical existence of James, as Paul visited him in Jerusalem (and referred to him as a literal "brother" of Jesus).

Having carried divinity in her womb, Mary's elevated status as a "divine vessel" meant that she never experienced sexual intercourse (the sin of lust). She now obtained a new title, *Theotokos*, that she "carried divinity in her womb". In reinterpreting the "brothers" of Jesus, Catholicism teaches that even though the Greek word *adelphoi* meant literal brothers, it should be interpreted as "cousins". In some Orthodox traditions, the brothers are "step-brothers", the sons of a previous marriage of Joseph, now deemed a widower.

In the Old City of Jerusalem today, you can visit two sites associated with Mary. The Dormitian Abbey (built in the Victorian period), is claimed to be the site where "Mary fell asleep" ("dormition"), and then her physical body was transferred to heaven by angels. In the traditional site of the Garden of Gethsemane is an underground tomb that claims to hold the body of Mary. This tomb-site is also honored by Muslims (there are 35 references to Mary in the *Quran*, far more than the gospels).

The Gospel of Peter

This text has only survived in fragments, and scholars continue to argue over the date—first century (pre-gospel) or second century? It begins in *medias res*, at the tomb of Jesus on Sunday morning.

This text (and later versions with more details) addressed two specific questions: (1) What was Jesus doing for a day and a half (between Friday evening and Sunday morning)? and (2) What about all the past dead who were no longer here to be saved by Jesus? Speculations began with a detail in Luke's Acts of the Apostles and 1 Peter. In Acts 2:27 and 2:31, Luke claimed that "Hades (*she'ol*) could not hold the crucified Christ". In 1 Peter 3:19–20, we have: "Jesus went and made a proclamation to the spirits in prison, who in former times did not obey, when God waited patiently in the days of Noah", and 4:6, saying that the gospel was "proclaimed, even to the dead ..." ("prison" being understood as Hades.)

In *The Gospel of Peter*, taking the idea of "guards" placed at the tomb from Matthew, it is the guards who first witness the resurrection, joined in some inexplicable way that morning by Herod Antipas and Pontius Pilate. They see three "beings" walking out of the tomb, two angels and Jesus, whose heads reach all the way up to the heavens. Included with this group is a cross that "talks". The cross says, "it is accomplished". As they watch this scene, a sound begins to roar, and they are aware of hundreds of souls following Jesus out of the tomb. These are the souls of the "righteous", or people who died since the dawn of time who, though not "Christians", nevertheless led righteous lives—Adam and Eve,

Abraham, Noah, Moses, the Prophets, but also Plato and Aristotle. This idea was picked up and taught by the Church Fathers, Melito of Sardis, Tertullian, Hippolytus, and Origin.

Ultimately, when the New Testament became canonized in the fourth century, this gospel was not included, but the idea was adopted by what will become the "Nicene Creed" (or the Apostles' Creed, in its shorter form). This creed simply says that Jesus "descended into hell, and on the third day, he arose again". In Christian theology, "the gates of Hell" remained closed until Jesus descended and opened them.

It is during the early Middle Ages that many more details were added to this story, particularly a duel between Jesus and Satan over releasing "the souls of the righteous" (ca. 1000). It became known as the "Harrowing of Hell", with the expression "to harry", understood as a military term, meaning "raids or incursions" (like Viking raids at the time).

Acts of the Apostles

"Acts", "deeds" of the Apostles narrated the legendary stories of what happened to the Apostles in their various mission areas, and how they died, allegedly all as martyrs. Most of these stories only survive in fragments. However, the stories of Thomas and Peter entail several volumes.

These writers utilized a very popular form of story-telling, the **Greek Romance Novel**. You know this genre because it became the stuff of fairy tales, westerns, Harlequin Romance novels, and "soap operas".

1. Boy meets girl and they fall in love. Either they belong to the wrong classes, or the parents disapprove, so that they are separated.
2. Girl gets kidnapped by pirates (or some evil villain).
3. Boy sets out to search for her.
4. They both have adventures, usually a ship-wreck or two and the girl is always being threatened with rape or near rape, but her virginity remains intact. There is often a magistrate or high-end official who is in love and tries to force her into marriage.
5. Sometimes the gods intervene to save them in these adventures.
6. Boy always has a best friend, a comic "side-kick".
7. They finally re-unite and get married and live happily ever after.

The "Acts of the Apostles" utilize all the above elements, but with a Christian "twist". The "twist" is supplied in utilizing the concepts of charismatic Christianity to the stories. By the second century, the belief was that if you had "the spirit of God", then you could *not* lead a normal life. That meant "no sex"; the stories represent all the Apostles and their converts as celibate and chaste.

There was a contemporary Romance novel written in the second century (and you may have encountered it in a literature classes): *The Golden Ass: The Metamorphoses of Apuleius*. A man named Apuleius somehow angered the gods and was turned into a donkey. He then has several adventures. Much of the story satirizes elements of Greco-Roman culture, particularly the popularity of "wonder-workers" and "charlatans". He is "saved" in the end by becoming a member of the Mystery cult of Isis (an Egyptian deity whose temples and rituals had spread through the Roman Empire). Frustratingly, while full of incredible details elsewhere, when it comes to the secret rituals of Isis, he tells us that "they cannot be revealed". We can only speculate if this novel was a model for Christian narratives.

The Acts of Thomas

This is the story of the apostle Thomas whose journeys took him as far as India. Indian Christians claim him as their founder; his tomb is located in the Indian state of Goa. Along the way, he traveled through all the empires of the Middle East, converting people everywhere.

We learn that his prior career was as a carpenter (again, this idea as Jesus' "twin"). In one story in India, the king gave him funds to rehab the palace, but Thomas spent it on charity. A typical Thomas story: he is invited (either by a local king or magistrate) to attend a wedding. Thomas then pulls the couple aside and talks them out of consummating their marriage that night. In one scene, Jesus himself appears sitting on the marriage bed, to list all the horrible things involved in "sex and child-birth". The story ends with his martyrdom, "pierced with spears" because he had converted the king's wives.

The Acts of Peter

The *Acts of Peter* is one of the longest and fullest stories that has survived. In this story, some of the information was obtained from the gospels and Acts, but other sources remain unknown. When Peter founded a community as a missionary, some of the original stories may have arisen in those communities but none have survived from the first century. Peter was one of the first disciples called by Jesus. Mark's first miracle takes place in the synagogue at Capernaum, and then they retired to Peter's house. There, we learned that Peter's mother-in-law was ill, so Jesus cured her. She then got up and cooked for them.

By the second century, Peter is now a widower (which kept him celibate). But we also learn that Peter had a daughter from his first marriage. She traveled everywhere with him and helped him with the mission. However, as she approached puberty, many men petitioned Peter for her hand in marriage. Peter was torn over what to do. He prayed to God (and/or Jesus) for guidance. His daughter was then struck with a thunderbolt and was crippled for life. This was understood as a divine miracle; no man wanted her after that. She could continue in her work with her father, as a virgin.

Simon Magus

Peter experienced many such "miracles" in his travels, but most of the "Acts of Peter" was devoted to the challenges between Simon Magus and Peter. Peter keeps running into Simon, everywhere he goes. From this story (and Irenaeus' version) we learn that Simon developed such hubris with his magic tricks that he began to claim that he was a "living god". Along the way he had picked up a follower he named Helen, whom he claimed was the reincarnation of Helen of Troy. Irenaeus said that he picked her up in a brothel in Lebanon.

By the time that Peter and Simon make it to Rome, Simon has finagled his way into being "a darling" of Nero's court and invited to perform his tricks at many state banquets. There are several stories of their "competitions" in Rome. The Roman crowds insist that Peter, like Simon, show them a "trick". Peter walked over to a stall where they were selling fish and "resurrected" the fish back to life. In another story, Simon at one point goes into hiding so as not to face Peter, but a stray dog finds him, "speaks" and "rats him out".

The ultimate contest ended with the hubris of Simon. He announced that everyone should meet him in the forum the next morning, when he would demonstrate that "he can fly". He built a sixty-foot tower. On top, he designed a crane that would be rigged with arms that were hidden under his cloak, so that down below it would seem that he could fly on his own. However, his sense of himself took over. When he got up there, he decided not to use the crane, and "flew". His body was smashed in the forum.

The Nero Traditions in the Acts of Peter

This is the text that detailed what happened to Peter during the (alleged) persecution by Nero. The Christian community in Rome urged Peter to leave, as his more important job was to preach the gospel. Fleeing Rome along the Appian Way, he encountered a vision of Jesus on his way to the city: *Quo vadis, Domine?* "Where are you going, Lord?" Jesus told him he had to go to Rome to "die again". Peter (feeling guilty) returned, was arrested, and then the famous story that he asked to be "crucified upside down", as he was not worthy to die the same way as Jesus. A site along the antique section of the Appian Way in Rome marks this event (see Figure IX.2).

Figure IX.2 Caravaggio's Crucifixion of Peter.

The Acts of Paul and Thecla

This was where the "Greek Romance Novel" was fully incorporated into a Christian tale. In Western Christianity, most people have never heard of Thecla, but she remains a cherished figure in Eastern Orthodoxy. This text became "a best-seller".

The story opens with our only physical description of Paul the Apostle: "middle-aged, short, bald, with a hooked nose, and bow-legged". This became and remains a popular way to portray Paul. Like the story of Mary and Joseph, this portrait emphasized that Thecla's attraction to Paul was not physical or sexual.

Thecla heard Paul preach and was converted. She wanted to become a follower of Paul, but (unfortunately) she was engaged to be married to the son of the local magistrate. But after hearing Paul, she admired his celibate life-style and so refused to get married. Thecla was then arrested, put on trial, convicted, and scheduled for execution (with her mother supporting the verdict). We must recognize the hyperbole here; there was no Roman law that condemned you to death if you refused to get married. In the narrative, this may be polemic or even satire against the marriage reforms laws that Augustus had instituted.

Thecla was sent to the arena and here we have a bit of a translation problem. In the known texts, she is condemned to jump into a tank of "man-eating seals". Perhaps a better understanding would be a Roman reference to "eels". Giant eels were bred in fish ponds by epicures. There was a famous story that when Augustus visited a client in Baiae (near Naples), a slave dropped and broke some of the glassware. The client, perhaps hoping to impress Augustus, had his guests watch as he had the slave thrown into the pond and eaten alive. Augustus was not impressed.

But before Thecla was thrown in, she jumped in herself, thereby as she stated later, "baptizing herself". Of course, they refuse to eat her. She was let go and moved on to another city, where the same problem occurred again (and everywhere she traveled). A local aristocrat falls in love, but she refuses to marry, continues to get convicted, faces other tortures, but always survives. Each time, the narrative contains long debates and speeches that highlight Christian teachings. Added to the story are sympathetic, upper-class Christian women (usually widows) who take her in and try to protect her.

An oddity in the story occurred with Thecla's efforts. We are told that she cut her hair and "dressed like a man" to follow Paul. However, Paul rejected her as a follower. This indicates that Christians condoned a cultural bias against "cross-dressing", or the merging of gender identities. Ultimately, Thecla escaped all her adventures and ended up living in a cave, where she became a Christian oracle, visited by many pilgrims seeking her advice. Although praised for her celibacy and chastity, one of the reasons that this story was not accepted as "canon" by the Western Church Fathers was most likely a reaction to the fact that, as a woman, and part of the laity, she baptized herself.

Apocalypses

The second century also produced additional "apocalypses". *The Apocalypse of Paul* only survives in a few fragments, but the **Apocalypse of Peter** is known from many ancient manuscripts. It is framed as a discourse of the risen Christ to Peter and the faithful, with first a vision of Heaven, and then Hell.

In Heaven, people have pure, milky white skin, curly hair, and are beautiful. They also wear shiny clothes, made of light, like the angels. Scenes of the reconstituted earth are there, with flowers and spices. Everyone spends their time singing hymns and praises to God.

In Hell we find the concept that "the punishment fits the crime". This idea may have been drawn from narratives concerning the "wicked" dead in the afterlife from Mesopotamia, Egypt, and some speeches in the book of Job.

Blasphemers are hung by their tongues. Women who adorn themselves for the purpose of adultery are hung by their hair over a bubbling mire. Male adulterers are hung by their "feet", (another euphemism) with their heads in the mire next to them. Murderers are restrained in a pit of "creeping things" that torment them. Men who take on the role of women in a sexual way, and lesbians, are driven up a great cliff by angels and are "cast off" to the bottom.

Women who have abortions are set in a lake formed from blood and gore, up to their necks. They are tormented by the unborn children who shoot flashes of fire into their eyes. The unborn are taken into the care of angels, who supervise their spiritual education. Those who charge too much interest on loans stand up to their knees in a lake of feces and blood. The idea is that all these punishments take place eternally; somehow the "tongues" grow back each night, etc.

How much did Dante know of this text when he wrote the *Inferno?* We do not really know, but he incorporated the same concept, that each sin results in a parallel and the appropriate punishment.

Summary

- Christians created legends and stories that provided more detail for the lives of the earliest Christians.
- Christians adapted contemporary literary styles and Greek Romance Novels to describe the adventures of the Apostles.

Suggestions for Further Reading

Ehrman, Bart D. 2005. *Lost Scriptures: Books that Did Not Make It into the New Testament*. Oxford University Press. Ehrman discusses this literature in the context of the various communities that may have produced them.

Russell, Noah and Williams, Anthony. 2018. *The Complete Apochrypha of Forgotten and Removed Scriptures*. Convent Press. For the primary documents, this is an anthology of Christian literature from this period.

INSTITUTIONAL DEVELOPMENT
BISHOPS AND THEIR AUTHORITY

X

- Elders and Bishops
- The Election of Bishops
- Deacons
- A Change in Leadership
- Candidates and Elections
- The Theology of Hierarchy and Election
- The "Absolution of Sin" (Penance)
- The Ritual of Penance
- The Power of the Bishop
- Excommunication
- Who Decides?
- The Liturgy
- The Holidays/Holy Days
- Theological Heights of One Bishop
- The First Christian Systematic Theology
- The Impact of the *Peri Archon*

Varieties of Early Christianity: The Formation of the Western Christian Tradition,
First Edition. Rebecca I. Denova.
© 2023 John Wiley & Sons, Inc. Published 2023 by John Wiley & Sons, Inc.

After reading this chapter you will be able to:

- Trace the institutionalization of Christianity and hierarchy of the clergy by the second century.
- Explore the obligations and duties of Bishops in relation to their congregations.

Elders and Bishops

The Greek term, *presbyteros*, meant "elder", or "senior". It had long been used in Jewish synagogue communities as an honorific title for older men as "sages", proficient in expounding the Law of Moses. Presbyter became a title for Christian clergy as a whole. *Episkopos* "overseer", (our term, episcopal) was the designation of an administrative official in the Eastern Roman provinces who oversaw a small section known as a **diocese**. The English translation became **bishop**. In some of the early Christian literature, "elder" and "bishop" are applied interchangeability and sometimes for the same individual. An easier way to approach the ideas is to assume that many "elders" were subsequently made bishops.

The earliest Christian communities apparently borrowed the dominant civic structure, where free citizens voted for various levels of magistrates who had different levels of administrative duties. Our earliest source for the office of bishop is found in 1 Timothy. This is one of the letters we deem "deutero-Paul", where the writer pretends to be Paul the Apostle. The others are 2 Timothy and Titus, and later deemed **The Pastorals**, as they show interest in issues that would concern a "pastor". Written perhaps by disciples of Paul (with a range of dates from the 80's to the end of the first century), the interest in hierarchy is understood by modern scholars not to be of interest to Paul. Paul did appoint "fellowworkers", but for the interim before the coming "kingdom" only; Paul saw himself and his Christians as the last of the "old generation".

The Election of Bishops

Here is a trustworthy saying: Whoever aspires to be an overseer (bishop) desires a noble task. Now the overseer is to be above reproach, faithful to his wife, temperate, self-controlled, respectable, hospitable, able to teach, not given to drunkenness, not violent but gentle, not quarrelsome, not a lover of money. He must manage his own family well and see that his children obey him, and he must do so in a manner worthy of full respect. He must not be a recent convert, or he may become conceited and fall under the same judgment as the Devil. He must also have a good reputation with outsiders, so that he will not fall into disgrace and into the Devil's trap.

(1 Timothy 3)

Note the similarity of Greco-Roman cultural traditions of the father as the head of household with responsibility over his family. The recognized cultural aspects of both private and public "honor/shame" apply in the selection of a bishop. The bishop should have a good and noble reputation not just in the Christian community, but in the larger city as well.

Deacons

The concept of a deacon was derived from the story of the election of deacons in the Acts of the Apostles. Deacons were to take care of every-day, practical matters, the distribution of charity (food and clothing) and setting up the shared meals and the cleaning-up afterwards.

> In the same way, deacons are to be worthy of respect, sincere, not indulging in much wine, and not pursuing dishonest gain. They must keep hold of the deep truths of the faith with a clear conscience. They must first be tested; and then if there is nothing against them, let them serve as deacons. In the same way, the women are to be worthy of respect, not malicious talkers but temperate and trustworthy in everything. A deacon must be faithful to his wife and must manage his children and his household well. Those who have served well gain an excellent standing and great assurance in their faith in Christ Jesus.
>
> (1 Timothy 3:8–12)

"In the same way, the women ..." indicates that women deacons were were elected in the earliest communities. (Recall that ca. 110, Pliny the Younger tortured two slave deaconesses.)

The Bishop became the head of each community with the office of deacon eventually transferred to the title "priest". As such, the deacon/priests later became the **clergy**, in their roles of aiding and serving the bishop. The word, clergy, derived from an Anglo-French term for the "learned". By the Middle Ages Christian clergy were the only educated class. However, in the earlier centuries, the clergy were not distinguished by educational levels, but designated as such as "inheritors" of the correct teaching (as earlier Temple priests in Jerusalem had inherited the traditions).

A Change in Leadership

Paul had included women apostles, disciples, prophetesses, and teachers. This was most likely because of his concept of a transformed universe, when social and status conventions would be transformed at "the coming of Christ". Paul had admonished widows not to remarry because of this. By the end of the first century however, problems concerning women had apparently risen in some communities.

Recall the importance of procreation for the role of women. There was social pressure for widows to remarry, supported by the Augustan legislation. Some historians speculate that one of the reasons for the increase of Christians was that Christianity promoted an ideal that for the first time, provided women with an alternative to this social pressure. We can speculate that in the earliest communities, women may have flocked to join. Where did they live? Most likely in the house or villa of the bishop. Apparently, this presence of widows created scandal. We now have "rules" for the admission of widows:

> Give proper recognition to those widows who are really in need. But if a widow has children or grandchildren, these should learn first of all to put their religion into practice by caring for their own family and so repaying their parents and grandparents, for this is pleasing to God. The widow who is really in need and left all alone puts her hope in God and continues night and day to pray and to ask God for help. But the widow who lives for pleasure is dead even while she lives. Give the people these instructions, so that no one may be open to blame. Anyone who does not provide for their relatives, and especially for their own household, has denied the faith and is worse than an unbeliever. No widow may be put on the list of widows unless she is over sixty, has been faithful to her husband, and is well known for her good deeds, such as bringing up children, showing hospitality, washing the feet of the Lord's people, helping those in trouble and devoting herself to all kinds of good deeds.
>
> As for younger widows, do not put them on such a list. For when their sensual desires overcome their dedication to Christ, they want to marry. Thus they bring judgment on themselves, because they have broken their first pledge. Besides, they get into the habit of being idle and going about from house to house. And not only do they become idlers, but also busybodies who talk nonsense, saying things they ought not to. So I counsel younger widows to marry, to have children, to manage their homes and to give the enemy no opportunity for slander. Some have in fact already turned away to follow Satan. If any woman who is a believer has widows in her care, she should continue to help them and not let the church be burdened with them, so that the church can help those widows who are really in need... .
>
> (1 Timothy 5:8–3)

> A woman should learn in quietness and full submission. *I do not permit a woman to teach or to assume authority over a man; she must be quiet.* For Adam was formed first, then Eve. And Adam was not the one deceived; it was the woman who was deceived and became a sinner. But women will be saved through childbearing—if they continue in faith, love and holiness with propriety.
>
> (1 Timothy 2:11–15)

By the second century, Christian men (absorbing the dominant cultural view of women) greatly diminished leadership roles for women. However, we have evidence that it was Christian women (known as "bone-gatherers") who rescued the remains of Christian martyrs for burial in the catacombs. Some of their tomb portraits have them holding scrolls or books, indicating a "teaching" role. We also have several writings by Church leaders denouncing women who continued to take on roles as leaders.

Candidates and Elections

We cannot determine exactly how the first "election" was carried out, but from the evidence of later literature, it became a standard process. Once there were established bishops, neighboring bishops would attend the election. Several men would be nominated as candidates (or nominate themselves). The congregation did not vote by ballot, but by popular acclaim—literally shouting out the names. The one who received the loudest acclamation was deemed the winner. The assumption was that the "holy spirit" had motivated the crowd, so that the winner was assumed to be selected by God.

However, it was not always a perfect process. If the crowd did not agree with the winner acknowledged by the other bishops, the people sometimes went out and "found their own". Ambrose, Bishop of Milan in the 380's was not even a Christian when they took him in; they had to baptize him first. In continuing debates over Christian doctrine, bishops often referred to "illegal" elections as a polemical denunciation of an oppositional bishop.

The Theology of Hierarchy and Election

Several factors were combined in the institution of bishops and the clergy. As usual, the gospels and Acts were gleaned for "proof-texts" to validate the process. The story of Pentecost (Acts 2) became the basis for the claim that when the original Apostles experienced the descent of "the spirit" upon them, they were imbued with this divine gift that could be passed on to other missionaries and the congregations. It was fundamental in the ritual of baptism, where the ritual conveyed "the spirit" to the believer.

Acts 8:14–17 related the story of Philip, another missionary, who went to Samaria. Many of the Samaritans "believed" and were cured, but Philip was not quite successful; they had not "received the spirit" (in a physical manifestation) when they were baptized: "When the Apostles in Jerusalem heard that Samaria had accepted the word of God, they sent Peter and John to Samaria. When they arrived, they prayed for the new believers there that they might receive the Holy Spirit because the Holy Spirit had not yet come on any of them; they had simply been baptized in the name of the Lord Jesus. Then Peter and John placed their hands on them, and they received the Holy Spirit".

This "laying on of hands" was a ritual at the Temple in Jerusalem. Only God could forgive sins, but the priests facilitated the process in the sacrificial rituals. Railings separated the sacred zones in the Temple (which later became the "communion rail" in Christian churches). The penitent brought his sacrificial animal to the rail and handed it over to a priest. The priest "laid his hands" on the head of the animal. This transferred the "sin" from the man to the animal, and that is why the animal had to die.

Using this first story with Peter and John, we have the evolution of another Christian ritual, that of the **ordination** of bishops and clergy. The claim was made that Peter's "laying on of hands" literally passed to the men that he had appointed as elders in his several communities. It passed through the Elders to imbue all elected clergy, almost as a spiritual, electric circuit that was passed on through the decades. Another passage from the gospel of John was utilized to support this claim: "'As the Father has sent me, I am sending you.' And with that he breathed on them and said, 'Receive the holy spirit. If you forgive anyone's sins, their sins are forgiven; if you do not forgive them, they are not forgiven'" (John 20:21–23). This elevated ordination with "sacredness", which simultaneously elevated the clergy above the congregation.

Peter's ability not only to pass on "the spirit" through himself, was combined with a passage originally in Mark but expanded in Matthew. In Mark, when Jesus asked the disciples, "'Who do men say that I am?' They replied, 'Some say John the Baptist; others say Elijah; and still others, one of the Prophets'. 'But what about you?' he asked. Peter answered, 'You are the Messiah'. Jesus warned them not to tell anyone about him" (Mark 8:27–30).

Matthew added a much longer response by Jesus to Peter: Jesus replied, "'Blessed are you, Simon son of Jonah, for this was not revealed to you by flesh and blood, but by my Father in heaven. And I tell you that you are Peter ("rock") and on this rock I will build my church, and the gates of Hades will not overcome it. I will give you the keys of the kingdom of heaven; whatever you bind on earth will be bound in heaven, and whatever you loose on earth will be loosed in heaven'" (Matthew 16:16–20).

"Bind and loosing" was a Scriptural term related to sages, designating who had authority "to forbid or to permit". If you have ever seen images (mostly cartoons) of St. Peter standing at the "gates of heaven", this is the source. The basis for ordination was the claim that Christ appointed Peter, who became Bishop of Rome, who then appointed others. When the institution of the Vatican emerged in the fifth century, this argument became the "primacy of Peter" combined now in the office of "pope". The Pope in Rome continues to share the office of the Bishop of Rome. If you have ever visited the complex of the Vatican, you will have noticed sculptural iconography on the walls of "crossed keys" (see Figure X.1, the "Crossed Keys" of Vatican City).

Figure X.1 Crossed keys. durantelallera / Adobe Stock.

Institutional Development   211

The "Absolution of Sin" (Penance)

The ability of Bishops to "forgive sins on earth" (not waiting for judgment after death) was a shared conviction by the second century. However, it is difficult to determine exactly when or where this began as there is scant literature that fully discussed it. What we find is the mention of it in various early texts where it is assumed that the audience understood it:

1. The *Didache*. This was a first century teaching manual (perhaps the first "catechism") that discussed the proper way to participate in the rituals: "Confess your sins in church, and do not go up to your prayer with an evil conscience. This is the way of life ... On the Lord's Day gather together, break bread, and give thanks, after confessing your transgressions so that your sacrifice may be pure" (*Didache* 4:14, 14:1).

2. The **Letter of Barnabas** (allegedly written by a companion of Paul): "You shall confess your sins. You shall not go to prayer with an evil conscience. This is the way of light" (*Barnabas* 19).

3. **Ignatius of Antioch**: "For as many as are of God and of Jesus Christ are also with the bishop. And as many as shall, in the exercise of penance, return into the unity of the Church, these, too, shall belong to God, that they may live according to Jesus Christ" (*Letter to the Philadelphians* 3). "For where there is division and wrath, God does not dwell. To all them that repent, the Lord grants forgiveness, if they turn in penitence to the unity of God, and to communion with the bishop" (*Letter to the Philadelphians* 8).

4. **Hippolytus** (a Bishop of Rome): "The bishop conducting the ordination of the new bishop shall pray, 'God and Father of our Lord Jesus Christ ... Pour forth now that power which comes from you, from your royal Spirit, which you gave to your beloved Son, Jesus Christ, and which he bestowed upon his holy apostles ... and grant this your servant, whom you have chosen for the episcopate, (the power) to feed your holy flock and to serve without blame as your high priest, ministering night and day to propitiate unceasingly before your face and to offer to you the gifts of your holy Church, and by the spirit of the high priesthood to have the authority to forgive sins, in accord with your command'" (*Apostolic Tradition* 3).

5. **Origen** (3rd century bishop): "[A final method of forgiveness], albeit hard and laborious [is] the remission of sins through penance, when the sinner ... does not shrink from declaring his sin to a priest of the Lord and from seeking medicine, after the manner of him who say, 'I said, "To the Lord I will accuse myself of my iniquity"'" (*Homilies on Leviticus* 2:4).

6. **Cyprian of Carthage**: "Of how much greater faith and salutary fear are they who ... confess their sins to the priests of God in a straightforward manner and in sorrow, making an open declaration of conscience ... I beseech you, brethren, let everyone who has sinned confess his sin while he is still in this world, while his confession is still admissible, while the satisfaction and remission made through the priests are still pleasing before the Lord" (*The Lapsed*, 28).

Cyprian added another concept that became a later element in the liturgy of "the Mass;" "The apostle [Paul] likewise bears witness and says: '... Whoever eats the bread or drinks the cup of the Lord unworthily will be guilty of the body and blood of the Lord' (1 Cor. 11:27). But [the impenitent] spurn and despise all these warnings; before their sins are expiated, before they have made a confession of their crime, before their conscience has been purged in the ceremony and at the hand of the priest ... they do violence to [the Lord's] body and blood, and with their hands and mouth they sin against the Lord more than when they denied him" (15:1–3). Penance became required before a participant could receive communion.

The Ritual of Penance

When the first Christians met in houses (most likely in the larger atrium or entrance way in a house) Christians all stood. The bishop however, had permission to sit in a chair. Any announcements or proclamations were given "from the chair", *ex-cathedra*, which became **cathedral**. In every town or city, the church of the bishop is denoted as the "Cathedral". The early emergence of what became the Catholic liturgy of "the Mass" derives from the weekly "assembly" of congregants on Sunday.

Christians required a three-year initiation period for converts. (Scholars speculate that the concept of an initiation was borrowed from the Mysteries.) After the opening greetings and ceremonies, anyone who was not yet baptized or who had not undergone penance were not permitted to remain. The bishop declared, *ita missa est* "you are dismissed". Hence, the term, "Mass" became the generic term for the full assembly of the baptized and penitent.

The ritual of penance was public on the premise that "all sin is sin not only against God but against our neighbor, against the community". Members of the congregation lay face-down on the floor before the Bishop's chair, and openly confessed their sins. In the early literature, we have some interesting complaints about this process. From Irenaeus: "[The Gnostic disciples of Marcion] have deluded many women ... Some of these women make a public confession, but others are ashamed to do this, and in silence, as if withdrawing from themselves the hope of the life of God, they either apostatize entirely or hesitate between the two courses" (*Against Heresies* 1:22). From Tertullian: "(Regarding confession, some) flee from this work as being an exposure of themselves, or they put it off from day to day. I presume they are more mindful of modesty than of salvation, like those who contract a disease in the more shameful parts of the body and shun making themselves known to the physicians; and thus, they perish along with their own bashfulness" (*Repentance* 10:1).

When Tertullian denounced the dress and jewels of women, he complained that women dressed like this to attend the assemblies to show off and find a rich husband (On the *Apparel of Women*). Apparently, "penitent Sundays" were more popular than regular ones. Then as now, people were overly-curious about the lives of the "rich and famous", and their sins became a topic of gossip. (In the later Middle Ages, the wealthy began hiring and housing "private" priests to hear their confessions in their castles.)

The Power of the Bishop

Bishops may or may not have been as overly-curious as everyone else, but the position of bishop was a powerful one because of the conviction that the bishop had an additional burden of being responsible for all the souls in his community. "The souls of his flock" were not only important in the here and now, but crucially important for the afterlife, and the "final judgment". When the bishop died, his elevation to heaven would be determined by how well he cared for the souls of his Christians.

Overseeing the congregation from birth to death (from "cradle to grave"), we have the eventual establishment of the **Sacraments**. The sacraments became embedded in the Western tradition that became the Catholic Church (see Box X.1).

Box X.1   The sacraments of the Catholic Church

There are seven official sacraments in Catholicism that mirror the concept of "rites of passage", or stages in human life. What distinguishes a "sacrament" from other rituals is the claim that in these seven, "the spirit" literally descends and is a vital presence in the ceremony.

1. Birth/Baptism. The earliest communities practiced adult baptism as the completion of an adherent's initiation. It was only in the third and fourth centuries (increased wars but also higher rates of infant mortality) that the practice of baptizing babies was introduced. Ancient Rome had a ritual of presenting a newborn to the father; the father had to acknowledge it as his, pick it up, and give it his name. Later Christians adopted this concept into that of "Christening", giving the baby a "Christian name" to indicate identity and loyalty to their religion. Many modern Christians combine the two, utilizing baptism as a Christening ceremony at the same time.
2. The Eucharist or Communion. We cannot determine when and where the "meeting in Jesus" name to replicate the "Last Supper" began, but they were doing it in Paul's community of Corinth in the 50's and 60's. Paul had castigated the Corinthians for their lack of respect and charity at "the Lord's Supper"; the rich were not sharing their food with the poor and some were getting drunk (1 Corinthians 11–27). Paul said that such behavior resulted in some of them becoming ill and dying. When Cyprian railed against those not doing proper penance before the eucharist, he quoted Paul: "'Whosoever shall eat the bread and drink the cup of the Lord unworthily, shall be guilty of the body and blood of the Lord'" (*Letters* 9:2).

    In the twelfth century, this became introduced into the Catholic canon as the concept of "transubstantiation". Transubstantiation is the belief that, through the "spirit" embedded in Catholic priests, every time this ritual is performed, the "bread and wine" miraculously turn into the literal "body and blood" of Christ (presentational). When Martin Luther denounced so many rituals of the Catholic Church, he claimed that this ritual should only be understood as symbolic (representational).

3. Penance. (See the evolution of the ritual of penance, above.) In modern Catholicism this is termed "reconciliation". In Catholic churches, many now perform this ritual "face-to-face".
4. Confirmation. One of the later official sacraments, this ritual mirrored ancient puberty rites, or when youth were ready to take their place as adults.
5. Marriage. Again, locating the first understanding of the marriage rite as a sacrament is difficult to locate. Several scriptural elements were combed for sources: Jesus' quote in the gospels that it was God who joined man and woman in Eden; Paul's urging that married couples should stay married, but widows should not remarry (because of the "impending crisis"); John's story of "the wedding in Cana" that condoned "marriage"; and the Church Fathers preaching against any other kind of sexual union as sin.

    It is a misunderstanding that the modern Catholic Church does not allow for divorce. Divorce is permitted, but the issue is re-marriage. Only a Catholic tribunal can provide an "annulment" of the original marriage sacrament to permit re-marriage. An "annulment" is a determination of something that was remiss in the original ceremony.
6. Ordination of the clergy. (See above.)
7. "Last Rites" (Death-bed rituals). This ritual was for those who were on the point of death. It mirrored the ancient concept of funeral rituals, where steps were taken to ensure that the passage to the eventual afterlife would be successful. The modern term is "anointing of the sick", which is done to effect successful healing. The "anointing" is conducted with holy oil and applied to the five senses. With no cure or alleviation, the final element is to prepare the person and the soul for death.

Excommunication

An important development in the literature of the Church Fathers was another instrument of authority for the bishops, that of **excommunication**. Hundreds of letters among and between Bishops discuss who should be excommunicated, for which sins, and the duration of the punishment.

The early concept came from Paul when he was appalled that a man in the community was "living with his father's wife" (step-mother), in 1 Corinthians 5:

> It is actually reported that there is sexual immorality among you, and of a kind that even pagans do not tolerate: A man is sleeping with his father's wife. And you are proud! Shouldn't you rather have gone into mourning and have put out of your fellowship the man who has been doing this? For my part, even though I am not physically present, I am with you in spirit. As one who is present with you in this way, I have already passed judgment in the name of our Lord Jesus on the one who has been doing this. So, when you are assembled, and I am with you in spirit, and the power of our Lord Jesus is present, hand this man over to Satan for the destruction of the flesh, so that his spirit may be saved on the day of the Lord.

This was followed by Paul's passage about not permitting the leaven (yeast) to infect the whole community. As Christians were to be the "righteous remnant" of the "final days", the community had to remain pure. The "expelling" of this individual, "excommunication" was then applied to the idea that "sinners" could not participate or now receive any of the sacraments.

What became the center of debate among bishops were the details: (1) which sins qualified for excommunication?; (2) depending upon the sin, was the excommunication extended from this world to the next?—were they condemned to Hell?; (3) for every-day sins, how long did the banishment last?; (4) how to help a penitent "re-enter" the community of the faithful?; (5) were there sins for which reentry should be eternally denied?

They debated whether or not the now Ten Commandments should be the guide (where it was understood that no ritual could ultimately atone for these sins). Most agreed on no atonement for murder, but "lying, theft, and adultery" were debated. What if "lying" were forced on someone because of the persecutions? What if you stole to feed your children? Equating "adultery" now with "prostitution", some bishops pointed out that "Christ himself forgave prostitutes".

Once someone was declared "excommunicate", this is when we had the creation of "public penitence". The traditional Scriptural elements of "ashes and sackcloth" were utilized in public parades and humiliation of the offenders. The excommunicates could attend the weekly assembly but had to stay in the back with their sackcloth and sometimes bound in chains. They had to leave before the ritual of communion with the rest of the unbaptized. Disagreements arose over how long this should last and how to judge the "true signs of repentence".

Once the liturgy of Easter week was established, penitents waited until the Thursday evening ritual of the "last supper" to be readmitted. But how many times should one "forgive?" Some communities condoned a "second baptism" before a penitent could be readmitted. In the next several decades, debates concerning a second baptism resulted in many Christians delaying baptism until their death-bed.

As we saw in Chapter IV on Martyrdom, schisms arose over the fact that some Bishops had either committed idolatry in a period of persecution or had "handed-over" their scriptures during the reign of Diocletian. The problem of a "lapsed" Bishop was directly tied to their elevated status and the "sacredness" of their office in the communities. If a Bishop lapsed, did all of his baptisms, absolutions of penance, marriages, and "last rites" have to be done again? How to save the souls of dead Christians in the afterlife who had the rites administered by a lapsed Bishop?

Who Decides?

With so many different Christian communities in the Empire, there was yet was no official, central authority to determine Empire-wide adherence and ritual practice. We have such an abundance of literature in this period on the topic because (as everyone did) bishops communicated with each through letter-writing. The style of ancient letter-writing opened with a greeting for the recipients, followed by the topic, and then ended with another greeting. This is the form that Paul used for his letters.

Many of the letters among Bishops opened with non-too-subtle hints that argued their claim for authority over other bishops. Clément's first letter to the Corinthians pointed out that it came from the "eternal city", and he emphasized that it was the site of the martyrdoms of Peter and Paul. Bishops in Jerusalem, Damascus, Antioch, Alexandria and other Eastern cities did the same, including details of why their views should dominate on any given topic. For example, the Jerusalem churches always cited that this was where Jesus had suffered his "passion"; Antioch always quoted Luke, that believers were first called "Christians" in their city.

The Liturgy

Liturgy is a form in which public religious worship is conducted. Liturgy was not a Christian invention; Jews and Gentiles had structures and dictates for the details of their worship. Jewish synagogues arose after the destruction of the first Temple by Babylon in 587 BCE. Those Jews who lived outside of the homeland, the Diaspora and more than a day's journey to Jerusalem, built synagogues as their community centers. Due to the scarcity of literature from Diaspora Jews, we know very little about the liturgy in the early synagogues. In fact, our earliest evidence is found in the gospel in Luke 4:16: "(Jesus) went to Nazareth, where he had been brought up, and on the Sabbath day he went into the synagogue, as was his custom. He stood up to read, and the scroll of the Prophet Isaiah was handed to him. Unrolling it, he found the place where it is written …".

Historians speculate that the liturgy of the synagogue included readings from the Scriptures, the Prophets, and then opportunities for "sages" to stand up and preach on the topics. The conclusion is reached that early Christians adopted this method in their weekly meetings and remains the "order" of Christian liturgy: a first reading from the "Old Testament", or a book of a Prophet, followed by an exposition of a Psalm or the "wisdom" books. After these two readings, a hymn of praise. The final reading is a selection from one of the gospels, followed by a sermon.

The Holidays/Holy Days

The second and third centuries saw a debate throughout the Empire known as the Quartodeciman Controversy. This was a debate over when churches should re-enact and celebrate the resurrection of Christ (Easter Sunday). Aligned with the events of Jesus during his last Passover in Jerusalem, many of the Eastern communities began literally following the Jewish Calendar for Passover each year. They claimed that Easter should be celebrated as the Jews did, on the 14th day of the Jewish month of Nisan. Jews utilized a lunar calendar, which meant that it fell on different times and different days during the Spring. (Others by this time were adapting to the solar calendar instituted by Julius Caesar which he had learned in Egypt.)

Some communities also began observing it on or around March 25 in relation to the Spring equinox. The cult of *Sol Invictus* was well established, and other native cults also celebrated the re-emergence of the sun. Thus, there was no conformity in the celebration and Christian communities were threatening to excommunicate each other over the date. **Synods** (church meetings) were called to resolve the issue. There were many arguments that Christians should no longer be held to compliance with Jewish traditions. Others argued that, despite when the events began (the "passion narrative") it had to end on a Sunday, as this was the glorious day of resurrection.

Have you ever wondered why Easter never falls on the same date every spring? **Bishop Victor I** (later deemed an early Pope) led the Roman church from 189–199. He made the determination that the Western churches should follow his lead in Rome. His communities celebrated Easter on the first Sunday after the first full moon of the Spring equinox. Eastern communities continued with variations. When Eastern Orthodox churches officially split with the Western churches in 1053, Orthodox Christians began following a separate calendar (the differences between the Julian and Gregorian calendars).

In the next few centuries more and more "holy days" were added and combined with incidents in the life of Jesus or his ministry. For example, January 6 became "Epiphany Sunday", claiming that this was the day that the Magi arrived in Bethlehem and declared the manifestation of "God in this child". But many Eastern churches also marked this date for the baptism of Jesus. After the rise of Christian monasticism and the "cult of the Saints", Christian martyrs were added with "feast days" in the calendar (see Chapter XII).

Tradition claims that it was Constantine I, after his conversion, who determined the celebration of **Christmas**. It was officially proposed for Rome in 336, although the evidence for an Empire-wide mandate is sparse. Rome had an age-old celebration of **Saturnalia** (December 17–24), a week-long event that combined the darkness of the Winter solstice with the expectation that "the sun", and all crops "would arise again in the New Year (January)". Many in Rome were participants of the cult of Mithras (a sun god) and celebrated his birth on December 25. It is from the traditions associated with Saturnalia that Christmas obtained many of its current elements (and then added some Celtic traditions in the conversion of Europe).

In anticipation of the coming restoration of fertility, pine branches were hung in the Temples and homes. Family celebrations were at the center of the festival, with attempts at reconciliation of family scandals or feuds. A "king" was selected in each family (usually a child) who had the authority to make people play silly games and take on humiliating (but funny) duties. Social conventions were relaxed. On the final night of Saturnalia, slaves were granted temporary freedom, and were served a banquet by the members of the family.

As an end of the year celebration, Saturnalia was the time to fulfill one's social obligations for patronage and help during the year. This was done through the exchange of gifts. Doctors and lawyers in Rome were forbidden to charge fees. But you showed your appreciation through gifts at Saturnalia. For most of Rome's poor, the cheapest gifts were candles. After the final dinner, Romans met in the forum for a "candlelight vigil".

Theological Heights of One Bishop

Not all bishops spent their time arguing the specific details of the differences over ritual practices and days. Many articulated what were considered "treatises" on a reflection of a theological concept or trying to explain the more esoteric nature of "the universe" to believers. One such Bishop, **Origen of Alexandria** (184–253) was a prolific Christian scholar, ascetic, and theologian. His writings included textual criticism, Biblical exegesis and hermeneutics (the science of literary interpretation), commentaries, and homilies. Origen is a good source for identifying which texts were in circulation and taught that ultimately made it into the New Testament.

In an earlier persecution in Alexandria, Origen's father was martyred, and he sought out martyrdom as well. (There is a legend that his mother hid his clothes so that he did not achieve this goal.) He studied at the catechetical school in Alexandria and was known as a vegetarian and a non-drinker. He traveled to Rome, studying under Hippolytus and was impressed by his teachings on *logos*. In 214, the governor of Arabia sent for him so that he could "learn more about Christianity" from this intellectual. The Roman philosopher Porphyry traveled to Caesarea for his lectures, although Porphyry accused him of "distorting Greek philosophy" for Christian interests.

Origen became ordained as a presbyter in 231 by the bishop of Caesarea while traveling through Palestine. Back home in Alexandria, Bishop Demetrius accused Origen of insubordination and accused him of self-castration in his ascetic ideals. This accusation cannot be historically verified because Origen never wrote about self-castration nor mentioned it in his commentary on Matthew 19 (a passage praising "eunuchs for the sake of the kingdom").

At Caesarea Origen founded his own school, teaching logic, cosmology, and natural history as well as Christian theology. Many future bishops of the East studied with him there, ultimately sharing his views with what became Orthodox communities. Among his followers were Athanasius of Alexandria and the Cappadocian Fathers of Eastern Orthodoxy (Basil and the Gregories). While traveling in Jericho (near the Dead Sea), allegedly Origen bought or discovered "in a jar", an ancient manuscript of the Hebrew Scriptures.

At Caesarea he produced his *Contra Celsus*, a response to the original critical work of Celsus. Another a major work in this period was what is known as the *Hexapla*. Promoted as the "first critical edition of the Hebrew Bible", this was a six-paneled text that contained Hebrew followed by a transliteration of the Hebrew letters into Greek, followed by the five variations of Greek texts (beginning with the Septuagint).

The First Christian Systematic Theology

Origen's most famous work was *Peri Archon*, "On First Principles". Most of it only survives in a Latin translation by an admirer, Tyrannius Rufus in 397, and we can only speculate whether Rufus added his own thoughts. It presumes a knowledge of Plato's universe (see Chapter V), but with the Christian understanding of how the system emerged and continues to influence believers. It is "systematic" in the sense that it explains the origin of souls and Christ, how evil got into the world, and how to overcome evil to obtain reunification with God.

1. "In the beginning …". God ("the highest good" of philosophers) existed alone.
2. God then emanated the souls. Their job was to worship and praise God.
3. When God emanated the souls, he gave them "free will".
4. Utilizing their free will, one day some of the souls began to "turn away", to look see what was out there, as it were. Doing so, some began to "cool and fall away".
5. As the souls began to fall, God in his compassion and mercy created "bodies" to protect them on their journey. This resulted in the creation of the physical universe and matter.
6. Some souls fell only a short distance and became the angels, others became the stars. Others fell further and became human beings. One soul fell the furthest from God, who became the Devil. Over time, many of the souls "forgot" their origin and purpose.
7. One soul remained loyal. This was Christ (the *logos*). Christ, of his own volition decided to "descend", to reawaken the souls and show them how to reunite with God. For Origen, this was the moment of "salvation" (not the "cross").
8. Because souls have free will, at any time they can choose to turn back to God. This could be done many times, "choosing" and then "forgetting" on a scale of different forms. In this sense it mirrors concepts of reincarnation.
9. At some time in the future, all of the souls would eventually find their way home, even the Devil. This was Origen's concept of traditional eschatology. God continued to emanate souls and the "kingdom" could be realized in the life of believers. Ultimately there would be a universal reunification of all God's creation.

Origen's view of beginnings and the place of souls in the universe was vastly different from what was being taught in the "mainstream" churches. As we saw, the Church Fathers emphasized that it was the "sins of the body and society" that led people to commit evil. For Origen, evil arises from individual, free will choice. One's place in the universe is one's own responsibility. In other words, do not blame the Devil, demons, others ("heretics") for your lot in life. You have the freedom to "turn back" at any time and be restored.

The Impact of the *Peri Archon*

I have taken the time to explain Origen's teaching because in the next chapters we are going to continually encounter his views in the major Christian debates of the next few centuries. His teaching provided the groundwork for the debate over Arianism concerning the "Trinity" at Nicaea in 325. Augustine later refuted it in the doctrine of Original Sin, and upended Origen's theory of "free will" (see Chapter XIII).

Modern Christians have never heard of or learned about Origen. At the Second Council of Constantinople in 553, his views were declared *anathema* (heresy). Two of the major reasons for this declaration were: (1) the creation of Christ as a soul made him subordinate to God (not equal); and (2) his conviction that even the Devil could turn back and be saved.

During the Decian persecution in 251, he was arrested and tortured in prison and later died of the abuse. However, in 1993 Pope John Paul II "reinstated" him and removed the ban of heresy.

Summary

- The institutionalization of Christianity as a religion with its own hierarchy began in the second century and evolved through the fourth century.
- The status, duties and obligations of Bishops were deemed "sacred", and thus the controllers of what became the sacraments.

Suggestions for Further Reading

Stewart, Alistair C. 2014. *The Original Bishops: Office and Order in the First Christian Communities*. Baker Academic. This texts attempts to distinguish differences of nuance between elders, presbyters, and eventual bishops as figures of authority.

Sullivan, Francis A. 2001. *From Apostles to Bishops: The Development of the Episcopacy in the Early Church*. The Newman Press. Sullivan traces the development of Christian understandings of the office and the responsibilities of Bishops.

THE CONVERSION OF THE ROMAN EMPIRE
CONSTANTINE AND NICAEA

The Battle of the Milvian Bridge (312)

The Edict of Milan (313)

Why Did Constantine Convert?

Constantinople

The Donatist Schism over the Persecution of Christians in Diocletian's Reign

Helena

Christian Art and Architecture

The Council of Nicea and the Trinity

Early Formulas

Alternate Views

Arius and Arianism (Nicaea)

The Doctrine of the Trinity

The Nicene Creed

The Original Nicene Creed

The New Testament

Varieties of Early Christianity: The Formation of the Western Christian Tradition,
First Edition. Rebecca I. Denova.
© 2023 John Wiley & Sons, Inc. Published 2023 by John Wiley & Sons, Inc.

222 The Conversion of the Roman Empire

The Immediate Aftermath of Nicaea

The Impact of the Trinity and the Creed

Julian the Apostate

Emperor Theodosius I (347–395)

Edict of Theodosius I (381)

What about the Jews?

After reading this chapter you will be able to:

- Trace the evolution of Christianity from a Roman cult to the only legal religion in the Empire.
- Explore the debates that gave rise to the concept of the "Trinity" and the Nicene Creed.
- Appreciate the Christian concept of relations between "Church and State".

As we saw in Chapter IV (Martyrdom), the Roman Empire experienced various crises between 250 and 300 CE. In the latter part of the third century, Emperor Diocletian was able to stabilize rule and divided the Empire into West and East through a **Tetrarchy** which appointed Caesars and Augustii in both the East and West.

Constantius was Caesar of the Western Empire. He was a participant in the cult of *Sol Invictus*. Although sources vary on the date of his birth (either 272 or 285), his son **Constantine** was born at Naissus (Serbia), to one of Constantius' wives, Helena. Because of his father's position, Constantine spent most of his early life at the Imperial court or in military duty with his father's legions. He was praised for his military skills and his loyalty to the Empire in wanting to keep it unified, assets he later put to use.

Constantine was with his father during a raid on the Picts in York, England when his father was killed in battle. The troops in the field proclaimed Constantine *imperator*. While fighting the Franks, he restored some church property that had been confiscated at Trier (Germany). With the death of Diocletian, challenges for the throne continued in both the East and the West. **Maxentius** was in charge in Rome. He had angered the people with tax increases, and a series of riots were put down with the massacre of several thousands. Watching the deterioration and seeing his chance, Constantine crossed the Alps and invaded Italy.

The Battle of the Milvian Bridge (312)

The forces of Maxentius and Constantine met at a bridge in a northern suburb of Rome. This is the site of his famous conversion. We have two written sources for the event where the details are slightly different and were written years after the event. Lactantius was the tutor for Constantine's son. He said that the event took place in Gaul, before the journey to Rome. Constantine (as well as the army) saw a "great cross in the sky". Beneath it were the words, *en toutoi nika*, "In this sign, conquer". Bishop Eusebius (who later wrote a biography of Constantine) said that he and his army experienced the vision the night before the battle of the Milvian Bridge. According to Eusebius, the sign

Figure XI.1 Gravestone for the boy Asellus. Catacomb picture of Peter and Paul with the Chi-Rho symbol between them. Marble catacomb inscription, *Pio Cristiano*: Vatican Museum. This figure is now a traditional symbol for Christ and is found throughout Vatican City. Vatican Museum.

was a superimposed "chi" and "rho", the first two letters of Christ. This was similar to the symbol known as the *staurogram* in the Christian manuscripts (see Figure XI.1).

Both versions reported that Constantine did not know which god gave him the sign but prayed and had a dream that night with a vision of Jesus. They both claim that he "sought out" details of this god. We do know that Bishops were traveling with his legions and they may have helped to inform him. The legend that he had his soldiers paint this symbol on their shields before the battle cannot be historically verified.

Leading his troops across the Milvian Bridge with the banner of *Sol Invictus*, Maxentius fell into the river and drowned. Constantine was now sole ruler in the West. Perhaps out of respect for "the cross", Constantine later banned the use of crucifixion as punishment. This is when Christians began promoting the symbol of the cross more extensively in their art.

The Edict of Milan (313)

In the East, Licinius still reigned. This portion of the Empire continued with persecutions of Christians and the usual coups challenging who ruled. Licinius also fought under the sign of the cross. He did it to gain the support of the Christians; his opponent, Maximinus, had promised to eradicate them. Perhaps with growing numbers of Christians in the legions Licinius suggested that he and Constantine both issue an "Edict of Toleration" for Christians. It was signed in Milan in 313. This was the edict that officially proclaimed that Christians could now meet in legal assemblies (*collegia*). This did not make the Empire Christian as yet. All other native cults continued. In 324 Constantine defeated Licinius and become sole Emperor (see Figures XI.2 and␣X1.3).

Figure XI.2 Head of a colossal statue of Constantine. V. Korostyshevskiy / Adobe Stock.

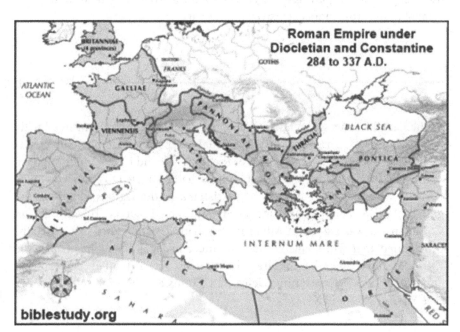

Figure XI.3 Roman Empire under Constantine.

Why Did Constantine Convert?

Recognized as "the turning point" in Western history, the "triumph of Christianity", scholars continue to debate Constantine's conversion. Was it because of the growing numbers of Christians, the politics of "the winds of change", or his "faith?"

At the same time, moderns continue to criticize him and point out what are considered incongruities. This always involves the question of how committed Constantine was to Christianity. Leaving native cults and traditions in place could appear that he was not so secure in his new faith, and so just added Christians as a legal assembly in the Empire. But Constantine could not directly eliminate the age-old ancestral traditions of the majority in his vast Empire. He did however, forbid Christians to make offerings at native temples in 321. (This edict reveals that some Christians continued doing so.)

Some scholars have suggested that Constantine was "pre-programmed" to accept Christianity through his background in the cult of *Sol Invictus*, which was popular along with Apollo/Helios, the sun god who was Augustus' favorite. All emperors promoted their family cults on their coins. Constantine issued coins with himself in the figure of *Sol Invictus* and *Helios*. However, we cease to find such coins after 319 CE, for unknown reasons.

One of his monuments which now stands next to the Colosseum is the triumphal Arch of Constantine. This was commissioned by the Roman Senate in 315 to celebrate the victory over Maxentius. However, a careful examination demonstrates that they incorporated parts of earlier arches, specifically images of Trajan, Hadrian, and Marcus Aurelius. Christian symbols are notably absent (see Figure XI.4).

Figure XI.4 Arch of Constantine. Yudai Ibusuki / Adobe Stoc.

But most of the debate focuses on the fact that Constantine did not receive baptism until he was on his deathbed. This most likely was not an issue of doubt. We have speeches and letters from Constantine where he appears to consistently uphold Christian teaching and rituals:

> This God I invoke with bended knees, and recoil with horror from the blood of sacrifices, from their foul and detestable odors, and from every earth-born magic fire: for the profane and impious superstitions which are defiled by these rites have cast down and consigned to perdition many, nay, whole nations of the Gentile world.
> (Eusebius, *Life of Constantine*, IV, chapter X)

He eventually banned native sacrifices, but we cannot determine if this was carried out everywhere.

The delay of his baptism can be better understood in the fact that, as Emperor, he knew he was going to have "blood on his hands" (all Emperors did). In fact, he executed one of his wives and a son for alleged conspiracies against the throne. At the time the churches were still debating if there would be a "second baptism". Constantine put his off until the end, when there would be no chance to "sin again".

Constantinople

Recognizing the vastness of the Roman Empire (from Britain to the Balkans and regions north of the Black Sea), Constantine saw Rome as too limited. He selected an older village on the shores of the Strait of the Bosporus, Byzantium, as a center of shipping and trade for both East and West. He called in artisans from all over the Empire, rebuilt the walls and created massive cisterns, amphitheaters, and race-tracks. He built both native temples and Christian churches, the most famous of which became Hagia Sophia. After the fall of the Western Empire in 476, Roman rule continued in the East for the next thousand years, designated the **Byzantine Empire**. Finally captured by the Ottoman Turks in 1453, the current name for this city is Istanbul.

The Donatist Schism over the Persecution of Christians in Diocletian's Reign

Recall that after the persecution under Diocletian, churches were embroiled in debates over what to do with bishops and Christians who sacrificed under pressure and turned over Christian scriptures to be destroyed. Upon the ascension of Constantine as a now Christian Emperor, the bishops decided to appeal to him as a mediator in the debate. One bishop, **Donatus**, insisted that those who had committed idolatry or blasphemy were now defiled. Re-admitting them would defile the entire community.

In almost everything that Constantine did, the motivation was unity of the Empire. As Emperor, he ordered a policy of "forgive and forget". In terms of propaganda, this meant "One God, One Emperor, One Church". Donatus refused to accept this order and moved his community to North Africa and created his own churches. We will meet these people again a hundred years later in Augustine's communities.

By serving as mediator, Constantine became the official "head of the Church", as the supreme patron of Christianity. This reflected Augustus' incorporating the position of *pontifex maximus*, the head priest of Roman religion, into his authority as the first Emperor. More importantly, utilizing the same concepts when Rome persecuted Christians, as Emperor and head of the Church, anyone who disagreed with *his* Christianity was deemed a heretic. *Heresy in this case became equivalent to treason* (you did not want the now Christian Empire to prosper). It is significant that more Christians (heretics) died in the arenas after his conversion than before. Most of their names are lost to history because as heretics, they were denied the status of "martyr".

The Empire continued to have a plethora of native cults, but Constantine favored the Christians. He gave them funds to build their churches and to acquire property, and to have any property that had been confiscated during the last persecution returned. A good percentage of this money was acquired by his confiscating native temples and melting down statues. Laws were issued against sexual immorality and ritual prostitution. He appointed Christians to high offices and exempted Christian clergy from taxes (the beginning of what remains a contemporary practice).

Helena

We know very little about Constantine's mother Helena prior to his conversion, but tradition claims that she was already a Christian. In 324 he sent her on a pilgrimage to the "Holy Land". She claimed to have visions which revealed the sites of both the nativity of Jesus in Bethlehem and the site of his tomb in Jerusalem. She claimed she found the "true cross" in a well at that site. Constantine built Christian basilicas over both sites (the Church of the Nativity and the Church of the Holy Sepulcher). The older levels remain, but during the Crusader period both were re-built as the edifices that remain today.

Christian Art and Architecture

Under Constantine, Christian art and architecture flourished, particularly the art of mosaics. With the promotion of the Emperor, Christians were permitted to "seize" native temples and build their own places of worship. The basic template was the *basilica*, the common public buildings in each city where magistrates and law courts met. Their characteristic shapes became the standard of churches, with a nave and apses (side altars which originally had statues of native gods). In Rome, Constantine built the basilica of St. John in Lateran (the first residence of later Popes) and St. Peter's basilica on Vatican Hill. He also built the Church of the Holy Apostles in Constantinople. In his will, he wanted to be buried there as the thirteenth apostle. The Church was sacked in the Fourth Christian crusade in 1204 and later destroyed (see Box XI.1).

Box XI.1 The Face of Christ

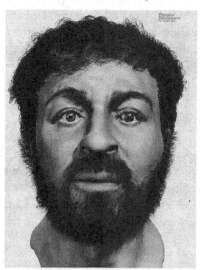

Popular Mechanics magazine created an anthropological image of Jesus by applying forensic techniques to a first-century skull from a tomb in Jerusalem. Credit Popular Mechanics

After the conversion of Constantine, the face of Christ was aligned with the famous statue of Zeus at Olympus (one of the Seven Wonders of the Ancient World). Only gods and philosophers were depicted with long hair. In contrast to the dominant society, Jews wore beards, but had short hair. The DJ / Wikimedia Commons.

The Conversion of the Roman Empire   229

The Council of Nicea and the Trinity

The Christian concept of the **Trinity** is a complicated belief for both Christians as well as non-Christians. While all Christians learn the ritual formula, "Father, Son, and Holy Spirit", most are unaware of the underlying concepts and historical context. When the followers of Jesus began worshipping him as a god, Christians struggled with a problem that was related to their claim that they inherited the Jewish concept of worshipping only one god; very soon they worshipped Christ as a god as well. At the same time, there was not a clear understanding of the relationship between God and Christ as Christians claimed that Jesus was pre-existent and present at creation but also lived on earth. And how did the "Holy Spirit" fit into this relationship?

In 1 Corinthians 8:6, Paul had taught, "Yet for us there is one God, the father, from whom are all things and for whom we exist, and one Lord, Jesus Christ, through whom are all things and through whom we exist." He consistently combined "God" and "Lord", but without a clear explanation of distinguished roles. When Paul referred to the spirit, it was the "spirit of Christ". The problem in the early centuries of Christianity was the struggle of how to properly interpret (and teach) what God and Christ must be like if all the things believed about them were true. Attempts were made to define God's oneness, transcendence, and immanence (in the manner of the schools of philosophy), but also his incarnate nature in Christ without misrepresenting or neglecting any of these attributes.

Early Formulas

The first time we encounter the formula is at the end of the gospel of Matthew when Jesus met the disciples in Galilee after his resurrection. He said: "All authority in heaven and on earth has been given to me. Therefore, go and make disciples of all nations, baptizing them in the name of the Father and of the Son and of the Holy Spirit, and teaching them to obey everything I have commanded you. And surely, I am with you always, to the very end of the age" (Matthew 28:16–20). Known as "the Great Commission" it remains difficult to determine if this ending was added much later to the extant manuscripts.

The early teaching manual, the *Didache*, directed Christians to "baptize in the name of the father and the son and the holy spirit". Bishop Clement of Rome had rhetorically asked in a letter: "Do we not have one God, and one Christ, and one gracious spirit that has been poured out upon us, and one calling in Christ?" Ignatius of Antioch exhorted obedience to "Christ, and to the father, and to the spirit". Justin Martyr also wrote … "in the name of God, the father and lord of the universe, and of our savior Jesus Christ, and of the holy spirit".

230 The Conversion of the Roman Empire

An early treatise known as the *Ascension of Isaiah* is dated anywhere from 70 to 175 CE. This is a detailed story of the martyrdom of the Prophet. Scholars label it a Judeo-Christian text, perhaps culled from several different sources (and writers), but with a final Christian redaction. The text "predicts" the suffering of Jesus and his betrayal. Isaiah's journey through seven heavens shows the angels in praise before the throne: "And there they all named the primal Father and his Beloved, Christ, and the Holy Spirit, all with one voice" (8:18).

Tertullian claimed that God is in essence and nature one, but within his oneness there are three real aspects, *personas* (persons). (The term "aspects" or "dimensions" conveys more of what he meant by *persona*.) Tertullian was the first to call this a "trinity", as three personas that worked in harmony.

Alternate Views

Attempts to fully define and understand Christ's relationship to God continued in several of the Churches:

Monarchianism. The idea of a "tritheism" was Monarchianism (God as "king"). God the father was the supreme God above the other aspects of the divine nature. This mirrored the concept of kings over their courts and courtiers in that kings designated bureaucratic elements to lower divisions of nobles.

Subordinationism. Subordinationism is a related position that subordinates the son to the father and (perhaps) the spirit to the son and father (Origen's view).

Sabellianism. Sabellianism was a view that can be characterized as monarchian and subordinationist. Sabellianism claimed that there was a perfect union (at least between the father and the son), so that it was also known as "Patripassionism", a reference to the father "suffering" and being "crucified in the son". This was popular with several Christians at Rome, who for some reason, thought that it was perfectly acceptable to "crucify God in Christ". They were later condemned as heretics in 381.

Arius and Arianism (Nicaea)

Early in the fourth century, a Presbyter in the church at Alexandria by the name of **Arius** (influenced by Origen's teaching), proposed what became a controversial doctrine. Using simple logic, he said that if you believe that God created everything in the universe (which Christians believed) then at some point, as creator, he *must* have created Christ. This placed Christ as not only subordinate but a "creature" of God. Riots arose over this in Alexandria and in other cities of the Empire.

With his goal of Church unity, in 325, Constantine called for a major conference to settle this issue and invited bishops to the city of Nicea (near Constantinople which was not finished yet). Roughly 217 bishops attended along with their entourages. He paid everyone's travel expenses and provided room and board. This was when Constantine settled the official date of Easter following the Roman practice.

The Doctrine of the Trinity

After days of debate, the conference settled on two choices: (1) was Christ *homo-iousios*, a being *like* God? or (2) was Christ *homo-ousios*, *identical* in essence with God? (Yes, the Greek had two different words; "like" and "identical" differ by one iota.) The Council opted for the second choice in that God and Christ were identical in essence and that Christ was a manifestation of God himself on earth.

Why Choose *homo-ousios*, "identical?" The debates centering on the concept of the Trinity are quite esoteric to most and include philosophical ideas of the universe that contributed to Christian thinkers. The concept of the Trinity may be easier to understand if we think not so much about the esoteric theology and philosophy, but the implications of the Trinity "on the ground".

First and foremost, having Christ identical to the essence of God theoretically kept the Christian heritage of "monotheism" of traditional Judaism, now defined as "belief in one God". With Christ identical to God, it validated the view that Christ was pre-existent and helped to create the universe. But perhaps more importantly, this choice bolstered the importance of the (now) Christian Emperor. Over time, the claim that the "kingdom of God" was imminent began to fade and was assigned to the future. In the interim, we now have the concept that the Christian Emperor "stands in" for Christ on earth, until he returns. If that is the case, then the Emperor must have the "identical" power of God and Christ on earth as he rules. The idea of "divine kingship" had always been accepted in the Eastern Empire and remained a concept in hundreds of native cults in the Empire.

Understanding this now, heightened position for the Emperor, this is when the worship of Emperors became the "new Imperial cult". As the "stand-in for Christ", portraits of Constantine and his successors have halos over their heads (see Figure XI.5). People bowed before the Emperor, recognizing his sacredness. The procession of the Emperor into the Senate with his priests and acolytes was adopted by the Catholic Church for the procession into Mass.

Figure XI.5 Constantine the Great and his Church. Анатолий Тушев / Adobe Stock.

The Nicene Creed

While he had all the bishops in attendance, Constantine had them work out what would become the **Nicene Creed**, another Christian innovation. (It is called a "creed", from the Latin of the first word "Credo, I believe …"). In the ancient world the concept of a creed did not exist. There was no central authority to dictate what everyone should believe. As both head of the state and head of the Church, Constantine now had the authority to mandate what every Christian should believe so as not to fall into the sin of heresy. The Creed included a "refutation of heresies", mostly Gnostic beliefs that were still dominant in some parts of the Empire. For example, the Creed emphasized that Jesus was "made man" against the Gnostic docetic view that he simply "appeared", and was never human.

The Original Nicene Creed

We believe in one God, the father Almighty, maker of all things visible and invisible. And in one lord Jesus Christ, the son of God, begotten of the father, the only begotten, that is, of the essence of the Father, God of God, light of light, very God of very God, begotten, not made, consubstantial with the father, by whom all things were made (both in heaven and on earth). Who for us men, and for our salvation, came down and was incarnate and was made man; he suffered, and the third day arose again, ascended into heaven. From thence he shall come to judge the living and the dead. And in the holy spirit. But those who say: "There was a time when he was not"; and "He was not before he was made"; and "He was made out of nothing", or "He is of another substance" or "essence", or "The Son of God is created", or "changeable", or "alterable"—they are condemned by the holy catholic and apostolic Church. ["Catholic" here is Greek for "universal".]

That "there was a time when he was not" refuted the claim of Arius and his followers. You will notice that the original Creed does not have much to say

The Conversion of the Roman Empire   233

about the spirit. In the next few decades this problem (and other issues) continued to be debated. A second meeting was called at the **Council of Constantinople** in 381 which resulted in a much more detailed and longer Creed:

> We believe in one God, the father almighty, maker of heaven and earth, and of all things visible and invisible. And one lord, Jesus Christ, the only begotten son of God, begotten of the father before all worlds (*aeons*), light of light, very God of very God, begotten, not made, consubstantial with the father, by whom all things were made; who for us men, and for our salvation, came down from heaven and was incarnate by the holy spirit and of the virgin Mary, and was made man. He was crucified for us under Pontius Pilate and suffered, and was buried, and the third day he rose again according to the Scriptures and ascended into heaven and sits at the right hand of the Father; from hence he shall come again with glory to judge the living and the dead, whose kingdom shall have no end. And in the holy spirit, the lord and giver of life, who proceeds from the father, who with the father and the son together is worshipped and glorified, who spoke through the Prophets. In the one holy catholic and apostolic Church; we acknowledge one baptism for the remission of sins; we look for the resurrection of the dead, and the life of the world to come, Amen.

Both creeds had claimed that Christ was "begotten of the father", adopting the term from the "begats" of the Jewish Scriptures, as a reflection of procreation. However, Christ was not formed through the traditional sense of procreation, but through God infusing Mary with the spirit. This kept Christ unique and different from the spirit; the spirit is not begotten, but "proceeds" from the father.[1]

That he was "crucified under Pontius Pilate" was most likely added for historical validity against continuing non-Christian criticism of the stories in the gospels. The Roman historian Tacitus had written in his description of Nero's persecution: "Nero fastened the guilt (for the fire) and inflicted the most exquisite tortures on a class hated for their abominations, called Christians by the populace. *Christus* (or *Chrestus*), from whom the name had its origin, suffered the extreme penalty during the reign of Tiberius at the hands of one of our procurators, *Pontius Pilatus*" (Annals 15:14).

Historians point out that the title of Pilate in the 20's in Judea is wrong. A stone inscription discovered in Israel calls him "Prefect". It was Emperor Claudius (in the 50's) who began appointing "procurators" to rule Judea. Written ca. 115, Tacitus applied the contemporary term. In the Western Tradition, the passage by Tacitus became associated as historical "proof" of the crucifixion, as the testimony of a non-Christian witness, and deemed essential for the creed.

---

1 In 1053 the Eastern Orthodox Churches officially separated from the Western Churches over the wording of the spirit in relation to "procession", or what is known as the *filioque* clause: Does power proceed from the father *and* the son, to the spirit? Or, does power proceed from the father, *through* the son, to the spirit? The Eastern Churches opted for the latter.

234 The Conversion of the Roman Empire

The New Testament

Without specific references or details, it is nevertheless apparent that Constantine adopted as dogma the views of the second century Church Fathers. His speeches and letters replicate many of their writings and teachings. These Church Fathers had claimed that only the four gospels of Matthew, Mark, Luke, and John were "orthodox", correct teachings against the Gnostic gospels. Eusebius later wrote that Constantine sent to Origen's library at Caesarea and ordered fifty copies of "the gospels" (assuming the four and other texts) to be distributed around the Empire. Thus, began the official canonization of the four gospels in the New Testament.

The Immediate Aftermath of Nicaea

The bishops in attendance were required to sign-off on both the Trinity and the Creed. Arius had been arrested earlier and brought to the Council in chains. Of course, he refused to sign. Eusebius, Constantine's court bishop refused as well. Both were sent into exile. One has to appreciate that, with the Emperor chairing this event (and the legions in town) it stands to reason that most of them would sign. However, after many of the bishops returned home, they symbolically ignored it and went back to the continued debates in their communities of the relationship between God and Christ. This is why there had to be a second meeting (and several more) to reconcile differences. We will encounter these continuing debates in Chapter XIII.

Eventually, those who remained loyal to the teaching of Arius, made their way east and north of the Black Sea area (the Balkans and Russia), converting people in those areas. These "Arians" were apparently quite successful. Two priests, Cyril and Melodius, created an alphabet, Cyrillic, which is still used in Eastern and Russian Orthodox Churches. Stemming from these regions would come the later invaders of Europe (Huns, Goths, Visigoths, Vandals), often referred to simply as the "barbarians" of late antiquity, who would topple the Western Roman Empire. However, many of them were in fact Christians, although for the most part, they remained enemies because they were heretic Christians.

It may surprise many to know that Constantine may have had a change of heart in later years although we do not know why. Before he died, he recalled both Arius and Eusebius from exile. Arius died in the capitol not long after, in circumstances shrouded in mystery. His followers claimed that he was poisoned, but his enemies considered his death as divine intervention. When he was dying, Constantine had Bishop Eusebius baptize him on his deathbed (see Box XI.2). After Constantine's death, the Empire was divided among his sons who continually fought each other, but also disagreed on Nicaea and some kept promoting Arianism. The reign of Constantius II (317–361) is notable that on his ascension to the throne he promoted Arianism as the only true faith in the Empire. However, he did not dictate any edict or change the creed.

> *Box XI.2   Eusebius of Caesarea*
>
> Eusebius of Caesarea (260–340) was a Christian exegete, polemicist, and historian. He wrote *Demonstration of the Gospel*, *Preparations for the Gospel*, and *Discrepancies Between the Gospels*. As the court bishop for Constantine, he remains the major source for almost everything we know about Constantine as well as events in this period. His *Ecclesiastical History* granted him the title of "the first Christian historian", despite his initial Arianism.
>
> After the death of Constantine, Eusebius wrote a eulogy, *Life of Constantine*, which detailed Constantine's religious policies and a detailed report of the Council of Nicaea. Not without criticism by modern scholars for factual mistakes, the value of both this and his *Ecclesiastical History* is found in the many quotes from writings that are now lost. Eusebius presented Constantine as a "god-like man", selected by the will of God to promote Christianity over all native idolatry. Eusebius declared Constantine an "immortal".

The Impact of the Trinity and the Creed

The greatest impact of the Trinity and the Creed was that it established the Empire-wide theological precepts of what made someone a Christian. Eliminating ties to ancestors, blood, language, local myths, and traditional social conventions, Christianity was a new system that emphasized theology (a belief system) over ancient practice and customs in society. Combining the Emperor with religion was not new but became elevated to a higher level of power than previous Roman Emperors had enjoyed.

The problem for the historian is finding evidence for both how the Creed was mandated and literally observed Empire-wide. The creation of a Creed did not settle continuing debates on some issues. Several bishops ignored the power of the Emperor or were willing to suffer the consequences (execution for heresy).

We know that local churches began their own alterations. In the Western Empire, at the Synod of Milan (390), the Creed was shortened and elements of it were incorporated into the ritual of Baptism. Earlier baptism formulas had included an "exorcism" clause ("Do you reject Satan and all his works?") The Milan formula opened with "Do you believe in God, the father almighty, creator of heaven and earth?" followed by shorter essentials of the Creed. This version spread through Gaul and Europe. When Martin Luther created his reforms of Catholicism, this shortened form became the "Apostles' Creed" that is recited by Protestant denominations.

Julian the Apostate

From (361–363), the Empire was ruled by a member of the dynasty of Constantine, Julian, known to history as **Julian the Apostate**. Although educated in Christianity from a young age, Julian attempted to reinstate traditional

236 The Conversion of the Roman Empire

Greco-Roman religiousness dominant in the Empire, and hence his title, "Apostate". (Apostate means a person who renounces a religion or religious principle.)

Much of Julian's anti-Church opinions were not so much theological as what he saw as the corruption of the Christian court in Constantinople. He often railed against the financial corruption (the rich life-style of bishops). But he also saw corruption in the traditional cults as well which still survived. Some die-hard traditionalists remaining in the Roman Senate welcomed his criticism of the Church, as did the Jews. Julian promised the Jews funds and permission to re-build the Temple in Jerusalem. Most likely he did this not out of sympathy for the Jews, but to irritate Christians.

The **Altar of Victory** was an ancient altar that depicted the winged goddess Nike and represented the power and might of Rome. Augustus had it moved into the Senate House (the *Curia*). Senators sometimes took their oaths at this altar after their election. Constantius II removed it in 357. This gave the conservative Senators a rallying cry that the removal upended the traditions and angered the gods. Julian approved and reinstated it. In a military campaign against the Sassanid Persians, he was killed in battle. Julian is often called upon in contemporary culture by some neo-pagan and New Age groups as a lamented hero.

Emperor Theodosius I (347–395)

Theodosius I (347–395), was Emperor from 329 to 395. He is remembered as a great champion of orthodoxy. We will learn more about him and his battles with the Latin Father Ambrose of Milan in Chapter XIII. Theodosius I made Christianity the *only* legal religion of the Empire:

Edict of Theodosius I (381)

It is Our Will that all the peoples We rule shall practice that religion which the divine Peter the Apostle transmitted to the Romans. We shall believe in the single deity of the father, the son, and the holy spirit, under the concept of equal majesty and of the Holy Trinity. We command that those persons who follow this rule shall embrace the name of Catholic Christians. The rest, however, whom We adjudge demented and insane, shall sustain the infamy of heretical dogmas, their meeting places shall not receive the name of churches, and they shall be smitten first by divine vengeance and secondly by the retribution of Our own initiative, which We shall assume in accordance with divine judgment.

This was the official end of native cults in the ancient world. Theodosius banned the Olympic Games in 396, dedicated to the gods (not to emerge again until 1896). All native temples and shrines were ordered destroyed or turned into churches. This is when Christians invented the term, *pagianoi* ("pagans") a negative slur against those who had not yet converted.

What about the Jews?

You may notice that the Edict said nothing about the Jews. Since the time of Julius Caesar, Emperors had continued to allow the Jews their "ancestral customs". However, Theodosius began to diminish Jewish life. One of his projects was an updated codification of Roman Law which became the **Theodosian Code** (later updated by Justinian I in the sixth century). This code now formulated specific laws against the Jews:

1. No Jew could own Christian slaves. This meant that Jews would have difficulty farming, especially the large plantations (*latafunda*) which relied upon slave labor.
2. No Jew could testify against a Christian in court.
3. Intermarriages between Jews and Christians was forbidden.
4. Jews could not conduct their services in Hebrew (in case they were plotting sedition).
5. No synagogue could be built higher than a church.
6. No Jews could proselytize Christians.
7. No Jew could be elected or appointed as a magistrate.
8. No Jews could work as doctors or lawyers for Christians. Doctors and lawyers learned intimate secrets which could be used against them.

Thus, began the slow economic privation of Jews, in that by the Middle Ages, they were forbidden many other careers. In turning to the "Scriptures", Christians found this: "If you lend money to one of my people among you who is needy, do not treat it like a business deal; charge no interest" (Exodus 22:26). Christians determined that the charging of any interest on loans was a sin, and therefore forbidden to Christians. Jews were permitted to charge interest in light of their ancient crime of having "money-changers" in the Temple. Hence, the beginning of the stereotype of "Jews and money". After several years, Christians realized they were missing profit, so this was when several Italian banking houses were established by Christians (as well as the Knights Templars in the 1200's).

Summary

- The evolution of Christianity from a Roman cult to the only legal religion in the Empire took several centuries.
- The debates that gave rise to the concept of the Trinity and the Nicene Creed created a unified system of belief.
- Through Constantine's conversion, the combination of "Church and State" became institutionalized.

Suggestions for Further Reading

Barnes, Timothy D. 2013. *Constantine: Dynasty, Religion, and Power in the Later Roman Empire*. Wiley-Blackwell Ancient Lives, Book 16. This is an updated version of one of the first modern biographies of Constantine.

Burckhardt, Jacob and Hadas, Moses. 1983. *The Age of Constantine the Great*. University of California Press. This text incorporates the changes in late antiquity in the Roman Empire as they relate to Constantine and his adoption of Christianity.

Schaff, Philip. 2007. *Nicene and Post-Nicene Fathers*. Cosimo Classics. This is an anthology of Church writings beginning with Nicaea and the Councils in the following centuries.

ASCETICISM AND MONASTICISM
THE DESERT FATHERS AND THE CULT OF THE SAINTS

XII

Anthony of Egypt (251–356)

Evagrius Ponticus (345–399)

The Deadly Sins

A New Martyrdom

Vigilante Monks

Radical Monastics

Monastic Literature

The Rise of the Cult of the Saints

Patron/Client

Tombs of the Martyrs

Ambrose of Milan (339–397)

The Incident at Minorca

The Necessity of Purgatory

Indulgences

Varieties of Early Christianity: The Formation of the Western Christian Tradition, First Edition. Rebecca I. Denova.
© 2023 John Wiley & Sons, Inc. Published 2023 by John Wiley & Sons, Inc.

After reading this chapter you will be able to:

- Trace the evolution of the institution of Monasticism.
- Understand the rise of the Cult of the Saints.

Monasticism in Christianity, which gave us **monk** and **monastery** originated in Egypt in the mid-third century. It eventually became a major institution in Catholic and Eastern Orthodox communities. Monasticism is defined as "an institutionalized religious practice or movement whose members attempt to live by a rule that requires works that go beyond those of either the laity or the ordinary spiritual leaders of their religions".

Anthony of Egypt (251–356)

Anthony of Egypt (251–356), was the first to renounce the traditional conventions of life in this world, for one of isolation and complete devotion to God. He was a rich young man (his parents had left him their estates), but he followed the gospel teaching of giving away his wealth and devoting himself to God's will. He retired to a cave in the desert to spend his life in prayer. He was not just "turning his back on society"; he was also frustrated with continual Church feuds.

Then as now, the Nile river valley has fertile, or black land for up to two miles on either side. The black is from the rich deposits of soil that were left behind in the yearly flooding of the river and what made Egypt a "bread basket" (always having food) in the ancient world. When Anthony left his village, it was just a short distance to the desert, so people often went out to see him and to check on what he was doing.

They found that every morning, Anthony emerged from his cave wounded and covered with bloody scars. He claimed that he had been engaged in "battling the Devil" all night. At the same time, Anthony deplored the crowds who came to see him and so he kept moving around to different caves. But the crowds followed him wherever he went. Soon, other men and women followed him to live as "hermits" in the desert. These recluses were eventually deemed "Desert Fathers" and "Desert Mothers" and their lives and writings became models of prayer and reflection for others. The term for those who want to live in isolation from society is **eremitic monasticism.**

Recall that some educated Christians had absorbed the concept of asceticism from the various schools of philosophy—from the Greek word *ascesis*, discipline, it was the idea of disciplining the urges and demands of the body so that the body would not distract from higher thinking and concentration. This resulted in chastity and celibacy for the clergy; bodily necessities and urges could lead one to sin. The monastics did not follow Gnostic ideas that the body was evil. The body was a gift from God but had to be "tamed", so that the mind could be focused on prayer.

The idea of taming the body was directed to those elements that caused the worst sins: the two most common temptations for desert hermits were women and food. Anthony claimed that the Devil often appeared to him at night as a seductive woman. At the same time, the asceticism practiced by the monks limited their food intake. They survived only on the bare essentials, such as one piece of bread a day and one glass of water. The physiological changes to their bodies from limitations of nutrition often produced visions. There were common dreams of banquets with huge tables of food. Anthony and the practices of his fellow hermits became famous when Bishop Athanasius wrote about him. *The Life of Anthony* became a best seller in its day.

As more and more people began moving to the desert regions, it was apparent that some kind of organization of these groups (and their living arrangements) was necessary. In 318 Pachomius began the first organized rules that eventually became **cenobitic (cells)** or communal living and now called a monastery. Women were initially housed in the same buildings, but there were concerns that men and women would accidentally touch each other, especially during communal meals. "Lauras" were built which became the first convents.

Pachomius developed his rules on the basis that if one were constantly busy, one could not be drawn into sin—a later adage would make this clear—"Idle hands are the Devil's playground." A monk's day was organized around what became "canonical hours". The day would begin with prayer, then work, then end with prayer (with prayers in the middle of the night as well). The work involved making the monastery self-sufficient in terms of growing food, craftsman shops for repairs, etc. This was to limit the contact with outside traders and craftsmen. Work would contribute to exhaustion by the end of the day, and thus less interference in dreams.

Work was determined by an individual's strength and how rigorously someone could fast. There were common meals of limited intake, necessary to strengthen the body. His monastery was visited by many and monasteries were established throughout the Empire (see Figure XII.1).

Figure XII.1 St. Pachomius Alchetron.

Pachomius' Rule was translated into Latin by Jerome who built monasteries in Palestine. In the East, monasteries were founded by Basil, Gregory of Nazianzus, and Gregory of Nyssa. Collectively, they are known as the **Cappadocian Fathers** or the founders of Eastern Orthodox churches (Cappadocia is a province of central Turkey). Their monasteries were established along similar lines of community life, liturgical prayer, and manual labor. Basil was known for his care for the poor and underprivileged. Rather than maintaining monasteries only in the isolated desert regions, he brought them to the cities and there established the first Christian hospitals. In this effort he was helped by his sister, Macrina, who became famous for her convent's work with the poor and sick.

Augustine made a trip to study Pachomius' monastery and built his own in North Africa. Benedict of Nursia (480–548) translated it to the first monasteries in Italy (Monte Cassino) and they spread throughout medieval Europe and Ireland. Throughout the Dark Age and the Middle Ages, one of their main tasks was to copy and preserve ancient manuscripts. These became the famous "scriptoriums" of monasteries.

(I have visited Pachomius' monastery in Egypt. Typical of modern Egypt, both ancient and contemporary religious concepts merge in what is known as "religious syncretism". The monastery shares its fields with neighboring Muslim farmers. Before entering the church, shoes are removed, and participants kneel on prayer rugs. Men and women are separated within the church.)

Evagrius Ponticus (345–399)

Evagrius Ponticus was an ascetic monk from Heraclea on the coast of Bithynia. His practices included eating only once a day, but no fruit, meat, or vegetables. He also refrained from bathing. He became influential with his writings and teachings on the monastic life. As one of the first to write down the teachings of the Desert Fathers, he also promoted education among all the monks. He was famous for categorizing sin, beginning with a book of recipes that he thought would help.

Much had been written by schools of philosophy of the relationship between the body and "sexual immorality". It was believed that the bodily fluid of semen contributed to sexual drives that led to adultery and masturbation. Evagrius developed a "cookbook" for monasteries that included only "dry" substances for intake by the monks—legumes, other forms of beans and wheat. The theory was that this would reduce the problem of seminal discharge ("wet dreams") experienced by monks through the night.

The Deadly Sins

Evagrius created a famous list of eight sins that must be avoided and were deemed "the deadly sins": gluttony, lust, greed, sorrow (despair), wrath, pride, vainglory (boasting), and sloth (laziness). Seven centuries later, Pope Gregory refined this list by claiming that pride and vainglory were the same, that sorrow led to sloth, and adding the sin of envy. What was the first and therefore the worst sin? For Evagrius, against the earlier Church Fathers, it was not "lust". As God had provided everything for their use in Eden, it was "gluttony" that first made the pair disobey; gluttony led to all the other sins.

A New Martyrdom

After Constantine's conversion and the elimination of Christian persecution, the concept of martyrdom was altered. It was no longer possible to seek out martyrdom and "die for one's faith". The growth of monasticism helped with the promotion of "living martyrs". The greatest sacrifice of earlier martyrs was to literally sacrifice one's life. Foregoing marriage, children and the benefits of social conventions, the monastic life was now deemed a "sacrifice". Like previous martyrs, such devotion would result in the monk being automatically translated to heaven after his death, "in the presence of God."

The Desert Fathers, by having to survive in such drastic environments, became legendary for having power over animals—they could stave off jackals and lions. They were admired for "taking on the terrors of the last judgment in this life." Considered living "holy men", they were the only ones who had immediate access to Emperors. By virtue of their devotion to God, those who did not wish to sacrifice a normal life nevertheless appreciated that someone else was willing to do it—to pray for the rest of us as it were. Wealth in the form of donations and treasures began to pour into the monasteries. It was understood that contributing to a monastery would earn one an easier passage to heaven and contribute to the "absolution of sins".

Vigilante Monks

Although in the stages of institutionalization, for periods in the fourth and fifth centuries, there was no official control over monks. An Abbot, the head of a monastery, was a later development. As the only ones who had direct access to Emperors, some Emperors could sometimes utilize them to enforce orthodoxy. This period saw bands of vigilante monks roaming the cities and the countrysides seeking out sinners and at times literally clubbing them to death. In North Africa Donatist monks, known as *Circumcellions*, carried cudgels called "Isaiahs" and attacked any remaining native shrines, non-Christians, and Christians they deemed heretics.

During the reign of Theodosius I, vigilante monks attacked and burned a synagogue in Callinicum (a town in the area of former Persia). After Theodosius I's edict, monks joined with Christian soldiers in 391 to destroy the great temple complex of the Serapeum in Alexandria, Egypt. Hypatia (350–415) was a

Neoplatonist philosopher, astronomer, and mathematician who ran her own school in Alexandria. Hypatia advised the Roman prefect of the city, Orestes, who was currently in the middle of a feud with Bishop Cyril. In 415, vigilante monks joined with Christian soldiers and the Christian mob and tore her limb from limb.

Radical Monastics

While monasticism began to take root throughout the Middle East, some men attempted radical heights of asceticism. One of the most famous was Simeon Stylites (390–459), or Simeon the Stylite (*stylite* in Greek means "pillar"). He had joined a monastery at the age of 16, but even for the monks, he was considered too austere (reportedly spending one entire Lenten period with no food or water).

When others saw this as a miracle and sought him out, he became irritated and moved to a pillar outside of Aleppo, Syria. There was a platform on top (some versions claim it was 50 feet high) and he arranged for village boys to haul up water and bread to survive. But even here, people would not let him alone. Crowds of pilgrims and tourists would gather at the foot of the pillar and so he began preaching. He sat up there for over 30 years. Others would imitate him and there were several pillar-sitters in the city of Constantinople, a practice which lasted until the conquest by the Turks. Many of the Stylites served as Christian oracles.

Monastic Literature

The teaching of the monastics was honored as enlightened understanding and began to be collected. *The Sayings of the Desert Fathers*, originally written in Coptic (the language of Egypt), were translated into Greek, Syriac, and Latin. They contain wisdom stories and experiences of the monastics in the desert. The traditional form was a penitent or pilgrim asking, "How can I be saved," and then the response of the monk. Histories of monks and monastics were written by John Cassian (360–435), Palladius' *Lausiac History* (420), and an anonymous work, *History of the Monks*, fifth century.

The Rise of the Cult of the Saints

Christians borrowed three elements from the dominant culture in relation to their martyrs: hero cults, pilgrimage and the concept of patron/client. As we saw, Greeks had hero cults for mythical heroes or founders of their cities. Several cities claimed to have the tomb of these figures. The Greeks borrowed a tradition that first began in ancient Egypt, that of pilgrimage. Egyptians traveled up and down the Nile to the memorial chapels of Pharaohs and to participate in religious festivals. Pilgrimage is a spiritual journey to a shared sacred site.

Patron/Client

The same concept that governed "how things got done in society", applied to the gods as well. Each city-state and town had a local god or goddess. The Olympians were far away (and thought to be too busy), so you appealed to your local god to "mediate" between you and the Olympians for your petitions, as a client would petition his patron for benefits. Hence, a "patron" god or goddess. The community cared for the deity and the temple functions through sacrifices; the deity showed gratitude by benefiting the prosperity of the community.

Tombs of the Martyrs

Beginning in the fourth century, Christians considered the tomb of a martyr as a sacred area where heaven and earth intersected. Martyrs' tombs became the object of pilgrimage and Christians petitioned the dead martyr through hymns and prayers. This was a direct borrowing of the patron–client relationship. Because martyrs were now in heaven with God, they could be called upon for the kind of mediation and protection that Greek and Roman gods and goddesses traditionally granted. The dead martyrs were now "patron saints", and towns and cities that had a martyr's grave became famous sites of pilgrimage. For non-Catholics, the importance of the saints can be confusing because it appears that believers are praying to other divinities in addition to God and Jesus. Historically, the Catholic Church has explained that this is not "worship" but "veneration"—a nuance that remains vague to non-Catholics.

Ambrose of Milan (339–397)

As Christians began taking over older temples and building new churches, debates arose on how to translate the ancient concept of "sacred space" into these buildings. Older native basilicas were "tainted" with idolatry; even "civic" functions in these buildings, like town council meetings, had begun with sacrifices to the gods.

Bishop Ambrose solved the problem when he was building his new church in Milan. He claimed that he had a dream of two earlier Christian soldiers who showed him where they were buried. He had their skeletons dug up, and literally buried in the walls of the new church. This endowed the building with sanctity, as a sacred place. The idea spread all over the Empire and beyond.

The Incident at Minorca

In the year 415, a British monk, Pelagius, was put on trial in Jerusalem for heresy. During the trial, a local parish priest had a dream that showed him where Stephen (the first Christian martyr from the book of the Acts of the Apostles) was buried They dug up Stephen and took the skeleton to sit at the tribunal in Jerusalem. This convinced the panel that it was a sign from God that Pelagius was a heretic, and thus condemned him. Augustine (bishop of Hippo) had sent his agent, Orosius, to attend the trial. Orosius was charged with taking the bones of Stephen and helping to distribute them in pieces across the Mediterranean so that others could share in "this wonderful power". By this time, the Vandals had invaded Spain, and he was afraid to go there, so he went to the small island of Minorca, off the Spanish coast.

There was a synagogue community at the small town of Mahon, and the governing magistrate was a Jew. (Apparently Theodosius' ban against Jews being magistrates was ignored.) Upon presenting the bones of Stephen to the Christians on the island, Bishop Severus recalled the death of Stephen at the "hand of the Jews". A Christian mob burned the synagogue and stole the gold lampstand and other articles from the synagogue. We know this story from a circular letter that Bishop Severus sent to other cities. He claimed that the bones of Stephen brought about repentance of the Jews who all asked to be baptized. In real terms, this is most likely the first incident of the forced baptism of Jews.

The rush was on. Christians sought out the tombs of the earlier Christian martyrs, exhumed the bones and established shrines and pilgrimage sites at their tombs. Christians believed these bodies had a divine power. **Relics** became the physical remains of people or objects that have been in contact with holy individuals. Relics are believed to have power and the ability to protect and endow a believer with good fortune.

To distribute this benefit to all, Christians broke up the skeletons to distribute bones, teeth, and hair. The competition was rife in terms of tourist and pilgrimage trade. Seven different churches in Asia Province claimed to have the head of John the Baptist. This is the period when martyrologies were enhanced with legendary details. Cyprian, a Bishop of Carthage, was martyred in 258. We now have the detail that as he died, people threw their handkerchiefs near his body to obtain droplets of his blood to cherish as relics.

There were two people for whom one could not claim such "body parts". Jesus had bodily ascended into heaven, and the tradition was that Mary's body had been taken to heaven by angels. Instead, you could have associated relics: a thorn from the crown of thorns, pieces of the true cross, a crucifixion nail, a piece of Mary's veil, the "spear" that pierced the side of Christ. (This relic sits today in a museum in Vienna. It was recovered after Hitler had stolen it during his conquest of Austria.)

However, some churches went beyond the norm, claiming what we can consider peripheral body parts. Several churches claimed to have the foreskin of Jesus after he was circumcised. Some later churches created "Mary fountains", statues of Mary where her "milk" sprouted from her breasts and was collected in bottles for sale to pilgrims. (You can still see these in the medieval churches of France, where a "cult of Mary" became popular throughout Europe. The cult of Mary elevated her above the martyrs and with the title "Queen of Heaven".)

Relics were placed within a reliquary, or an ornate receptacle often covered with gold and jewels. Beginning in late antiquity and throughout the Middle Ages, the production and traffic in relics was big business. Christian communities with famous relics benefitted from the pilgrims and tourists by providing housing, food, and selling items associated with the saint. At the same time, there were many fake relics. The traffic in relics became one of the elements for Martin Luther's criticism of the Catholic Church and the practice was rejected by Protestant Christianity.

In Catholicism, every Catholic church is made sacred with the presence of a relic of a saint. The relic is either buried in the cornerstone (Christ as the "cornerstone"), under the altar, or in a separate chapel with a statue of the saint. Thus, the names of churches: St. Agnes, St. Catherine, St. Stephen, etc. Today, the Vatican controls the distribution (and confirmation of a true relic).

The Necessity of Purgatory

The elevation of past martyrs to that of "saint" eventually became problematic in relation to all other Christians. If all good Christians "went to heaven" when they died, how did this distinguish them from the martyrs? The death of a martyr was a sacrifice of their lives, an "atonement of sins" for themselves and others. They were held as a special group and had to remain elevated above all other Christians.

In the twelfth century, the concept of Purgatory became Christian doctrine at the Second Council of Lyon in 1247 (although the problem had been debated for several centuries). Purgatory, "purging", "cleansing", borrowed from Anglo-Norman and Old French, became an intermediate state for non-martyred Christians. Non-martyred Christians were given time to "burn off", purge themselves of ordinary sins. These sins were considered "venial sins", and contrasted against "mortal sins" (such as murder). Only after this purging could believers enter Heaven. Some theologians claimed that "mortal sins" were punished by automatic condemnation in Hell.

Indulgences

The concept of Purgatory influenced the practice in the later Middle Ages of **indulgences**, or the ability to reduce one's time in Purgatory. Indulgences were offered to those who contributed large donations to churches, had donated a reliquary to a church, and paying the clergy to say special masses for a dead relative. As such, many sins were forgiven. During the period of the Crusades, any Crusader was granted absolution of sins by Popes for their great sacrifice against the Infidels.

Among many other elements, one of Martin Luther's protests against the Catholic Church was this practice of Indulgences. Pope Julius II was renovating St. Peter's Basilica in Rome (when Michelangelo painted the Sistine Chapel). To pay the craftsmen, sculptors, and artists, Julius was openly selling Indulgences.

The modern Catholic Church upholds the practice of Indulgences through masses for the dead. Catholic funerals have "mass cards" for donations to the priest for this special mass. Modern Catholic pilgrimage sites allocate indulgences for pilgrims who make the journey: The holy sites in Jerusalem, the four major basilicas in Rome, the Shrine of Lourdes in France (St. Bernadette), and Saint James in Compostela, Spain. Each shrine offers a set number of years to reduce one's time in Purgatory (but you must be in a "state of grace" to receive it).

The Vatican continues the process of "sainthood", first with a designation as Beatification, and then Canonization. Prayers to a saint must result in three miracles (usually a cure for a disease). The miracles require medical confirmation. John Paul II began the process of increasing the numbers of saints by including martyred Christians in Asia, Africa, and Latin America. The concept of martyrdom has been adjusted to one in which the person does not necessarily have to die as a martyr, but one who "sacrificed" a normal life to devote themselves to the Church.

The nun known as Mother Teresa of Calcutta, who received the Noble Peace Prize, was beatified in 1979 and canonized as a Saint in 2016 by Pope Francis. Pope John Paul II was canonized in 2014. He was recognized for his struggles and resistance to Nazism in Poland in WWII and his support for Christians in Eastern Europe against Communism.

In the modern world, we have adopted the concept of martyrdom to include those deemed "secular martyrs". One of the criteria for this designation is that it reflects someone's decision to uphold different values and teachings, knowing full-well that it could lead to his or her death. A modern example is Dr. Martin Luther King. Islam adopted the traditional concepts of martyrdom (those who die for the faith) but also added "suffering" to the concept. Cancer victims and others who suffer through life-long disease are deemed martyrs.

Summary

- The institution of Monasticism began in Egypt with ascetic attempts to devote one's life to God.
- The rise of the "cult of the Saints" evolved from hero cults and concepts of martyrdom to distinguish martyrs from other Christians.

Suggestions for Further Reading

Brown, Peter. 2014. *The Cult of the Saints; Its Rise and Function in Latin Christianity*. University of Chicago Press. Brown surveys the various religious and cultural concepts that led to the worship of early martyrs as saints in late antiquity.

Harmless, William. 2004. *Desert Christians: An Introduction to the Literature of Early Monasticism*. Oxford Press. This is an anthology of the literature of the early monastics.

EXCURSUS IV
THE LATIN FATHERS

Ambrose, Bishop of Milan (339–397)

The Fight over the Basilica

The Power of the Emperor

Church and State Relations

John Chrysostom (347–407)

Jerome (347–420)

Excursus IV The Latin Fathers

Just as the earlier Christian writers were retrospectively given the title, the "Church Fathers", so a group of men in late antiquity became designated the **Latin Fathers**, as **Doctors of the Church**: Ambrose, John Chrysostom, Jerome, and Augustine.

Ambrose, Bishop of Milan (339–397)

We have already seen that it was Ambrose who solved the problem of creating "sacred space" for Christian churches. But he began to take on more important roles as he was often involved in disputes with Emperor Theodosius I.

Ambrose was the son of a prefect of Gaul but was educated in Rome. Most likely learning much about Christianity, he had nevertheless remained a non-Christian. He was appointed governor of the province of Aemilia-Liguria in northern Italy in 370. He was called upon to keep order at the election of the successor to the Arian Bishop of Milan, Auxentius. Apparently not being happy with the selection, the crowd went to the streets, grabbed Ambrose, who agreed to take on the position and was baptized.

The Fight over the Basilica

After Nicaea, there were still Arian sympathizers in the Empire. When Ambrose was building his church in Milan, the Emperor's mother Justina, wanted a church for Arians, but Ambrose (a good Nicaean) refused. This argument went on for a few years, with councils being called and people excommunicating each other back and forth. It was finally settled when the Emperor needed to call upon Ambrose to send some troops against a rebellion in Gaul. Ambrose traded military support and succeeded in keeping the Arians out.

The Power of the Emperor

When the vigilante monks destroyed the synagogue in Callinicum, Theodosius ordered them to compensate the Jewish community. Ambrose bridled at this, telling Theodosius that if he did this, people would accuse him of "being a Jew". Theodosius backed down. A second incident occurred in Thessalonica. A magistrate had a local chariot driver put to death for alleged homosexual activity and the residents of the city revolted and tore the magistrate (a non-Christian) limb from limb. Theodosius ordered in the troops, with the result of a massacre of 7000 citizens.

Ambrose objected that since the magistrate was a pagan, Theodosius over-reacted. Ambrose ordered the Emperor's excommunication and informed clergy to deny him communion. This was an incredible action—as the Christian Emperor, he was head of the Church. Did this put everyone in the Empire under the ban.? At first, Theodosius angrily argued back, "Who's in charge of the Empire?" Ambrose's response: "The Church". After several days Theodosius was forced to do penance and Ambrose removed the ban.

Church and State Relations

In a later writing, Ambrose established the relationship between the Empire and the Church:

1. The "state", understood as a function of human relationships, was created by God in Eden. In principle, it was natural and preceded the Fall. The divinely appointed fellowship of Adam and Eve is the germ of the State, for fellowship implies mutual help and so justice and goodwill, the twin principles of community and society. It is true that, but for sin, society would be freer, and more equal than it is; some of its institutions, like slavery and private property are the result of the Fall. So indeed, is monarchy.
2. While the State itself is natural, coercive power is the fruit of sin. Not as an invention of the Devil, but as the divinely approved remedy for sin. Thus, where there is a monarch, he must be accepted as the power ordained of God and given his due.

But what is his due? The Emperor is free to control or suppress religious cults and associations in the interests of politics or morals; the "anointed king" of the Jewish Scriptures. Problems arose when individual Emperors began to enforce their own views (or the views of lobbying bishops) into the Church. "What has the Emperor to do with the church?" asked Bishop Donatus in 347 (North Africa). Bishop Hosius of Cordova in 355: "God has put the kingdom in your hands; he has entrusted the affairs of the Church to us…. Render to Caesar the things that are Caesar's, and to God the things that are God's".

Ambrose started from some such dualist theory of the separate spheres of church and state, and never denounced it, but handed down to posterity his own version:

The Emperor derives his power from God and within his proper sphere is to be obeyed. But he is not above the Church. In God's cause, the bishops are the judges and are directly responsible to God. On the one hand, the State has far-reaching duties towards the Church. While the Christian Emperor must not try and impose his own views in matters of morals or faith on the Church, he should put the decisions of the Church into execution, even by force. He should protect the Church against all rivals and all heresies and prohibit native cults.

On the other hand, the Church, as guardians of the moral law, will speak its mind through the bishops to the Emperor whenever political decisions or actions are held to be un-Christian, and if necessary, it will use the threat of excommunication and even damnation. An Emperor is after all, a Christian layman, and as such, is subordinate to the bishop. Although kings are above man's laws, they are subject to the punishment of God for their sins.

Ambrose was Augustine's mentor when Augustine lived for a time in Milan. A we will see in Chapter XIII, Augustine will fine-tune this teaching that will establish State and Church relations in the Middle Ages and beyond.

John Chrysostom (347–407)

"Chrysostom" means "golden-tongue" and refers to John's eloquent oratory. John had at first tried being a desert monastic but developed ulcers. He was famed for his preaching and asked to come to the court at Constantinople. However, most of his sermons were addressed to the corruption of the court, especially against the women and their finery and schemes. The Emperor soon sent him back to the East, to become the bishop of Antioch. He became famous in his preaching concerning celibacy; all Christians should now practice celibacy because "the world was fully populated".

In his fiery sermons, John is famous for a series delivered during Easter week in 387. John was apparently upset over the fact that his Christians "attended Synagogue on Saturday and Church on Sunday". In some of the most repugnant anti-Jewish denunciations ("synagogues are brothels", and "their sexual immorality has the sound of snorting pigs") it also reveals something very interesting about late antiquity.

Ignoring the higher educated writings of the Bishops against the Jews, Christians in Antioch apparently had no problem "mixing with the Jews". John railed against them sharing their holidays and festive meals. We find this in several communities throughout the Empire. In the Council of Elvira, Spain in 312, Christians were admonished for continuing to have Rabbis bless their fields. He also railed against Christians continuing to be involved in traditional native elements, such as the theater and the chariot races. Unfortunately, John's Easter sermons continued to be quoted against the Jews in medieval Europe and beyond.

Jerome (347–420)

As a student, Jerome engaged in the superficial escapades and sexual experimentation of typical students in Rome. He indulged himself quite casually, but he suffered terrible bouts of guilt afterwards. To appease his conscience, on

Sundays he visited the sepulchers of the martyrs in the catacombs. Although initially skeptical of Christianity, he eventually converted.

In Rome, Jerome was surrounded by a circle of well-born and well-educated women, including some from the noblest Patrician families, such as the widows Lea, Marcella, and Paula, with Paula's daughters Blaesilla and Eustochium. His written correspondence with these women has been preserved. Dominant cultural social conventions did not disappear with the conversion of the Empire to Christianity. Marriages were still the way in which to achieve higher status and political clout. As widows, all these women had inherited vast resources of their husbands. As admirers of Jerome, he encouraged them to accept the celibate life.

The resulting inclination of these women towards the monastic life, "away from the indulgent lasciviousness in Rome", made him an enemy of the upper-class lay Christians. His unsparing criticism of the life-style in Rome resulted in the same opposition. Soon after the death of one of his patrons in 384, Jerome was forced to leave his position at Rome after an inquiry was brought up by the Roman clergy into allegations that he had an improper relationship with the widow Paula.

In August 385, Jerome, with Paula and Eustochium, who had resolved to end their days in the Holy Land, moved to Bethlehem. Jerome moved into a cave (the cave where Jesus was born, he claimed) and spent the rest of his life there. Although later Renaissance art would present this as an austere life, Paula and others made sure he was "comfortable"—fine furniture, oriental rugs, all the books he wanted in the cave.

It was here that he finished what would eventually be deemed his greatest work. He translated the Hebew Scriptures and the Greek New Testament into Latin. In Latin, "vulgar" means common, or the common tongue—hence the **Vulgate Bible**. This bible would remain the most popular one in Europe until the beginning of the production of bibles in German, English, and French.

We detail the life and accomplishments of Augustine in Chapter XIII.

AUGUSTINE (354–430)

XIII

- The Conversion (386)
- Back to North Africa
- Why Do Humans Sin?
- Back to the Garden
- The Doctrine of Grace
- Predestination
- Pelagius and Free Will
- Julian of Eclanum (386–455)
- Augustine's Concept of Free Will
- The Donatists
- The Circumcellions
- The Sin of Suicide
- The Barbarian Invasions and the City of God
- Just War Theory
- "Slay Them Not"

Varieties of Early Christianity: The Formation of the Western Christian Tradition,
First Edition. Rebecca I. Denova.
© 2023 John Wiley & Sons, Inc. Published 2023 by John Wiley & Sons, Inc.

Augustine (354–430)

After reading this chapter you will be able to:

- Chronical Augustine's conversion and why it resulted in the Doctrine of Original Sin.
- Appreciate that the reflections and writings of Augustine determined relations between the body and society and the Church and State for the Middle Ages and beyond.

Aurelius Augustinus Hipponensis, Augustine of Hippo (a city in the Roman province of North Africa), is extolled as the greatest of the Christian Church Fathers. More than any other writer, he developed what would become known as "systematic theology", or an explanation of how Christianity fit into views of the universe, creation, and humankind's relationship with God. When Martin Luther (an ex-Augustinian friar, 1483–1546), protested against the Catholic Church, he created the Protestant Reformation utilizing the teachings of Augustine. Through the various Protestant denominations and their missions, the Christian Western tradition is indebted to the teachings of Augustine.

You may have encountered some of Augustine's books. His *Confessions* is one of those Great Book classics (found in any bookstore) and is considered the first autobiography in the West. His other major work *The City of God*, is also referenced in Political Science courses for his "just war" theory and as a source for the lost manuscripts of ancient philosophers (see Figure XIII.1).

354—born in Thagaste, North Africa, to Patrick and Monica

370—the death of Patrick

371—Augustine began a 15-year relationship with a woman

374—Professor of rhetoric and philosophy at Carthage. He joined a Manichaean sect as a "hearer"

384–86—Milan and conversion. Monica died shortly afterwards

391—Back at Hippo, coerced to become a presbyter

395—Co-adjutor Bishop, and then Bishop of Hippo. Augustine created his own monastery and order

397—*The Confessions*

410—The sacking of Rome by Alaric and the Goths

411–12—Emperor Honorius formally proscribed and executed the Donatists

412–13—Writings against Pelagius and "free will"

413–27—*The City of God*

430—Death at Hippo, with the "Vandals at the gates"

Augustine has left a catalogue that contains 113 books, 218 letters, and 500 sermons.

Figure XIII.1 Augustine's Life (354–430).

Augustine's writings are among the most complicated of the Latin Fathers because over the course of his life, he would often go back to a theological concept and "update" it or add to it as his thoughts evolved and he matured. For example, his doctrine of Original Sin emerged in *The Confessions* (397) but it is not fully articulated until *The City of God* (413). We also have many of his letters to other Bishops who challenged his ideas and his teachings. The other complication is that throughout his literature and especially in *The City of God*, Augustine quoted from both past and contemporary philosophers.

Augustine was born to a non-Christian, Patrick, and Monica, a Christian (something very common in the late Empire). We don't know much about Patrick, but we can describe Monica as a "stage-mother". She constantly pushed Augustine to better himself all the while nagging for him to become a Christian. She was very ambitious for her son, and once the Empire was converted, believed that he could only get ahead in the world if he was a Christian.

Augustine had an excellent education in rhetoric. After Patrick died in 370, Augustine left home and took a position as a professor of rhetoric in Carthage. Apparently sharing interests with other intellectuals and philosophers, Augustine became a "hearer" in the sect of Manichaean Christians, a heretical but popular sect in the Empire at the time (see Box XIII.1).

Box XIII.1   Manichaean Christians

Mani (d. ca. 254) was a Persian Christian who founded a sect of believers based upon Gnostic ascetic principles. Mani claimed to be the last Prophet sent by God in a long chain of Prophets. His teachings were very popular among intellectuals and even the uneducated, defying Imperial bans against it being a heresy. Manicheanism also became popular in the East, traveling along the Silk Road and other caravan routes into central Asia and China.

Augustine enjoyed this group because they were fellow intellectuals, but also because it was a Christian sect that had two tiers. Even though a zealous ascetic, Mani only demanded celibacy and other sacrifices for the leaders of each group. The second tier, the "hearers", did not have to give up a normal life. Later in life, after his conversion to Imperial Christianity, Augustine would refute Manicheanism and take on the Manichaeans in his writings and public debates in North Africa.

It was at this time that Augustine lived with a woman outside of marriage for fifteen years. Augustine could have the best of both worlds—stimulating discussions and the companionship of a woman. There were still class restrictions involving marriage in late antiquity. You could marry into a different class, but ideally it had to be "marrying up", never down. Apparently, this woman was of a lower class than Augustine's family. If he had legally married her, his status would be reduced. They had a son together, Adeodatus ("gift of god") who died young.

Monica still had plans for her son. Together they moved to Milan, Italy where she began negotiations for a marriage contract with a girl from a better family.

Augustine knew that there was an impressive philosophical school near Milan that he could join. Augustine said goodbye to his companion; we never learned her name.

The Conversion (386)

We know the details about Augustine's conversion because he wrote about it later in *The Confessions* (397). Considered the first autobiography in Western literature, it is psychological retrospective ("looking back") on his life. It is not a history of events in the sense that we can analyze the events as they took place. Augustine wrote about his experiences years later, after he had time to reflect upon the decisions he had made.

As a dutiful son he took Monica to mass at the Cathedral in Milan each week (Ambrose's cathedral). He was intellectually interested in Ambrose's sermons. After the sermon, he would sit on a bench outside waiting for his mother. On one of his visits, he heard what he thought was a child playing a sing-song game "Take up and read". When he did not see anyone, he realized that it was a supernatural calling. He said he found a New Testament and opened it to Paul's letter to the Romans. It changed his life and he became a Christian.

This must have thrilled Monica. However, Augustine was a perfectionist. If he was going to be a Christian, then he was going to be a celibate Christian. He told Monica to cancel the marriage negotiations. Monica then died. This must have been traumatic for Augustine, and it is perhaps here that he began to articulate the metaphysics of guilt (*reatus*). It went something like this: God made everything from nothing and each created thing is good, with natural faculties. All owe a debt to God for their creation. When they misuse their faculties (sin), this misuse results in guilt because of the debt.

Back to North Africa

The Roman provinces of North Africa had originally been settled in the late Republic by legionary veterans and the *Equites* class ("middle-class" commercial businessmen and traders). Being transferred to one of the provinces, there was an inherent obsession of still wanting to be perceived as traditional Romans. Thus, North African Romans were extremely conservative in relation to culture and religion. Augustine inherited this view in upholding both conventional society and the now, new "Imperial religion" as dictated by the state.

In Hippo, Augustine became one of those Bishops who was coerced into taking the position after a vote where the outcome for someone else was challenged. He made a trip to Egypt to study the monasteries and built his own when he returned.

Augustine's commitment to celibacy never bothered him in the physical sense. The philosophical concept of asceticism, against "losing control" of the bodily urges was condoned by Augustine. He now had his own body under control. When I described Augustine as a "perfectionist", he reached beyond for attempts of "perfection of the mind" as well. With a controlled body, nevertheless, he could not control his thoughts of thinking about sexual intercourse. He assumed that "such thoughts" would go away with old age. But when a seventy-year-old parishioner announced the birth of a son, he was dismayed. His struggles with *why* he could not control his thoughts led to the bigger question of why people commit sin when they, at least intellectually, know better (like Augustine)?

Why Do Humans Sin?

In one of the most famous sections of *The Confessions*, Augustine related an incident when he was a teenager. He and his friends broke into a neighbor's garden and stole some pears. He thought about this incident over and over—none of them were hungry, none of them were poor. Why did they do it? Augustine was a great admirer of Paul and realized that Paul had undergone a similar struggle. He went to a passage from Paul's letter to the Romans 7:14:

> We know that the law is spiritual; but I am unspiritual, sold as a slave to sin. I do not understand what I do. For what I want to do I do not do, but what I hate I do. And if I do what I do not want to do, I agree that the law is good. As it is, it is no longer I myself who do it, but it is sin living in me. For I know that good itself does not dwell in me, that is, in my sinful nature. For I have the desire to do what is good, but I cannot carry it out. For I do not do the good I want to do, but the evil I do not want to do; this I keep on doing. Now if I do what I do not want to do, it is no longer I who do it, but it is sin living in me that does it. So, I find this law at work: Although I want to do good, evil is right there with me. For in my inner being I delight in God's law; but I see another law at work in me, waging war against the law of my mind and making me a prisoner of the law of sin at work within me. What a wretched man I am! Who will rescue me from this body that is subject to death? Thanks be to God, who delivers me through Jesus Christ our Lord!

Back to the Garden

Augustine, as a Biblical exegete and Bishop, like so many others, turned to Genesis, the beginning of all creation, to analyze how evil got into the world and why humans sin. The human proclivity for sin and evil began with Adam and Eve who passed it down to every generation because after their expulsion from Eden, they began to populate the world. Augustine reinterpreted Genesis 3, as a way in which to help people "read between the lines" in terms of "what really happened".

As we saw with earlier Christian theologians, Eve was blamed for introducing the sin of lust into human intercourse. But in Genesis, there is no sexual intercourse until after they leave Eden. Augustine's contribution to the story was to move their sexual intercourse back to *before* the expulsion. This highlighted sexual intercourse as the first "sin", and not just disobedience against God's command not to eat of the two trees.

In the last line of the second creation story (Genesis 2), after God created Eve out of Adam's rib: "And the man and his wife were both naked and were not ashamed". Genesis 3, enter the serpent and Adam and Eve disobey God and eat from the tree of the knowledge of good and evil: … "their eyes were opened, and they knew that they were naked; and they sewed fig leaves together and made loincloths for themselves". When God came to look for them, they were hiding because now they are "naked and ashamed". Augustine claimed that between the two passages (naked and not ashamed/naked and ashamed) something "evil" had happened—the sin of lust in sexual intercourse.

But didn't God also create genitals? Wasn't God's first commandment in Genesis, "to be fruitful and multiply?" Yes, Augustine said. God did create genitals (and human sexuality), but originally, this human activity was to be simply a natural function of humans, like walking or eating. The initial "fall" was in the fact that Adam and Eve introduced the "passions" into it, creating the sin of lust.

According to Augustine, Adam and Eve's intercourse left an indelible mark, a stain, on the fetus and this stain was passed on to all. Without using the term, or understanding the science of genetics, Augustine claimed that we "inherited it", somewhat like a "sin gene". Located in the semen, it was transmitted to the woman, and so both are guilty.

Augustine claimed that his concept of this (now) **Original Sin** was not new. He quoted Paul in Romans 5:12: "Therefore, just as sin came into the world through one man, and death came through sin, and so death spread to all because all have sinned". In the Vulgate Latin translation of the letter, the phrase, "because all have sinned," was "Wherefore as by one man sin entered into this world and by sin death; and so, death passed upon all men, in whom all have sinned". One should be an expert philologist in both Greek and Latin to perceive the nuances of differences in the phrase. Scholars still debate if Paul had the same concept as Augustine. Augustine had studied Greek, but he was more comfortable with Latin.

Augustine's concept of Original Sin was an incredibly fatalistic view of humankind. He referred to the human race as "the condemned masses" because we are "conceived in sin", and thus damned from the moment of conception. Baptism was the initiation ritual that admitted you to the Church to "wash away this Original Sin", but did not totally eliminate the human proclivity for evil. As he knew, baptized Christians continued to sin.

Over the centuries, natural disasters, high infant mortality rates, and plagues led people to begin baptizing babies. With the doctrine of Original Sin, this became the practice by the fifth century. Augustine originally declared that unbaptized babies went to Hell. By the Middle Ages, this was softened with the concept of **Limbo**, from *limbus*, for "hem" or "edge", an intermediate state between Purgatory and Heaven. But the unbaptized had to be buried in a special "unsanctified" section of cemeteries and not with their family. Always viewed as harsh teaching for grieving parents, the Vatican's International Theological Commission under Pope Benedict XVI officially eliminated the teaching of limbo for unbaptized babies.

The Doctrine of Grace

If we are all condemned at conception, what is the way out? This is where he adopted another theme from Paul; the only thing that can save humans is "the grace of God". Grace in this sense is derived from the Greek *charis*, which means "gift". God's gift to us was sending Christ who would lead the way to salvation. This was truly a gift because humans (being condemned) could never achieve salvation on their own merits. Augustine may have utilized Plotinus' concept of "pride" in humans that kept them from thinking they could overcome sin on their own. Humans remain unreconciled without this, and it has to come from God as the world is now corrupted by evil and the distractions of evil, applying the concepts of Plotinus (see Figure XIII.2).

Why do humans commit evil? Why do humans continue to disobey?

Augustine summarized the beliefs of divergent Christians: Gnostics, Manicheans, and other heretics. They explained the existence of evil as ignorance alone which does not constitute sin. Once you are enlightened, you remember your true origins and re-join with God. The Gnostic view of evil was found in the very nature and origins in matter. Humans are not held responsible for evil because they are not responsible for having bodies and they do not know any better. What is the solution? Finding the truth (*gnosis*) which is what Christ came to teach us. All of these ideas were deemed heresy by Augustine.

He summarized his own views (with his reading of Paul). First and foremost, the existence of evil results from a weakness of willpower. "Sin" is the inability to resist the temptation of the power of sin in the universe. What is evil? Matter itself is not evil, but overindulgence in matter, and one's attitude toward matter can be evil. Humans are held responsible for their evil. They will be judged by God. What is the solution? Faith in Christ and practice in self-discipline.

For Paul and Augustine, evil results from weak willpower in both physical and mental aspects: (1) physical, the desire to satisfy bodily instincts; and (2) mental, the desire to disobey for its own sake (the way in which Augustine understood his stealing of the pears).

For Augustine, God is all-good, all-powerful, and omnipotent. He did not create anything evil. When calamity or natural disaster strikes, this is all part of the divine plan to teach us, to form us, so that through suffering, we can re-direct our souls (and bodies) upward. As a typical philosopher, Augustine dealt with abstractions: evil is nothing but the privation or absence of good; not a substance in and of itself. It is a manifestation of what happens when we turn away from God, from the good.

Figure XIII.2 *"Unde hoc malum?* Whence comes all this evil?".

264   Augustine (354–430)

This concept of God as abstract however, did not indicate a totally new understanding of the universe. As a product of his culture, Augustine nevertheless railed against the existence of the "demons" at work in his communities.

Figure XIII.2   (Con't)

Predestination

How does one receive grace? Augustine added a complication to his doctrine of grace. Because God is omniscient (all-knowing), God already knows who will be saved and who will be damned. The omniscience of God had been debated by various Jewish sects. The Pharisees claimed a theory of providence (culturally, the power of the divinity Tyche or Fate), while the Sadducees disagreed. Augustine wrote that the Church had always believed in the doctrine of predestination, citing Paul:

> We know that in everything God works for good with those who love him, who are called according to his purpose. For those whom he foreknew he also predestined to be conformed to the image of his Son, in order that he might be the first-born among many brethren. And those whom he predestined he also called; and those whom he called he also justified; and those whom he justified he also glorified.
>
> (Romans 8:11)

In his earlier writings, Augustine claimed that predestination was based on God's foreknowledge of whether individuals would believe, that God's grace was "a reward for human assent". He later refined his ideas which were challenged by other Christians.

Pelagius and Free Will

Pelagius (354–418), was a British monk who was also an itinerant preacher, traveling around the Western Empire. The gist of his preaching was on the story of the Fall in Genesis. If God is omniscient, then why didn't he *know* that Adam and Eve would disobey and eat from the tree? To solve this conundrum, both the early Rabbis as well as Christian theologians read something back into the text which was not there: God did not want slaves; when he created humans, he gave them "free will". (Recall that this was the teaching of Bishop Origen in the third century.)

Pelagius could not conceive of a God who would create humans whom he knew would sin. Thus, giving them free will, God had created humans with the ability to choose. It was possible for humans to freely choose to be moral and good. The model for this is the life of Christ, who was even obedient to God through death, and so all Christians should strive to be imitators of Christ.

Christians had free will, the Law of Moses, and the teaching of Jesus to help them. God's grace was a gift to help discipline us and bring us to salvation. Free will was a matter of human *will* and not human *nature*.

Pelagius was put on trial in Jerusalem in 415. This was when a parish priest had a dream of where to find the bones of Stephen. The tribunal took this as an omen to condemn Pelagius. The last we hear of Pelagius is that he went to Egypt, where he died, but we don't know the details. Excepting a few fragments, all of his writings were destroyed.

Debates followed, particularly through letters and treatises. In the beginning, both Augustine and Jerome praised the teaching of Pelagius, particularly his asceticism and teachings on morality. As more details became known however, it was evident that Pelagius disagreed strongly with Augustine's concepts of Original Sin and the role of divine grace. Pelagius opposed Augustine's concept of a flawed humanity, as well as the idea that God provides "grace", more or less "on a whim". If God did not want humans to ultimately be saved, he would not have sent his son into the world to die for their sake.

Julian of Eclanum (386–455)

Julian was a leader of Pelegians in Benevento, Italy. From 419 on, he and Augustine waged a war on the issue of free will through books, pamphlets, letters, and sermons. He wrote in a letter to Augustine:

> We maintain that men are the work of God, and that no one is forced unwillingly by his power either into evil or good, but that man does either good or ill of his own will; but that in a good work he is always assisted by God's grace, while in evil he is incited by the suggestions of the Devil. Strengthened by baptism, everyone possesses enough self-control to reject evil.

Julian wrote that our laws are rational and mirror the attributes of God himself. God would not condemn every human because of one sin committed by Adam. He accused Augustine of importing Manichean teachings into his concept. Augustine responded: "Our notions of justice are too fallible to be attributed to God; his ways are inscrutable" (*Against Julian*).

Augustine's Concept of Free Will

In Augustine's earlier work, he agreed that God conferred free will in humans. But Christian communities were still embroiled in debates over baptism, grace, and predestination. Augustine pulled all these issues into his **Doctrine of Free Will** (see Figure XIII.3 for a summary of the contending views).

Origen (which influenced Arianism)

There were two stages of creation, a first spiritual cosmos (eternal), containing God and pre-existent souls. The Fall began when the souls "cooled" and turned, utilizing their free will. God created the material universe to shelter souls in their various stages. The Incarnation of Christ is when the soul of Christ adjoined with a human soul and descended to show us the way back to God. This was the moment of salvation, not the cross. Grace is the illumination provided to understand scripture. Redemption is found in utilizing the free will to return to God where the body is left behind in the world; its material nature evaporates.

Pelagius

The creation of the cosmos is spiritual and physical and created at the same time. Human's Fall into sin is the willed rebellion against God, where humans have total freedom of choice; mortality is the "wages of sin". The Incarnation was an historical expression of God's love. The gift of grace is sent to help humans discipline themselves. Humans can be redeemed through their moral efforts; the soul is perfected through love.

Augustine

God created the universe peopled with bodies and souls created new together at conception. The Fall produced a flaw in humans through sexual intercourse in Eden, Original Sin, passed down to all humans. Humans commit sin because they want to, because it is forbidden. The Incarnation of Christ was the manifestation of God himself on earth. Without God's free gift of grace, all humans are damned without it (*massa condemnata*), but it is always God's choice to provide grace. God chooses us, we do not choose him.

Augustine's contribution to these debates was another analysis of Genesis. God did grant free will to Adam and Eve in the beginning, but with their sin, total freedom was lost to humans. Through the procreation of the first couple (with the sin of lust which was the stain that was passed down), humans are only "free to choose evil". The "choice" is found in man's perverse will against the divine Will—the soul pays the penalty. This is why Christians need both grace and the Church; the sacraments confer grace through the "spirit" to disciple them. Redemption for Augustine involves a raised body and soul (which also has to change) and residing in a heavenly "city of God". We will all exist as the same age of Christ (30) and be perfect.

The nuances of these various views can be complicated and esoteric and it is difficult to understand the distinctions. For Origen and Pelagius, free will and the choice to sin was mainly intellectual. Augustine began from the same premise but now understood that the "locus of sin" *began and remained in the body*. Through this teaching, the Western tradition inherited an almost obsessive aspiration to control and tame the body. Modern discourse still debates the relationship between the body and society, instituting government, religious, and cultural limitations on what we can and cannot do with our bodies.

Augustine won and opposing views were condemned as heresy at later Councils. In one of those ironies of history, Augustine's preference for Latin meant that he most likely never read Origen's *Peri Archon* (in Greek). Pelagius had journeyed to Hippo to meet with Augustine, but Augustine was away at one of his monasteries. If these two had met, perhaps the fatalistic view of being "condemned at conception" could have been softened.

Figure XIII.3
Summary of the Debates on Free Will.

The Donatists

Recall that when the Diocletian persecution was ended, several Bishops debated whether to forgive those Christians who had handed over their Scriptures or committed idolatry. Constantine reconciled this by decreeing that they should be forgiven, but Bishop Donatus disagreed and took his group to North Africa. Donatist churches were established throughout the area. Constantine condemned them as heretics and ordered the confiscation of their church property, but they simply refused to turn over the buildings.

Donatism was popular with the common people of North Africa, as well as the now converted Berber (nomad) population. Most Donatist clergy in rural Numidia spoke the vernacular languages (Libyan or Punic) whereas the Catholic clergy used Latin. Donatus argued that Christian clergy must be faultless for their ministry to be effective and their prayers and sacraments to be valid. The church must be a church of "saints" (not "sinners"), and sacraments administered by any previous *traditores* (the compromisers) were invalid.

The *Circumcellions*

This was the name given to bands of Donatist clergy, monks, and anti-Roman, Punic-speaking rebels. The term may have been used by critics to mock them *circum cellas euntes* "go around larders", because "they roved about among the peasants living off those they sought to indoctrinate". These men claimed to be reforming social grievances by condemning property, promoted canceling debt and freeing slaves. They attacked both Christian and native landlords and colonists and redistributed their property to the poor. They preferred their own name, *agonistici*, "fighters for Christ".

The object of the random beatings of both Christians and non-Christians was to provoke the victim or the government to kill them, thereby bringing on martyrdom. They regarded martyrdom as the true Christian virtue and strove to bring about their own. In the hope of "getting to heaven", many of them committed suicide by throwing themselves off cliffs, drowning, or deliberately trashing a pagan shrine to get themselves arrested and condemned. Some burned themselves at the stake.

Augustine held a series of town hall meetings and campaigned against the Donatists. His response to their claim that clergy who sinned should be expelled, was to apply an analogy of Noah's Ark: "Just as the Ark had both clean and unclean animals, so the Church will always have sinners and saints". The later Council of Trent (1545–1563), utilizing Augustine, taught that the value of the sacraments conducted by the clergy does not depend on the status of the celebrant, but on the "worth of the victim and on the dignity of the chief-priest, Christ himself."

Augustine quoted from the parable of the banquet in Luke 16:23, where a man gave a banquet, but no one came: "And the lord said unto the servant, 'Go out into the highways and hedges, and compel them to come in, that my house may be filled.'" Augustine, influenced by Ambrose's understanding of church and state, petitioned Emperor Honorius (384–423) in 410 to send in the legions to enforce "orthodoxy". Donatist churches were destroyed and their clergy massacred. The slaughter at times was so great that even Augustine protested.

The Sin of Suicide

It is during this period that Augustine wrote on the nature of suicide. As we saw, in both Greco-Roman culture and early Christianity, suicide was not a sin. In his debates with the Donatists, Augustine criticized their "seeking out" martyrdom. He argued that these Donatists should never receive the title of martyr, because they died of their own volition and were not forced. At this point he declared suicide as "the sin that cannot be forgiven". He used the example of Judas. Judas could have been forgiven, but his suicide is why he would forever remain in Hell.

The Barbarian Invasions and the City of God

We have focused on the personal elements of Augustine and his theological concepts, but this did not take place in vacuum. The Western Empire was besieged by many and continuing invasions; Goths, Visigoths, and Vandals. The city of Rome, in fact, had fallen to Alaric and the Visigoths in 410; Rome had never been invaded or conquered for 800 years. This trauma motivated remaining non-Christians to claim that it was the fault of Christians for "angering the gods".

Augustine's second great opus, *On the City of God Against the Pagans* (413–426) was his response to these critics. Considered another classic in Western thought, Augustine fine-tuned his earlier writings on the suffering of the righteous, the existence of evil, the conflict between free will and divine omniscience, and the concept of Original Sin. Its value is found in his arguments for the superiority of Christian philosophy over other schools and his skill in summarizing and chronicling philosophical treatises.

The book presented human history as a universal conflict between God and the Devil. The "earthly city" is defined as one of corruption and evil, where people immerse themselves in the cares and pleasures of the present world. The "city of God", a new Jerusalem, contains those who devote themselves to the eternal truth of God and the eventual Heavenly realm for all believers. This period also saw many Christian writers describing details and differences in the realms of Heaven and Hell (which influenced Dante's The Divine Comedy, 1320).

Turning the criticism on its head, Augustine wrote that Christianity did not cause the sacking of Rome. The pagan gods had often failed to protect Rome against disasters and military defeats such as the sack of Rome by the Gauls in 390 BCE (Book III). Rather, God, in his foreknowledge was responsible for the successes of Rome. He knew that Roman military victories and expansion, with those Imperial roads and the conversion of Constantine, would provide a coherent system for the conversion of the Empire.

When Alaric sacked Rome, many Christian women who had been raped committed suicide. Culturally, rape resulted in shame for both the woman and current or future marriages. In *The City of God*, Augustine emphasized his view that suicide was not necessary after a rape, because it could never be forgiven. Rather, victims of rape should not marry, but dedicate their lives to the Church and good works.

Just War Theory

The City of God contains what became known as "just war theory". How to determine if a war was morally justified? Augustine applied the criteria of the "right to go to war", and "right conduct in a war". He reviewed ancient traditions and philosophical writings on war as he developed his views. Individuals should not commit violence on their own. God gave the sword to governments, validated by Paul in his letter to the Romans 23:4: "For the one in authority is God's servant for your good. But if you do wrong, be afraid, for rulers do not bear the sword for no reason. They are God's servants, agents of wrath to bring punishment on the wrongdoer".

One of the problems with the theory of a "just war" is that Augustine did not detail the conditions, particularly of who gets to decide if a war is justifiable or not. But summarizing his views on church and state, Augustine believed that the Christian government, motivated with "divine necessity", had the right to determine if any war was morally waged. Augustine's "just war theory" was reviewed and adapted for centuries where it most likely influenced the later Geneva Conventions (1939–1945), that addressed war crimes, the protections for prisoners of war, and the treatment of civilians during war.

"Slay Them Not"

What about the Jews? Augustine's familiarity and study of the Jewish Scriptures led him to be at variance at times with fellow Christians. As we saw, by the late fourth century, the Theodosian Code began diminishing Jewish life and culture. At the same time, their continuing existence led to more *Adversos* treatises over the centuries. Augustine's admiration for Paul and his admiration for the Scriptures led him to urge that Jews should be protected.

Augustine fully condoned all bans against pagans and heretics. However, he argued that Judaism had laid the foundation for the Church and provided the beginnings of understanding God and Christ. Augustine claimed that one of the purposes of the Church was to protect that legacy. In late antiquity with its constant wars and invasions, "end-time" scenarios were drawn from the Book of Revelation (then as now). Paul had written that when Christ returned "his brother Jews" would see the light and convert. Augustine wrote, "slay them not"; Jews had to survive to be part of the end-time scenario. This view remains dominant in some Evangelical Christian circles who vigorously support the Jewish state of Israel for this reason.

Augustine died in 430 during the Vandal invasion of North Africa. Augustine lamented not the invasion per se, but that the Vandals (by now Arian Christians) were heretic Christians. His monks rescued many of his books and sermons and took them to southern France where they spread throughout monasteries in Europe and Ireland.

Summary

- Augustine's conversion was influenced by cultural and religious ideas in the context of the Roman Empire in late antiquity.
- Augustine's Christianity was transferred to Europe and became the dominant teaching of the Church throughout the Middle Ages and beyond.

Suggestions for Further Reading

Augustine and Bettenson, Henry, trans. 2004. *City of God*. Penguin Classics.
Augustine and Chadwick, Henry, trans. 2017. *Confessions*. Oxford's Word on Fire Classics.
Peter, Brown. 2013. *Augustine of Hippo: A Biography*. University of California Press. First published in 1977, Brown's biography remains a classic study of Augustine and his world.
Young, Frances M. and Teal, Andrew. 2010. *From Nicaea to Chalcedon: A Guide to the Literature and Its Background*. Baker Academic. This is an anthology to both the literature and the context of late antiquity.

EXCURSUS V
CHALCEDON AND BEYOND

The Struggle among the Sees

Paulinism

Novationism

Nestorianism

What Type of Human?

Council of Chalcedon (451)

Consequences of Chalcedon

Orthodox Christianity

The reader should not be surprised by now that despite revised editions of the Creed and Imperial Edicts against heretics, various Christian communities either ignored them or suffered persecution as a result. The barbarian invasions did not only affect ecclesiastical dictates, but the local populace as well. Through the period, Christians were urged to be "patriotic Christians", in line with the Imperial Church. But which Imperial Church? The Antiochene and Alexandrian communities continued to debate which Emperors had such authority (legitimacy), depending upon their views of continuing Arianism at their courts and other topics. The Empire contained ethnic diversity of every kind which also had to deal with local, cultural "ancestral traditions", as well as periodic, localized rebellions in districts that had nothing to do with religion.

The Struggle among the Sees

The major "sees", (dioceses) of Bishops) were Jerusalem, Antioch, Alexandria, Constantinople, and Rome. The First Council of Constantinople in 381 elevated Rome as above all others (as the site of the martyrdoms of Peter and Paul). Alexandria saw this as an insult to their prestige. Antioch resented it because they claimed the first "Christian" community. Jerusalem was the most insulted, as this was the site of Jesus' passion, crucifixion, and resurrection. Thrown into this mix were three more "heresies" that ultimately required more Imperial *anathemas* (a formal curse or denunciation of dogma), dictates, and Councils: **Paulinism**, **Novationism**, and **Nestorianism**.

Paulinism

Paul of Samosata (200–275), from which we have the term "Paulinism", was the Bishop of Antioch from 260–258. In the earlier Trinity debates, he supported the concept of Monarchianism. Jesus was born a man but infused with the divine *logos*. Through this adoption, Jesus was not "a god who became man", but "a man who became God". But as a man, Jesus shared God's divine will. Paul was condemned as a heretic after the official doctrine of the Trinity was established at Nicaea, but there were followers of his teaching throughout the Empire. Paulinist baptism was deemed unacceptable and required re-baptism. A source for the life of Paul of Samosata is contained in Eusebius' history. He claimed that Paul took money for his services and that he had immoral sexual relations with his women (standard levels of polemic).

Excursus V Chalcedon and Beyond 273

Novationism

Novatian (ca. 200–258) was a Christian theologian (like Donatus) who refused lapsed Christians during the persecution of Decius (251). Their forgiveness had to await God in the final judgment. The only source we have for Novation is found in Eusebius' history, where he was accused of the standard crimes: taking money for his services, living a "high life-style", and sexual immorality with his women parishioners. Novatian believed that membership in the Church was not required for salvation. But as the Church is made up of "saints", re-admission of these "sinners" would threaten the community. Novatian's followers extended the idea of "no re-admission" to all who committed "mortal sins" (idolatry, murder, and adultery). Many of them also forbade re-marriage.

Nestorianism

Nestorius (386–450) was the Archbishop of Constantinople from 428 to 431. Among other issues, his most controversial teaching was a rejection of the elevation of Mary as *Theotokos* ("God-bearer", the second-century claim that Mary was elevated because she carried "divinity in her womb"). Rejecting *Thetokos*, he preached *Christotokos* ("Christ-bearer") instead. Whether he intended to or not, by the fifth century, Nestorianism was denounced as teaching two distinct **hypostases** in the Incarnate Christ, or two "realities," one human and one divine.

The Council of Nicaea was largely concerned with the relationship of God and Christ; it did not delve into the "nature" of Christ (**Christology**). Was Christ human or was he divine? Was he first divine and then human, or human who was exalted to divinity? Continuing debate concerning Christology led Emperor Theodosius II to call a Councils at Ephesus in 431 (see Box XIII.2).

Box XIII.2   The Debates at Ephesus

The choices in defining Christology at Ephesus involved the cities of Jerusalem, Antioch, Alexandria, Rome, and the communities which still contained Jewish-Christians. All of them sent Bishops and delegations to Ephesus.

1. Jewish-Christians (Ebionites): Affirm his humanity and God's revelation in him, with the result of his moral excellence. Jesus was born human but was vindicated by his death and exalted to Heaven (with the concept of the Maccabee martyrs). This was condemned as heresy.
2. Docetism ("appearance"): Affirm the pre-existent divinity of Jesus but deny his humanity. This was the view of Gnostic systems which made the Incarnation meaningless. All docetic views were condemned.
3. Rome: Tertullian had set the tone for the Western churches, by simply claiming that two substances were joined in a single person (nature), including a rational soul (but without elaborate explanation). This union was formulated in the Trinity at Nicaea and followed in the Western Empire and certain communities in the East.

274   Excursus V Chalcedon and Beyond

4. Antioch. In and around Antioch, Christians preferred the gospel traditions of a more human Jesus. Jesus' humanity meant that he could more sympathetically understand the normal struggles of humans. Divine elements were present in the human Jesus, but full divinity was only achieved at his resurrection and exaltation.
5. Alexandria. The remaining Arians in Alexandria (Christ is subordinate to God), claimed that if the "word" can combine with flesh, it receives sense impressions. Therefore, it is "mutable," not "identical" to God, who was "immutable," unchanging. The Hellenistic-influenced schools in Alexandria insisted that the union between the divine and human in Jesus be such that there was a true communication—so identical to the divine will, that Jesus lacked a rational (human) soul.

"How can the immutable word unite with mutable humanity?" The union of the word with flesh, transforms this particular flesh. In Christ, the word = spirit, and the body and soul are thus joined to the divine and can't be acted on or changed. This was a union without forming a new nature.

What Type of Human?

Throughout the proceedings, Bishops argued over the extent of Jesus' humanity. Bishop Clement of Alexandria had earlier claimed that Jesus lacked human passions. The line in the gospel of John, that "Jesus wept," was an allegorical symbol of the loss of God's plan for humans. Origen taught that Jesus's body was different, purer than all other humans. As an original soul before creation, the soul of Jesus was different than human souls. They even debated if Jesus physically ate or performed other human functions (such as defecation).

All these theologians agreed on the union of divinity and human but disagreed on the physics of how it was achieved. In relation to salvation, "Why become a man to save other men?" Athanasius of Alexandria claimed that it was not to give God an opportunity to participate in human life, but so that humans could participate in the divine life "for man to become God".

At the Council of Ephesus, Nestorius' views were supported by Bishop John of Antioch, and Cyril of Alexandria (who had a monastery). Bishop Celestine of Rome opposed him. But then Cyril of Alexandria sent Nestorius a letter with twelve anathemas that had to be accepted and included in all Alexandrian theology. Both Nestorius and John of Antioch were late in arriving and were condemned in *abstentia*. John arrived four days later and condemned Cyril. Bishops' legates arrived from Rome in the next few days. They suggested ratifying the condemnation of Nestorius but removing the ban on John's group and re-admitting them.

Ephesus was notorious for the constant excommunications and charges of *anathema* by Bishops on both sides. Theodosius II threw most of them in prison, but Cyril talked his way out. All three major heresies (Paulinism, Novationism, and Nestorianism) were condemned. Because the first Council of Ephesus resolved nothing, a second one was called in 439. The conclusion was that the duality of natures existed only in the ideal moment, before the Incarnation. The conclusion of this Council was that after the "the union", there was only one nature.

Council of Chalcedon (451)

After the death of Theodosius II, those discontented with Ephesus still objected. In 451, Emperor Marcian called for a Council at Chalcedon (near Constantinople). The purpose was to finally settle the issue of the two natures of Christ and how to word the doctrine of Incarnation. It was attended by 520 Bishops and their entourages and was the largest and best documented of all the Councils. Marcian wished to bring proceedings to a speedy end and asked the council to make a pronouncement on the doctrine of the Incarnation. It was decided that no new creed was necessary.

The Council issued what was called the **Chalcedonian Definition** or the Chalcedonian Confession:

> Following then, the holy Fathers, we all with one voice teach that it should be confessed that our Lord Jesus Christ is one and the same God, the Same perfect in Godhead, the Same perfect in manhood, truly God and truly man, the Same (consisting) of a rational soul and a body; *homoousios* with the Father as to his Godhead, and the Same *homoousios* with us as to his manhood; in all things like unto us, sin only excepted, begotten of the Father before the ages as to his Godhead, and in the last days, the Same, for us and for our salvation, of Mary the Virgin *Theotokos*, as to his manhood. One and the same Christ, Son, Lord, Only-begotten, made known in two natures [which exist] without confusion, without change, without division, without separation; the difference of the natures having been in no wise taken away by reason of the union, but rather the properties of each being preserved, and [both] concurring into one Person and one hypostasis (essence)—not parted or divided into two persons, but one and the same Son and Only-begotten, the divine *Logos*, the Lord Jesus Christ; even as the prophets from of old [have spoken] concerning him, and as the Lord Jesus Christ himself has taught us, and as the Symbol of the Fathers has delivered to us.

In other words, the two natures of Christ remained distinct in the union; neither nature was diminished in any way through their joining. The final answer at Chalcedon to the question, was Christ human or divine, was "Yes". How was it physically achieved? "It is a mystery".

The Council also issued twenty-seven disciplinary canons governing Church administration and hierarchy (to stem the life-styles and corruption of the clergy). Canon 28 declared that the See of Constantinople (New Rome) had the patriarchal status with equal privileges to the See of Rome.

Consequences of Chalcedon

The immediate result of the Council created more schisms. Some Bishops claimed that the declaration of "two natures" was equivalent to Nestorianism. The Alexandrian churches did concede "two natures" from the beginning, but they emphasized the "divine nature" as dominant. The Alexandrians were now labeled "monophysites" ("one nature"), and thus "heretics". This was technically not their position, but they broke from both Constantinople and Rome and created the independent Coptic Christian Church of Egypt with their own Pope. They suffered persecution and executions until the time of the Islamic Conquest, which granted them status as "people of the Book", Jews and Christians.

In the East, the Nestorian survivors carried his teachings into Persia and other regions of the Byzantine Empire and beyond. Nestorian communities existed along the silk road into China and India. Periodically vestiges of "heretical teachings" arose, so that we had continual rounds of excommunications and denouncements from Constantinople. The continuing existence of these divergent communities ultimately contributed to the separate creation of Eastern Orthodox Christianity. They utilized both inherited teachings (from the Cappadocians Fathers), as well as contemporary views. As we saw, the differences contributed to the Great Schism of 1054 between Rome and Constantinople.

Orthodox Christianity

With the collapse of the Western Empire, Constantinople maintained the entity of what became known as the Byzantine Empire, until the invasion and conquest of the Ottoman Turks in 1453. The survivors transferred the concept of a "Holy Roman Empire" into the Balkans and Russia. The later Romanovs adopted the title of "Caesar", to "Tsar", and their symbol on coins was the "two-headed eagle" of Rome. The two heads indicated the "new or second Rome of Constantinople", now surviving as both church and state in Russia.

Referred to as Orthodox Christianity, there are fifteen autocephalous (autonomous) Orthodox churches. They are self-governing in communion with each other, but with internal self-government. They have the right to choose their own leaders, Patriarchs, and Metropolitans, and resolve their own problems. Often aligned with governments and geographic areas, the four ancient Patriarchates include Constantinople, Antioch, Alexandria, and Jerusalem. The others are found in Russia, Serbia, Romania, Bulgaria, Georgia, Cyprus, Greece, Poland, Albania, Czechoslovakia, and Slovakia. Orthodox Christianity can be found throughout the Americas, Africa, and the East. Byzantine Catholic Churches are those that identify with the spiritual traditions of Orthodoxy but recognize the primacy of the See of Rome.

EPILOG
THE LEGACY OF CHRISTIANITY IN THE WESTERN TRADITION

The religion of Christianity evolved over several centuries by incorporating the concepts of ancient Judaism and Greco-Roman religion and culture. Applying new interpretations, Christians developed their own ideas of sacrifice, rituals, myths and sacred stories, hymns and prayers, a priesthood, martyrdom, patron mediators in heaven (saints), and the language of philosophy to explain their views.

For millennia, ancient cultures had claimed a direct line from their ancestors to their contemporary religious customs. Hence, traditional cults were simultaneously ethnic. Christianity introduced the idea that ancestry and bloodlines were irrelevant to membership in the assemblies. In practical terms this meant that Christianity was not confined to a people or a geographic area; Christianity became a portable religion as assemblies were found in every city. This aspect of the new religion was one of the elements that contributed to its spread throughout the Mediterranean. At the same time, Christianity provided an assured afterlife in heaven for those who adhered to the dictates and rules of the Church.

The ancient concept of the full integration of divinity with everyday life remained essentially the same. However, Christianity eliminated the ancient recognition of "all the gods" as "gods," by reducing them to demons. This was achieved through the innovation of defining orthodoxy against heresy, now enforced by the power of both the Church and the state. The Creed became the standard measurement to determine permissible thoughts and practices.

Christians also upended the ancient understanding of human sexual intercourse for the sole purpose of procreation. Augustine's claim that humans are "conceived in sin" created a new understanding of the burden placed on bodily behavior and the body and its relationship to society. Only the Christian Church and the society that it created can save humanity.

Varieties of Early Christianity: The Formation of the Western Christian Tradition, First Edition.
Rebecca I. Denova.
© 2023 John Wiley & Sons, Inc. Published 2023 by John Wiley & Sons, Inc.

278   Epilog

The Roman Empire in the West

When Constantine moved the capitol to Constantinople, that city became both the center of the Church as well as the administrative center of the Roman Empire. There were "Emperors" in the West (with the traditions of "Caesars", and "Augustii") but diminished in authority. Over the centuries, as circumstances changed in the West, and with the barbarian invasions, Western Emperors ultimately failed to maintain Imperial rule.

The Huns were nomads who arose in Central Asia, the Caucasus, and Eastern Europe in the fourth and fifth centuries. Their migrations pushed other tribes (Goths, Visigoths, Vandals) into Europe (Germany, Gaul, Italy, Spain) and North Africa. Attila was the most famous leader of the Huns (see below). Many of these tribes had adopted Arian Christianity.

The fall of the Western Empire resulted from the inability of leaders to keep the West stable financially, militarily, and theologically. In addition to the invasions, drought and food shortages, inflation, a series of devasting plagues, recurring theological debates, and constant civil wars contributed to the decline. In 476, the Germanic king Odoacer deposed the last Emperor in the West, Romulus Augustulus. The Senate officially sent the Imperial signa to Emperor Flavius Zeno in Constantinople.

The Rise of the Institution of the Papacy

Bishop Leo I (400–461), also known as Leo the Great, is credited with the creation of the **Institution of the Papacy**. He continued to conduct many synods and debates on the existence of Arians and other heresies. He upheld the Nicaean Creed and the results of Chalcedon on the nature of Christ.

In 451, Attila invaded Italy, sacked several cities and headed for Rome. Leo was among the delegation who met with Attila to negotiate the sparing of the city. According to the story, the preaching of Leo convinced Attila to change his mind. In 455, the Vandal king Genseric succeeded in sacking Rome, but tradition claimed that the efforts of Leo reduced the carnage and spared the Basilicas of St. Peter, St. Paul and St. John where many Christians were holed up as refugees. After the fall of the West, there was no equivalent secular authority as there was at Constantinople.

The Petrine Supremacy

In 450, Leo appealed to the Byzantine Emperor Theodosius II, and was granted the title of "Patriarch of the West". This included the first usage of the title "Pope" for Leo. The word, *popa*, is derived from the Greek, "father", and had been used in the Eastern Empire for some Bishops and monastics. In the Latin West, however, *popa* was the title of the priest who slaughtered sacrificial animals. This may be a remnant relating the position of the Pope as overseer of all "sacraments" of the Church.

Leo emphasized the importance of the Church of Rome (and his position) by utilizing the historical traditions of Peter, retrospectively declared the first Bishop of Rome, and thus the first Pope. As the "heir of Peter", Leo was authorized to demand the extradition to Rome of any heretics. Succeeding Popes took on this role, ultimately acquiring territory in central Italy in the Middle Ages (the Papal States) and leading their own armies. All elected Popes simultaneously serve as the Bishop of Rome.

A second level of clergy evolved with the appointment of **Cardinals** in the sixth century. They were originally drawn from the deacons in the various dioceses in Rome. The word may have derived from *cardo*, which meant "pivot" or "hinge" in the sense that it was someone incorporated into the community who was not an original member. Organized into the "College of Cardinals", their primary responsibility is electing a new Pope after the death of a prior one by meeting in **conclave**.

"Conclave" derives from the Latin, *clavi*, a key. It refers to the fact that the Cardinals were literally locked in a chamber while they voted, so as not to receive any outside influence or bribes. Throughout the later Middle Ages, conclaves became infamous because of the integration of political influence of the emerging nation-states. From 1309–1376, in protest of a decision, many Cardinals moved the Papacy to Avignon, France (in the kingdom of Arles), under the auspices of several French kings.

The Church from Late Antiquity to the Middle Ages (476–1500)

The use of the Greek word, *catholic* ("universal") in the Nicene Creed became official as the title of the "**Catholic Church**" in the West in late antiquity. As Christianity spread through Europe, the Catholic Church became the dominant institution that ordered the daily lives of everyday Christians, from birth to death to the afterlife. This was understood as the "kingdom of God on earth" until the return of Christ. The Catholic Church remained the dominant Church in the West until the Protestant Reformation in 1519.

The Holy Roman Empire

In the year 800, Pope Leo III crowned Charlemagne (the king of the Franks) as the Holy Roman Emperor (a concept and title that had not been used since the fall of Rome). This renewed the conviction that the Emperor remained the head of the Church as well. Historians continually point out that it was "neither holy,

Roman, nor an Empire." Monarchs and princes vied with each other for the title and control throughout the history of Europe, often clashing with the contemporary Popes. It was dissolved in 1806 through the conquests of Napoleon.

Ancient Concepts Redefined

"Everything old is new again ..." All the debates over the Trinity and Christology continued into the Middle Ages (and continues in some modern Christian denominations). Augustine's systematic theology spread throughout Europe and was utilized for the work of a new group of "Doctors of the Church," the Humanists and Scholastics. They continued to analyze the unity of the divine nature, free will, the nature of evil, divine grace, and Original Sin. They combined rationality with theology, in that God was the source of both.

Anselm, Bishop of Canterbury (1033–1109), began writing on a problem inherent in the exegesis of Genesis. How can we prove that God exists? He presented what is known as "the ontological argument," a rational way in which to prove the existence of God through an a priori argument: God exists an as idea in the mind; if it exists in the mind, then it is a reality. There is nothing beyond God, so God is the source of all, and thus proof of his existence. Thomas Aquinas (1225–1274) produced his magisterial work, *Summa Theologica*. He applied the principles of Aristotle to argue that faith and reason were compatible. In the *Summa*, the proof of God's existence is found in creation. In other words, the very nature of creation requires a first creator.

Mendicant Orders (Twelfth Century)

By the Middle Ages, the great monastic orders owned large tracts of farm lands and incorporated castle keeps (places of refuge in case of war) into their monasteries. They accumulated great treasures from Christian donations of relics and art. But several monks led a movement that rejected both the ownership of property as well as the life-style to become itinerant orders known as **mendicants**.

"Mendicant" from the Latin, "to beg", was someone who survived through alms. They took the monastic ideal of asceticism from the monastery to the cities, administering to the poor and the sick. Members of these orders were known as "Friars," and became infamous in their critique of both the monasteries and the Catholic Church. They often attacked the villas of Bishops and redistributed their wealth to the poor. The two most famous orders were the Dominican Friars (by Dominic Guzman, 1170–1221) and the Franciscan Friars. The Franciscans originated with followers of St. Francis of Assisi (1181–1226) who had donated his family's wealth to the poor.

Epilog 281

The Millennium

In the eleventh century, a remnant of the last of the Ice Ages created crop failures and famine in Europe. Turning to Scripture, calculations of the age of the earth were combined with the "1000-year reign of Christ on earth" from the Book of Revelation. People believed that the reign of Christ was equivalent to the reign of the Church in the last 1000 years. In anticipation of the imminent "final days" and the return of Christ, many Christians did not plant crops. This only added to famine and hardship when the kingdom did not materialize.

Nevertheless, the renewed interest and popularity of the Book of Revelation continued in every generation and beyond. Modern Christians still turn to the book to analyze contemporary crises and "signs" as they arise in line with John of Patmos' predictions.

The Inquisition

The problem of heresy did not go away. The Second, Third, and Fourth Lateran Councils (1139, 1179, 1215) prescribed imprisonment and confiscation of property as punishment for heretics and threatened to excommunicate princes who failed to punish them. During the twelfth century, Christian sects known as the Albigenses in Southern France (*Cathari*) and the Waldenses in the Balkans, led to the formation of the "**Episcopal Inquisition**". These branches of Christianity were accused of teaching Gnostic-like doctrines.

The Episcopal Inquisition was formally instituted by Pope Gregory IX in 1231. Gregory mandated that heretics be sought out and tried before a church court. This task became entrusted to the Dominican and Franciscan orders. The independent authority of the inquisitors was a frequent cause of friction with the local clergy and Bishops. Infamous for its notoriously harsh procedures (torture), the Inquisition was defended during the Middle Ages by appeal to Biblical practices and to Augustine, "Compel them to come in ...").

When the Inquisitors arrived in a city, a period of grace was given for any heretic to renounce his/her beliefs. Denunciations could be made by anyone, even other heretics. The court conducted an interrogation and attempted to gain a confession. The accused was tortured which included burning with live coals, cutting off fingers, toes, tongues, testicles, and breasts, or the *strappado*, stretching on a vertical rack. The Church was not permitted to shed blood; the torture was carried out by secular authorities who executed by burning at the stake. Notable victims of the Inquisition included Galileo (who was saved by recanting), the philosopher Giordano Bruno, the religious order of the Knights Templar, and Joan of Arc.

The Inquisition grew to include sorcery, alchemy, blasphemy, sexual immorality, and infanticide. The number of witches and sorcerers burned after the late fifteenth century was greater than the number of heretics (approximately 60,000). At the urging of Ferdinand II of Aragon and Isabella I of Castile, the Inquisition developed a special relationship with the crown in Spain. Their Inquisitor, Tomas de Torquemada, was charged with ridding Spain of the Moors and Jews. He extended this to the Marranos (converts from Judaism), and Moriscos (converts from Islam) who had been Christians for generations. Torquemada accused them of secretly continuing to practice their original faith. Jews and Muslims were expelled from Spain in October,1492.

This is when behavioral theory and racial theory were added to the persecution of Jews and Muslims, as behavior was "in the blood." In other words, their "conversion" would always be suspect. This idea spread throughout Europe and became embedded in emerging racial theories as Europeans encountered indigenous populations during the Colonial Period.

The Spanish inquisitors followed the Conquistadors to the colonies in America and applied their procedures to resistant indigenous populations. The Inquisition was finally suppressed in Spain in 1834 and in Portugal in 1821. During the Catholic Counter Reformation (mid-sixteenth century), Pope Paul III created what became the Congregation of the Roman and Universal Inquisition, also known as the Holy Office, whose task was to watch over the correct doctrine of faith and morals for the Roman Catholic Church. It was redefined by Pope Paul VI in 1965 as the Congregation of the Doctrine of Faith, where the disciplinary tool currently used is excommunication.

The Bubonic Plague

In the ancient world and the Middle Ages (as well as contemporary society, Covid-19), mass incidents of plague created theological crises. In the fourteenth century in Europe, the "Black Death" (Bubonic Plague) killed roughly a third of the population. We know of earlier incidents of Bubonic plague from ancient manuscripts, but the increased trade between Europe and the East during this period brought rats from ships (who carried the plague in their fleas) to European cities. The Plague was spread by respiratory transmission, killing a person within a few days of contact.

A "sign of the end?" A punishment from God? A movement of **Flagellants** began, from the Latin, "to whip." This was a mortification of the flesh through whipping the skin with different instruments. Fasting, hair-shirts, and other forms of discipline of the body, they cited Paul when he said: "I chastise my body" (perhaps scourging) in 1 Corinthians 9:27).

Sharing in the passion of Jesus through this process, sins were forgiven not only for the practitioner, but the perception of the "sins of the Church" through their wealth and corrupt life-styles. Recurrences of the Plague, and views of both Mendicant Friars and the Flagellants contributed to highlighting the "failures of the Church", that led to the later Protestant Reformation. Modern Catholicism still honors groups of Flagellants as "confraternities of penitents".

Many Christians blamed the Jews for the "Black Death". Jews in the Middle Ages resided in their own communities (later to be limited to ghettoes in the fifteenth century). The impact of the plague was less in Jewish communities, perhaps due to their isolation and having their own doctors. Rumors began that the Jews were poisoning wells. In the city of York in the twelfth century, the Jews were arrested and burned to death because of the plague. In other cities, attacks on Jews became normal events.

The Crusades

The concept of a **crusade** was derived from the Book of Joshua, when God told him that the wars against the Canaanites involved the destruction of people, crops, and herds, as "devoted to God." Certain wars were "holy wars", with the spoils sacrificed to God.

The Church issued a call for "crusades" against the Islamic rule of the "Holy Sites" in Jerusalem and the Galilee. Originally called "pilgrimages," the word "crusade" only came into use much later in the Middle Ages. In 1095, Pope Urban II called for a crusade at the Council of Clermont. Considered a sacrifice, anyone who became a Crusader was absolved of sins.

A committed Crusader had to undergo long journeys by land or by sea; many never reached the Holy Land. But "fighting for the cross of Christ" could be achieved by attacking both Jewish and Muslim communities nearer to home. In the first crusade, Jews in the Rhineland were forced to be baptized and slaughtered when some refused to do so (1096).

The First Crusade (1096–1099) established the Kingdom of Jerusalem (the most successful Crusade). The Third Crusade (1189–1192) is famous for the participation of Richard II (the "Lion-heart") and Saladin (who reconquered the city of Jerusalem). The Fourth Crusade (1202–1204) is the most infamous. Instead of attacking Muslims, the Crusaders attacked the Byzantine capitol of Constantinople, stealing many of the treasures that were transferred to Venice. They remain incorporated into St. Mark's Cathedral and plaza in that city.

Modern historical analysis of the Crusades focuses on the historical context of the periods, emphasizing the economic changes in trade between the West and the East. The Italian cities of Venice and Genoa relied upon the caravan routes of the Middle East for imported spices and other wares. Muslim control was considered a threat to their prosperity.

The term, "crusade", became attached to efforts to eliminate any group or movement that was deemed heresy or sought to challenge the Catholic Church, either religiously or politically. It is also utilized by some Protestant denominations in planned recruitment efforts, most famously through the late Reverend Billy Graham.

284 Epilog

Passion Plays

In a world where literacy was confined to the upper-classes and the Church, teaching the majority of the population was done through art as well as what became known as "the **Passion Play**", or the reenactment of the Passion of Christ. First presented as part of the Easter liturgy (with an expansion of choirs) they also became an essential element of "carnival season" in various cities. An unfortunate result of the Passion plays was periodic increased persecution of the Jews.

Passion plays remain a popular element in Catholic countries all over the world, where select men often volunteer to "be crucified" (especially in the Philippines and Mexico). One of the more famous European passion plays is presented every ten years in Oberammergau, Germany. Protestant Christian denominations in America present Passion plays as part of their educational efforts throughout the mid-West and South in the circuits of summer-stock theater.

Renewed controversy in the production of Passion plays was generated in 2004, with Mel Gibson's *The Passion of the Christ*. Claiming to be "historical", Mr. Gibson added several extra elements to the story, culled from the visions of a nineteenth century German nun. Both Rabbinical leaders and Christians reacted negatively to the film, with conferences around the country and the publication of several books and articles. Mr. Gibson belongs to the Catholic Traditional movement, a Catholic sect which rejects the reforms of the Second Vatican Council of 1964–65.

The Renaissance (15th to 16th Centuries)

The Renaissance ("re-birth") is often described as the "flowering of classical literature and art" in the Middle Ages, transitioning from late antiquity to the modern age. It coincided with the discovery of ancient manuscripts that had been preserved by Arab scholars. Christian intellectuals scoured philosophical treatises and updated them for Christian understanding to be applied to art, architecture, politics, science, and literature. This period produced the great artists and masterpieces of Christian art and architecture: Leonardo da Vinci, Michaelangelo, Bernini, Raphael.

As an increased interest in the cult of Mary, paintings and statues proliferated with what is known as "the Madonna" (from "my lady"). A seated Mary with the baby Jesus on her lap may have evolved from the popular cult of the Egyptian goddess Isis in the late Empire holding her son Horus (See Figures 1 and 2).

Epilog 285

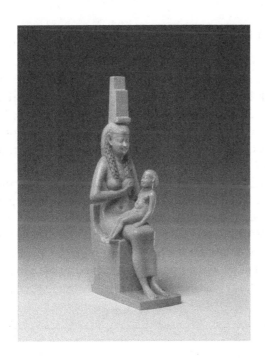

Figure 1 Isis and Horus. The Metropolitan Museum of Art / Wikimedia commons / CC BY 1.0 Universal Public Domain Dedication.

Figure 2 Rest on the Flight into Egypt, Gerard David, 1510. National Gallery of Art / Public Domain.

The Protestant Reformation

From the fourteenth to the sixteenth centuries, criticism of the institution of the Catholic Church began to spread throughout Europe. Early reformers such as John Wycliffe (1330–1384) and Jan Hus (1369–1415) advocated for the production of Bibles in local languages instead of Latin. The invention of the printing press (credited to Johannes Gutenberg) in 1436 helped to spread their ideas in several countries.

Martin Luther (1483–1546) was a German professor of theology, and an Augustinian monk and priest. Luther advocated against the practice of saints, relics, indulgences and other abuses by the Catholic Church in his *Ninety-five Theses* of 1517. When he refused to renounce his criticism he was excommunicated by Pope Leo X and the Holy Roman Emperor Charles V at the Diet of Worms in 1520. Luther was declared a heretic and an outlaw.

Justification by Faith Alone

More than any other medieval theologian, Luther promoted Augustinian theology. Sinners are saved through "faith alone", with the gift of God's grace. Original Sin eliminated the human capacity to work out their own salvation. There is no free will because the will is overpowered by sin. Only God can overpower the influence of the Devil. Luther extended Augustine's concept by adding that when God redeems a person, he redeems the entire person, including their will. Only after this is done is a believer liberated to serve God.

Sola Scriptura

Luther declared that the only true knowledge is found in *sola scriptura*, "scripture alone". Scripture can be mediated through creeds and Councils. However, humans are fallible, but scripture is divinely revealed. We are saved through the divine scriptures and God's gift of grace. As only God can do this, the clergy are not sacred mediators between God and humans. Nor is the Church. When he married Katharina von Bora, a former nun, he renounced the idea of clerical celibacy as well as the Catholic meaning of the sacraments. Luther's ideas were also spread by another reformer, John Calvin (1509–1564) and his community at Geneva, Switzerland. Both upheld Augustine's doctrine of predestination.

Luther and the Jews

Initially, Luther wanted to convert the Jews. But a later work, *On the Jews and Their Lies*, he called for the burning of synagogues, schools, and books. They should have their property confiscated and no access to legal protection. The Jews should be drafted into forced labor, and "We are at fault for not slaying them." His writings on the Jews remain infamous, especially after Hitler called him "one of history's greatest reformers," in *Mein Kampf*. Analysis of his rhetoric however can be confusing at times. It lacks references to contemporary Jews and Judaism in Germany, focusing on past, Biblical "sins of the Jews". The other problem is that in his critique of the Vatican, he often applied the analogy of the Pope and the Cardinals to that of "Pharisees". Modern Lutheran and Protestant churches have renounced Luther's views on Jews and Judaism.

The Enlightenment (Seventeenth and Eighteenth Centuries)

Often described as the "Age of Reason," the period known as the Enlightenment presented new intellectual and philosophical ideas that also coincided with scientific revolutions in technology. Major contributions to the Enlightenment are assigned to Francis Bacon, Rene Descartes, Isaac Newton, Emmanuel Kant, Denis Diderot, Spinoza, David Hume, John Locke, Montesquieu, Jean-Jacques Rousseau, Adam Smith, and Francois Arouet (Voltaire).

Enlightenment writers in France focused on individual liberty (against absolute monarchy) and religious tolerance (against the power of the Catholic Church). These views contributed to the French Revolution of 1789, and the ideas spread throughout Europe and eventually to the American colonies, creating the modern nation-states.

The Enlightenment writers did not outright reject religion but became noteworthy for what is described as "**Deism**". From *deus*, Latin for god, it is the rational application to the study of the natural world, concluding in the belief of a supreme creator of the universe. It eliminates "miracles" as "proof" of divine intervention. The description of miracles was the way in which the ancients described natural events without rational thought. Influenced by this idea, Thomas Jefferson wrote *The Life and Morals of Jesus of Nazareth* (also known as the "Jefferson Bible"). He highlighted the teachings of morality and values in the gospel message as useful to society and eliminated all the miracle stories.

Both Thomas Jefferson and Benjamin Franklin lived in Paris (as delegates from the American colonies). Influenced by Enlightenment ideas (including political theory), the Declaration of Independence reflects traditional Christian tenets:

> We hold these truths to be self-evident, that all men are created equal, that they are endowed by their Creator with certain unalienable Rights, that among these are Life, Liberty and the pursuit of Happiness—That to secure these rights, Governments are instituted among Men, deriving their just powers from the consent of the governed …

Simply called the "Creator" here, "God" became iconic in the great seal, in the currency, eventually in oaths in court-rooms, in the national anthem and the pledge of allegiance, "In God we trust" in the currency is the God of Israel mediated through Christ. George Washington began the continuing practice of the president of the United States taking his oath of office on a Bible. Soldiers' funerals are replications of martyrs' funerals, as they "sacrificed their life for God and country." The later "Federalist Papers" gave us the "separation of Church and State". This does not eliminate the "religiousness" of American culture; it is a ban on the government imposing any one religion on the populace.

Enlightenment thought also led to the "scientific study of the Bible", which coincided with the emerging social sciences of Archaeology, Anthropology, Sociology, and Psychology in the nineteenth century. Social Scientific methods of analyses are now incorporated into theological and academic disciples of the study of the history of both Testaments.

Varieties Galore

The Protestant Reformation coincided with political changes throughout Europe, the Balkans, and Russia. Various church leaders followed Luther's lead and broke with Rome, while simultaneously aligning with the emerging nation-states. Henry VIII broke with Rome over the Vatican's refusal to grant him an annulment. As the monarch, he became the head of the Church of England. Mirroring the beginnings of Christianity itself, Protestant groups broke into "sects" which were now aligned with geo-political demographics.

The Lutheran Churches in Germany were different from the Anabaptists in Munster (where they rebelled against the local government), Dutch Reform Churches, the Calvinist Churches in Switzerland, the Anglican Church in England, and the Huguenots in France. They agreed on the basic anti-Vatican position, but differed in terms of church governance, which rituals to maintain and which to eliminate.

Many Protestant sects experienced persecution in some countries: Anabaptists, Huguenots, Puritans, Pilgrims, Quakers. The persecutions coincided with the discovery of the New World which was perceived as the new "promised land", for a new "kingdom on earth". Protestantism in America became characterized by periodic movements known as "the Great Awakening", which included critiques of various denominations and a renewed understanding of individual salvation, branching into Presbyterians, Baptists, and Methodists. There are at least 65,000 Protestant denominations in the United States alone.

These movements gave rise to a concept known as "Christian Fundamentalism" which proclaimed the "inerrancy of Scripture". As a response to growing liberal and nonliteral interpretations of the Bible, inerrancy declares: "The Bible speaks with infallible divine authority in all matters upon which it touches." The appeal to inerrancy continues in Christian debates concerning creationism (and evolution), gender equality (women ministers), social justice, racism, homosexuality, same-sex marriages, and abortion. Contemporary debates argue these issues by validation to Scripture and the relationship between church and state. Should the government (especially the Supreme Court) mandate laws concerning human behavior and society, especially if they are contrary to Scripture?

The Colonial period provided more opportunities to missionize in the Middle East, Africa, Asia, and Latin America. Like their forefathers, Christian missionaries often adopted elements from the dominant culture. As one religion, Christianity throughout the world incorporates many local traditions and customs.

Martyrdom

Maintaining the original concept of martyrdom (sacrificing one's life for one's beliefs) remains an important concept in the modern world. We have incorporated the concept into what we consider "secular martyrs", people who risk political or social denunciation, and at times their life, for their beliefs, despite knowing that it could lead to death. The Reverend Dr. Martin Luther King combined religion with social justice, but we also consider others as martyrs to a cause: Abraham Lincoln, John and Robert Kennedy, Matthew Shepherd, Harvey Milk, civil rights advocates, and those who have died a violent death for a cause.

Technically, modern criteria for martyrdom involves a voluntary choice to risk one's life. However, we collectively assign it even when a choice was not available. The victims of the Two Towers on 9.11 are collectively denoted martyrs, and the site as "sacred space". Ideologically, as "Americans", they are juxtaposed to the ideology of Islamic terrorists.

Christianity is the world's largest religion, with an estimate of 5.2 billion followers. Unfortunately, the persecution of Christians continues to be a problem, particularly in those countries that have experienced the rise of the Islamic State (ISIS). In Iraq, many of the remaining Christian communities fled to refugee camps where they remain. Muslim-dominated countries in both West and East Africa, Malaysia and Indonesia periodically target Christians and kidnap Christian missionaries. China has recently renewed limitations of missionizing on both Christian and Muslim communities.

In some countries, however, the Christian response to persecution is also one of violence. Particularly in West Africa, Evangelical "mega-churches" promote equal atrocities against their Muslim neighbors. Both sides validate their actions as "killing in the name of God", searching their scriptures for ways in which to justify such slaughter. And both sides claim martyrs in this struggle. The stakes are high. "Religion" remains the way in which humans can achieve "salvation", variously defined.

Jewish–Christian Relations

On October 27, 2018, an anti-Semitic shooter attacked the Tree of Life Synagogue in Pittsburgh, Pennsylvania, resulting in the death of eleven people and injuring four police officers. The shock of this incident highlighted the renewal of attacks on synagogues in Europe, Canada and the United States in recent years.

Renewals of what became modern anti-Semitism began in Russia and Europe in the early twentieth century, with the publication of a forgery known as *The Protocols of the Elders of Zion*. This text claimed to have knowledge of a secret cabal of Jews who sought world domination through economic control. It became elementary reading in Nazi Germany and was widely distributed in America through Henry Ford's publication of it in his newspaper, *The Dearborn Independent*. (Ford later recanted with the beginning of WWII.) The English translations of this document often substituted "Communists" for "Jews". Hence, the document was useful for the McCarthy hearings on "the Red Scare" of the 1950s. Modern anti-Semitic groups continue to utilize the *Protocols* for evidence of Jewish conspiracy.

Modern analyses on the root causes of the Holocaust as well as continuing anti-Semitism has expanded to consider the relationship of Christianity among all world religions. There is increased interest in ways to express and respect the diversity of all peoples and a focus on the way in which "words matter". All religions remain challenged with promoting their own "true faith", while respecting the views of others. Understanding the historical context of the origins of religious views can help to appreciate both the construction of worldviews that incorporate social, cultural, and religious meanings as well as their changes over time.

Suggestion for Further Reading

Logan, Donald F. 2012. *A History of the Church in the Middle Ages*. Routledge. This history combines the theological elements with its historical context.

APPENDIX I: A BRIEF OUTLINE OF THE HISTORY OF ROME

753 BCE—According to legend the city of Rome was established by Romulus and Remus.

715-673—The reign of King Numa Pompilius, legendary founder of Roman religion.

509 BCE—Overthrow of the kings and the creation of the Roman Republic.

390 BCE—The Gauls invade Rome and sack the city.

264-146 BCE—The Three Punic Wars against Carthage.

204-202 BCE—Scipio Africanus defeats the Carthaginian general Hannibal at the Battle of Zama in North Africa.

146-141 BCE—Carthage destroyed; Macedonia and Greece conquered.

110 BCE—The first of several invasions by German tribes, which were eventually defeated by Gaius Marius who reformed the army.

98-88 BCE—Social War, the last rebellion of the Italian peoples against Rome.

88-66 BCE—Wars against King Mithridates VI of Pontus (northern Anatolia): Rome conquers Asia Province (Anatolia), Syria, Israel, and Armenia.

60-54 BCE—The First Triumvirate of Caesar, Pompey, and Crassus.

58-50 BCE—Caesar's Gallic Wars.

Varieties of Early Christianity: The Formation of the Western Christian Tradition, First Edition.
Rebecca I. Denova.
© 2023 John Wiley & Sons, Inc. Published 2023 by John Wiley & Sons, Inc.

49 BCE—Caesar crosses the Rubicon; civil war against Pompey and the Republicans.

48–45 BCE—Pompey defeated at Pharsalus and assassinated in Egypt; Republican forces defeated in North Africa.

44 BCE—Caesar assassinated; Octavian, Anthony, and Lepidus form the Second Triumvirate.

31 BCE—Octavian defeats Anthony and Cleopatra at the Battle of Actium.

27 BCE—Octavian declared Augustus; end of the Republic and beginning of the Roman Empire.

14–68 CE—Julio-Claudian Emperors: Tiberius, Caligula, Claudius, Nero.

69–9 CE—Flavian Emperors: Vespasian, Titus, Domitian.

98–117 CE—Trajan (101–107, Dacian Wars).

117–138 CE—Hadrian—the building of Hadrian's wall in Britain; The Bar Kokha Revolt

161–180 CE—Marcus Aurelius.

212 CE—Roman citizenship offered to all for tax revenue.

250–300 CE—the Empire suffers from foreign invasions, plague, inflation and military coups.

284–306 CE—the Emperor Diocletian restores the Empire; divides the Empire into East and West with a hierarchy of Augusti and Caesars.

312/313 CE—Constantine, the first Christian emperor; the Edict of Milan proclaims Christianity as a recognized religion in the Rome Empire.

330 CE—The center of the Roman Empire is moved from Rome to Constantinople.

381 CE—Theodosius I forbade all forms of paganism; Christianity becomes the sole religion of the Empire.

410 CE—Alaric and the Goths sack Rome.

476 CE—The last Roman Emperor is defeated by the Germanic leader Odoacer; the Roman Empire ceases to exist in the West but continues for the next thousand years at Constantinople/Byzantium.

APPENDIX II: TIMELINE FOR THE EARLY HISTORY OF CHRISTIANITY

6 BCE–6 CE	The range of dates for the birth of Jesus; traditional reckoning places it at 0.
20's–30's	Ministry of Jesus.
26–36	Jesus of Nazareth crucified during the reign of Pontius Pilate in Judea.
36–40?	Call of Paul, the apostle.
50's–60's	Establishment of various Christian communities in the Eastern Mediterranean, Greece, Egypt, and Rome; the letters of Paul.
64	The great fire in Rome; legendary persecution of Christians.
66–74	The Jewish Revolt against Rome.
70	The city of Jerusalem taken, and the Second Temple destroyed.
69/70?	The Gospel of Mark.
85?	The Gospel of Matthew.
95?	The Gospel of Luke and Acts of the Apostles.
83–95	Reign of Domitian.
95–100?	The Gospel of John.
95–100?	The *Apocalypsis* of John of Patmos (Revelation).

Varieties of Early Christianity: The Formation of the Western Christian Tradition, First Edition.
Rebecca I. Denova.
© 2023 John Wiley & Sons, Inc. Published 2023 by John Wiley & Sons, Inc.

294   Appendix II: Timeline for the Early History of Christianity

110–113   The correspondence between Pliny and Trajan; the first documented "Christian trial".

112–115?   The letters of Ignatius of Antioch.

132–135   The Second Jewish Revolt against Rome, under Hadrian; Jews are banished from Jerusalem.

140   Marcion and his congregation arrives in Rome; popularity of Gnostic beliefs, literature.

150–200   The writings of Justin Martyr, Irenaeus, Tertullian and others, and what will eventually become orthodoxy; apologetic writings to pagan intellectuals; writings against Gnostics as "heretics"; writings against Jews.

200   Clement of Alexandria.

202?   Martyrs in Carthage (Perpetua and Felicity); empire-wide citizenship granted to everyone.

250?   Anthony (Egypt) leaves the world for the desert.

251   Decius issues edict for everyone to propitiate the gods; first semi-official persecution of Christians by the state; Christian communities break into "schism".

257   Second similar persecution under Valerian.

250–300   Empire-wide conflicts: wars on the borders, inflation; famine; plague— Christian leaders take over functions previously carried out by magistrates.

284   Aurelian ("one empire, one emperor, one god") is succeeded by Diocletian.

303   The "Great Persecution" under Diocletian, and the last persecution; he ordered Christian leaders to turn over their sacred writings; again, "schism" occurs.

312   The Battle of the Milvian Bridge in Rome; Constantine is ruler of the West and becomes a Christian.

313   The Edict of Milan, which legitimized Christianity in the Empire; Constantine invited to mediate Christian schisms.

324   Constantine sole ruler of the Empire, East and West; Helena makes a pilgrimage to the Holy Lands.

325   The Council of Nicaea; confirmation of the "Trinity"; Constantine moving the capitol from Rome to Constantinople (Istanbul).

330   The death of Constantine; he is baptized on his deathbed.

350   The Rise of Monasticism; The birth of Augustine.

360–363   The reign of Julian; the renewal of paganism.

Appendix II: Timeline for the Early History of Christianity   295

386/7	The conversion of Augustine; 390's, "The Confessions".
407	The Emperor Honorius proscribes the Donatists of North Africa.
410	The Goths sack Rome.
415–420's	"The City of God".
417	Trial of Pelagius in Jerusalem; Minorca synagogue burned and first mass conversion of Jews.
430	Death of Augustine, with "Vandals at the gates" of Hippo.
451	The Council of Chalcedon; Jesus attains two natures.

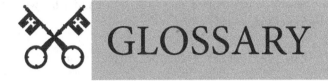

GLOSSARY

Aaron the brother of Moses and the first high-priest of Israel.

Abraham the founder of the nation of Jews in Canaan.

Acts of the Apostles Luke story of the history of the movement from Jerusalem to the cities of the Empire.

Adam and Eve the first created couple; the progenitors of humans.

adultery the violation of another man's property.

Adversos Literature the collective term for the writings of the Church Fathers against Jews and Judaism, as "adversaries".

afterlife the general term for the belief in some form of existence after death.

Alexander the Great conqueror of the Middle East and Persia who introduced Greek culture and language to the region (330 BCE).

allegory a method of interpretation that provides a picture or a story to devise another meaning, often applied for religious, moral, or political exposition.

altar an outdoor table or stone slab, usually a stone slab, where sacrifices were offered to deities.

altar of victory the altar to Nike in the curia of the Senate; a rallying point for Roman senators against its removal under Christian Emperors.

anachronism placing something outside of its place and time.

angels divine beings who serve in the court of God; messengers between God and humans.

Varieties of Early Christianity: The Formation of the Western Christian Tradition, First Edition.
Rebecca I. Denova.
© 2023 John Wiley & Sons, Inc. Published 2023 by John Wiley & Sons, Inc.

annunciation stories the announcement of the birth of a child who will demonstrate greatness by God or an angel.

Anthony of Egypt (251–356) the founder of Christian monasticism.

anti-Christ the "lawless" individual who will appear in the "end times."

Antiochus Epiphanes IV the Seleucid king who forbade the Jewish religion (167 BCE).

anti-Semitism the modern term for the continuing hatred and denigration of the Jewish people.

Antonia Fortress the seat of the Roman magistrate in the corner of the Temple complex.

apatheia the philosophical concept of not letting the passions of the body control one's life.

apocalypse "hidden things revealed" concerning the "final days."

Apocalypse of Peter an early review of what awaits dead Christians in Heaven and Hell.

apocalyptic the description of a mindset that sees the world divided between good and evil, thus awaiting God's final intervention.

apocalyptic eschatology the study of apocalyptic ideas of "the final days."

apochrypha Second-century writings of legends of the journeys and experiences of the apostles.

Apokalysis of John of Patmos the Book of Revelation, a Christian apocalyptic view of the eventual destruction of the Roman Empire.

apologia/**apology** the literary genre of a work that explains concepts and rituals.

apotheosis the Greek concept of the elevation of a hero to the place of the gods after death.

apostle a "herald" who brings news; the name of the Disciples as missionaries.

Apostle to the Gentiles   Paul's self-identification for his role in the salvation of Gentile believers.

Apostolic Council   the meeting in Jerusalem where it was decided that Gentiles who joined the movement did not have to undergo the identity-markers of Judaism, circumcision, dietary laws, and Sabbath observance.

Apostolic Fathers   a group of Christians from the end of the first century who are understood to have been commissioned by the disciples of Jesus.

Apostolic Tradition   the claim of the Church Fathers against the Gnostics that the words of Jesus were passed down only through the disciples and those whom the disciples commissioned.

Arius   the presbyter of Alexandia who taught that Christ had been created by God; the motivation for the Council of Nicaea and the creation of the Creed.

Ark of the Covenant   the wooden chest that held the tablets of the Laws of Moses received on Mt. Sinai.

ascension   Luke's story of what happened to Jesus after his death.

ascesis/**asceticism**   the philosophical concept of not indulging the desires of the body in order to concentrate on the mind and soul.

Assyrians   the empire that invaded the Northern Kingdom of Israel in 722 BCE and removed its population; the loss of the "ten tribes".

astrologers   experts in the study of the influence of the stars and planets on individual lives.

atheism   the disbelief/disrepect of the gods, equivalent to treason.

atonement   a "covering over" or "fixing" of a violation of God's commandments; Paul's concept that Jesus died for the punishment of the sin of Adam.

augurs   a form of divination where thunder, lightning, and the flights of birds were studied as an indication of the approval or disapproval of the gods.

Augustus   successor to Julius Caesar and the first Roman Emperor.

Babylon   the city of exile/the code word applied by John of Patmos for the Roman Empire.

300 Glossary

Babylonians the empire that defeated the Assyrians, then conquered and destroyed Jerusalem and Solomon's Temple in 587 BCE.

baptism "dunking," a ritual washing after repentance by John the Baptist; this became one of the earliest Christian rituals.

Bar Kokhba Revolt 135 CE, the second and last major revolt by Jews against Rome.

Barabbas the rebel chosen by the crowd and released at the trial of Jesus.

Barnabas a traveling companion of Paul's.

barren women a literary device in biblical literature that allows for eventual "motherhood" through divine intervention.

"begats" the genealogical lists of the tribes of Israel in the Pentateuch, created by priests.

"the beloved disciple" the special disciple in the fourth gospel.

Bestiarii the "beast-men" who conducted animal hunts in the games.

Birkat-ha-minim the synagogue dictate against "dissenters".

Bishops the first elected overseers of the Christian communities.

Bishop Victor I Bishop of Rome who set the dates for the celebration of Easter.

blasphemy the charge against Jesus at his trial by the high-priest.

calendars the marking of both sacred and secular time.

call of Abraham the selection by God for Abraham to move to Canaan and be protected in return for worship and faithfulness; the beginning of the nation of Israel.

Canaan the "promised land" of the Jewish Scriptures, in the areas of ancient Phoenicia, parts of Syria, Lebanon, and Israel.

canon a measurement, applied in the decisions of which would books would eventually be "sacred" for the Jewish Scriptures and the New Testament.

canonical gospels   the four gospels that make it into the New Testament, Mark, Matthew, Luke, and John.

Capadocian Fathers   the collective term for the founders of what became Eastern Orthodoxy.

Capitoline Trinty   the major dieties of the state cults of Rome, Jupiter, Juno, and Minerva.

Cardinals   the second tier below the Pope; responsible for the election of new popes.

catacombs   "near the tombs"; the burial methods popular during the second and third denturies CE.

catharsis   the ecstactic release of emotions experienced in some of the Mysteries.

cathedral   the first Christian basilicas, from "ex-cathedra", "from the chair" of the Bishop.

celibacy   not entering into a formal, marriage contract.

Chalcedon   the Council that determined the dual natures of Christ, 451 CE.

charismatic exorcist   the most common portrait of Jesus in Mark's gospel, charismatic exorcists were itinerant wonder-workers who were understood to have gifts from the gods or God that allowed them to drive out demons.

chastity   not indulging in sexual intercourse.

circumcision   the removal of the loose foreskin of the penis; the physical mark of identity of Jews.

Chosen people   the understanding that God choose Israel as his special people at Sinai.

Christian trials   the trials of Christians who refused to sacrifice to the Imperial/State cults.

Christianoi   Luke's term for Christians, "followers of the Christ".

Christmas   the celebation of the nativity of Jesus.

Christology the study of the nature of Christ (divine or human).

Christos the Greek form of "messiah".

Church/*ecclesia*, "assembly", and the most common term for the earliest communities of Christians.

Church Fathers the collective term for the Christians writers in the second century who created Christian dogma.

collegia groups of similar trades and classes who met under the auspices of a god or goddess.

The Commandments this is what Moses received on Mt. Sinai — 613 dictates that created a constitution for the nation of Israel.

"conflict dialogues" in Mark a literary device to demonstrate the Pharisees' opposition to Jesus and to provide the opportunity for Mark's Jesus to discourse on issues.

Constantine I the first Christian Emperor.

conversion the change from one religious system (or worldview) to another, often requiring changes in life-style.

corpse contamination impurity that derives from the nearness of corpses, removed with a sprinkling of ashes and water at the Temple in Jerusalem and by priests in the funeral rituals of Rome.

Covenant an ancient form of contract between gods and people. Later termned, "testament".

Covenant with Abraham the promise by God to protect the descendants of Abraham if they make "the sign" of the covenant through circumcision.

Covenant with Moses Essentially the "Law of Moses", or the 613 commandments received at Mt. Sinai.

crucifixion the Roman punishment for slaves and traitors.

crusade the calling of a special mission to either deal with a perceived crisis or recruitment.

cthonic a term for the deities dominant in the underworld, or the land of the dead.

cult from *cultus*, all the elements involved in the worship of the gods. Also, a sociological term for members who move away from a sect and begin to develop their own views.

Cyrus the Great the "king of kings" of the Persians who provided funds for the Jews in Babylon to return home and rebuild Jerusalem and their Temple.

daemons originally lesser powers in the universe, many would be deemed "evil" to explain evil in the world.

Damnatio memoriae the process utilized by the Church Fathers to condemn the writings of the Gnostics; the concept of annihilation through no memory of the person.

David although a sinner, the greatest of the kings of Israel, who founded the "United Monarchy".

Davidic Covenant the covenant when God promised David that one of his descendants would always sit on the throne of Israel. It became part of the "final days" scenario in the first century.

deacons men first elected to take care of organizational details of the communities, later the first priests.

Dead Sea Scrolls the library of the Essenes that was discovered in 1947, which contained copies of the biblical texts and treatises on their apocalyptic worldview.

Decius Roman Emperor who required a receipt for visiting the Imperial Temples (251 CE).

deism the belief of some intellectuals after the Enlightenment in some power of creative power that instituted all of creation.

Demeter the goddess of grain and agriculture; one of the more popular of the Mystery cults.

demi-urge the Platonic and Gnostic concept of a secondary, lower creator god.

Deutero-Pauline the scholarly designation for the letters in the New Testament written in Paul's name by disciples of Paul.

Deuteronomy the "second law", this book summarizes the first four books of the Jewish Scriptures and contains Moses' farewell speech to the people.

diaspora "the dispersion", a term for Jews living outside the land of Israel.

Didache an early teaching manual for Christian rituals.

diocese the Roman section of a province that was adopted for the rule of a Bishop.

Diocletian Emperor who ordered the last persecution of Christians in 302–303 CE.

Dionysius the god of fertility and wine-making; his festivals coincided with drama contents in Athens.

disciple "student", the common name for members of a philosophical school and the inner circle around Jesus.

divination the way in which humans communicate with the gods, and the gods with humans. Often found in "oracles", both the place and term for the individual who became possessed and then spoke the words of the deity. The Jewish equivalent was Prophets.

divine the general term for all the powers in the "heavens" as well as the powers "under the earth".

docetism ("appearance") the belief that Jesus only appeared in a body, but did take on physical flesh.

Documentary Hypothesis developed in the nineteenth century, this was the scholarly device to identity different "sources" in the Scriptures, as well as their historical contexts.

dogma an accepted belief system by a group.

Donatus/Donatism Bishop Donatus refused to re-admit Christians who had lapsed during the Diocletian persecution. He created his own churches in North Africa.

dualism the later Persian and Greek concept that humans consist of two elements, a physical body (matter) and a nonphysical "essence" known as the "soul".

Edict of Milan 313 the official permission for Christians to assemble as a *collegia*.

Encratities radical Christians who taught the ways in which to eliminate the sexual urges and appetites of the body.

epiphany the literal manifestation of a deity on earth; in the modern world, a "sudden insight" or awareness.

Episcopal Inquisition the special commission by Gregory IX in 1231 to hunt out and convict heretics.

eremitic monasticism the term for monastics who reside in community buildings.

Essenes the Jewish sect identified as the writers of the Dead Sea Scrolls; an apocalyptic group that lived at Qumran on the edge of the Dead Sea; apocalyptic in outlook.

ethnic cults/groups the way in which native cults were identified as groups that shared language, common ancestors, and religious traditions.

etiologies explanations of the origins of ideas and things.

eucharist "thanksgiving" in Greek, the ritual meal in memory of the dead.

Eusebius of Caesarea (317–361) deemed the writer of the first Christian history; court Bishop to Constantine I and author of *Life of Constantine*.

Evagrius Ponticus (345–399) the creator of monastic menus and the "deadly sins."

excommunication the later Christian practice of expelling members from the community and denying them the sacraments; derived from a passage in 1 Corinthians.

The "Exile" the period ca. 587–539 when the Jews were carried as captives to the city of Babylon after the destruction of Jerusalem and the Temple. They were released under Cyrus the Great.

ex nihilo what became the doctrine that God created the universe out of nothing.

Exodus the second book of the Pentateuch, it relates the story of the Jews as slaves in Egypt and their liberation under Moses, who brought them to Mt. Sinai. It contains the rituals for the Jewish holiday of Passover.

exorcist   someone who "drives out demons" from a person possessed.

faith   in the New Testament, *pistis*, "loyalty", in the sense of loyalty to certain teachings.

family   the basic social unit of ancient cultures.

fertility   the most crucial element in ancient societies, the clan or tribe did not survive without fertility of people, crops, or animals. The concept of fertility was manifest in the idea of every god having a female goddess.

Flagellants   orders of monks who took on the punishment for sins during times of crisis in the Middle Ages.

foundation myths   those stories that claimed the founding of a city or community by one of the gods.

Four Horsemen of the Apocalypse   the four riders, released from one of the scrolls in heaven who bring inflation, war, famine, and death.

funeral games   the honoring of the dead that consisted of athletic games, chariot races, religious festivals, plays, and Gladiatorial games.

funeral rituals   the specific rites for an easy journey to the afterlife; keeping the dead in the land of the dead.

Gentiles   the general Jewish term for anyone who was not a Jew, and then not a Christian.

Gentile-Christians   the designation for Gentiles who became believers.

Gethesemene   the garden where Jesus and the Discples went after the "Last Supper".

gladiator games   always presented as part of funeral games, trained fighters known as gladiators fought each other, and sometimes to death.

glossolalia   the scientific term for "speaking in tongues."

"God-Fearers"   non-Jews who were attracted to Judaism and the synagogues, while remaining within their ancestral cults.

Gospel   the "good news" of Jesus of Nazareth that "the kingdom of god was coming soon."

Gnostics "gnosis", "knowledge", portrays groups of Christians who claimed to have secret knowledge of the nature of the universe and the nature of Christ.

Gnostic Gospels the writings of Gnostic Christians.

Greek romance novel the literary genre for the legendary stories of the Apostles.

Hades the Greco-Roman name for both the god and the place of the dead.

Hanukah a medieval Jewish holiday, it is taken from the story of the rededication of the Temple after the Maccabee revolt when they had driven out the Greeks.

haeresis the term for a school of philosophy.

Haruspix an expert on reading the entrails of sacrificial animals.

Heaven the domain of the gods; the realm of the God of Israel.

Hebrews the term used to designate the Israelites in the book of Exodus.

Helena the mother of Constantine I who discovered the sites of the nativity and burial of Jesus in Jerusalem.

Hell equivalent to the Jewish *she'ol* and the Greco-Roman Hades, Hell became the place for the punishment of the wicked.

Hellenism the general term for the implementation of Greek culture, language, education, philosophy, and religion by Alexander the Great in his conquests of the Middle East.

Hellenistic Judaism a scholarly construct to described Judaism after the conquest by Alexander.

Heresiologists the collective term for the writings of the Church Fathers that created orthodoxy from heresy.

Herod Antipas the son of Herod the Great, he inherited the Galilee as his territory. He was responsible for beheading John the Baptist.

Herod the Great the client-ruler under Rome, he was granted the title "king of the Jews" by Augustus and Anthony.

308   Glossary

Herodians   the collective term for the descendants of Herod the Great.

Herodias   married to several of her uncles, she is infamous for influencing her daughter to ask for "the head of John the Baptist."

high-god   a deity over and above all other divinities; sometimes a "king of the gods."

high-priest   most temples designated one among them who had increased duties and increased privileges in the rotations of priesthoods.

honor/shame   the public and private reputation, standing, and status of a person.

hymns   prayers set to music; a way to communicate with the gods.

hypostases   "realities", "natures" in relation to the natures of Christ.

idolatry   the collective term by Jews to refer to all the other native cults; lapses into idolatry were considered a great sin in Judaism.

Imperial Cult   the Roman religious practice of deifying Emperors after their death.

impiety   disrespect for the gods.

Incarnation   the concept from the gospel of John, in that Jesus, descending from God, "took on flesh" in order to communicate with humans.

indulgences   the reward for donations to the Church and pilgrimage that granted a reduction of time from one's existence in Purgatory.

initiation   a training and learning period before the admission into a cult.

Israel   the collective term for the descendants of Abraham through the name change of Jacob to Israel.

James   the brother of Jesus who led the Jerusalem church.

Jewish-Christians   the designation for Jewish believers who claimed that Gentile believers had to convert and follow the Law of Moses.

Jewish–Christian relations   the study of the ways in which Jews and Christians related to each in the cities of the Roman Empire; it also includes debates over which Jewish elements should remain as part of Christianity.

Jewish tax reparations to be paid by Jews for the Jewish Revolt against Rome, 66–73.

Jewish Restoration Theology the scholarly rubric to describe the "message of hope" in the books of the Prophets; the Prophets' predictions of the events of the "final days".

Jewish Revolt (66–73 CE) the Zealots convinced most Jews to official rebel against the Roman Empire. The result was the Roman destruction of Jerusalem and the Temple complex. The Revolt is also the immediate historical context for Mark's gospel.

Jewish Scriptures the collective books of the Jewish canon; a less offensive designation than "the Old Testament."

Jewish sectarianism the scholarly description of the various sects of Jews that began to emerge after the Maccabee Revolt (c. 150 BCE).

John the Baptist "John the dunker," John began immersing people in the river Jordan after they had repented; all four gospels have Jesus going to John for baptism.

John of Patmos the author of the Book of Revelation.

Joseph one of the twelve sons of Jacob, he was sold into slavery by his brothers and rose to become vizier in Egypt.

Joseph of Arimathea allegedly the individual who asked Pilate for permission to bury Jesus in his tomb.

Josephus, Flavius the Jewish general in the Jewish Revolt who became a traitor to the Jews and an adviser to Rome; an eyewitness to the Jewish Revolt, his writings are a source for many events in the first century.

Joshua the right-hand general of Moses, he takes the generation from the wilderness into the "promised land".

Judaizers the collective term for the followers who insisted that Gentile believers convert to Judaism first.

Judas Iscariot the individual who allegedly betrayed Jesus to the Jewish authorities.

Judges a book reflecting the time when God raised up "judges", redeemer figures during the Tribal Confederation. Its "downward spiral of violence" sets up the reader for the rise of King David.

Julian the Apostate The Emperor who wanted to restore the traditional ethnic cults of the Roman Empire.

"Kingdom of God" a shorthand phrase for the events predicted by the Prophets "in the final days". This was an early tradition that the teachings of Jesus incorporated the list from the Prophets and declared the "kingdom" imminent.

1 and 2 Kings two scrolls that describe the "united monarchy" under David and Solomon, and then the splitting of the tribes into two kingdoms, North and South.

kingship Israel differed from their neighbors in their views of combining kingships with divinity; their kings were judged on whether or not they let idolatry continue in the land.

"L" source a scholarly designation for the sources of Luke (particular his parables) not found in either Mark or Matthew.

Lamentations a book devoted to grief concerning the Babylonian destruction of the Temple and the city of Jerusalem.

"The Last Supper" the Passover meal in which Jesus recites what becomes the ritual communion formula, and an early ritual in Christianity.

Latin Fathers Church leaders who wrote in Latin, Ambrose, John Chrysostum, Jerome, Augustine.

lauras the term for the first convents of monastic women.

Law of Moses what Moses received on Mt. Sinai, the constitution of the nation of Israel.

Leviticus the third book of the Pentateuch, the book is also known as "the priests' manual" because it contains the dietary laws, incest codes, and all the details on how to carry out the various sacrifices.

Limbo Augustine's original concept for the place of dead, unbaptized Christians.

logos the doctrine of rationality from the schools of philosophy, applied by John's gospels as the concept of Christ emanating from "the one god".

Lucifer the most popular name for Satan in the Middle Ages.

Ludi "games", the general term for the combination of religious festivals, plays, and chariot races.

Luke the alleged writer of the third gospel in the canon and the Acts of the Apostles.

Luke-Acts the scholarly designation for the combined works of the third gospel and the Acts of the Apostles.

"M" source the scholarly designation for sources of Matthew's gospel not found in Mark or Luke.

Maccabee Revolt the Jewish revolt against the forbidding of "Jewish customs" by Antiochus Epiphanes in 167 BCE.

2 Maccabees the book that contains the story of the Maccabee martyrs, Hannah and her seven sons. This work introduces the concept of "martyr" (witness) as well as the reward for martyrdom, resurrection of the dead and being instantly taken into the presence of God.

Magi the three court astronomers who visit Bethlehem in Matthew's gospel.

magic/magicians a term for the power to manipulate nature, for good or harm.

Magna Mater an ancient fertility goddes of Anatolia (Cybele), she ws transferred to Rome; her priests castrated themselves.

Manichaean Christians the followers of the Persian Prophet Mani who taught Gnostic elements.

manumission the legal freeing of slaves.

Mark the designation for the first gospel in the New Testament. The tradition claims that it was dictated to a follower named John Mark who followed Peter to Rome.

martyr "witness", as in "witnessing" to one's belief. It was a term applied to anyone who had died for their beliefs.

Mary Magdalene a female follower of Jesus and a witness to the resurrection in all four gospels.

Masada the desert fortress taken over by the Zealots after Jerusalem was destroyed. From that position, they kept up resistance to Rome until they agreed on a mass suicide.

mass   the term for the weekly assembly in Christian churches; from "ita missa est," "you are dismissed" for those not baptized.

Matthew   the alleged writer of the first gospel in the canon, identified by the name "Matthew" for the tax-collector called by Jesus.

Maxentius   the last pagan Emporer in the West; died at the Battle of the Milvian Bridge in 312.

mendicants   Chrisitans in the Middle Ages who renounced all possessions and begged for the necessities of life.

messiah   "anointed one", favored by God to be raised up "in the final days" to lead the armies of Israel (like King David).

metaphor   a figure of speech in which a word or phrase is applied to an object or action to which it is not literally applicable; a favorite literary device in the gospel of John.

mikvaot   the stone tanks for ritual washing in Second Temple Judaism.

millennium   the 1000-year reign of Christ on earth in the Book of Revelation.

misogyny   "the fear of women", an attitude from the dominant culture as well as the schools of philosophy that women had the power to seduce men.

Mithras   a Persian sun god popular with the legions and a competitor in early Christianity.

monism   an ancient concept of the person consisting of a physical body and a personality, in one unit.

monk   the term for an ascetic hermit of the dessert monasteries.

monastery   the residence of monastics.

monasticism   the collective term for those who go beyond the norm and dedicate their lives to God.

monotheism   the belief in one god, always in juxtaposition to polytheism.

Moses   the individual in the book of Exodus who pleads with Pharaoh to "let my people go"; Moses brings the people to Mt. Sinai where he receives the constitution for the nation of Israel (the Commandments).

Glossary 313

Munera sine missione a function of Gladitorial games when men fought to the death.

myth a story to explain the origins of a civilization, usually called upon to explain contemporary society.

Mysteries Public and private cults that required a period of initiation and offered benefits in this life and the afterlife.

Nag Hammadi Library the collection of Gnostic writings.

The Nativity stories in Matthew and Luke that provide the details of the birth of Jesus.

necromancers experts in communicating with the dead.

Nero Emperor of Rome (50s–60s) but more infamous as the first to persecute Christians after a fire that destroyed much of Rome in the year 64.

Nicene Creed the creed that was established in 325, listing all the items that a Christian should believe; also known as "the Apostles' Creed".

noble death the term for honorable, voluntary suicide.

Northern Kingdom of Israel the ten tribes that seceded after the rule of Solomon, where they set up a separate kingdom.

Numbers the fourth book of the Pentateuch, it lists all the individuals who "came out of Egypt", as well stories of their wilderness experience.

Olympians the 12–14 major gods of Greece who lived on Mt. Olympus.

Oracle a place or an individual who was "possessed" by one of the gods; the way in which the ancients received messages from the gods.

ordination the "laying on of hands" sacrament to initiate a priest or Bishop.

Origen 180–254) Bishop of Caesarea and Christian theologian; arthur of *Peri Archon*.

Original Sin Augustine's doctrine for the stain of sin that is born in all humans at conception.

orthodoxy "correct belief", arguments made by the Church Fathers in the second century as to what could be accepted and what could be rejected (heresy).

orthopraxy correct rituals or practices.

paideia the collective term for higher education.

pagans a derogatory term for those individuals who had not yet converted to Christianity from the hinterlands. It retained its negative connotations throughout the middle ages and into modern culture.

Palm Sunday this is when Christians celebrate the "triumphal entry into Jerusalem" by Jesus as reported in the gospel.

Pan the god of forests and fertility; the first iconography of the Devil.

parables the common method of teaching by Jesus as reported in the Synoptic gospels; parables use homey examples as a method of analogy.

parousia the "second appearance"; the claim that Jesus would return to earth to carry out the rest of the elements of the Prophetic "final days".

Passion Narrative the story of Jesus' suffering and crucifixtion during his last days in Jerusalem.

Passion play the re-enactment of the trials and suffering of Jesus for the benefit of uneducated Christians.

Pastorals the letters of 1 and 2 Timothy and Titus that develop rules for bishops, deacons, and widows.

Passover the Jewish holiday from the book of Exodus, to be re-enacted as a ritual meal every year. This is celebrated as the time of year when Jesus was crucified in Jerusalem.

Patricians the aristocratic upper classes of Rome.

Patristic Literature the body of writings from the Church Fathers

patron/client the way in which "things got done" in the ancient world; favors and obligations between classes.

patron saints the Christian adaptation of the patron/client system now applied to Christian martyrs in Heaven.

Glossary   315

Pax Romana   Augustus' term for the normalization of the Empire after the death of Julius Caesar.

pedagogus   "tutor", "guide", Paul's analogy for the reason why God gave the Law.

Pentateuch   the Greek term ("penta" means five) for the first five books of the Jewish Scriptures. By tradition, they were assigned to Moses.

Pentecost (*Shavuot*)   the spring holiday fifty days after Passover; the "descent of the spirit" on believers in Acts.

Pelagius (354–418)   the British monk who taught that existence of free will in humans; later condemned as a heretic.

Perpertua and Felicity   two female martyrs during the persecutions in Carthage, 202 CE.

Persia   the empire that conquered the neo-Babylonians. Their first king, Cyrus the Great, permitted and funded the captive Jews to return to Jerusalem to rebuild the city and the Temple.

personification evil   the process of demonizing anyone who disagrees or opposes one's worldview.

Peter   One of the first followers of Jesus, famous for his three-time denial of Jesus at the trial.

Pharisees   a sect of Judaism that emerged ca. 150 BCE. Pharisees were concerned with living according to the Law of Moses. Pharisees claimed "oral law" that had been passed down to them from the elders at Sinai.

Philistines   the "sea peoples" who invaded lands of the eastern Mediterranean c. 1180 BCE. They established five cities in what is now the Gaza Strip. The Philistines introduced iron and chariots into the region and became formidable foes of the Israelites.

philosophical monotheirsm   the shared belief of the schools of philosophy in the existence of a higher god, the source of all creation.

Plebeians   the next class below the Patricians of Rome; the "people".

polemic   the written or verbal attack against an opponent. Polemic is found throughout the Jewish Scriptures and the New Testament.

Polycarp Bishiop of Smyrna martyred in 151 CE.

polytheism the worship of many gods, always in juxtaposition with monotheism.

Pontius Pilate the procurator of Judea, the Roman official who condemned Jesus to crucifixion.

prayers the way in which people communicated with the divine.

predestination Augustine's theory that God already knows who will be saved and who will be damned.

priests/priestesses the religious experts of the ancient world, most of whom served in rotation at the Temples.

Prophets the Jewish concept of oracles.

Prophets of Israel the collective term for the writers of the books of prophecy in the Jewish Scriptures.

pseudepigrapha "false writing", the term for common writings in antiquity that claimed to be written in the name of a famous person to grant validity.

Purgatory the later concept of a place for ordinary Christians to "purge" their sins before going to Heaven.

"Q" source/*quelle* the scholarly term for the alleged document that contained only teachings of Jesus, found verbatim in Matthew and Luke.

Rabbinical Judaism after the fall of the Temple, the remnants of the Pharisees moved to Yavne and began focusing on the "book". Their writings evolved into Rabbinical Judaism, which remains the form of modern Judaism.

religio from the Latin, "those things which bind one to a god."

religio licta "legal" or "licensed" religious groups recognized by the Senate of Rome.

religion a modern term to describe religious systems, from the Latin, *religio*, or "those things that bind one to a god".

religious festivals Community events celebrating a god, goddess, or the foundation of a community and agricultural cycles.

religious pluralism   the ability of people to move to one ethnic cult to another without the process of conversion.

resurrection   the concept of "life after death", in that the body and soul are reunited and dwell in either Heaven or Hell.

rhetoric   "the art of persuasion", a verbal and literary device involved in presenting one's arguments.

rites of passage   religious rites that celebrate important stages of development, birth, puberty rites, marriage, death.

rituals,   the actions involved in communicating with the gods and in the sacrificial worship of the gods.

ritual purity   "a state of being", related to separating the "mundane" from "sacred objects".

Roma   the concept of the idea of "Rome" as a divine power.

Romans   the last known letter of Paul to the community in Rome. This letter fully articulates the atonement for believers who are "in Christ".

sacraments   Christian rituals and rites of passage that were later deemed as having the literal presence of "the holy spirit" involved: baptism, communion, penance, confirmation, marriage, ordination of the clergy, death (now known as "anointing of the sick").

Sacred scriptures   a term to designate teachings and law-codes that were revealed or "given by the gods".

sacred space   the areas separated by zones of holiness that are believed to have been "touched" by a deity; all temples and shrines were sacred space, as well as some rivers, groves of trees, and mountaintops.

sacred time   denoting foundation myths, or events in the lives of the gods.

sacrifice   the idea of offering something of value when petitioning the gods, or as atonement for a violation; sacrifices consisted of animals, birds, wheat cakes, and wine.

sacrilege   destruction of a sacred space or site.

Sadducees a sect of Jews who were in charge of running the Temple in Jerusalem. They also sat in the Sanhedrin, the city council. They were at odds with the Pharisee interpretation of the Law of Moses.

Samuel the first Prophet, priest, and judge, Samuel anointed David and was the adviser to the people during the Philistine era and the Tribal Confederation.

salvation from the Greek "*soter*", "to save", this became the core teaching of Christianity, in the concept of atonement, in that Jesus died to remove the physical punishment of death. As Christians began to die, the idea evolved into the hope of "life after death," but now in Heaven.

Satan/the Devil (*ha-Satan*) the name of the concept of an oppositional force in the universe, derived from Zoroastrianism in Persia. The Devil is a major force that Jesus combats in the gospel of Mark.

schisms early Christian disagreements over what to do about "lapsed" bishops.

Second Temple the new Temple that was built by Jews returning from Persia.

Second Temple Judaism the collective term for Judaism after their return from Persia and under both the Greek and Roman occupations; the term utilized for the Judaism of the communities of Jews in the Diaspora.

Sectarianism the process of groups in a religion who call for reforms; the scholarly term for the groups of Jews that began to form c. 150 BCE, highlighting differences in the interpretations of Scripture and daily living.

Seers the later version of Prophets; seers underwent out-of-body experiences and were shown secrets in the heavens.

Septuagint the Scriptures that were translated into Greek c. 200 BCE.

Sermon on the Mount the teachings of Q that are found in Matthew and Luke.

Shavuot the festival of "weeks" in Jerusalem which becomes the Christian celebration of Pentecost.

sola scriptura Martin Luther's concept that all that is necessary for salvation in found in Scripture alone; this was his argument against the sacraments of the Catholic Church.

Glossary   319

Solomon   the second king of the United Monarchy and the son of David and Bathsheba. He built the first permanent Temple in Jerusalem; known for wealth and wisdom. He was ultimately condemned by later writers for permitting his many foreign wives to erect shrines to their deities in Jerusalem.

"Son of man"   a character known from the books of Enoch and Daniel, the "son of man" was a pre-existent entity whom God appointed as the judge of humankind in the "final days". "The son of man" is Mark's favorite title for Jesus.

Sophia   the feminine concept of wisdom; the self-generating archon who produced the Demi-urge in Gnostic thought.

Southern Kingdom of Judah   the tribes of Benjamin and Judah who remained when the ten tribes moved north to form a separate kingdom, ca. 920 BCE. They were eventually conquered by the Babylonians in 586 BCE.

"spirit"   in the Jewish Scriptures and the New Testament, this is the spirit of God, understood as the breath of God that gave life to Adam, and the spirit that possessed the Prophets. Jesus received the spirit at his baptism, and the spirit was understood to be at work in various "gifts" in the first generation of Christians.

Stephen   the first Christian martyr after Jesus; a witness to Jesus "standing at the right hand of God".

suffering servant passages   passages from the book of Isaiah, personified in the sufferings of the nation of Israel. Early Christians reinterpreted these passages as a way in which to explain why God permitted Jesus to be tortured and killed.

symposium   dinner party where philosophy was discussed.

synagogue   "assembly", communal places for Jewish worship and community activities.

Synagogue of Satan   John of Patmos' term for a community in Asia Province.

syncretism   the method employed by Alexander the Great in his conquered territories to combine older, local systems of belief and worship with Greek concepts.

Synoptic gospels   the scholarly term for Mark, Matthew, and Luke in that they all contain a similar narrative structure and similar stories.

Synoptic problem this is the scholarly debate concerning the relationship among the first three gospels in terms of dating, redaction, and reinterpretation.

Syria-Palestina the official name of Judea after the Bar Kokhba Revolt.

table-fellowship the way scholars describe Jewish–Gentile social relations.

Talmud the collected writings and commentaries of Rabbinic Judaism.

temples the "sacred spaces" of religious participants in the ancient world.

ten plagues of Egypt the battle between God and the gods of Egypt.

tent of meeting the portable shrine that was shared among the various tribes during the Tribal Confederation.

Tetrarchy the division of the Roman Empire under Diocletian.

theodicy the modern term for the analysis of how a good God nevertheless permits evil.

Theodosian Code the re-working of Roman Law by Theodosius I which began to limit the civil and social rights of Jews.

Theodosius I (347–395) the Christian Emporer who mandated Christianity as the only legal religion of the Empire.

thirty-nine lashes the communal form of discipline in Synagogue communities.

Titus, Emperor the son of Vespasian who laid siege to Jerusalem and destroyed the city and the Temple in 70 CE; later emperor of Rome (81–83).

Torah "teaching", an abbreviation for the teaching of Moses contained in the first five books, and the Law he received at Sinai.

Tribal Confederation the shared governance after the tribes settled in Canaan during the Iron Age.

the Trinity the doctrine agreed upon at Nicea in 325 that made Christ identical in essence with God.

Triumphal Entry Jesus' entrance to Jerusalem when the crowds welcome him as the deliverer of Israel.

Glossary 321

Twelve Tribes of Israel the twelve sons of Jacob who ruled in Canaan.

United Monarchy the period under the reigns of David and Solomon when the tribes were united until the governance of kingship, rather than a Tribal Confederation; centralized rule from Jerusalem.

venatio the animal hunts in the arenas of Rome.

Vespasian as a Roman general, he led the armies against the Jewish Revolt. He then was declared emperor upon the death of Nero, and became emperor of the Flavian dynasty.

virgin martyrs legendary stories of Christian women who undergo miracles so as to be martyred as virgins.

Vulgate Bible the translation from the Hebrew and Greek by Jerome which became the Latin Bible of the Middle Ages.

worship the collective term for religious rituals whose most important element was sacrifices to the gods.

Yahweh the Hebrew name for the God of Israel.

Yavne the town along the coast where the remnant of the Pharisees reinterpreted Judaism in light of the destruction of the Temple; the beginning of Rabbinic Judaism.

Zakkai, Johanan, ben the leader of the Pharisees at Yavne.

Zealots the Jewish sect who promoted the sole rule of the Jewish god on earth; the group that promoted the Jewish Revolt against Rome.

Zoroastrianism the state religion of Persia, founded by the prophet Zoroaster. A system of belief that incorporated dualistic ideas of the universe.

INDEX

Aaron, 30, 32
Abbot, 243
Abel, 172
abominations, 151–52, 233
abortion, 167, 204
Abraham, 21, 24, 26–29, 44, 80, 91, 93, 96, 185–87, 194, 199
Absalom's rebellion, 61
absolution of Sin, 205, 211, 243
Achilles, 14, 107
Actium, 102
Acts of the Apostles, 19, 56, 62–63, 75, 80, 82, 85–86, 92, 149, 164, 195, 198–201, 207, 246
Acts of Paul and Thecla, 202–3
Adam, 17, 24, 26, 52–53, 56, 89–90, 155, 162, 208, 261–62, 264–66
Adeodatus, 259
adultery, 27–28, 147, 150, 152, 154, 170, 203, 215, 242, 27
Adversos Literature, 124–25, 179, 181–82, 189–91, 269
Aelia Capitolina, 183
Aesculapius, 137
afterlife, 1, 8, 10–14, 43, 76, 111, 131, 203, 213–15
agents of Satan, 55–56
agnostic, 160
Agrippa, Marcus, 183
Ahitophel, 61
Ahriman, 53
Ahura Mazda, 53
Ajax, 107
Alaric, 258, 268–69
Albigensians, 175
Alexander the Great, 24, 39–41, 118, 135, 161

Alexandria, 41, 110–11, 124–25, 127–28, 135–36, 140, 166–67, 216, 218, 230–31, 243–44, 272–74, 276
Alexandrian theology, 274
Alighieri, Dante, 57
allegory, 6, 129, 135–36, 159, 162, 176, 179, 181, 186, 188–89, 195
altars, 6, 41, 154, 228, 236, 247
Ambrose, 209, 239, 245, 251–54
  cathedral, 260
  understanding of church and state, 268
amphitheaters, 93, 103, 139, 226
anachronism, 2, 18, 182
Ananias, 73
anastasis, 42
Anatolia, 8, 39, 128
ancestors, 14, 26, 28, 30, 44, 146, 149, 189, 235
ancestral traditions, 6, 19, 272
ancient Egypt, 11, 27, 43, 245
ancient Greece, 5, 13, 151
ancient Israel, 22–23, 25, 28, 60
ancient Judaism, 1, 12, 15, 52, 85
ancient manuscripts, 203, 218, 242
ancient Mesopotamia, 26
ancient Persian religion, 53
ancient Rome, 17, 132, 150, 213
ancient world, 2–7, 9–11, 15, 17–18, 41, 45, 125, 128–29, 142, 145–46, 150, 228, 232
ancient writers, 18, 182, 195
androgyny, 162, 165
angels, 3, 27–28, 52–55, 62, 94, 151, 153, 162, 166, 171–72, 195, 198, 203–4
  archangels, 54
  creation, 171
  fallen, 3, 54, 153

Varieties of Early Christianity: The Formation of the Western Christian Tradition, First Edition.
Rebecca I. Denova.
© 2023 John Wiley & Sons, Inc. Published 2023 by John Wiley & Sons, Inc.

324 Index

Angra Mainyu, 53
animals,
　sacrificial, 10, 209
　unclean, 267
annihilation, 175
annulment, 214
anointing, 34, 214
　sick, 214
Anthony, Marc, 102
anti-Christ, 56
Antinous, 184
Antioch, 99, 109, 124, 211, 216, 229, 254,
　272–74, 276
Antiochus Epiphanes, 24
Antipater, 45, 106
anti-Semitism, 78, 181, 191
Antitheses, 160, 173
Antonia Fortress, 71
Aphrodisias, 84
apocalypse, 106, 193, 203
　eschatology, 22, 44
　literature, 12, 44
　traditions, 62
Apochrypha, 193
Apokalypsis, 106
Apollo, 10, 120
apologia, 124
Apostate, 189, 222, 235–36
apostles, 56, 62–63, 79–80, 82, 85–87,
　91–92, 97–98, 155, 164–66, 193–95,
　198–99, 202, 204, 206–7, 209
Apostolic Council, 84, 86
　fathers, 124
　tradition, 159, 165–66, 211
Apparel of women, 156, 212
Aquinas, Thomas, 141
arenas, 78, 93, 105, 110–13, 115, 181, 202,
　227
Arianism, 220, 221, 230, 234
Arians, 234, 252, 274
Arimathea, Joseph, 60, 62, 76
Aristotle, 39, 56, 147–48, 168, 199
ark, 26, 31, 34–35, 267
Armenian Church, 185
asceticism, 134, 148, 157, 239–41, 244, 251,
　261, 265
Asia Province, 106, 109, 117, 140, 157, 246
Asphodel Fields, 12
Assyria, 36, 41
astrology, 1, 9–10

Athanasius, 124, 218, 274
atheism, 99, 105, 121, 137–38
　atheists, 129, 141
Athens, 8, 128, 130–31, 151
atonement, 31, 42, 89, 151, 215
augurs in Rome, 10
Augustine, 88, 156, 220, 242, 246, 252,
　254–55, 257–72
　free will, 257, 265
　conversion, 260, 270
　Original Sin, 262, 265
　life, 258
Augustus, 7, 24, 46, 99, 102, 104, 149,
　202–3, 227, 236
Aurelius, Marcus, 225

Babylon, 24, 36, 41, 53, 56, 216
　destruction, 184
　empire, 22, 36
　the great whore of, 106
Babylonian Talmud, 190
Bacchus, 100
baptism, 80, 82, 96, 166, 169–70, 213, 215,
　217, 226, 233, 235, 262, 265
　delaying, 215
　adult, 213
　babies, 263
second, 215, 226
baptisms and marriages, 121
Baptist, John, 47
baptizing babies, 213, 262
Barabbas, 60, 74
barbarian invasions, 257, 268, 272
Bar Kokhba Revolt, 182–83, 189
Barnabas, 211
barren women, 27
Basil, St., 124, 218, 242
basilica, 97, 227–28, 248, 251–52
　Rome, 97, 248
Bathsheba, 35
battle, final, 39, 44, 54, 56, 65, 67, 180
　final eschatological, 94
Beelzebub, 54
behavior, 2, 15, 65, 95, 131–33, 135–36, 140,
　169, 176, 182, 188
　bodily, 194
　ecstatic, 194
Benedict, 242
Bethany, 69
Bethlehem, 34, 65, 217, 227, 255

betrayal, 57, 61, 77, 230
 Jesus, 61, 73, 77
 Judas, 77
bishops, 120–21, 157–58, 160, 165, 167,
  205–16, 218, 220, 223, 226, 231–32,
  234–36, 251–54, 259–61, 272–75
 Ambrose, 246
 Athanasius, 241
 Celestine, 274
 Clement, 97, 120, 229, 274
 Cyril, 244
 Demetrius, 218
 Donatus, 253, 267
 Eusebius, 222, 234
 Hosius, 253
 Irenaeus, 117–18, 124–25, 139–40, 167,
  169, 172–73, 175, 188, 201, 212
 Tertullian, 100, 105, 109, 125, 139, 156,
  173, 188, 190, 199, 212, 230, 273
 Ignatius, 109, 124, 211, 229
 John Chrysostom, 252, 254
black market, 119
Blandina, 118
blasphemy, 73, 173, 226
body and society, 158
bondage, 139, 157
 to Satan, 139
 to sin, 157
Borgia Pope Alexander VI, 158
brothels, 154, 201, 254
Brutus, 57
Buddhism, 161, 168, 176
burial, 113–14, 117, 208
 clubs, 100
 rites, 13
 rituals, 62
burning bush, 187
Byzantine Catholic Churches, 276
Byzantine Empire, 226, 276
Byzantium, 226

Caesar, Julius, 45, 100–101, 181, 217, 237
Caesarea, 83, 124, 218, 235
Cain, 26, 172
calendars, 9, 217
 lunar, 216
 solar, 217
Caligula, 99, 102–3, 135
Callinicum, 243, 252
Calvin, John, 169

Canaan, 22, 24, 26–27, 29, 32–34, 187
 ruled, 31
Canaanites, 34
canon, 15–16, 42, 158, 174, 195, 203, 275
 official, 129, 195
canonical gospels, 15–16, 59–60, 169–71
canonization, 174, 248
Canon/Old Testament/Jewish Scriptures, 15
Capernaum, 173, 200
Capitoline Trinity, 7, 108
Cappadocia, 81, 197, 242
Carthage, 110, 118, 139, 156, 211, 246,
  258–59
Cassian, John, 244
catacombs, 113–14, 117, 208, 255
catechism, 211
cathedral, 212, 260
Catholic Church, 158, 171, 175, 213, 231,
  245, 247–48, 258
celibacy, 145, 157, 165, 203, 240, 254, 261
 clerical, 157
Celtic traditions, 217
cemeteries, 13, 263
 public, 14
centurion, 83, 93
Cephas, 61
Chalcedon, 270–76
 definition, 275
chariot races, 9, 105, 254
charismatic, 55, 193–94
chastity, 145, 157, 165, 203, 240
 life-long, 157
 temporary, 157
Christ, 56–57, 67–68, 78, 88–96, 105–6,
  108–9, 136–41, 159–60, 162,
  164–76, 180–81, 186–88, 215–16,
  219–20, 228–31, 233–34, 263–64,
  266–67, 270, 273–75
 crucified, 56, 198
 emanated, 167
 in imitation of, 107
 pre-existent, 136, 162, 175
 risen, 83, 203
Christening, 213
Christian Art, 75, 221, 227
Christian communities, 44, 65, 109–10, 124,
  157, 160, 207, 215, 217, 265, 272
Christian doctrine, 209, 247
 defining, 163
Christian literature, 157, 204

326 Index

Christian missionaries, 48, 180
Christian philosophy, 130, 268
Christian pilgrims, 114
Christians, 15–17, 85–86, 89–92, 97–98,
    99–100, 103–21, 132–43, 145–58,
    160–61, 179–82, 184–91, 212–17,
    223, 225–27, 229–30, 237, 243–49,
    254–55, 259–60, 264–68
Christian transformation of sexual morality
    in Late Antiquity, 158
Christian trials, 100, 108, 117
Christian women, 113, 208, 269
    upper-class, 203
Christmas, 217
Christology, 273
    defining, 273
church and state, 222, 238, 253,
    268–69, 276
Church Fathers, 15–16, 62–63, 123–25, 127,
    132–33, 136, 140, 153, 155–56,
    160–61, 163–65, 173–75, 179,
    181–82, 214
City of God
Codex Sinaiticus, 195
Colossians, 87
commandments, 3, 19, 31–32, 34–35, 38,
    63, 89, 96, 179, 185, 188
    first, 27, 152, 156, 262
    original, 188
Confessions, Augustine, 258–61
Constantine, 121, 184, 191, 194, 217,
    221–28, 231–32, 234–35, 238, 267,
    269
    conversion, 225, 238, 243
    death, 234
    mother Helena, 227
Constantinople, 220, 221, 226, 228, 231,
    233, 236, 244, 254, 272–73, 275–76
Constantius, 222
Constantius II, 234, 236
Corinth, 92, 166, 213
Corinthians, 55, 61, 67, 69, 73, 87, 90–92,
    152, 174, 213–14, 216
Cornelius, 83, 90
covenant, 16, 26, 28–29, 31, 34–35, 37, 44,
    91, 96–97, 180–81, 189
    new, 16, 185
creation, 23–25
creation myths, 52
creative-fiction

creator, 164, 173, 230, 235
cremation, 13, 114
crucifixion, 59–60
    historical, 73
Crusades, 248
cult, 1, 4, 7–9, 43, 100, 217, 222, 225,
    239–40, 244, 247, 249, 251–52
the cult of Bacchus, 100
the cult of Dionysus, 8
the cult of Mithras, 217
Cult of the Saints, 217, 244–45, 252
Cyrus the Persian, 24, 36, 53

daemons, 3, 52
Damascus, 15, 45, 83, 190, 216
Daniel, 24, 36, 106, 115–16
    in the lion's den, 114
Dante, 57, 176, 204
Dark Age, 242
David, 21, 24, 34–35, 39, 61, 64–65, 67, 71,
    94, 180
Davidic Covenant, 35
DaVinci Code, 170
deacons, 82, 158, 173, 205, 207
Deadly Sins, 239, 242
Dead Sea, 44–45, 48, 56, 218
Dead Sea Scrolls, 44, 51, 54
death, 11–14, 40–42, 46–47, 61–64, 67,
    69–70, 73–78, 89–91, 94–97, 101–4,
    107, 109–12, 120–21, 131–32,
    138–39, 172–73, 186–87, 213–14,
    246–48, 261–62
    angel of, 30
    sacrificial, 90
    voluntary, 106–7
Demeter, 8, 140
Demi-Urge, 161–62, 167, 171
demonization, 156
demon-possession, 10
demons, 3, 52, 54–55, 57, 60, 95, 125, 137,
    153, 162, 220
Deuteronomy, 3, 21–22, 24, 31–33, 52
Devil, 3, 10, 12, 51–57, 64, 153, 155–57, 206,
    219–20, 265, 268
    lore, 54
Didyma, 120
dietary laws, 32, 83, 88–89, 136, 182
dioceses, 206, 272
Diocletian, 100, 119–21, 184, 215, 222, 226
    court advisers, 120

persecution, 267
reign, 221, 226
Dionysus, 8, 100, 140
disciples, 60–61, 63, 69, 73, 77, 81, 85, 87, 165–66, 170–72, 206–7, 210, 229
first, 63, 200
divination, 1, 9
divine, 2, 4–5, 26–27, 41, 52, 56, 128–29, 142, 153, 168, 172, 266, 272–75
Divine Comedy, 176, 268
divinity, 11, 41, 102, 129–30, 162, 196, 245, 273–74
pre-existent, 273
divorce, 27, 68, 150, 153, 214
Docetism, 273
dogma, 124, 128, 141, 234, 272
Domitian, 99, 104, 106
Donatism, 267
churches, 267–68
clergy, 267
Donatists, 257–58, 267–68
Schism, 221, 226
Donatus, 226–27, 267, 273
Dormitian Abbey, 198
drink offerings, 11

Easter, 61, 215–17, 231, 254
celebrated, 217
liturgy, 69, 215
Easter Sunday, 216
Ebionites, 273
ecclesia, 17
Ecclesiastical History, 235
Eden, 12, 26, 53, 56, 60, 157, 162, 243, 253, 261–62, 266
Egypt, 3–4, 24, 27, 29–33, 39, 41, 102, 105, 184–85, 189, 239–40, 242–44, 249
Eleusis, 8
Elijah, 34, 42, 187, 210
Elisha, 34
Elysian Fields, 12, 101
Embassy to Gaius, 135
Emmanuel, 67
Encratities, 157
Enoch, 42, 44, 54, 153, 180, 187, 194
Ephesians, 55, 87
Ephesus, 63, 92, 166, 273–75
Epicurus, 127, 131–32
epiphany, 41

Epiphany Sunday, 217
eremitic monasticism, 240
eschatological Israel, 91
eschatology, 38, 165
Essenes, 43–45, 54, 125
Esther, 36
ethnic cults, 7, 15, 36
ethnos, 15, 91
Etruscans, 13–14
rituals, 10
eucharist, 61, 67, 116, 169, 213
eunuchs, 154, 218
Eusebius, 222, 226, 234–35
history, 272–73
Eustochium, 255
Evagrius Ponticus, 239, 242
evangelist, 60
Eve, 26, 52–53, 56, 155–56, 162, 190, 198, 253, 261–62, 264, 266
evil, 26, 44–45, 47, 52–56, 95, 131–32,
exaltation, 94, 180, 274
of Christ, 180
to heaven, 94
excommunication, 173, 205, 214–15, 254, 276
Existentialism, 161
exorcisms, 60, 95
Exodus, 3–4, 21–22, 24, 29, 32, 181, 237
story, 30
Ezekiel, 34, 81, 106
Ezra, 24, 36

faith, 2–3, 16–17, 78–79, 89–90, 93, 103, 108–10, 135, 140–41, 207–8, 211, 248, 253
justified by, 89
family, 4, 13–15, 26, 42, 45–46, 102, 104, 110, 114, 148–50, 206–8, 217, 259
celebrations, 217
famine, 11, 29, 115, 118, 146
Canaan, 29
Faust, 57
feast days, 217
ferryman, 12
Fertile Crescent, 36
fertility, 4, 8, 14, 27, 32, 57, 146–47, 156, 158, 217
rituals, 15
festivals, 8–9, 22, 46, 71–72, 74, 77, 81, 117, 185, 217

328 Index

Flavius Josephus, 22, 46, 74
foreskin, 28, 247
forgiveness, 120, 174, 211, 273
fornication, 84, 152
forty lashes minus one, 92
freedom of religion, 100
free will, 219–20, 257–58, 264–66, 268
Friday, good, 109
fulfillment, 39, 186, 189
  of Prophecy, 80
funeral games, 1, 14, 101, 111–13
funeral, 13–14, 111, 115
  industry, 13
  monuments, 6
  processions, 13

Galatians, 79, 87, 89–90
Galen, 127, 133–35
  criticism, 135
Galilee, 36, 42, 46–47, 61, 63, 69, 73, 185, 229
games, 9, 111, 113, 217
  venatio, 113
Gehenna, 39, 43
gender roles, 2, 6, 25, 110, 145–47, 153, 155, 158, 171
genealogies, 26
Gentiles, 14–15, 64–65, 68–69, 71, 79–80, 83–97, 110, 114, 139–40, 142, 153–54, 180–81
Gentiles and Pagans, 1, 14
Gentiles in Israelite tradition, 88
Gethsemane, 61, 198
gifts, 55, 155, 158, 167, 194, 196, 211, 218, 259, 263, 265–66
  charismatic, 194
  of grace, 266
Gilgamesh Epic, 26
gladiators, 112–13
Gnostic/Agnostic, 159–60
Gnostic Christians, 160–61
Gnostic Gospels, 159, 167, 169, 177, 234
Gnosticism, 159–77
Gnostic myth, 161
Gnostic Rituals, 159, 168
Gnostics, 159–66, 168–69, 171, 173, 175–77, 196, 240, 263
  schools, 164, 169
  teacher, 166, 173

God, 2–4, 9–12, 26–45, 52–56, 63–65, 80–86, 88–91, 93–96, 104–9, 135–40, 152–54, 156–59, 171–75, 185–89, 211–12, 219–20, 228–33, 253–54, 257–66, 268–70
goddess, 4, 8–10, 14, 27, 100, 102, 154, 245
gods of Egypt, 3–4, 30
Golden House, 103
  good shepherd, 115
Gospel of Judas, 159, 171–72
Gospel of Mark, 59, 62
Gospel of Peter, 56
Gospel of Truth, 167, 169
gospels, 15–18, 33, 55–56, 59–80, 86–87, 89, 164–65, 167–75, 177, 185, 187–88, 197–201, 209–10, 216, 233–35
Goths, 234, 258, 268
the Great Commission, 229
Great Schism, 276
Greece, 5, 12, 14, 18–19, 28, 39–40, 101, 140, 150, 184, 276
Greek and Roman gods and goddesses, 245
Greek culture, 155
Greek myths, 19
Greek philosophers, 63, 136, 142
  schools of, 40
Greeks, 15–17, 22, 38–43, 52, 66–68, 81, 89, 91, 134–35, 140–41, 151–52, 184, 231–32, 244, 262–63
Greek underworld, 12
Gregorian calendars, 217
guerilla warfare, 42

Hades, 8, 12–14, 43, 56, 198, 210
Hadrian, 183–84, 225
Hagia Sophia, 226
Hanukah, 42
Haran, 26
Harrowing of Hell, 51, 56, 199
Hasmoneans, 42–45, 190
  brothers, 42
  princess, 46
heaven, 2–4, 39–40, 42–44, 53–54, 81–82, 90, 93–95, 136–37, 162–64, 194–95, 198, 203, 210, 229–30, 232–33, 243, 245–47
Hebrew Bible, 218
Hebrews, 2–3, 14, 29–30, 32, 34, 52, 54, 81, 141, 219, 237
Hebrew Scriptures, 56, 218

Index   329

Hecate, 10
Helios, 225
hell, 4, 43, 54, 56–57, 121, 153, 175, 199,
  203, 262, 268
  hell and heaven, 43
Hellenism, 40, 44
Hellenistic period, 49, 161, 167
Herakles/Hercules, 101
heresiologists, 124–25, 160
heresy, 124–25, 160, 163–64, 172, 175–76,
  220, 227, 232, 235, 259, 263, 266,
  272–74
heretics, 56–57, 125, 139, 175, 227, 230, 243,
  246, 263, 267, 270, 272, 276
Hermes, 12
hermits, 240
Herod, 24, 45–46
  Agrippa, 78
  Antipas, 73, 198
Herodians, 22, 45, 64
Herodotus, 19
heroes, 12, 93, 101, 153, 194
  ancient, 194
  deifying, 140
Hesiod, 168
high-priest, 6
  Caiaphas, 73
Hippolytus, 118, 199, 211, 218
Holocaust, 74, 191
Homer, 2, 138, 168
homosexuality, 145, 150, 153
honor, 4, 8–9, 13–14, 23, 101, 108, 112,
  136–37, 150
  public, 148
Hosea, 24, 38
hospitality, 151, 208
human intercourse, 145, 148, 155–56, 158,
  262
human sexuality, 145–46, 153, 155, 157–58,
  262
hymns, 7, 10, 22, 94–95, 216, 245
Hypatia, 243–44
hypostases, 273, 275

iconography, 31
  earliest, 114
idolatry, 15, 18, 32, 35, 38, 42, 53, 89, 92–93,
  152, 188–90
idols, 32, 38, 84, 140, 186
Ignatius of Antioch, 109, 124, 211, 229

Iliad, 2, 14, 107
Imperial Christianity, 259
Imperial Cult, 8, 99, 101–2, 104, 108
  new, 231
impiety, 100
impurity, 32–33
incantations, 10
Incarnate Christ, 273
incest-codes, 158
Infancy Gospel, 196
infanticide, 147
Inquisition, 175
institutionalization, 243
  of Christianity, 206, 220
Intermarriages, 237
Irenaeus, 118, 125, 127, 139, 164, 167, 169,
  172–73, 175, 188, 201
Irkalla, 11
Isaac, 29, 54, 185
Isaiah, 24, 34, 38, 44, 56, 64, 70–71, 75–76,
  94–95, 97, 173–74, 185–86
Isis, 154, 200
Islam, 3, 28, 42, 52, 100, 248
  Conquest, 276
Ismael, 28
Israel, 3–4, 10, 12, 15–16, 21–49, 51–52,
  59–60, 63–65, 80–81, 84–87, 94–97,
  135–36, 152, 164, 173–74, 180–81,
  188–90
  evil kings, 43

Jacob, 29, 81–82, 93, 97, 183, 185,
  187, 238
James, 49, 63, 67, 78, 84–85, 196–98
  decision, 86
Jeremiah, 24, 34, 38, 70–71, 85, 185
Jericho, 69, 218
Jeroboam, 35
Jerome, 56, 190, 242, 251–52, 254–55, 265
Jerusalem, 22–24, 31–33, 35–36, 41,
  45–48, 53, 61–63, 69–72, 74,
  76–85, 90–91, 96–97, 180–82,
  184–87, 189–90, 198, 209, 216,
  246, 272–73
Jesus, 16–17, 55–56, 59–78, 80, 82–90,
  93–95, 109, 114–15, 134, 164–67,
  169–75, 180–81, 187, 189–91,
  194–201, 210, 216–17, 227–30,
  245–47, 272–74
Johannine letters, 56

330 Index

John, 55–56, 59–66, 68–69, 72–73, 76,
    81–82, 106, 165–66, 168, 170,
    174–75, 209–10, 254, 274
John Chrysostom, 251–52, 254
Jonah, 76, 210
Joppa, 83
Jordan, 48
Jordan river, 60
Joseph, father of Jesus, 21, 23, 29, 60, 62, 76,
    194, 196–98, 202
Joshua, 21–22, 24, 33–34
Jubilees, 54
Judah, 16, 23, 34–36, 43, 64, 185
Judaism, 3–4, 7, 42–43, 47, 52, 80–81,
    83–84, 86, 88–89, 92–95, 124,
    133–34, 179–91
Judaizers, 79, 90
Judas Iscariot, 61, 171
  suicide, 61
Judea, 12, 22, 24, 46, 73–74, 81,
    183–84, 233
judgment, 3–4, 11, 142, 180, 185, 206, 208,
    211, 243
  final, 39, 65, 171, 213, 273
  seat, 120
Julian, 217, 222, 235–36, 257, 265
  anti-Church, 236
Julio-Claudians, 47
Juno, 7, 108
Jupiter, 7, 108, 137, 184
Justin Martyr, 124–25, 136–39, 153, 173,
    181–82, 185, 190, 229
Justinian, 237

kingdom, 21, 24, 34–35, 39, 60–61, 65,
    91–93, 97, 152–53, 155, 157,
    171–72, 218–19
  of God, 39, 46, 60, 87, 152, 165
  of heaven, 171, 210
Kings, books of, 21, 24, 33–36, 41–43, 45,
    52, 56, 61, 69, 71, 230
Knights Templars, 237

Lactantius, 222
Last Supper, 61, 115, 160, 213, 215
  words of the, 69
Lausiac History, 244
law, 28, 31, 79, 85–89, 91–92, 95–96,
    131–32, 140–42, 153, 156, 185–87,
    261, 265

  of Moses, 87
lawyers, 64, 218, 237
laying on of hands, 209–10
Lazarus, 114, 116
Leah, 29
Lenten period, 244
Leo, Pope, 278–80, 286
Leonidas, 118
lesbianism, 151–52
letters of Christ, 223
Levi, 63
Levites, 32
Leviticus, 21–22, 24, 31–33, 44,
    151–52, 211
Licinius, 223
literary devices, 18, 27, 85, 124, 129, 162,
    194
Literature of Early Monasticism, 249
liturgy, 173, 205, 212, 216
Locke, John, 141
logos, 63, 67–68, 127, 130, 135–39, 159, 162,
    164, 167, 169, 218–19, 272, 275
Lucifer, 56–57
lust, 145, 152, 156, 198, 242–43, 262, 266
Luther, Martin, 88, 213, 235, 248, 258

Maccabees, 24, 42–43
  martyrs, 93, 99, 107, 273
  revolt, 22, 42, 44, 106, 184
Magdalene, Mary, 160, 170
Magi, 10, 217
magic, 10, 54, 133
  formulas, 147
  rituals, 133
magicians, 1, 9–10
magistrates, 95, 102, 119–20, 124,
    142, 146, 149, 199–200, 206,
    246, 252–53
Magna Graecia, 13
Magus, Simon, 164, 201
Manasseh, 43
Manichaeans, 259
manifestation, 41, 63, 88, 91, 162, 164, 167,
    169, 187, 263, 266
  of God on earth, 63
Mark, John, 62
marriage, 7, 121, 145–58, 169, 198–200,
    214–15, 243, 255, 259, 269
  contract, 27, 149, 157, 259
  gender roles, 1

Index   331

martyrdom, 42–43, 97, 99–121, 123–24, 140, 215–16, 218, 222, 243, 248–49, 267, 272
martyrologies, 99, 109–10, 246
martyrs, 42, 107, 109, 111, 113, 120, 128, 239, 243–45, 247–49, 255
  secular, 248
masturbation, 242
Mattathias, 42
Matthew, 10, 16, 55, 59–61, 63–66, 72–74, 76, 174, 194, 197–98, 210, 229, 234
Maxentius, 222–23, 225
Maximinus, 118, 223
meals, 61, 72, 83, 150
  common, 241
  eucharistic, 95
  festive, 254
  funeral, 116
meat, 7, 9, 32, 84, 186, 242
  eating, 84, 157
medical knowledge, 147, 156
medicine, 129, 147, 211
medieval alchemy, 160
Mesopotamia, 35, 81, 203
Mesopotamians, 26
  ancient, 11
messiah, 34, 61–62, 64–65, 67, 93, 106, 180, 183, 187, 196
Metamorphoses, 200
metaphors, 5, 38, 41, 55, 67, 72, 103, 106, 152,
  marriage, 152
  of marriage and sexual intercourse, 169
metaphysics, 128, 260
Michelangelo, 248
Middle Ages, 110, 114, 134, 141, 173, 175, 237, 242, 247–48, 254, 258, 262
Middle Kingdom, 11, 43
midwives, 29, 197
Milan, 209, 221, 223, 235–36, 239, 245–46, 251–52, 254, 258–60
Milton, John, 176
Milvian Bridge, 221–23
Minerva, 7, 108
ministry, 39, 55, 61, 65–67, 69, 71, 77, 86, 155–56, 158, 172
miracles, 17, 42, 60, 67, 80–81, 110–11, 134, 194, 201, 244, 248
Mishnah, 189
misogynism, 155

missionaries, 78, 80, 84, 156, 180, 200, 209
  early, 196
  first, 17
missions, 4, 15, 55, 79, 83, 85, 87, 165, 172, 200, 258
Moabite, 43
Modern anti-Semitism, 16, 181, 191
Molech, 43
Monarchianism, 230, 272
monasteries, 240–44, 258, 260, 266, 270, 274
Monasticism, 158, 239–49, 251–52
money-changers, 70, 237
monism and dualism, 40, 159, 167–68
monks, 158, 175, 240–44, 267, 270
monotheism, 1, 3, 189, 231
  ancient, 3
Moriah, 28
mortality, 52, 266
  infant, 52, 213
Moses, 22, 24, 30–33, 42, 44, 79, 81, 85–89, 91–93, 95, 134–36, 138, 140, 185, 187–89
motherhood, 111
  surrogate, 27
mother religion, 7, 43
mothers, 27, 30, 42, 57, 110, 149, 153–54, 158, 171, 196, 202
Mystery Cults, 8, 141, 200
mysticism, 167
mythological characters, 12
mythology, 2, 19, 113
myths, 1, 5–6, 8–9, 11, 22, 25, 129, 133, 147, 155, 182
  ancient, 25
  fabulous, 129

Nag Hammadi, 161, 169, 175
  library, 159–61
  scriptures, 177
nations, 3–4, 14–15, 28, 31–32, 42, 44, 60–61, 64, 81, 91, 173–74, 185–86, 226, 229
native cults, 7–8, 14–15, 17, 19, 22, 27, 129, 154, 157, 223, 225, 227, 231
nativity, 10, 227
Nazarenes, 190
Nazareth, 10, 33, 48, 59–60, 64–65, 68, 95, 180, 197, 216
Nazianzus, 124, 242

332 Index

Nazism, 248
necromancers, 9–10
Nehemiah, 24, 36
Nephilim, 153
Nero, 46–47, 99, 102–3, 201, 233
Nestorianism, 271–75
Nestorius, 273–74
netherworld, 11
New Testament
    canon, 160, 174
Nicaea, 220, 221–22, 230, 234–35, 238, 252,
        270, 272–73
Nicene Creed, 56, 199, 221–22, 232, 238
Nile, 29–31, 184, 245
Noah, 24, 56, 93, 135, 187, 198–99, 204
    Ark, 267
    sons, 26
North Africa, 110, 113, 139, 227, 242, 253,
        257–60, 267, 270
Northern Israel, 35, 60
Northern Kingdom, 35, 38, 174
Novationism, 271–74
Nyssa, Gregory of, 124, 242

oaths, 42, 73, 236
Octavius, 141, 145, 154
Odyssey, 2
Old Testament, 16, 188, 216
Olympians, 245
omnipotence, 52, 54
omniscience, 264
oracles, 1, 9–10, 22, 120, 154
    ancient, 34
oral Law, 44, 189
oral traditions, 22–23, 67
orgy, 8
Origen, 133, 190, 211, 218–20, 230, 266, 274
Original Sin, 156, 220, 258–59, 262, 265–66,
        268
origin myths, 6
Origin of Satan, 57
Orthopraxy, 163
Osiris, 11
overseers, 30, 157, 195, 206

Pachomius, 241
pagans, 1, 14–15, 17, 56–57, 84, 125, 191,
        214, 237, 268, 270
Palatine Hill in Rome, 103
Palestine, 140, 184, 218, 242
Palestinians, 184

Palm Sunday, 61
Pan, 155
Pandora, 155
Papias, 124
parables, 67, 72, 171, 195
Parthian Empire, 45
Passover, 30, 61, 72–74, 77, 81–82, 187, 190,
        216
    festival, 70, 74
    in Jerusalem, 216
    meal, 61, 72
Patmos, John of, 56, 99, 106, 117
patriarchs, 24, 93, 188, 276
Paul, 15–17, 55, 61, 63, 67–69, 73, 75,
        78–80, 82–83, 85–98, 152–53,
        174–75, 202–3, 206–7, 211–16, 229,
        261–64, 269–70, 272
    arrest, 85
    belief, 155
    description, 92
    disciples, 55
    Eschatology, 79, 87
    innovations, 98
    letters, 63, 66–68, 78, 81, 86–87, 89, 92,
        97–98, 152, 155, 260–61
    missions, 63, 87
    ordeals, 92
    preaching, 93
    trial, 97
Paulinism, 271–72, 274
Pelagius, 246, 258, 264–66
Pelagius and Free Will, 257, 264
penance, 205, 211–15, 253
penitent Sundays, 212
Pentateuch, 22
Pentecost, 79, 81, 209
Peri Archon, 205, 219–20, 266
period of exile, 12
Perpetua, 100, 110, 118
persecution, 56, 78–79, 82, 106, 115,
        117–21, 190, 215, 221, 223, 226–27,
        272–73, 276
    of Christians, 99–100, 103–4, 106, 108,
        115, 117, 121, 137, 153, 223, 243
Persephone, 8
Persia, 22, 24, 36, 41, 45, 53, 185,
        243, 276
Persian Empire, 36, 53
Peter, 56, 61–62, 67, 83, 85, 103, 164, 166,
        170, 198–203, 209–10, 270, 272
Phaedo, 107, 166

Index   333

pharaoh, 11, 29–30, 35, 41, 245
Pharisees, 18, 43–44, 48, 60, 63–64, 77, 86,
    88, 94, 180, 182
Philemon, lett of, 87
Philippians, letter of, 87
Philistines, 34, 184
Philo, 74, 127, 135–36, 188
philosophers, 124, 128–29, 133–34, 137,
    139–40, 142–43, 147–48, 219, 228,
    259, 263
    Aristotle, 147
philosophy, 124–25, 127–32, 135–42,
    146–48, 150, 155, 161–62, 167, 229,
    231, 240, 242
Phoenician Empire, 26
Phrygia, 81
physicians, 134, 212
Picts, 222
piety, 110, 141, 186
Pithom-Rameses, 29
plagues, 11, 52, 54, 115, 118, 262
    final, 30
    ten, 30
Plato, 40, 99, 107, 127, 130–31, 134, 136,
    138–41, 161, 166, 168
    Plato's universe, 219
Plebeians, 101
Pleroma, 162, 167, 171
Pliny, 108, 207
    Letter to Trajan, 99, 108
Plotinus, 263
polemic, 17–18, 38, 56, 77, 79, 86, 92, 125,
    166, 181, 202
    anti-Jewish, 92
Polybius, 19
Polycarp, 99, 109–10, 124, 165, 173
Polytheism, 1, 3
polytheists, 3
Pompeii, 156
Pompey Magnus, 22, 24, 45
Pontius Pilate, 46, 62, 73, 198, 233
Pontus, 45, 81, 172
    wolf of, 173
pope, 195, 210, 228, 248, 276
    Benedict XV, 158
    Benedict XVI, 263
    Francis, 248
    Gregory, 242
    Gregory I, 170
    John Paul II, 220, 248
    Julius II, 248

pornea, 152
pornography, 152
Praetorians, 102, 104, 109
presbyters, 158, 195, 206, 218, 220, 230, 258
Priapus, 155
Pricilla, 114
priestesses, 6, 149
priesthoods, 2, 5–6, 71, 77, 86, 100, 102,
    104, 181
priests, 6–7, 9, 13, 36, 44, 46, 71–72, 74,
    77, 196–97, 207, 209, 211–12,
    231, 234
    high, 187, 211
procreation, 110, 138, 140, 146, 148–49,
    152–53, 156, 158, 208, 233, 266
profane, 83, 154, 226
proof-texts, 73, 209
propaganda, 75, 112–13, 119, 227
    ordinary political, 84
Prophetic books, 38
Prophetic elements, 64
Prophets, 9–10, 15, 33–35, 37–39, 44, 60,
    63, 65, 67, 70–71, 85, 95, 145–46,
    152, 173–74, 181, 186–87,
    216, 259
    Amos, 84
    Elijah, 187
    false, 186, 195
    Hosea, 76
    Isaiah, 216
    Jeremiah, 184
    Zechariah, 69
prostitution, 28, 170, 215
Protestant Christianity, 247
Proverbs, 73
Psalms, 3, 61, 75, 216
Pseudepigrapha, 193–94
Ptah, 27
Ptolemaic Egypt, 135
Ptolemies, 41
Ptolemy Soter, 41
puberty, 7, 27, 149–50, 197, 200
Punic War, 8
Purgatory, 239, 247–48, 263
purification, 13, 166
purity, 33, 157
Pythagoreans, 147

Queen of Heaven, 247
Quo vadis, Domine, 201
Quran, 198

334 Index

rabbi, 16, 48, 183, 189
Rabbinic Judaism, 185
Radical Christians, 145, 157
Radical Monastics, 239, 244
Radical Monism, 168
Rameses II, 29
rape, 52, 92, 199, 269
redeemer, 161, 176
Red Sea, 30
reincarnations, 166, 201, 219
relics, 246–47
  associated, 247
  fake, 247
religion, 1–2, 4–7, 18–19, 41, 43, 124,
    127–29, 142, 208, 213, 235–36, 238,
    240
religious festivals, 1, 9, 72, 81, 111–12, 117,
    119, 134, 149, 190, 245
restoration of Jerusalem, 24
resurrection, 39, 42, 67, 76, 92–94, 96, 134,
    136, 138, 164–65, 216–17, 272, 274
  bodily, 138
  general, 12
return of Christ, 90–91, 165
Revelation, book of
Rhadamanthus, 138
rhetoric, 17–18, 128, 258–59
rituals, 2, 6–8, 10, 13–14, 16–17, 30–31, 33,
    41, 44, 168–69, 186, 188, 209, 211,
    213–15
Roman Church, 173, 217
Roman Empire, 2, 7, 9, 15, 19, 100, 105–6,
    118, 121, 143, 145–46, 149–50,
    222–38
Romans, 14–15, 43, 46–47, 60–61, 87, 89,
    93–97, 100, 102, 111–12, 151–52,
    221, 224, 260–62, 264
  Senate, 101, 225, 236
  society, 151
  worship, 102
  writers and philosophers, 124
Rome, 7–10, 12–14, 22, 44–48, 69–71,
    73–78, 92–93, 97, 100–106, 108–15,
    117–19, 149, 180–83, 195, 201,
    217–18, 226–30, 254–55, 268–69,
    272–76
Romulus, 2, 183
Rufus, 219

Sabbath day, 216
Sabellianism, 230

sacraments, 7, 109, 121, 213–14, 220,
    266–67
sacrifices, 3–4, 7, 9–10, 21, 23, 26, 28,
    30–32, 70–72, 104, 118–19, 186–87,
    243, 245, 247
sacrilege, 12, 100
Sadducees, 18, 43–44, 60, 77, 182, 264
Saint James, 248
saints, 239–40, 244–45, 247–49, 251–52,
    267, 273
  cult of the, 217, 249
salvation, 83, 88–89, 95–97, 140, 165–66,
    172, 174, 212, 219, 232–33, 263,
    265–66, 273–75
Samaria, 164, 20
Samuel, Book of, 34
Sanhedrin, 62, 67, 72–73, 85, 190
Sarah, 26–28
Sardis, 199
Satan, 3, 10, 45, 51–57, 106, 139, 155, 157,
    164, 208, 214
satire, 141, 154, 202
Saul, 34, 82–83, 174
savior, 161, 167
scapegoats, 103, 117
scribes, 36, 60, 64, 72–73, 194
Second Temple, 24, 36–37, 86, 182, 184
  Judaism, 37, 67–68, 88, 94
  literature, 94
  period, 43
Second Triumvirate, 102
sectarianism, 43
sects, 7, 43–44, 163, 169, 182, 184, 190, 259
Sejanus, 102
Seleucid dynasty, 41
self-castration, 218
semen, 28, 33, 146–48, 152, 242, 262
  involved, 6
Senate, 100–102, 104, 112, 133, 231
Senate House, 236
Seneca, 97
Septuagint, 219
Serapeum, 243
Serapis, 41
Seth, 26
sexual abstinence, 140, 149
sexual deviation and sins, 153
sexual identity, 158
sexual intercourse, 6, 27, 33, 151, 155–58,
    169, 261–62, 266
shame, 4, 81, 107, 147–48, 150, 158, 269

public, 107
shepherds, 30, 133, 147, 195
shrines, 7, 34–35, 43, 97, 153–54, 237, 248
   established, 246
Sicarii, 44
siege of Jerusalem, 45, 48
Sinai, 3, 19, 30, 81, 188
sins, 28, 33, 38, 88–90, 95–97, 140, 151,
       155–58, 186, 209–15, 232–33,
       240–43, 247–48, 253–54, 260–66
Sixtus II, 118
slave labor, 237
slavery, 1, 5, 112, 253
Slavery in ancient Greece and Rome, 5
   ancient society, 5
   commercial, 5
   female, 150
   freed, 5
   freeing, 267
   public, 14
   rebellious, 5
slave testimony, 108
Smyrna, 99, 109, 124, 165, 173
social conventions, 8, 85, 88, 133–34, 137,
       142, 146, 153, 155, 176, 217
society, 1–2, 4–6, 11, 132, 135, 137, 141–42,
       146–47, 151, 158, 253, 258, 260
Socrates, 99, 107, 127, 130, 138, 148
Socrates and Plato, 99, 107
sodomy, 151
Solomon, 24, 35, 43
   death, 35
   Temple, 12, 24, 31, 36, 184
son of David, 67
sons by adoption, 91
sons of God, 3, 54, 67, 94, 153, 156, 232
sorcerer, 164, 189
sorcery, 134
souls, 11–13, 40, 42, 56–57, 130–32, 136–39,
       166–69, 186, 198, 213–15, 219–20,
       263, 266, 274
Southern Kingdom, 36
spirit, 17, 81–82, 88, 94–95, 164, 167–68,
       211, 213–14, 229–30, 233, 266
spring equinox, 217
stigmata, 75
Stoicism, 127, 130–31, 140
Stoics, 117, 131, 139, 147
Stromateis, 120
St. Stephen, 247
study of religion, 5

suffering servant, 64, 95
suicide, 103, 107,
superstition, 10
symbols, 6, 17, 26, 32, 106, 114, 156, 187,
       223, 275–76
   allegorical, 162, 274
synagogue of Capernaum, 173
synagogue of Satan, 106
synagogues, 31, 84–85, 92–93, 185, 189–90,
       216, 237, 243, 246, 252, 254
syncretism, 40
Synoptic, 65
gospels, 73
problem, 65
Syria, 22, 26, 39, 41, 157, 173, 244
systematic theology, 87, 182, 205, 258

Talmud, 48, 185, 189
Tantrism traditions, 168
Tartarus, 12
Tatian, 157
tax-collector, 63
taxes, 36, 104, 222, 227
tax rolls, 118
telos, 88
Temple, 6–7, 22, 24, 32–33, 35–36, 41–42,
       44, 46–48, 70–74, 82, 84–85, 101–2,
       153–54, 180–84, 196–97
"Temple Incident", 71
Temple Schematic, 37
temptations, 55–56, 153, 263
tenements, 104
Tertullian, 105, 109, 125, 127, 139, 156, 188,
       190, 199, 212, 230
Tetrarchy, 46, 119, 222
Theodosius I, 236–37, 243, 246, 252–53
   Theodosian Code, 237, 269
Theotokos, 198, 273, 275
Titus, 47–48, 103, 140, 206
transcendence, 229
transubstantiation, 213
treason, 46, 64, 101, 105, 111, 121, 175, 227
trials and tribulations, 8
tribal bloodlines, 28
tribes, 15, 23–25, 29, 32, 34–36, 60, 82, 87,
       176, 187
   northern, 23
   southern, 23
Trinity, 220, 221–22, 229–31, 234–35, 238,
       272–73
Trypho, the Jew, 182, 185–88

336 Index

uncleanness, 137
underworld, 3, 10–12, 14, 40, 43, 95, 171
universalism, 83
universe, 3, 86, 88–89, 91, 128–33, 136, 138,
        160–61, 163–64, 219–20, 229–31,
        263–64, 266

vagina, 147, 151
vainglory, 242–43
Valentinian Gnosticism, 168
Valentinus, 167, 175
Vatican, 2, 97, 114, 210, 247–48
Vatican City, 210, 223
Vatican Hill, 103, 117, 228
Vatican's International Theological
        Commission, 263
Vedantism, 168
Venus Libitina, 14
Vespasian, 46–47, 103–4
Vestal Virgins of Rome, 149
Vibia Perpetua, 110
Victorian period, 198
virgin, 111, 201, 275
virgin girls, 111
virginity, 111, 149, 199
    cradle to grave, 157
Virgin Mary, 173, 233
visions, 67, 82–83, 86–87, 92–93, 106, 110,
        195, 201, 203, 222–23, 227
voluntary cults, 1, 8

Vulgate Bible, 255

Waldensians, 175
winter solstice, 217
wisdom books, 216
witch, 10
wives, 35, 46, 155, 158, 171, 187, 226
    foreign, 35
    king's, 200
woman, 146, 149, 152, 154, 156, 170–71,
        195, 203, 208, 214, 258–59, 262, 269
    educated, 150
    sinful, 170
women, 8, 13, 27–28, 33–34, 62, 110–11,
        146–52, 155–58, 169, 171, 203–4,
        207–8, 212, 240–42, 254–55
    church leaders denouncing, 208
worship, 3, 6–8, 15–16, 39, 42, 93–96, 100,
        102, 104–5, 108, 187–90, 216, 219

Yahweh, 4

Zadock, 43
Zealots, 43–44, 46–48, 71
Zeus, 40–41, 155, 228
Zion, 97, 189
Zipporah, 30
Zoroaster, 40
    prophet, 53
Zoroastrianism, 36, 40, 51–53, 161